ASIAN DEVELOPMENT OUTLOOK 2000

Special Chapter
As the Century Turns
The Social Challenge in Asia

Published for the Asian Development Bank
by Oxford University Press

OXFORD

UNIVERSITY PRESS

Oxford University Press is a department of the University of Oxford.
It furthers the University's objective of excellence in research, scholarship,
and education by publishing worldwide in

Oxford New York

Athens Auckland Bangkok Bogotá Buenos Aires Calcutta
Cape Town Chennai Dar es Salaam Delhi Florence Hong Kong Istanbul
Karachi Kuala Lumpur Madrid Melbourne Mexico City Mumbai
Nairobi Paris São Paulo Singapore Taipei Tokyo Toronto Warsaw
with associated companies in Berlin   Ibadan

Oxford is a registered trade mark of Oxford University Press

First published 2000
This impression (lowest digit)
1 3 5 7 9 10 8 6 4 2

Published in the United States
by Oxford University Press, New York

Published for the Asian Development Bank by
Oxford University Press

British Library Cataloguing in Publication Data
available

Library of Congress Cataloging-in-Publication Data
available

ISBN 0-19-592533-5
ISSN 0117-0481

Printed in Hong Kong

Published by Oxford University Press (China) Ltd.
18th Floor Warwick House East, Taikoo Place, 979 King's Road, Quarry Bay
Hong Kong

Foreword

The *Asian Development Outlook 2000* is the 12th in a series of annual economic reports on the developing member countries of the Asian Development Bank. The *Outlook* provides a comprehensive analysis of salient macroeconomic and development issues in individual countries as well as at the regional level, from both positive and normative perspectives.

In 1999 the world economy finally shook off the effects of the 1997 Asian crisis and the economic disturbances in Russia and Brazil that followed. Within Asia a moderate to strong upswing replaced negative growth in several countries; interest rates decreased and exchange rates stabilized. Domestic demand and export growth improved. Increased confidence in the region's economic prospects is evident from strengthened capital inflows from overseas investors, increased vitality of equity markets, and revived consumer confidence. All of the countries that were directly affected by the crisis and experienced negative economic growth in 1998 — Indonesia, Republic of Korea, Malaysia, Philippines, and Thailand — recovered to positive growth. The strength of the rebound varied from a strong recovery in the Republic of Korea to a more modest revival in Indonesia. The People's Republic of China (PRC) and South Asia were insulated from the crisis to a certain extent and as a result fared better. In 1999 growth slowed slightly in the PRC, while accelerating by a similar margin in South Asia. Growth in Central Asia showed a strong increase as the effect of the Russian crisis dissipated, and the performance of the Pacific economies improved from the previous year.

To sustain and further reinvigorate the growth process, developing Asia will have to continue with its agenda of reforms and institutional innovations in areas that are considered weak and vulnerable. In particular the crisis has exposed weaknesses in the banking system, capital markets, and corporate sectors of the affected countries. The scale and complexities of the issues involved are enormous. The crisis has rendered a large part of the banking and corporate sectors financially insolvent. In the immediate aftermath of the crisis, the ADB cooperated with other donors in providing emergency financial assistance to stabilize the affected economies and to support urgent structural reforms. On its part, the ADB focused on a structural agenda that included restructuring insolvent financial institutions, improving corporate governance, and deregulating and opening domestic markets. In this regard, the ADB provided loans to assist Indonesia, Korea, and Thailand in implementing financial sector reforms. The crisis countries have made significant progress in bank and corporate sector restructuring and have created new organizational entities to deal with these issues. While much progress has been made, much remains to be done.

However, given the willingness and dedication of the governments to address this unfinished agenda of reform and restructuring, we are confident that the results of these structural reforms and review of policies and institutions will result in improved economic efficiency, greater transparency, better governance, and improved social equity. The region will emerge stronger and more able to fulfill its potential for sustained economic growth and development.

Part I of this year's *Outlook* comprises two chapters. The first chapter provides a comprehensive review of economic developments in the Asian and Pacific region against a background of developments in the world economy. In the second chapter, the *Outlook* presents a progress report on financial and corporate restructuring in the countries most affected by the crisis. This chapter develops elements of such a strategy, as well as an agenda for strengthening ongoing reforms, improving governance, reducing fiscal imbalances, and developing financial markets.

Part II discusses the recent economic performance and short-term prospects for each of the 37 developing member countries of the ADB. It also reviews and assesses economic management and policy and development issues from a medium-term perspective.

Part III discusses the social challenges the Asian region faces as it moves into the new millennium. It reviews the record of social achievement, analyzes salient factors behind the social challenge, and recommends policies for change. In addition to poverty, this challenge has many dimensions: low literacy, unsatisfactory education, poor health and nutrition, environmental degradation, income and wealth disparities, and discrimination. Several conclusions follow from the analysis, including the importance of openness and market orientation in sustaining vibrant economic growth that includes the poor and disadvantaged. For growth to be inclusive, renewed and more focused efforts to invest in human resources and physical infrastructure are crucial. The ability and will of governments to address social issues through the political process and good governance must be strengthened. Finally, national governments should create a fiscally prudent social safety net to safeguard the nonpoor from a sudden push into poverty, and the poor from a descent into extreme poverty. While developing an agenda to address social issues is primarily the task of national governments, the international community can assist by increasing foreign assistance (which has declined sharply in recent years); providing international public goods, such as research on tropical diseases and tropical agriculture, which concern the majority of the poor; and improving the global trading environment, which remains encumbered by many restrictions in areas of interests to poor countries.

The ADB has recently adopted poverty reduction as its overarching objective. This *Asian Development Outlook 2000* provides a useful addition to our stock of knowledge on both the location and dimensions of the poverty problem, as well as specific policies to address this crucial social challenge in individual countries.

TADAO CHINO
President

Acknowledgments

The *Asian Development Outlook 2000* has benefited from the support and valuable contributions from many individuals, both inside and outside the Asian Development Bank. The following individuals provided critical support, guidance, and advice on various matters relating to the preparation of the *Outlook*: Shamshad Akhtar, Nihal Amerasinghe, Thomas Crouch, Gunther Hecker, Yoshihiro Iwasaki, Kazi Jalal, G.H.P.B. van der Linden, Bruce Murray, Rajat Nag, Shoji Nishimoto, Filologo Pante, Jr., Kazu Sakai, Karti Sandilya, Marshuk Ali Shah, Christine Wallich, and Y. Zhang. Special thanks are due to the following ADB staff for comments on various parts of the *Outlook*: John Boyd, David Green, E. Manes, Henrike Feig, P. Ghosh, Keiko Hioki, Joo-Hyun Kim, Hisashi Ono, Ernesto M. Pernia, Stephen Pollard, Brahm Prakash, Frederick Roche, S.D. Tamondong, Hong Wei, Hyong-Jong Yu, and Tao Zhang. Ian Gill, Tsukasa Maekawa, Lynette Mallery, and Robert H. Salamon of the Office of External Relations provided advice and assistance in disseminating the *Outlook*. The prepress work was done by the Printing Unit under the supervision of Raveendranath Rajan. The assistance of the Resident Missions, Office of Administrative Services, and Office of Information Systems and Technology in the preparation of the *Outlook* is also gratefully acknowledged.

A select group of economists and social scientists from the region, as well as other international organizations, participated in the *Twelfth Workshop on Asian Economic Outlook*, which discussed a set of background materials for this *Outlook*. Those who prepared papers or acted as designated commentators for the workshop include Douglas Brooks, James Chamberlain, Daniela Klingebiel, James Knowles, Flemming Larsen, Joseph Lim, Cayetano Paderanga, Yung Chul Park, and Veerathai Santiprabhob. Additional background papers were prepared by Ismail Alowi, Dongchul Cho, Nguyen Dinh Cung, Teresa K.B. Fung, Mohammed Jaleel, Eshya Mujahid-Mukhtar, Chirathep Senivongs, Nimal Siripala, Myat Thein, Chung Shu Wu, and Sajjad Zohir.

The *Outlook* has benefited from comments and guidance from a distinguished panel of external advisors consisting of Mohamed Ariff, Pranab Bardhan, Jere Behrman, Yih-Peng Chia, Gary Fields, Basant Kapur, T.N. Srinivasan, and C. Sussangkarn. Zanny Minton-Beddoes was the principal economic editorial consultant for some chapters of the *Outlook*.

Several international institutions shared their research and data with the *Outlook* team. In particular, we would like to acknowledge the contributions from the International Monetary Fund and the World Bank, which shared their research on global economic prospects and on the financial and corporate restructuring in developing Asia. Staff from both these organizations also participated in the *Twelfth Workshop on Asian Economic Outlook*.

JUNGSOO LEE
Chief Economist

The Team

The *Outlook* has been prepared by the Economic Analysis and Research Division, in collaboration with the Programs Departments of the Asian Development Bank. The core team that prepared the *Outlook* was led by M.G. Quibria, Assistant Chief Economist and assisted by Rana Hasan, Sailesh Jha, Yun-Hwan Kim, and Rajiv Kumar, along with James Villafuerte, who was responsible for coordination. The other members of the core team included Dilip Das, Shew Huei Kuo, Yeo Lin, Soo-Nam Oh, Narhari Rao, Purnima Rajapakse, Emma Banaria, Laura Britt, Charissa Castillo, Edith Lavina, Elizabeth Leuterio, Aludia Pardo, Joy Quitazol, Marcus Ynalvez, and Cherry Lynn Zafaralla. The core team was assisted by the following members of the Programs Departments and the Office of Pacific Operations, who prepared most of the country reports in Part II of the *Outlook*: Shiladitya Chatterjee, Brett Coleman, Padmini Desikachar, V. N. Gnanathurai, Barry Hitchcock, Sophia Ho, Cindy Houser, Suganya Hutaserani, Neeraj Jain, Hun Kim, Bruce Knapman, Seung Beom Koh, Srinivasa Madhur, Sultan Hafeez Rahman, Yumiko Tamura, Min Tang, Almud Weitz, Hong Wang, Lan Wu, and Joseph Zveglich. Charito Arriola, Franklin de Guzman, Marichu Duka, Carmela Espina, Ma. Olivia Nuestro, and Marriel Remulla provided additional support in the preparation of country reports. The principal editing responsibility for the *Outlook* was borne by John Malcolm Dowling, who also made many important substantive as well as advisory contributions, and Sara Henry. The work was carried out under the overall direction of Myoung-Ho Shin, Vice-President (Region West), and the supervision of Jungsoo Lee, Chief Economist.

Many others inside and outside the Asian Development Bank wrote background papers, provided helpful comments, and participated in the *Twelfth Workshop on Asian Economic Outlook*, held in Manila on 23 November 1999 to discuss some of the background materials. Contributors and participants are listed in the Acknowledgments. The statistical database and country tables were prepared by staff from the Economic Analysis and Research Division with some assistance from the Statistics and Data Systems Division. James Villafuerte and Anicia Sayos were responsible for the *Outlook* data management and Statistical Appendix preparation. Ma. Teresa Cabellon and Socorro Fajardo provided the main secretarial and administrative support, with additional assistance from Zenaida Acacio, Ma. Lourdes Antonio, Patricia Baysa, Eva Olanda, Nilo Sandoval, and Anna Liza Silverio. Alex McLellan and Amanda McGrath designed the cover and dividers. Mercedita Cabañeros was responsible for typesetting, assisted by Ma. Lourdes Maestro and Edmond Sid M. Pantilo. Cherry Lynn Zafaralla coordinated prepress work. Charissa Castillo and Elizabeth Leuterio coordinated printing of the volume with Oxford University Press.

Contents

TEXT FIGURES

BOX FIGURES

BOX TABLES

Acronyms and Abbreviations

ADB	Asian Development Bank
AMC	Asset management company
APEC	Asia-Pacific Economic Cooperation
EU	European Union
FDI	Foreign direct investment
GDP	Gross domestic product
GEM	Growth Enterprise Market
GNP	Gross national product
IBRA	Indonesian Bank Restructuring Agency
ILO	International Labour Organization
IMF	International Monetary Fund
INDRA	Indonesian Debt Restructuring Agency
IT	Information technology
MENA	Middle East North Africa
NASDAQ	National Association of Securities Dealers Automated Quotations
NGO	Nongovernmental organization
NPL	Nonperforming loan
NPRT	Nauru Phosphate Royalties Trust
OECD	Organisation for Economic Co-operation and Development
OPEC	Organization of Petroleum Exporting Countries
RERF	Reserve Equalization Reserve Fund
SME	Small and medium-size enterprise
SOE	State-owned enterprise
UNCTAD	United Nations Conference on Trade and Development
WHO	World Health Organization
WTO	World Trade Organization

Definitions

The classification of economies by major analytic or geographic groupings such as industrial countries, developing countries, Africa, Latin America, Middle East, Europe, and transitional countries follows the classification adopted by the International Monetary Fund. Latin America, however, is referred to as developing countries in the Western Hemisphere in the IMF classification. Transitional economies in Asia include Kazakhstan, Kyrgyz Republic, Mongolia, Tajikistan, and Uzbekistan.

For purposes of this *Outlook* the following apply:

■ **Developing Asia** refers to the 37 developing member countries of the Asian Development Bank discussed in this *Outlook*.

■ **Newly industrialized economies (NIEs)** comprise Hong Kong, China; Republic of Korea; Singapore; and Taipei,China.

■ **South Asia** comprises Bangladesh, Bhutan, India, Maldives, Nepal, Pakistan, and Sri Lanka.

■ **Southeast Asia** comprises Cambodia, Indonesia, Lao People's Democratic Republic, Malaysia, Myanmar, Philippines, Thailand, and Viet Nam.

■ **Central Asian republics** comprise Kazakhstan, Kyrgyz Republic, Tajikistan, and Uzbekistan.

■ **The Pacific** comprises Cook Islands, Fiji Islands, Kiribati, Marshall Islands, Federated States of Micronesia, Nauru, Papua New Guinea, Samoa, Solomon Islands, Tonga, Tuvalu, and Vanuatu.

■ **East Asia** comprises the NIEs, the People's Republic of China, and Mongolia.

■ **Crisis-affected countries** comprise Indonesia, Republic of Korea, Malaysia, Philippines, and Thailand.

■ **G7** comprises Canada, France, Germany, Italy, Japan, United Kingdom, and United States.

■ **Other non-Asian developing economies** refer to Argentina, Brazil, Chile, Colombia, Egypt, Mexico, Morocco, Turkey, and Venezuela.

Unless otherwise specified, the symbol $ means US dollars.

This *Outlook* is based on data available up to 8 March 2000.

Developing Asia and the World

Economic Developments and Prospects

The year 1999 saw the resolution of the financial crisis in developing Asia and acceleration of global growth, propelled primarily by a buoyant US economy. Led by the newly industrialized economies (NIEs) and the People's Republic of China (PRC), Asia posted strong growth that meant almost tripling the growth rate from the previous year. Prospects for further acceleration of growth in the region in the next two years depend on the sustainability of domestic demand, favorable global economic conditions, and progress in corporate and financial sector reforms in the crisis-affected economies.

In the fall of 1998, many economies in Asia were in recession, capital flows had turned negative, Russia had just defaulted on its official debt, and the outlook for the region and the world economy were generally pessimistic. Stock markets were languishing and there was a very real fear that the world economy would tip into recession. The sharp decline in worldwide economic growth had brought commodity prices to historical lows, with oil prices plummeting by 30 percent. The contagion effect from the Asian crisis was threatening Latin America, where the Brazilian currency, the real, was under siege. European banks, currencies, and stock markets were badly affected by the Russian devaluation and subsequent default during July and August, and the euro currency area appeared to be faltering. In its fall issue of the 1998 World Economic Outlook, the International Monetary Fund (IMF) slashed its forecast for 1999 world growth from 3.7 percent to 2.5 percent, stating, "The risks to this projection, however, are predominantly on the downside. Indeed a significantly worse outcome is clearly possible." The IMF would later downgrade its world growth forecast even further, to 2.3 percent.

A year and a half later the outlook for the world economy is, however, much more bullish. The year 1999 turned out to be much better than anyone had expected. The sharp rebound in global growth has now generated the fear of excess growth and inflation. How was such a turnaround possible?

The turning point was probably October 1998, when the Federal Reserve lowered the discount rate for the second time in two weeks. This sent a strong message to the world financial community that the United States (US) was ready to take whatever measures necessary to stem the threat. Markets responded quickly and enthusiastically. At about the same time, the Japanese government passed legislation to deal with bad loans in the banking system, and a month later, passed a stimulus package that worked to bring about positive growth the coming year. Between November 1998 and April 1999, the European Central Bank also lowered interest rates in tandem with US rates. Lower interest rates in industrial countries were matched by a further relaxation of monetary policy and fiscal policy in the countries that had been hit by the crisis in Asia.

These coordinated efforts on the part of both the industrial world and the crisis-affected developing countries in Asia were largely responsible for the upturn of the world economy in 1999, as it finally shook off the effects of the 1997 Asian crisis and the economic disturbances in Russia and Brazil that followed. Growth resumed in some countries and accelerated in others. The US continued to be the primary engine of growth among industrial countries and showed no signs of a deceleration in growth, as equity markets continued to surge while unemployment and inflation remained low. The misery index—the combination of the unemployment rate and the inflation rate—continued to fall (see figure 1.1).

Strong US growth also helped drive the rest of the North American Free Trade Area, with Canada and Mexico also performing well. Europe ended the year on an increasingly positive note, with Germany and France providing much of the impetus for growth in the region. Some countries in Asia moved to a higher growth path while others emerged from recession. Eastern and Central Europe made a modest recovery, supported by improved conditions in Russia, Poland, and the Czech Republic. The result was robust growth in the world economy and a low inflation rate for both industrial and developing economies.

Despite widespread economic success in 1999, there remained reasons for concern. The current account deficit of the United States remains large and the Japanese internal public debt has increased dramatically the past few years. There is also the issue of how long the "new industrial revolution," born of the development of the Internet, information technology, and e-commerce, can continue to increase productivity and boost equity prices without causing inflation (see box 1.1).

In contrast to the 19th century industrial revolution, which featured numerous innovations in manufacturing, today's revolution seems to permeate a wider segment of the economy. However, traditional industries are not benefiting much from these innovations as reflected in a growing disparity in equity markets between the new and older sectors of the economy.

It is difficult to gauge the overall long-run impact of the productivity gains from the new industrial revolution on global growth. In the short run, however, it is probably reasonable to assume that advances in computer and information technology will help drive growth in industrial countries. The positive synergies from globalization and new technologies should also spread to the more progressive developing countries.

THE WORLD ECONOMY

World GDP growth increased to 3 percent in 1999 and it is likely to improve further, to about 3.5 percent in 2000. World trade volume also increased slightly to 4 percent in 1999, compared with the downturn of 1998 when trade growth moderated to 3.6 percent from 9.9 percent the previous year. World trade volume is projected to grow further, to nearly 6 percent in 2000. In 1999, world inflation declined to its lowest level in 40 years. This exemplary record reflects the intensified commitment among monetary authorities to focus on price stability.

Industrial Countries

GDP growth in the industrial economies rebounded to 2.6 percent in 1999 from 2.4 percent in 1998. The United States and Canada continued to perform strongly in 1999, supported by buoyant domestic demand. Overall growth in GDP in the euro area declined to 2.1 percent in 1999 from 2.8 percent the previous year. In Japan, stimulative macroeconomic policies and the rebound in the Asian economies underpinned a modest economic recovery.

Inflation in the industrial economies was 1.3 percent in 1999, close to the decade low of 1.2 percent the previous year. Productivity increases exerted downward pressure on prices of final goods. Prices of services, which are primarily determined by labor costs, also remained low, because real wage increases lagged behind productivity growth. Inflation in 2000 may escalate to 1.7 percent, largely due to higher oil prices in the first quarter of the year and some modest upward pressure on wages as labor markets tighten further.

While interest rates bounced back in the latter part of 1999 from the crisis-depressed lows of late 1998, equity markets enjoyed stellar performance due to the vigor of output and earnings growth. The tightening of monetary policy by the major industrial economies in 1999 caused nominal bond yields to rise.

Figure 1.1 Misery Index, United States, 1963-1999

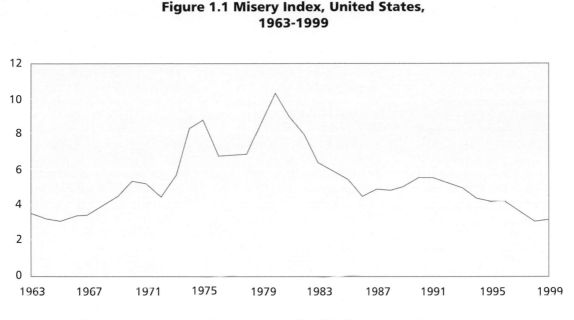

Note: The misery index is a weighted average of the CPI inflation rate and unemployment rate.
Source: US Bureau of Labor Statistics.

In 1999 there was a net outflow of capital from Europe into Japan (particularly into the equity market) and the US. The US attracted inflows of $85 billion in direct investment and $241 billion in portfolio investment. Direct investment was primarily used for foreign acquisition of US companies. These two sources of inflows, net of outflows, financed the US current account deficit of $316 billion (3.5 percent of GDP) in 1999. Much of the net capital outflow from the European Union (EU) was spent on foreign mergers and acquisitions and liabilities issued internationally by regional banks. Record levels of foreign investment in Japanese equities took place in 1999 as economic growth prospects brightened. This helped support the yen and contributed to the buoyancy of the Japanese stock market.

The outlook for industrial countries suggests a trend toward convergence of economic growth. Growth in the euro area and in Japan is expected to be higher and US growth similar to that in 1999. Growth convergence within industrial countries will help maintain overall macroeconomic stability within the global economy. Nevertheless, policymakers need to address imbalances in foreign trade among the major regions.

Transition Economies

The transition economies showed clear signs of revival in 1999 as growth of nearly 1 percent was recorded following a slight contraction in 1998. Industrial output was particularly strong in Hungary and Poland, as Eastern European countries benefited from the economic strength of the EU, which replaced Russia as the major trading partner of many countries in this region. Countries that have undertaken structural reforms, such as Hungary, were well positioned to take advantage of improved trade linkages and growing import demand from the EU. For example, the Czech Republic, Hungary, and Poland sent a third of their exports to Germany and two thirds to Western Europe. Hungary and Poland led the region in growth performance in 1999, while in the Czech Republic, strong exports to Germany offset the effect of a strong krona to halt economic deceleration. Boosted by higher oil prices and the 75 percent depreciation of the ruble in the fall of 1998, Russia reported the strongest growth in industrial output in seven years as overall GDP grew by 1.7 percent. The improved performance of the region led to large capital inflows and boosted currency and equity markets. Greater sta-

Box 1.1 New Economy: Much Ado about Nothing?

The New Economy doctrine—sometimes grandiosely labeled as the New Economy paradigm—holds the view that information technology, in conjunction with globalization, has led to a permanent upsurge in productivity of US workers. This has in turn pushed up the growth rate the US economy can achieve without running up against capacity limits. The conventional view, which is based on economic theory and historical evidence, holds that the US economy has a "speed limit" of around 2-2.5 percent growth. The proponents of the new economy believe that the growth potential of the US economy has now been pushed to the range of 3-4 percent, stemming from productivity and efficiency gains arising from information technology and globalization.

What do data tell us about productivity growth in the United States? It is clear from historical analysis that productivity growth comes primarily from technology and not from improved workforce quality or equipment per worker. Using a method that isolates technology from the other two sources, the evidence suggests that the technology component of US productivity slowed down after 1973 and never really picked up again. There were surges for short periods (1977-1978, 1983-1986, and 1990-1992), but they all followed recessions. The current productivity boom began in 1996, but what differentiates it from the other surges is that it did not follow a recession, and it has not reversed after a few years.

Is the current surge in productivity permanent? Are we in the middle of a new industrial revolution created by the computer, information technology, and the Internet? Several issues must be resolved before we can answer these questions with any certainty. First, the computer has been in use for many years but productivity didn't accelerate until the early 1990s. Why was there such a lag? It could be because computers were not nearly as productive until they were linked together, either in local area networks or through the Internet, and this interconnectedness took time to develop and to be "sold" to the public. Second, even if the lag can be explained, how has the productivity in a small sector of the economy had such a beneficial effect on the entire economy? Third, and perhaps not quite as important, can the contributions of these three components of the new industrial revolution—the computer, information technology, and the Internet—be separated and analyzed individually?

As we try to answer these questions, we acquire a better understanding of whether this is actually in a "new economy," and if so, precisely what is raising productivity. A plausible answer to

Source: http://www.brookings.org.

bility in Russia, along with increased import demand from the EU, improved current account balances in the region. Inflation also dropped in most countries.

Growth is likely to strengthen further to 2.8 percent in 2000, fueled by accelerating export growth to the EU. The downward trend in inflation and nominal interest rates is likely to continue as risk premiums in these countries decline. Entry negotiations into the EU will continue to dominate the policy agenda for some countries. The political situation in Eastern Europe should continue to improve, which will boost business confidence and foreign investment.

THE DEVELOPING ECONOMIES

Growth in the developing regions of the world improved from 3.2 percent in 1998 to 3.5 percent in 1999. This was underpinned by the strong rebound in developing Asia, where GDP expanded by 6.2 percent from 2.3 percent in 1998 on the back of strong export growth and a revival of domestic demand. Greater strength in the global economy and the dissipation of the contagion effects of the Asian crisis also contributed to the improved performance of developing countries.

In growth, the NIEs, the PRC, and South Asian economies were the strongest performers among developing countries. Aside from a few countries such as Mexico, growth in Latin America was modest as political uncertainty dampened economic performance and market expectations. In Africa, growth varied substantially. Performance improved in several smaller countries that adopted structural reforms, while growth in the larger countries remained modest.

the first question, why the computer is only now so affecting the economy, is provided by a look at history. Economic historian Paul David argues that it takes decades for new technology to spread to the rest of the economy. His research shows that it took several decades for the technology of the electric dynamo to diffuse sufficiently to raise industrial productivity significantly. The same could be true for computer use in business, reinforced by the new information technology and the Internet.

To look for an answer to the second question regarding how productivity gains may have spilled over from the computer and information technology sections, consider inventory control, more efficient sourcing of inputs by canvassing suppliers, and Internet retailing. Certainly inventory control has been improved by the use of computers, but the cost savings are not great. Input sourcing and Internet retailing may yield productivity advances in the future,

but the savings up to now are small. Instead, it may be that the acceleration in productivity in the 1990s results from productivity gains in the computer industry alone. There is no doubt that a genuine productivity miracle has occurred in this industry, and some evidence suggests that it could have been responsible for the small overall acceleration in productivity in the entire economy. This suggests that there has been very little measurable diffusion of technology beyond computers.

The third question regarding how much each of the three factors have contributed individually to growth may be answered by the sheer strength in productivity in the computer industry. So far, whatever productivity gains have been made probably result primarily from the technology revolution in the computer industry alone and less from the Internet or information technology.

However, it is also plausible that the increased productivity has not been responsible for the reduced

inflation and unemployment and higher growth. The International Monetary Fund (IMF), in its latest *World Economic Outlook 2000* suggests that a strong dollar and lower import costs reduced consumer price inflation between 1996 and 1998, masking the signs of overheating. Moreover, the IMF argues that the financial crisis in 1997-1998 helped boost capital inflows, which in turn helped lower interest rates and strengthen the dollar despite the widening trade deficit, thereby raising demand. The IMF also increased its estimates of trend productivity, suggesting that the surge in productivity in the past few years is not as significant as previously estimated.

Whether the US economy has moved to a higher and seemingly sustainable growth rate, maintaining full employment without inflation, is therefore still debatable. Only time will tell whether the present upsurge in productivity heralded the arrival of the New Economy, or just another spike in the productivity chart.

The Non-Asian Developing Economies

GDP growth in Africa in 1999 was slightly lower at 3.1 percent, down from 3.4 percent the previous year. In the Middle East, GDP growth slowed to 1.8 percent from 3.2 percent in 1998 because of lower oil output. In 1999, growth in Latin America expanded by 0.1 percent as most countries in the region, except Mexico and Peru, experienced recession.

Africa. Growth performance varied across the region, with many of the smaller countries—Cameroon, Côte d' Ivoire, Ghana, Mozambique, Sudan, Tanzania, Tunisia, and Uganda—performing remarkably well, with growth of 3.9-7 percent. Implementing appropriate macroeconomic policies and favorable weather conditions contributed to this relatively strong ex-

pansion. Algeria implemented an extensive set of structural reforms over the past five years, and in Tunisia consistently strong growth was underpinned by healthy export performance supported by fiscal consolidation and a flexible exchange rate policy.

However, growth in three of the largest African economies was modest. Growth in South Africa recovered to 0.7 percent in 1999, only a slight improvement over 0.5 percent in 1998. Renewed financial market confidence; much lower interest rates; and improved prospects for exports, particularly to Asia, contributed to this recovery. Despite rising oil prices following the reduction in Organization of Petroleum Exporting Countries (OPEC) quotas in the second half of 1999, lower oil prices in 1998 and early 1999—and the subsequent reductions in oil production in compliance with lower OPEC quotas—reduced GDP growth in Nigeria to 0.5 percent in 1999. This was accompanied by rising budget and current account deficits. Morocco also grew slowly, as the economy was adversely affected by a drought that decreased agricultural output.

The implementation of structural reforms in Africa has been constrained by the economic difficulties brought about by depressed non-oil commodity prices in recent years, and this continued in 1999. However, increased attention to privatization efforts, public sector reforms, and other structural measures have in part been instrumental in improving the business and investment environment in some countries. Positive developments in trade and political cooperation have included the common external tariff implemented by the West African Economic and Monetary Union, bilateral trade agreements between the EU and some African economies, and plans for free trade areas in Eastern and Southern Africa.

Latin America. Many of the countries in this region experienced negative growth in 1999 following the 1998 Brazilian currency crisis. The recession and devaluation in Brazil—a major export market for the rest of the region—combined with political instability in some countries to cause regional GDP growth to slow in 1999 to 0.1 percent from 2.2 percent in 1998. The three big Latin American countries, Argentina, Brazil, and Mexico, faced varying economic situations. Mexico enjoyed relatively robust growth of 3 percent, while Argentina and Brazil were in a recession, with negative growth rates of 3 and 1 percent, respectively. All three faced difficult conditions in international financial markets: credit conditions hardened, and debt-market access was more difficult following the Brady bond default in Ecuador and the consequent possibility of involving private creditors in restructuring. The region weathered the storm largely through forced adjustment of exchange rate, fiscal policy, or both. Mexico had essentially separated itself from the rest of the region through its strong trade dependence on the US, which accounts for more than four fifths of its exports. Besides Mexico, Peru is the only other country in the region that achieved growth. It took advantage of the recovery in the global demand for industrial materials to expand production and increase revenue in its primary and mining sectors.

Investors' demand for a greater risk premium in view of exchange rate volatility and political instability, have kept real interest rates at extremely high levels in the region. Following the Brazilian devaluation in January 1999, secondary market spreads increased for most of the major developing country borrowers, including Latin America. However, there was a partial recovery later in the year as spreads fell somewhat. The high-risk premium has curbed net capital inflows that are needed to finance domestic investment. Foreign fund flows into local equity and money markets are being deterred because of poor growth prospects and exchange rate risk.

Much of the volatility in the region's currency and equity markets in 1999 resulted from the elections in Argentina, the chance of debt default in Argentina and Mexico, and slow or negative growth through much of the region. The recession in Latin America and large public sector debt service worsened the region's public finances in 1999. Even Chile, which had fiscal surpluses in the past five years, incurred a deficit. Despite the difficult environment, every major Latin American country achieved a primary surplus in 1999.

The Middle East. Many countries in this region emerged from the global financial crisis relatively unscathed. The use of foreign exchange reserves and external portfolios to finance the fiscal deficits and trade balances in the short term were used to avert the contagion effects from other financial markets. In countries with tighter financing constraints, contractionary expenditure policy, exchange rate devaluation, and rescheduling of external debt were used to regain stability.

Saudi Arabia, the main driver of growth in the Arabian Peninsula and the Gulf, did not adjust its spending to the fall in oil prices in 1998, and its government was forced to draw on its substantial overseas assets to meet budgeted spending commitments. Fiscal austerity measures were implemented in 1999 and growth is expected to resume in 2000. Egypt continued to drive growth in the Eastern Mediterranean area. Despite a change in the cabinet in 1999, progress in economic reform and liberalization propelled GDP growth to 6 percent. Growth also increased in Israel, due to greater foreign investment and political stability. Foreign direct investment (FDI) in the Middle East and the North Africa (MENA) region continued to lag behind other emerging markets because of the low level of integration with global capital markets. While global FDI inflow rose by 38.7 percent in 1998 to $643.9 billion, inflows into the MENA region fell by 6 percent to $7.2 billion and accounted for only 1.1 percent of global levels, down from 1.7 percent in 1997.

The Asian and Pacific Developing Economies

The Asian economic outlook changed dramatically in 1999 (figure 1.2). In the fall of 1998, several economies were in recession, capital flows had turned negative, and the outlook was generally pessimistic. In early 1999, an average annual growth of 4.4 percent was forecast for the region. This was revised to 5.7 percent in the fourth quarter of 1999, and the actual outcomes for the year have exceeded 6 percent.

The recovery has been uneven across developing Asia. Growth in the Republic of Korea (henceforth referred to as Korea) was particularly strong, along with the PRC and India. In tandem with the economic recovery in Russia in 1999, most countries in Central Asia experienced higher rates of growth, although inflation and external imbalances continued to be relatively high.

The faster-than-expected recovery in the first half of 1999 in most of the crisis-affected countries – Korea, Malaysia, Philippines, and Thailand—resulted from stimulative monetary and fiscal policy and increased exports, led by a surge in worldwide demand for electronics. Consumer sentiment also improved, bolstering domestic demand and economic growth. In the second half of 1999, the recovery was supported by continued expansionary policies and progress on implementing structural reforms to deal with the financial crisis.

In the NIEs and in Southeast Asia, either a resumption of growth or increased growth, combined with generally buoyant equity markets, helped improve aggregate demand and consumer confidence. Consumers began to spend after two years of belt tightening. A decrease in consumer goods prices in some countries further increased purchasing power, partly offsetting selective wage cuts and high unemployment.

Korea, one of the countries most affected by the financial crisis, led the region with double-digit economic growth in 1999. Stock rebuilding, increases in private consumption and investment, and increased exports boosted Korean production to above precrisis levels. Among the other crisis-affected countries growth ranged from 0.2 to 5.4 percent, as these countries also experienced a stronger-than-expected recovery from the crisis. Growth in the PRC slowed from 7.8 percent in 1998 to 7.1 percent in 1999, as its pump priming of the economy through expansionary fiscal policy weakened and export growth remained modest. South Asia continued to be a strongly performing region with an aggregate growth rate acceleration of 5.5 percent in 1999. Growth in India, the largest economy in the region, was robust at 5.9 percent. A strong increase in industry sector activity was partially offset by weak agriculture output growth. Other countries in the region, including Bangladesh and Sri Lanka, also did reasonably well.

Currency markets in Asia stabilized in 1999 because of structural reforms, interest rate cuts in most of the industrial countries, positive expectations about the Japanese economy, and increased financial commitments from the international community. Consequently, foreign capital started returning to Asia. Private capital flows returned to five crisis-affected countries—Indonesia, Korea, Malaysia, Philippines, and Thailand—with net private inflows of $5.1 billion in 1999, as opposed to a net outflow of $38.6 billion in 1998. In the PRC, net private flows slowed from about $40 billion in 1998 to around $27 billion in 1999, as FDI eased and debts were repaid. At 6.2 percent, growth in the Asian region is expected to remain virtually unchanged in 2000. Slower growth in the NIEs and the PRC will be offset by more rapid growth in Southeast Asia, South Asia, and the Central Asian republics.

The Newly Industrialized Economies. The NIEs rebounded strongly in 1999. GDP growth was 7.0 percent compared with a contraction of 1.9 percent in 1998. There was slight deflationary pressure as the aggregate price level fell by 0.4 percent.

Despite the overall revival of the NIEs, economic performance varied significantly among countries. After a severe recession in 1998, the economy of

Figure 1.2 ADB's Forecast Growth Rate, Asia, November 1998 - March 2000

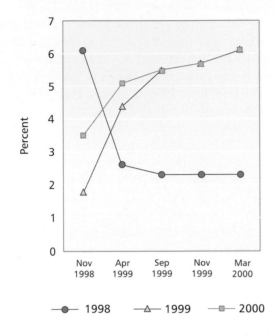

Sources: ADB (1998c, 1999b); Kumar (1999); Siregar (1998).

High unemployment rates and low wage growth continued to dampen consumer demand in the NIEs. Private consumption expenditure increased a modest 1.6 percent in 1999 for the subregion, although there were substantial differences among countries. In 1999, high real interest rates and an uncertain business outlook contributed to weak consumption in Hong Kong, China, while in Taipei,China consumption demand was weak compared with previous years. Conversely, in Korea consumption spending increased significantly, rising to 7.4 percent from a decline of 8.2 percent in 1998. In Singapore, consumer demand also increased because of falling unemployment, wage increases in the private sector, and more tourist arrivals.

Inflation in the NIEs in 1999 averaged negative 0.4 percent. In Hong Kong, China deflation continued at a more rapid pace than in 1998 as the consumer price index fell by 4 percent. Fierce price competition, flat rental prices, and a freeze in government fees and most public utility charges contributed to the sustained fall in the consumer price index. Weak world commodity prices (except for fuel), and deflation in the PRC—Hong Kong, China's major trading partner—also kept imported inflation at bay. Singapore's inflation rate was 0.5 percent in 1999, primarily due to weak domestic demand. In Taipei,China, the inflation rate continued to be low, averaging 0.2 percent. Weak domestic demand coupled with the government's strategy of increasing imports helped contain inflation. In Korea, the appreciation of the won contributed to the drop in the inflation rate from 7.5 percent in 1998 to 0.8 percent in 1999, the lowest level recorded in 50 years.

Exports, which had declined in 1998 because of the crisis, staged a moderate recovery and increased by 4.5 percent in 1999 in the NIEs. Net exports of services rose in 1999, led by regional demand for financial and business services. In Singapore, the services balance benefited from regional recovery and more than offset the smaller trade surplus. Consequently, the current account surplus was 18.5 percent of GDP in 1999. In Taipei,China imports of industrial raw materials and capital goods used primarily for export production began to increase at the end of 1999, although imports of consumer goods remained sluggish. Overall, Taipei, China recorded a current account surplus of 3 percent of GDP in 1999. The trade deficit

Hong Kong, China posted growth of 2.9 percent in 1999. This recovery was mainly sustained by accelerated growth in government spending, and increased exports of services combined with decreased imports of goods. In Korea, real GDP grew by 10.7 percent in 1999 after declining by 6.7 percent the previous year. Several large fiscal stimulus packages combined with foreign capital inflows and more accommodating monetary policy helped renew domestic demand in Korea. Along with more expansionary monetary and fiscal policy, electronics exports to the US to meet Y2K standards provided a major boost to growth in Singapore. Taipei,China experienced a 15-year low GDP growth rate of 4.6 percent in 1998, although it edged up to 5.7 percent the next year. Some additional growth resulted from a surge in exports of electronic, information, and communication products, which emanated from an expansion of the information technology (IT) sector in industrial countries and Y2K-compliance requirements.

Table 1.1 **Selected Economic Indicators, Developing Asia, 1997-2001**
(percent)

	1997	1998	1999	2000	2001
Gross domestic product (annual change)					
Developing Asia	6.0	2.3	6.2	6.2	6.0
Newly industrialized economies	5.7	-1.9	7.0	6.5	6.0
PRC and Mongolia	8.7	7.8	7.1	6.5	6.0
Central Asian republics	3.3	0.8	2.8	3.0	3.6
Southeast Asia	3.7	-7.5	3.2	4.6	5.0
South Asia	4.7	6.2	5.5	6.4	6.6
The Pacific	-3.2	1.2	4.4	—	—
Inflation (change in CPI)					
Developing Asia	4.3	5.5	1.6	3.0	3.3
Newly industrialized economies	3.5	3.9	-0.4	1.8	2.6
PRC and Mongolia	2.8	-0.8	-1.4	1.8	2.0
Central Asian republics	21.4	11.4	21.9	15.1	10.7
Southeast Asia	5.5	21.3	7.4	4.7	4.6
South Asia	5.6	7.1	4.1	5.0	5.4
The Pacific	3.9	9.9	10.4	—	—
Current account balance/GDP					
Developing Asia	0.5	4.1	3.8	1.5	0.5
Newly industrialized economies	1.6	9.3	6.4	3.7	2.4
PRC and Mongolia	3.3	3.0	1.2	-0.4	-0.9
Central Asian republics	-4.0	-4.5	-2.0	-2.4	-2.3
Southeast Asia	-3.4	7.0	7.6	3.3	0.8
South Asia	-1.4	-1.9	-2.2	-3.9	-3.0
The Pacific	-0.9	1.8	—	—	—

— Not available.
CPI consumer price index.
Sources: Appendix tables.

narrowed, as there was a significant rebound in re-exports to and from Asia, especially Indonesia, Japan, Korea, and Singapore. In Hong Kong, China exports recovered but growth was still negative in 1999. In Korea, export growth recovered strongly to more than 10 percent from a 4.7 percent deficit in 1998, as a result of stronger competitiveness vis-a-vis Japan and recovery in Asian markets.

Future economic expansion in the region will be driven by growth in domestic demand, efficiency gains resulting from progress in structural reforms and IT-related exports. GDP growth in 2000 is forecast to be 6.5 percent for the NIEs (see figure 1.3). This growth rate, while quite robust, is still somewhat lower than in 1999, primarily because of a decline in Korea's growth,

where double-digit growth is not expected to be sustained. Export growth in the NIEs is projected to increase more, to 8.9 percent in 2000. This would be the highest growth rate in exports since 1995, but it falls short of the average of nearly 15 percent between 1992 and 1995. A large-scale restructuring of capacities and policy measures to regain competitiveness may be required before the NIEs regain such export dynamism. Import demand will recover sharply as growth returns and the increased exports in turn drive up demand for raw materials and components.

PRC and Mongolia. Despite the Asian financial crisis, the PRC maintained a robust growth rate of 7.8 percent in 1998, and did not fall into recession for two

Figure 1.3 Real GDP Growth Rates, Newly Industrialized Economies, 1999-2001

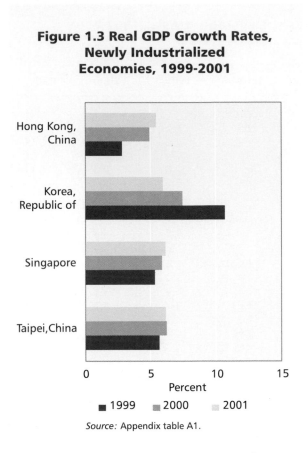

Source: Appendix table A1.

reasons. First, the PRC has capital controls and a fixed exchange rate, and these policies insulated the economy from the financial turmoil that besieged other countries. Second, the PRC adopted an expansionary fiscal policy in the form of public spending on infrastructure projects. GDP growth slowed to 7.1 percent in 1999, partly because of a tapering of the stimulus from the 1998 fiscal packages. An increase in sales of durable goods and commodity prices in 1999 helped ease deflationary pressures. The economic recovery within the Asian region, which absorbs half of the PRC's exports, helped accelerate export growth to 6 percent in 1999, from less than 1 percent the previous year. This is far short of the rapid export growth recorded before the crisis, but is on a par with many of its competitors in the region. Clearly, some of the deceleration in export growth may be due to greater competition from other regional exporters, which have more competitive exchange rates after the Asian financial crisis. Imports grew by 18.2 percent in 1999,

primarily because of increased demand by export- oriented industries for imports to replenish inventories and to satisfy the demand for investment and consumer goods. The combination of a narrowing trade surplus and a chronic deficit in the services balance reduced the current account surplus to 1.2 percent of GDP.

Interest rates were lowered four times since 1998, to boost consumption and investment spending and ultimately break the deflationary spiral. The relaxation of monetary policy also reduced the debt-service burden of state-owned enterprises.

FDI fell 9.7 percent during 1999, and there may have been portfolio capital outflow. Consequently, foreign reserve accumulation was minimal. However, this is not a serious concern because the growth of foreign exchange earnings kept pace with the growth of foreign liabilities, with foreign exchange reserves still five times the level of short-term debt.

Growth in 2000 is forecast at 6.5 percent, primarily due to slowed industry and construction sector activity (see figure 1.4). The PRC's reform strategy over the last two decades has centered on the agriculture and manufacturing sectors, while the service sector has lagged in productivity growth because of heavy protection. Liberalization of the service sector over the next two to five years, as a result of entry into the World Trade Organization, could potentially overhaul the sector and unleash a second wave of dynamic productivity gains, which may spur growth in the medium to long term (see box 1.2).

After several years of a relatively well-managed transition to a market-based economy, Mongolia has faced a financial sector crisis and problems with macroeconomic stabilization. The Asian and Russian financial crises caused a severe drop in FDI and bilateral aid flows. In addition, cashmere, copper, and gold, the main exports, suffered from low world prices, which decreased export revenues. Economic growth remained at 3.5 percent in 1999.

As large enterprises faced cash shortages, a drawdown on bank deposits and a growing volume of nonperforming loans led to a weakening of the banking system. This increased the fiscal liability of the government, as the distressed banks need to be recapitalized. The public sector fiscal imbalance, which has been compounded over the years due to budgetary

Figure 1.4 Real GDP Growth Rates, PRC and Mongolia, 1999-2001

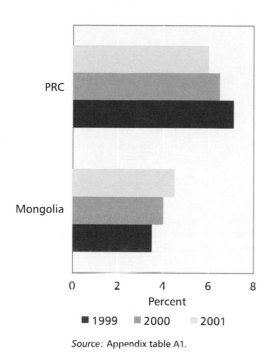

Source: Appendix table A1.

cent contraction the previous year. The Kyrgyz Republic's economy was in the middle of a major fiscal and financial adjustment process, but the GDP growth rate in 1999 was 3.6 percent, up from 2.1 percent in 1998. The engine of growth was the agriculture sector, which grew by 8.7 percent. Tajikistan made substantial progress in macroeconomic stabilization and its transition to a market economy in 1998. Its three-year IMF reform program is largely on track. However, GDP growth was only 3.7 percent in 1999, considerably lower than the 1998 rate of 5.3 percent, reflecting stagnant growth in both agriculture and industry. Uzbekistan, the country with the largest population in Central Asia, is following its own gradual reform program. Foreign exchange controls, the country's policy of self-sufficiency, and rudimentary financial markets all impede more rapid economic progress. GDP growth in 1999, at 4.4 percent, was the same rate recorded in 1998.

Future economic performance in the Central Asian republics will depend on Russia's continued economic recovery and improvement in international commodity prices (see figure 1.5). The extent to which the respective countries are affected by these two factors varies considerably. Political stability will also play a role in the future development of these former Soviet republics.

mismanagement, has begun to threaten the government's ability to complete ongoing reforms.

Mongolia's short- to medium-term prospects depend on the success of banking sector reforms, whether fiscal imbalances are addressed, and the strength of export performance. GDP growth in 2000 is forecast at 4 percent, with the main sources of growth expected to be mining and manufacturing. Reforms in the agriculture sector, promotion of small-scale industries, and escalating private sector activity (which constituted 60 percent of GDP in 1998) are expected to stimulate growth.

The Central Asian Republics. The economies of Central Asia grew at 2.8 percent in 1999, up from the previous year's 0.8 percent. Kazakhstan implemented major policy adjustments, including floating its currency, the tenge. Stabilization of commodity prices and prudent fiscal policy provided breathing space for implementing reforms, which helped the economy grow to 1.7 percent in 1999, compared with a 1.9 per-

The Southeast Asian Economies. The V-shaped recovery in the crisis countries in this region can be viewed partly as a snapback given the sharp negative growth the previous year. Nevertheless, various positive factors, both domestic and external, contributed to the recovery, including increased consumption, stock rebuilding, massive fiscal stimulus, and loose monetary policy. New policy measures to address corporate and financial sector problems also supported the recovery, and helped contain and even reduce the level of nonperforming loans. The recovery was stimulated also by the strengthened Japanese economy and increased financial resource flows from the international community, which resulted in improved balance-of-payments position in most of the subregion. Together with inflows of foreign aid and progress on foreign debt rollovers, capital flows were stabilized, and confidence in these countries was restored. The availability of fiscal surpluses, a legacy of

Box 1.2 The People's Republic of China's Entry into the World Trade Organization: Who Wins and Loses?

With merchandise exports of nearly $200 billion in 1998, the People's Republic of China (PRC) is the ninth largest exporter in the world. The PRC is expected to join the World Trade Organization (WTO) in 2000, an event of major economic significance for the Chinese and global economy. One of the major obstacles to the PRC's 13-year bid to gain accession to WTO was cleared in November 1999, when the United States and the PRC signed a bilateral trade agreement detailing a far-reaching set of commitments that the PRC will have to meet as a WTO member. Although the PRC will now have to negotiate similar agreements with the European Union and several other smaller trading partners before it can join WTO, the agreement with the US is pivotal, because the concessions it extracted from the PRC are likely to satisfy many other countries. The terms of the bilateral agreement with the US include the following

- *Agriculture:* Overall tariffs for all agricultural products are to be cut from an average of 22 percent to 17.5 percent by January 2004, with even lower rates for beef; cheese; wine; and a range of fruits, including grapes, oranges, apples, cherries, and almonds. Moreover, market access will be further enhanced by a progressive increase in quotas on

bulk commodities such as corn, cotton, rice, soybean oil, and wheat, and the elimination of health and hygiene standards that are not based on scientific evidence. The PRC has also committed itself to eliminating export subsidies and liberalizing domestic trade in agriculture by allowing private entities to engage in importing and distributing agricultural products without going through state trading enterprises.

- *Industry:* Average tariffs on all industrial products are to be cut from the 1997 average of 24.6 percent to 9.4 percent by 2005, with sharper reductions for tariffs on automobiles (from 80-100 percent to 25 percent by 2006), chemicals, wood, and paper. Quotas for fiber optic cables and other products are to be eliminated upon the PRC's accession to WTO, and most of the remaining quotas will be increased before being phased out by 2005. The PRC will also join the Information Technology Agreement and eliminate tariffs on semiconductors, computers, and all Internet-related equipment by 2005.

- *Services:* The PRC is committed to eliminating most foreign equity and geographical restrictions on its service sectors within two to six years. It will also accede to WTO's Basic Telecommunications and Financial Services agreements. The Basic Telecommunications agreement will

allow up to 49 percent foreign ownership in mobile, domestic, and international land and sea services within five to six years and 50 percent ownership in paging and value-added services within two years. The Financial Services agreement will phase out all geographical restrictions on foreign insurers within three years and expand their scope of activities to include group, health, and pension policies within five years. The PRC will also allow 50 percent foreign ownership in life insurance joint ventures and 100 percent ownership in reinsurance and nonlife insurance within two years. Foreign banks will gain full market access within five years and will be able to conduct local currency transactions with Chinese enterprises and individuals within two to five years. Joint venture firms with minority foreign stakes will also be able to underwrite domestic- and foreign-currency-denominated securities.

- *Trading and distribution rights:* The PRC will grant full trading and distribution rights to foreign firms within three years of accession to WTO. This will give foreign firms the right to import and export directly without Chinese intermediaries, and to handle wholesaling, retailing, maintenance and repair, and transportation.

Source: Institute for International Economics (1999).

---

past prudent policies, and a favorable external environment permitted the easing of fiscal and monetary policy and reduced interest rates without causing volatility in foreign exchange market.

After an initially tenuous start, Southeast Asia's recovery has proved more rapid and broad-based than anticipated. All the countries in the subregion registered growth in 1999 (see figure 1.6). The GDP growth rate for the subregion was 3.2 percent in 1999, in sharp

contrast to a negative growth of 7.5 percent in 1998. Nevertheless, domestic consumption and investment, on average, remained well below precrisis levels.

In the first half of 1999, the recovery in global demand for semiconductors, which emanated from preparations for achieving Y2K compliance, led to a surge in exports from Malaysia, Philippines, and Thailand. Among the crisis-affected countries, only the Philippines escaped negative export growth in

Foreign firms will also be able to engage in such auxiliary services as leasing, air courier, warehousing, packaging, and advertising.

These sweeping reforms are likely to have far-reaching domestic and international implications. In the short term, many analysts expect the reforms to lead to a considerable loss of output and a sharp increase in unemployment. For instance, in farming, cuts in tariffs and increases in tariff quotas will probably result in a substantial increase in wheat imports, as domestic prices remain far above world market prices. This will bring about a sharp reduction in output and an increase in unemployment. The auto industry will probably experience a similar sharp reduction in output and jobs, as the new WTO regime slashes tariffs and allows foreign carmakers to provide financial assistance to buyers. This may cause rationalization of the fragmented and inefficient car industry that currently has more than 100 manufacturers of vehicles and components. Many domestic vehicle makers will not survive the cost cutting needed to remain competitive.

WTO membership also will bring far-reaching changes to the financial sector. As foreign banks will eventually be allowed to conduct local currency business with both Chinese firms and individuals, competition within the domestic financial sector is certain to intensify.

Domestic banks will need to improve their banking practices and strengthen their balance sheets. Otherwise, they could face a loss of deposits to foreign banks that have fewer nonperforming loans and can, therefore, offer higher interest rates to depositors.

However, over time the efficiency gains from reallocating both capital and labor to more competitive sectors within the Chinese economy should more than offset these short-term losses. This should result in increased productivity, profitability, investment, and employment. Accession to WTO would then deepen and accelerate Chinese liberalization and help lock in the tenuous domestic reform process.

What will be the probable impact on the rest of the world when the PRC joins WTO? Apart from increased access to the PRC's internal market, WTO membership would make all investors who use the PRC as a production and export platform feel more secure about access to third markets as well as the domestic market. Foreign retailers and distributors will also be able to sell products and services directly to Chinese consumers for the first time. This will give Chinese consumers greater choice at lower prices. Regional economies are likely to be among the main beneficiaries of the PRC's liberalization measures. Established producers of quality consumer durable goods, including

Japan; Republic of Korea; and Taipei,China, could gain significantly from better access to the region's second largest market. Southeast Asian exporters of natural resources such as Indonesia and agricultural producers such as Thailand could gain from greater access to the PRC markets, while Indian pharmaceutical manufacturers could potentially gain access to the PRC's highly protected pharmaceutical market. On the export side, the PRC's accession to WTO will make it an even more formidable competitor in labor-intensive products in the world market such as shoes, toys, bags, and textiles. Some regional economies will lose export markets to the PRC in the textile and apparel sector when the Multi-Fibre Agreement quotas are phased out by 2005. Finally, given that the PRC's accession commitments to WTO are considerably more liberal than the commitments of a number of regional member countries, this could prompt a further round of competitive liberalization within the region, as the PRC begins to implement its WTO commitments.

The PRC's accession to WTO should not be seen as a zero sum game where one side loses and the other gains. Although there may be short-term costs for both sides, the long-term benefits from an expansion and liberalization of the world trading system from the PRC's membership would no doubt far outweigh these short-term costs.

the past two years, achieving an export growth rate of 16.9 percent in 1998 and 18.8 percent in 1999. It was less constrained by the crisis, as it had undergone a major restructuring in the 1980s. Its exports also were more geared to the US market, which remained buoyant.

Consumer spending began to recover in the first half of 1999. In the four crisis-affected countries, consumer confidence indicators stabilized and are improving. Even Indonesia, which lags behind the other

countries in the region in terms of consumer confidence, registered a private consumption growth rate of 2 percent in 1999, while the Philippines and Thailand registered 2.5 percent. Nevertheless, the 1999 level of private consumption expenditures remained below precrisis levels.

Pump priming of the regional economies through large fiscal stimulus packages was used extensively in 1998 and 1999, causing concern that fiscal imbalances

Figure 1.5 Real GDP Growth Rates, Central Asian Republics, 1999-2001

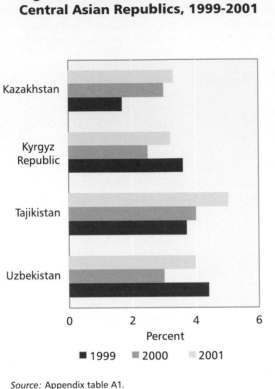

Source: Appendix table A1.

were getting out of hand. Assuming a recovery of 50-60 percent of nonperforming loans in these economies, the cost of fiscal support for bank recapitalization was expected to be about 15 percent of GDP in Malaysia and more than 30 percent in Indonesia and Thailand. Actual recovery rates in 1999 were, however substantially lower.

The improvement in economic performance, combined with the return of portfolio capital to the region, resulted in a surge in the equity market prices by 25.4 percent in dollar terms during 1999. This was significantly above the 6.7 percent and 4.5 percent recorded in the US and world stock markets, respectively. This boosted confidence in domestic markets and stimulated consumption spending.

Price stability continued to improve in the region. In Cambodia, Lao People's Democratic Republic, Philippines, Thailand, and Viet Nam, inflation fell in 1999, reflecting lower food prices. Indonesia displayed a dramatic decline in its inflation rate, from 58.5 percent in 1998 to around 20.5 percent in 1999, because of

lower food prices and unused industrial capacity. A more stable political environment and increased foreign capital inflows also helped stabilize prices, particularly during the second half of the year.

Short-term nominal interest rates across the region remained below precrisis averages, with the exception of Indonesia. Thailand's three-month interest rate of 4.00-4.25 percent in December 1999 is significantly below the 10.7 percent recorded for 1991-1996. The interest rate declines result from improvements in the balance of payments combined with an expansionary monetary policy. Central banks in the region kept short-term interest rates low to keep financial sector reforms on track and bolster demand.

On the external balance, the substantial current account surpluses that accompanied the initial collapse in economic activity lifted foreign exchange reserves to record levels in Malaysia and the Philippines during 1998. Combined with the announcement of structural reforms and macroeconomic stabilization programs, this led to a resumption of foreign capital inflows and boosted investor sentiment. Strong FDI offset the low level of domestic investment somewhat. Import growth tended to outstrip export growth by a large margin in several countries because of rising demand from increased industry sector activity. However, imports continued to decline in Indonesia, so the trade and current account balances in the region's totals changed only slightly compared with 1998.

Growth in 1999 emanated from continued improvement in domestic demand that arose from expansionary macroeconomic policies, combined with improved external demand that resulted from expanded world and intraregional trade. The 2000 forecast for Southeast Asia is for a modest strengthening of growth to 4.6 percent. This upward trend should be supported by the boom in the electronics industry, continued economic growth in the US, likely upturn in euro area, and the possible continued recovery of the Japanese economy.

South Asia. South Asia continues to be a strong performer, largely because of the strength of the Indian economy. Growth in the subregion was 6.2 and 5.5 percent in 1998 and 1999, respectively. In India, the industry sector showed signs of an increase after three years of sluggish performance. Combined with in-

Figure 1.6 Real GDP Growth Rates, Southeast Asia, 1999-2001

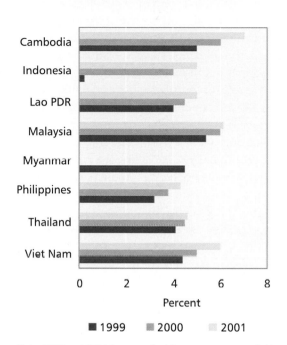

Note: 2000 and 2001 forecasts for Myanmar are not available.
Source: Appendix table A1.

creased exports and a weaker performance in the agriculture sector, GDP growth was 5.9 percent in 1999. Pakistan's continued political instability, weak agriculture sector performance, and macroeconomic imbalances constrained growth to 3.9 percent in 1999. In Bangladesh, manufacturing sector activity was seriously hampered because of the floods in the first half of 1999 and political demonstrations. The Maldives recorded 8.5 percent growth, with strong performance in the tourism, fisheries, and construction sectors. GDP growth in Nepal was a modest 3.3 percent in 1999, higher than 2.3 percent growth in the previous year. The recovery of the agriculture and industry sectors supported Nepal's growth momentum. Growth in Sri Lanka decelerated to 4.2 percent in 1999, primarily due to declining industrial output.

Inflation dropped in the subregion during 1999 to 4.1 from 7.1 percent in the previous year, primarily due to increased agricultural production that offset a 25 percent hike in diesel prices in India. Rising business competition put downward pressure on prices, while the relatively stable exchange rate dampened imported inflation. In Pakistan, the downward trend in inflation continued in 1999 because of tight monetary and fiscal policies, combined with weak aggregate demand growth. Severe floods disrupted industrial production in Bangladesh, which contributed to inflation.

The fiscal balance continued to be a cause for concern in most major countries in the subregion. In India, the gross fiscal deficit of 5.5 percent of GDP is particularly worrisome because the real interest rate on public debt exceeds the GDP growth rate. Not only does the growing fiscal deficit seriously threaten macroeconomic stability, but it will limit the amount of public investment available for physical and social infrastructure required to support an industrial recovery. In Bangladesh, the shortfall in government revenues, combined with expenditures associated with flood-relief programs, further strained the fiscal balance. Structural reforms in the form of tax increases, subsidy reductions, and current expenditure reduction improved the fiscal balance in Pakistan. However, development program spending is expected to rise in the next few years to promote economic growth, which, combined with a decline in foreign aid, will exert pressure on the fiscal balance in the short to medium term.

On the external balance, export growth decelerated in most major countries, with the exception of India. Manufacturing exports, which accounted for 80 percent of India's exports, was stimulated by the recovery in Asia and global trade. The export competitiveness of Bangladesh, Pakistan, and Sri Lanka was adversely affected by the large devaluation of major Southeast Asian currencies. The drop in prices of textile products and non-oil commodities such as tea and rubber also contributed to the export slowdown in Bangladesh and Sri Lanka.

The current account deficit for the subregion widened to 2.2 percent of GDP in 1999 from 1.9 percent in 1998, the highest recorded in the 1990s. Most of this resulted from increased import growth in the subregion, because of the substantial climb in the prices of crude oil and petroleum products.

Political stability and a positive economic outlook for India led to resumed foreign capital inflows into India and raised investor confidence. This encouraged foreign investors to pour in portfolio investment, which recorded a net inflow in 1999 rather than a net outflow as in 1998. However, a deterioration of the political environment in Pakistan and Sri Lanka slowed the inflow of foreign capital into these countries. FDI decreased to $225 million in Bangladesh in 1999 from $317 million in 1998. Most of the inflows were to the natural gas and power sectors, which account for 60 percent of total FDI.

Aggregate growth in South Asia for 2000 is forecast at 6.4 percent (see figure 1.7). Growth in India will increase slightly, with industry and service sector growth remaining strong. Political stability in the region will be essential in determining the course of economic policy in the subregion and the prospects for reaching the per capita income levels attained in the NIEs and Southeast Asia. The opening of domestic capital markets and integration with international financial markets will increase net capital inflows and improve the access to international financial markets. These synergies will help alleviate the negative effects of chronic fiscal deficits, which otherwise would have crowded out private sector investment in a relatively closed economy.

Figure 1.7 Real GDP Growth Rates, South Asia, 1999-2001

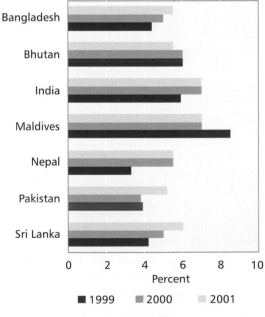

Source: Appendix table A1.

The Pacific. The Pacific subregion as a whole grew by 4.4 percent in 1999, compared with 1.2 percent in 1998. Sound macroeconomic management and tight monetary policy in those countries that have their own currency contributed to the improved economic performance in most of the subregion. Papua New Guinea, the subregion's largest economy, experienced an acceleration in real GDP growth of 3.9 percent in 1999, despite intensified macroeconomic instability. Faster growth resulted from higher commodity prices and increased exports. With the exception of Kiribati, Tuvalu, and Vanuatu, all the economies registered faster growth in 1999, including the Fiji Islands, where the recovery in agricultural production and growth in garment manufacturing contributed to a 1999 GDP growth of 7.8 percent. Inflation in the subregion rose to 10.4 percent in 1999, mostly because inflation in Papua New Guinea rose to 16 percent. The government failed to secure external funding to finance fiscal imbalances, and had to rely on domestic financing of the budget deficit and accumulation of arrears on debt-service payments.

The economic prospects in the short to medium term will depend on the success of public sector reforms, sustained macroeconomic stabilization, and private sector development. The potential of this subregion will not be realized unless macroeconomic stability is sustained and improvements made in the economic policy environment. In some countries, economic policy continues to be characterized by lack of transparency and predictability that discourages prospects for both domestic and foreign investments.

RISKS AND UNCERTAINTIES

Recovery in Asia was robust during 1999. The transformation of developing Asia from financial crisis in 1997 and 1998 to the world's fastest-growing region has exceeded all expectations. It took developing Asia less than two years to return to the precrisis level of industrial production. Prospects for 2000 depend on sustainability of domestic demand growth, not only through growth in consumption, but also an upturn in investment demand and favorable global economic conditions. Investment may have to rise as capacity utilization rates go up and capacity restructuring occurs in response to technological advance and competitive pressures. However, this is predicated on an upturn in credit growth, which is still uncertain because bank lending remains weak.

Rapid growth in intraregional trade feeding into increased domestic demand and higher real incomes is also expected. For these effects to prevail in the Asian subregion, the external environment will also have to be favorable. The continued expansion in global GDP and the expected rise in international trade volumes, combined with continued firmness in commodity prices, are crucial in maintaining export growth momentum. The major concern will be the nature of correction in asset prices in the US, the strength of the cyclical upswing in the euro area, and the prospects for Japanese recovery. A favorable external environment requires a soft landing for the US economy as a further tightening of monetary policy accomplishes a smooth transition to slower growth. It also requires a strengthening of the cyclical upswing in the euro area despite more monetary policy tightening by the European Central Bank and a continuation of the Japanese recovery.

Even as domestic demand conditions in the world economy improved, OPEC decided in April 1999 to cut back production. Unless oil prices moderate, another oil shock could derail Asia's recovery as well as the rest of the world economy (see box 1.3).

From a domestic aggregate demand perspective, expansionary domestic policies and rallies in equity markets in developing Asia have helped to improve business and consumer sentiment, and have had a salutary effect on consumption. These factors seem to be offsetting the constraints on domestic consumption imposed by high unemployment rates, slow wage growth, and reluctance of banks to lend. The fiscal expenditures required to fund financial sector bailouts, combined with ongoing development and recurring expenditures, will put additional pressure on government budgets throughout the subregion. The cost of financing these expenditures will increase budget deficits further, pushing up prices and interest rates. Unless handled prudently, these pressures could dampen growth prospects for the Asian region, particularly in the crisis-affected countries where bailouts are the most costly.

It is worth noting that domestic demand and the stabilization of savings ratios are two sides of the same coin. Where savings ratios fell in 1999, noticeably in Indonesia, Korea, Singapore, and probably Thailand, domestic demand rallied. However, during 2000, the strength of that rally may moderate in these countries, unless asset markets continue their upward trend. In those countries where 1999 saw little or no saving rate decline—Hong Kong, China; Malaysia; Philippines; and Taipei,China—domestic demand is likely to be better supported in 2000.

Another concern is the continued large external imbalance in the US. Some of the funding for the US deficit has come from those seeking a safe haven during the financial crisis. But with the restoration of growth, these funds are beginning to return to Asia and other countries. Convergence of growth between the US and the euro area in the next few years may help raise US exports to that area and cut the deficit. However, if US interest rates must be raised to sustain the capital inflows required to service this debt, it will have a depressing effect not only on the US economy, but also on the rest of the world. It would result in upward pressure on interest rates in Asia and threaten the strength of the economic recovery.

Continued commitment to and speedy implementation of structural reforms is necessary in the crisis-affected countries in developing Asia. In most of the crisis-affected countries, progress in establishing a modern legal and regulatory framework has occurred, but there is more to be accomplished. Public administration reforms are required to improve bureaucratic and corruption-prone administrative procedures. Corporate governance reforms for changing ownership structure of large business groups and adoption of modern financial management techniques remain a priority. The region still has an extensive agenda for restructuring the banking and corporate sectors and making business transactions more transparent and accountable. Progress in implementing these will ensure efficiency in resource allocation and help stimulate investment spending. (The next chapter of this *Outlook* addresses these topics in depth.)

In the case of the Central Asian republics and Mongolia, risks are related to the success of policy measures aimed at completing the transition to a market-based economy and building the necessary institutional structures. Higher energy and primary commodity prices in 2000 and the emergence of a recovery in Russia, if realized, will affect these economies positively.

Increased investments and innovative policies are required to raise productivity levels and enhance the international competitiveness of the region. Raising labor productivity would entail investments in human resources in education, knowledge, and skills. Raising the international competitiveness of Asia's developing economies would require adopting and generating new and innovative technologies, which would, in turn, require greater investments in research and development as well as a conducive environment that fosters greater creativity and innovativeness.

Box 1.3 A Crude Reminder: Will Oil End the Boom?

Does the sharp increase in crude oil prices from $10 a barrel in 1998 to more than $30 a barrel by March 2000 mean the possible return to the bad old days of stagflation? Simulation exercises for industrial countries reported by the Organisation for Economic Co-operation and Development (OECD) suggest that doubling the oil price from $10 a barrel to $20 a barrel raises inflation by less than 1 percent after one year. The OECD simulations also suggest that economic growth can be slowed by between 0.2 and 0.4 percent. The impact will be larger on Japan than the United States and the European Union, because Japan is more dependent on imported oil and exports much less to the Organisation of Petroleum Exporting Countries (OPEC).

So far the actual effect of the oil price increase has yet to be felt on the general level of consumer prices, which are still remarkably steady in the industrial economies. The impact on growth is more difficult to determine but there apparently has been no appreciable growth slump within the OECD in the past few months. One difficulty with estimating the effects of an oil price increase on growth or the general price level is the lag between the increase in prices and the feed-through to the rest of the economy.

A more worrisome possibility is the secondary effect that higher oil prices might have on policy. In previous oil shocks the increase in prices accelerated inflation, which was then followed by contractionary monetary policy and recession. The effect on oil-importing developing countries was also quite severe.

Is such a scenario likely to reoccur? This will depend on several factors, including pass-through to inflation, the actions of oil suppliers, and the response in demand.

The pass-through to inflation will be lower than during the earlier two oil shocks simply because the oil economy is dramatically smaller.

On the supply side, oil prices increased primarily because OPEC lowered quotas in April 1999, and most members have stuck to the quotas. The response of non-OPEC members to higher prices has been and can be expected to remain marginal. First, putting new capacity into operation takes time and second, the scope for increased supply by nonmembers is limited, even in the long run. Compared with previous oil shocks, there is very little scope for additional non-OPEC supply. There are no more untapped sources such as Alaska and the North Seas once provided. Also, industrial countries are putting enormous pressure on OPEC to increase supply. OPEC probably prefers to avoid the experience that followed the second oil shock, when longer-run adjustments to demand resulted in unusually low oil prices for a decade.

This was reflected in the March 2000 meeting when nine of the 11 OPEC oil ministers agreed to raise production by about 7 percent from current levels. Following this announcement, oil prices declined and are in the range of $25 per barrel as this *Outlook* goes to press.

Is more oil price volatility likely? In the short run, supply factors probably will not change quickly, because the lag between increased pumping and delivery of the new output to the local service station is still several months. Current prices probably reflect these delays.

Aside from the influence of the weather, demand factors are not very significant in determining price in the short run. Milder weather in Europe and North America with the end of winter tends to moderate demand. Otherwise, the reduction in demand will be insignificant as a few people buy smaller cars, drive less frequently, or turn down their thermostats.

In conclusion it is unlikely that oil prices will start back up, given the higher production quotas recently agreed upon, continued leverage exerted on OPEC and the memories of two previous recessions caused by oil shocks. In addition policymakers presumably have learned from experience, and will be able to adopt macroeconomic policies that deal with the potential inflationary effects of higher oil prices without tipping the world economy into recession.

Source: OECD (1999).

Corporate and Financial Sector Reform: Progress and Prospects

This chapter examines and appraises the corporate and financial sector reforms undertaken so far in the crisis-affected economies in Southeast Asia and East Asia. It considers what must be done—both in the short and medium term—to create vibrant and healthy corporate and financial sectors. The chapter concludes that sustainability of the region's short-term recovery, as well as its long-term economic prospects, depends largely on how effectively and comprehensively the corporate and financial sectors are restructured.

The 1997-1998 Asian financial crisis was the biggest economic and social shock to befall the region since the Great Depression. After decades of rapid growth, output plummeted. In little over a year, the five crisis countries—Indonesia, Republic of Korea (henceforth referred to as Korea), Malaysia, Philippines, and Thailand—saw their combined economic loss reach approximately 30 percent of gross domestic product (GDP). As a result, once again, the unemployment and poverty problems came to the fore. In Korea, for instance, where unemployment and poverty were almost nonexistent before the crisis, the unemployment rate almost tripled in 1998, while urban poverty incidence more than doubled at the peak of the crisis. Such a devastating economic shock, in turn, precipitated substantial social turmoil. The crisis-affected countries experienced food riots and labor unrest, and in Indonesia a dramatic political upheaval occurred.

Fortunately, 1999 brought a clear shift from crisis toward recovery. As current account balances improved while inflation remained subdued, investor confidence returned. This allowed the region's currencies to stabilize and interest rates to fall, which in turn fueled recovery in output. Estimates indicate that all the crisis countries except Indonesia saw substantial GDP growth in 1999, ranging from 3.2 percent in the Philippines to around 10.7 percent in Korea.

The improvement in financial market conditions has been particularly impressive. Most of the region's currencies have appreciated dramatically. The Indonesian rupiah and the Korean won, for instance, strengthened by 35 and 25 percent, respectively, against the dollar between early 1998 and the end of 1999 (see figure 1.8). Malaysia, which introduced capital controls in September 1998 and maintains a fixed exchange rate, is the exception. Yield spreads on international bonds issued by the crisis countries have

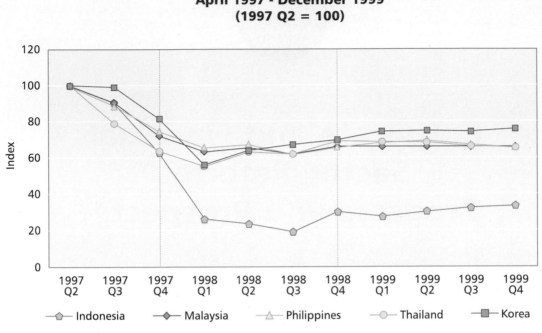

Figure 1.8 Nominal Exchange Rate Indices, Crisis Countries, April 1997 - December 1999 (1997 Q2 = 100)

Note: Exchange rates are in US$ to local currencies.
Source: Based on average-of-period data from BLOOMBERG.

fallen sharply (see box 1.4). Domestic short-term interest rates have also fallen. With the exception of Indonesia, where higher inflation and greater political uncertainty have kept rates high, interest rates in crisis countries are in line with their precrisis averages. Stock markets have soared. Since the fourth quarter of 1998, stock prices in these countries have increased, on average, by 50 percent in local currency terms. With currencies also appreciating, the rise has been even larger in dollar terms (see figure 1.9). Market capitalization in most crisis countries is now approaching or even exceeding its precrisis level.

This recovery, while impressive, masks substantial problems, particularly in the corporate and financial sectors. Distress in the financial sector and restructuring costs have proved far larger than anticipated. One estimate suggests that total financial restructuring costs for the four worst-hit countries will reach 58 percent of GDP in Indonesia, 16 percent

in Korea, 10 percent in Malaysia, and 32 percent in Thailand.

The main problem is the overhang of corporate debt. Burdened with an enormous stock of nonperforming loans (NPLs), banks are undercapitalized and reluctant to lend. Saddled with heavy debt burdens, many firms are technically insolvent. Private sector financial analysts estimate that as many as 60-85 percent of loans in Indonesia are nonperforming, compared with 20-30 percent in Korea and Malaysia and 50-70 percent in Thailand (see table 1.2). Comparisons between countries must be made cautiously, because the definition and measurement of NPLs differ considerably. Official estimates of the share of NPLs are much lower, but even these indicate a dramatic increase since the onset of the financial crisis.

Overall, the sheer size of NPLs reflects the poor health of the corporate sector. However, all firms did not suffer equally. In general, export-oriented

Box 1.4 **Improved International Confidence in Crisis Countries**

The yield spread of a government bond is the difference between the yield on that bond and the yield on a "safe" instrument of similar maturity (usually US Treasury notes). The size of the yield spread represents the degree of international investor confidence in a country's economy: the higher the yield spread, the lower the investor confidence. Tracking yield spreads over time is therefore a useful gauge of how investor confidence shifts. Yield spreads tend to have an inverse relationship with GDP growth, so lower yield spreads suggest an improved economic outlook.

The government of the Republic of Korea issued two foreign currency bonds in April 1997 to mobilize foreign exchange: a five-year $1 billion bond and a ten-year $3 billion bond. At that time the spreads of these bonds over US Treasury notes of the same maturity were 3.35 percent and 3.55 percent per year, respectively. The yield spreads reached a peak of 7.2 percent in the third quarter of 1998 following Russia's debt moratorium.

Since then, the Republic of Korea's yield spreads have been on a broad downward trend. The same pattern is true for sovereign bonds in other crisis countries. Yield spreads peaked in the third quarter of 1998—16 percent for Indonesia, and 7 percent for both Philippines and Thailand—but have dropped significantly since. In the fourth quarter of 1999, yield spreads over comparable US Treasury notes for the Republic of Korea and Thailand were around 1.8 percent, while those for the Philippines and Indonesia stood at 3.1 and 5.5 percent, respectively.

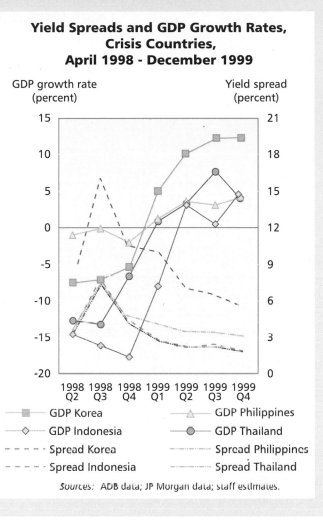

Yield Spreads and GDP Growth Rates, Crisis Countries, April 1998 - December 1999

Sources: ADB data; JP Morgan data; staff estimates.

companies fared better than those that produce nontraded goods and services, and, except in Korea, small firms were hit harder than large firms. In Malaysia, for instance, about 75 percent of the NPLs are to firms in the nontradable sector. In Thailand, small firms and households account for 50 percent of the NPLs.

Each of the crisis countries has embarked on comprehensive restructuring strategies to deal with this financial and corporate distress. While considerable progress has been made, the magnitude of NPLs suggests that much remains to be done. The risk is that economic recovery will dull the momentum for restructuring. A variety of vested interests, including financial institutions, business corporations, labor unions, and politicians have exerted pressure to slow and limit structural reform.

FINANCIAL AND CORPORATE RESTRUCTURING

Plummeting currencies, collapsing confidence, and financial system paralysis characterized the early phase of the financial crisis. Uncertainties about the likely behavior of depositors and foreign creditors and fears about the financial health of borrowers led banks vir-

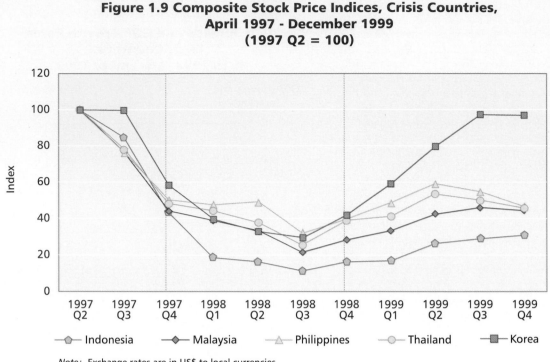

Figure 1.9 Composite Stock Price Indices, Crisis Countries, April 1997 - December 1999 (1997 Q2 = 100)

Note: Exchange rates are in US$ to local currencies.
Source: Based on average-of-period data from BLOOMBERG.

tually to stop lending. To prevent a complete collapse in bank intermediation, financial reform strategies initially focused on measures to restore market confidence and attract capital inflows. The most popular method was government guarantees, and in the early stages of the crisis, governments gave broad guarantees both to foreign creditors and depositors.

As the crisis deepened and the extent of corporate and financial insolvency became clear, the reform strategy shifted toward restructuring in the financial and corporate sectors. The goals were twofold: to escape from the crisis and to address the structural weaknesses that had helped trigger the financial collapse. The focus was on restructuring insolvent financial institutions by closure, merger, or recapitalization; improving corporate governance; reducing labor market rigidities; and deregulating domestic markets.

In all the crisis countries, three broad principles governed financial restructuring: (a) minimizing the risk of moral hazard associated with using public money for bank recapitalization by ensuring that government ownership increase commensurately with the infusion of public recapitalization; (b) maximizing the participation of the private sector by providing fiscal and administrative incentives; and (c) ensuring that the restructuring process was comprehensive and covered the institutional, legal, and regulatory aspects of the banking sector as well as its financial health. Banks were mandated to meet international standards of capital adequacy, loan classification, loan-loss provisioning, accounting, and disclosure.

Similar goals drove corporate restructuring efforts. It was necessary to find quick and effective ways of allocating losses and facilitating asset mobility to remove the paralyzing debt overhang that stymied the corporate sector. Developing an efficient bankruptcy regime and modernizing corporate governance were also critical.

Again, strategies were broadly similar across the crisis countries. All countries developed new out-of-

Table 1.2 **Nonperforming Loan Ratios and Fiscal Costs of Restructuring, Crisis Countries**
(percent)

Country	Share of nonperforming loans to total loans			Unofficial estimate, peak level	Fiscal costs of restructuring as share of GDP
	Official estimate				
	End of 1997	End of 1998	September 1999		
Indonesia	—	—	—	60-85	58
Korea	—	7.6	6.6	20-30	16
Malaysia	—	18.9	17.8	20-30	10
Philippines	5.4	11.0	13.4	15-25	—
Thailand	19.8	45.0	44.7	50-70	32

— Not available.

Note: NPLs are measured on a three-month basis, and the unofficial estimate includes assets carved out for sale by the asset management companies.

Sources: Central banks and financial supervisory agencies; World Bank (1999a); Deutsche Bank (1999); J.P. Morgan (1999); Bank of America (1999); staff estimates.

court systems to restructure the debts of large firms, variants of the London approach to corporate restructuring (see box 1.5). Indonesia set up the Jakarta Initiative, Korea and Malaysia set up corporate debt restructuring committees, and Thailand used a corporate debt-restructuring advisory committee. Tax incentives encouraged out-of-court workouts, while regulatory obstacles that hindered mergers and debt-equity swaps were removed. Simultaneously, the crisis countries strengthened domestic bankruptcy laws to accelerate resolving bankruptcy cases, protect creditors' rights, and discipline managers. Policies to improve corporate governance included attempts to reduce ownership concentration, increase market competition, reduce government monopolies, strengthen the rights of minority shareholders, and increase the transparency of financial reports and transactions.

An Individual Look at Crisis Countries

Though the broad principles of financial and corporate restructuring have been similar in the crisis countries, the details and rates of progress have varied considerably. Korea and Malaysia have gone furthest

in restructuring their corporate and financial sectors, but with different approaches. Korea adopted tight macroeconomic policies under an International Monetary Fund (IMF) program and aggressively closed, merged, or suspended insolvent financial institutions. Malaysia declined an IMF rescue plan, opting for capital controls, and closed no financial institutions. After dramatically downsizing the financial sector by closing virtually all its finance companies, Thailand adopted a more gradual, market-based approach to restructuring, with banks allowed to raise equity capital over a long period through phased-in requirements for loan provisioning. Indonesia lags behind the other three countries, and has only recently taken steps to deal with banking problems and corporate distress. As a less severely affected economy, the Philippines adopted a market-led reform process, with the government and the central bank focusing on reforming the supervisory systems.

Indonesia. Indonesia's first step toward structural reform in the financial sector was to create new institutions. The Indonesian Bank Restructuring Agency was formed in January 1998 as an independent body to

Box 1.5 Models of Corporate Restructuring

There are three popular approaches to corporate sector restructuring: centralized, decentralized, and the London approach.

In the centralized approach, the government plays a leading role. This is effective when the size of problematic debts is small, corporate structure is simple, and the government enjoys high levels of confidence. Sweden in the early 1990s and Hungary in the mid-1990s used a centralized approach to corporate restructuring.

At the other extreme, interested parties use a decentralized approach to reach voluntary restructuring agreements. This is considered more useful than the centralized approach if the bad debts are large and the corporate structure is complex. Corporate restructuring in the United States tends to follow this model.

The London approach evolved in the United Kingdom when numerous firms faced bankruptcy in the recession of the early 1990s.

During this period, more than 160 British companies used the London approach, in which creditor financial institutions and indebted firms work under the close coordination of a government institution (in the British case, the Bank of England), but outside the formal judiciary process. The London approach includes
- Full information sharing between all parties involved in a workout
- Collective decision making among creditor banks on whether and on what terms a company should be given a financial lifeline
- Standardized agreements between debtors and creditors and among creditors themselves
- A clear timetable to achieve timely resolution
- Binding agreements between banks and firms to participate in and honor the restructuring agreements
- The principle of "shared pain" in the allocation of losses, meaning

equal treatment for all creditors of a single category
- The possibility of penalties if the agreements are not adhered to.

To be successful, this approach demands strong confidence in the official mediating institution. In the British case, the parties concerned held the Bank of England in high regard, a crucial ingredient for success.

Superficially, the corporate debt workouts under government coordination in Indonesia, Korea, and Thailand resemble the London approach. However, the Asian countries lacked the equivalent of the Bank of England, a government institution with high credibility. They also suffered a lack of mutual trust and confidence between financial institutions. This process is now gradually changing, as both financial institutions and corporations become more confident in the ability of government to oversee corporate debt restructuring.

restructure troubled banks and their assets. Within this agency, a specific Asset Management Unit was created in April 1998 to acquire NPLs from troubled banks. By the end of 1999, it held around two thirds of all NPLs. So far, however, the Indonesian Bank Restructuring Agency has done little to recover these assets, although the legal, organizational, and regulatory framework is in place.

Greatest progress has been made in restructuring private banks. At the end of July 1997, before the onset of the crisis, Indonesia had 160 private banks. In September 1998, all private banks were classified into categories of A, B, or C, based on their capital adequacy. All group C banks and nonviable group B banks were closed in March 1999. In the span of one year, 66 banks were closed and 12 taken over by the state. Consequently, the state banking system accounts for 75 percent of the liabilities of Indonesia's banking

system and 90 percent of its negative net worth. Unfortunately, the restructuring of these state banks has just begun. By some estimates, around 80 percent of all outstanding loans are nonperforming. As a result, most Indonesian financial institutions remain insolvent or undercapitalized, and lending operations are severely curtailed.

One of the major causes of the collapse of the banking system was the absence of an effective bank supervision system. Realizing this weakness, Indonesia has taken steps to improve prudential regulations, bank supervision, and enforcement capabilities. Nevertheless, bank supervision remains limited because of weak enforcement capacity and a lack of trained staff.

As in the financial sector, Indonesia's efforts at corporate reform initially focused on creating new institutions and improving legislation. First, the government set up the Indonesian Debt Restructuring

Agency in July 1998 to help restructure foreign debt. This agency allows debtors and creditors to insure themselves against exchange risks, once they have reached rescheduling agreements. Indonesia then created the Jakarta Initiative for out-of-court corporate settlements, following the example of the London approach to corporate workouts. Legislation to improve corporate governance included new bankruptcy and anticorruption laws. In August 1998 a new bankruptcy law was introduced, which modernized the legal infrastructure for bankruptcy and facilitated the rapid resolution of commercial disputes. In 1999 a law against corruption, collusion, and nepotism was passed.

Despite this comprehensive legal and institutional framework, the progress of corporate restructuring has been disappointing. The Indonesian Debt Restructuring Agency has registered little debt. By the end of June 1999, only 80 bankruptcy cases had been registered, although almost half of Indonesian corporations were insolvent and experiencing increased difficulties in meeting debt service obligations. One of the biggest constraints on the speed of corporate debt restructuring has been the lack of financial system reform. Weak undercapitalized banks lack the resources or technical skills to resolve corporate debts within the framework of the Jakarta Initiative. Another constraint is the enormity of Indonesia's foreign debt. Without relief from foreign creditors, including Japan, Indonesia probably cannot service this debt, in particular the $36 billion owed to foreign banks.

Korea. Korea's financial sector strategy initially focused on restoring market confidence with government guarantees to prevent a run on the banks. However, once the situation stabilized, priority shifted to restructuring or closing insolvent financial institutions and rehabilitating viable ones. At the same time, adoption of international standards of regulation and supervision was emphasized, as well as capital market development.

In December 1997, the Korean Parliament passed 13 financial reform bills, and streamlined bankruptcy law. In January 1998, the government, corporations, and unions agreed on a national council to discuss economic restructuring. A legal framework for corporate sector restructuring was created in February 1998. In April 1998 the powerful Financial Supervisory

Commission was created to monitor and supervise all financial institutions. During the crisis, however, it focused on financial and corporate restructuring, accelerating the reform process.

In early 1998, two of Korea's largest banks, Korea First Bank and Seoul Bank, were recapitalized with public funds and effectively nationalized. Korea First Bank was subsequently sold to a foreign consortium. On 29 June 1998, the Financial Supervisory Commission announced that five insolvent commercial banks would be closed and absorbed by healthier banks. Mergers involving the five largest banks have been completed. Two years after the crisis, the number of banks has been reduced from 33 to 23 through closures and mergers. The government has also closed down or suspended 21 of 30 merchant banks, and 22 other financial institutions.

The public sector contribution to this restructuring has been huge. At the beginning of the crisis, the government earmarked W64 trillion ($53.3 billion) in public funds to support financial sector restructuring. By the end of 1999, the government had used the entire allocation of funds to purchase W20.5 trillion ($17.1 billion) in NPLs from banks and secondary financial institutions through the Korea Asset Management Corporation. It also provided W43.5 trillion ($36.2 billion) in recapitalization and deposit repayment support through the Korea Deposit Insurance Corporation.

Korea has taken a three-pronged approach to reforming the corporate sector. First, the four largest *chaebols* (conglomerates of corporations), known as the Big Four, were restructured through specific plans to improve capital structure. These required the four chaebols to reduce their debt-equity ratios to below 200 percent by the end of 1999, remove existing cross-guarantees between subsidiaries in different lines of business, and consolidate businesses by exchanging noncore businesses with other chaebols, a process known as "Big Deals."

Second, the mid-ranking chaebols and other large corporations have been subject to out-of-court workouts with their designated lead creditor banks, based on the London approach.

Third, the restructuring of small- and medium-size enterprises (SMEs) has been left to the creditor banks and largely postponed. To prevent insolvency and preserve employment, these firms were allowed easy access to working capital loans. In Korea, compared with other crisis countries, SMEs account for a relatively small fraction of outstanding bank loans. While this justifies the delay in restructuring SMEs, a comprehensive program to work out these debts is urgently needed.

The restructuring of the Big Four and out-of-court workouts of other large corporations have had mixed results. The lead banks have been accused of including firms that should have been immediately liquidated. Given their financial fragility, the banks have been reluctant to absorb losses, and are trying to keep many troubled firms on their balance sheets that in fact are unlikely to survive the crisis. The lead banks have also been unable to devise a comprehensive set of workout criteria involving debt-equity swaps, debt write-downs, and debt rescheduling. The absence of comprehensive criteria has raised concerns about the fairness and effectiveness of using differential measures to support different firms in various industries. Disagreements over loan-loss provisioning, disputes over asset valuation, and managers' resistance to losing control all have further complicated the process. Consequently, many firms are likely to fail to meet their obligations to their lead banks.

The restructuring impact of the Big Deals is also mixed. Whether or not the excess capacity problems that plagued Korea's chaebols have been solved is not clear. Evidence is also mixed on whether the Big Four has fulfilled its commitments to improve corporate governance and slim down to a few core businesses.

Most of the banks, including restructured ones, have seen substantial improvement in the quality of their assets and profitability of their operations. Their lending capacity also has increased, supporting the ongoing economic recovery. However, financial restructuring is far from over. The Financial Supervisory Commission has been struggling to restructure the three largest investment trust companies, which hold many corporate bonds issued by corporations engaged in out-of-court workouts. Many nonbank financial institutions, including life insurance companies, also need rehabilitation.

The banks have faced major losses from the corporate workouts. For instance, the restructuring of Daewoo, Korea's second-largest chaebol until domestic creditors decided on a debt-rescheduling program for its subsidiaries, caused bank losses estimated at $10.4 billion. The requirement that the Big Four reduce their debt-equity ratio to less than 200 percent by the end of 1999 also led to debt write-downs and debt-equity swaps that cut the earnings of major commercial banks.

These costs made it difficult for Korean banks to build the capital and loan-loss provisioning needed to absorb the losses from further corporate restructuring. Some progress has been made, however. The average capital adequacy ratio of the commercial banks reached 10.5 percent by the end of 1999. Nonetheless, estimates suggest that the Korean government will need additional public funds besides the W64 trillion ($53.3 billion) already used for reforming the financial sector.

Malaysia. Malaysia's experience of financial restructuring differed from the other crisis countries in two crucial aspects. First, Malaysia began with a stronger financial sector. Before the crisis it had developed more effective bankruptcy and foreclosure laws, as well as a stronger supervisory capacity. The banking sector was also well capitalized, with capital-asset ratios exceeding 10 percent. Second, Malaysia altered its macroeconomic course in September 1998, choosing to impose capital controls rather than accept an IMF rescue package.

However, like the other countries, Malaysia began its financial and corporate restructuring effort by creating new institutions. In June 1998, the authorities set up Danaharta, an asset management company (AMC) to acquire nonperforming bank loans. In August 1998, Danamodal was created to recapitalize financial institutions whose capital adequacy ratios fell below 9 percent. In the same month the Corporate Debt Restructuring Committee was established to facilitate the out-of-court restructuring of corporate debt.

Both Danaharta and Danamodal made significant progress in restructuring banks. Danamodal injected $1.6 billion into ten financial institutions, while Danaharta purchased 50 percent of outstanding NPLs, about the same ratio as Korea. The level of NPLs appears to have peaked in mid-1999 at over 20 percent of total loans. The total fiscal cost of the restructuring is estimated at around 10 percent of GDP.

In an effort to accelerate the rationalization and consolidation of the banking system, instead of closing affected institutions as in Korea and Thailand, Malaysia continued to encourage financial institutions to merge and consolidate. The central bank approved the formation of ten banking groups and the selection of the anchor banks and their respective partners in January 2000. Accordingly, 54 domestic banking institutions—reduced from 88 at the end of 1997—will be further consolidated. With a relatively sound legal system and a good institutional framework for financial restructuring, the prospects for Malaysia successfully restructuring its financial system seem bright.

Before the crisis, Malaysia's corporations were less heavily indebted than firms in other crisis countries in East Asia. Consequently, corporate distress in Malaysia was less acute than elsewhere, although firms were hit hard by the rise in interest rates because of heavy dependence on bank financing. Malaysia's troubled firms are concentrated in the real estate, construction, and infrastructure sectors.

Nonetheless, debt workouts and operational restructuring through the Corporate Debt Restructuring Committee have been slow, partly because of a lack of adequately trained staff. To address the problem, the government has established agencies to deal with corporate restructuring: the Loan Monitoring Unit of the central bank assists small corporate borrowers in restructuring, a rehabilitation fund helps viable SMEs restructure, and the Finance Committee on Corporate Governance works on reforming corporate governance practices.

Philippines. While the Philippines was affected by the Asian crisis, it suffered significantly less than the other four crisis economies. No broad banking crisis occurred and no emergency rescue assistance from the IMF was needed. The country was resilient because it had virtually no short-term foreign currency borrowing, its banks were well-capitalized after two decades of financial sector reform, and its manufacturing sector was smaller and less leveraged than the other economies.

The mildness of the Philippines' crisis affected the scope and nature of the country's financial and corporate reforms. Compared with the four worst-hit crisis economies, the Philippines followed a market-led reform process with less government involvement.

Its major reform elements included (a) strengthening the prudential and supervisory systems overseeing the financial sector, (b) adopting an early intervention system to deal effectively with problem banks and keep the banking system sound, (c) strengthening and modernizing state banks through privatization, (d) reducing the intermediation costs of financial institutions, and (e) improving the legal and regulatory framework.

To improve the supervisory framework, the central bank required banks to set up 2 percent general loan-loss provisions, as well as increasing specific loan-loss provision on individual loans, which reached 2 percent by 1 October 1999. The central bank also limited banks' exposure to the real estate sector to 20 percent of total loans, and reduced the allowable loan value of real estate security from 70 to 60 percent. It imposed a 30 percent liquid cover on all foreign exchange liabilities from foreign currency deposits.

To deal more effectively with problem banks, the central bank adopted an early warning system that included formalizing sanctions on undercapitalized banks. To strengthen and modernize state banks, the government concentrated on selling shares to private investors. Statutory reserve requirements were reduced from 10 to 8 percent in May 1998 to reduce the costs of financial intermediation.

Regulatory improvements have been significant. The central bank has proposed major revisions to key banking laws to (a) limit the ability of universal and commercial banks to invest in firms; (b) redefine the functions, authority, and minimum capitalization of trust entities; (c) adopt the Basle Capital Accords, a set of standards for measuring capital adequacy; (d) strengthen provisions to guard against bank overexposure to risky assets; (e) guard against credit concentration among borrowers; (f) grant the central bank the right to examine banks once a year; and (g) authorize the central bank to issue regulations requiring bank subsidiaries and affiliates to maintain a balanced position in foreign exchange transactions.

These reforms contributed to the early recovery of financial markets. Nonetheless, problems remain. First, many of the new prudential norms and international standards are poorly implemented. Second, banks still hold many real estate NPLs, which continue to curtail banking sector operations and stall overall economic activity. The illiquidity of property markets also means that loan-loss provisioning may not reflect all real losses. Informal loan-for-property swaps without formal legal foreclosure proceedings pose an additional problem.

Thailand. Like other crisis countries, Thailand began structural reform in the financial sector by creating new institutions. In October 1997, three months after the onset of the financial crisis, the government established the Financial Sector Restructuring Authority to organize the workout of failed finance companies, and the Asset Management Company to buy nonperforming assets and recover them. In December 1997, the Financial Sector Restructuring Authority closed 56 of 58 suspended finance companies, and since then has been disposing of their assets. The Asset Management Company purchased its first NPLs at a Financial Sector Restructuring Authority auction in March 1999.

After closing the finance companies, to help regain investor confidence the government adopted a market-based approach to restructuring and recapitalizing the remaining financial institutions. By gradually introducing stricter loan classification and loan-loss provisioning requirements, the Thai authorities hoped to give private investors the incentive— and time—to provide fresh capital.

However, this strategy did not succeed because private investors had little incentive to invest in those banks and in other financial institutions that were amassing large numbers of NPLs because of continuing recession. The government shifted to a more interventionist approach in August 1998, announcing a new comprehensive financial restructuring package. This package allowed viable financial institutions to recapitalize using public funds under clear safeguards. It offered incentives for accelerating corporate debt restructuring and promoting new lending to the private sector. It also created a legal basis for establishing private AMCs and clear resolution strategies for financial institutions in line with the government's long-term objective of strengthening the financial system.

Even this interventionist approach faced problems. Thai bank owners remain as reluctant to take advantage of public funds as they were determined to maintain ownership and control of their institutions.

By January 2000, only four banks had accepted the government's recapitalization scheme, and most banks limited new lending and resorted to complex private arrangements to raise capital. The level of NPLs in commercial banks is so high—as much as 50 percent of total loans or more—that for banks to recapitalize through normal business operations seems impossible.

Thailand's strategy for corporate restructuring, like that of the other countries, consisted of new institutions, better incentives, and improvements in the legal framework. In August 1998, the government created the Corporate Debt Restructuring Advisory Committee. It also endeavored to create an effective legal framework for recovering debt through bankruptcy legislation, and provided tax and other incentives to encourage corporations and banks to restructure bad debt.

Progress has been made, and the results of the corporate restructuring account for about 25 percent of NPLs. The growth of NPLs has outpaced the rate of corporate restructuring completion. SMEs account for more than two thirds of this aggregate corporate debt, which makes restructuring complex: transactions are small, costly, and diffuse, with firms scattered over the country. Banks have also been reluctant to deal with the debts of SMEs, preferring to scale back lending.

Thailand has made greater progress in improving the supervisory and regulatory framework surrounding the financial sector. The authorities are enforcing new loan classifications and provisioning requirements, and the supervisory functions of the Bank of Thailand are being strengthened. All financial institutions have signed a memorandum of understanding that describes their plans to raise capital. The more stringent provisioning requirements for nonperforming assets are being phased in from the second half of 1998 until the end of 2000. The Bank of Thailand also began implementing a modernization program aimed at redesigning the bank's organizational structure, streamlining work processes, and improving corporate governance. As part of these efforts, experts from some central banks of industrial countries have offered recommendations on strengthening central banking and bank supervision. The Bank of Thailand has also set up a school for bank examiners.

Assessment of Reforms

Almost three years after the onset of the Asian crisis, financial and corporate restructuring is best seen as a work in progress. All the crisis countries have begun to lay the foundations for stronger financial and corporate sectors. Throughout the region, new accounting standards, improved disclosure requirements, and better rules for corporate governance were introduced. However, effective implementation and enforcement of these rules are still lacking.

Similarly, all the crisis countries have made progress in the immense task of financial and corporate restructuring, but much remains to be done. Banks remain undercapitalized and still hold large amounts of NPLs on their balance sheets. The ratio of NPLs to total loans remains well above 20 percent in all the crisis countries, far higher than in any previous major emerging-market banking crisis. Public sector involvement has been much higher than anticipated: while restructuring, governments nationalized many weak financial institutions. Although all the region's governments have placed a high priority on divesting state-owned banks and assets, willing and qualified buyers have been scarce. Consequently, the restructuring process will likely require a further infusion of public money (see table 1.3).

The strength of the crisis countries' public commitment to structural, financial, and corporate reform may have contributed to their economic recovery. Market confidence—and hence the return of foreign direct and portfolio investment—has been boosted by the expectation that Asia will emerge from the crisis with more stable and efficient financial sectors than before (see box 1.6).

Unfortunately, it is too early to be certain of such success. Despite continuing pressure from international financial institutions, corporate and financial reform has slowed, and backtracking is evident in some cases. Moreover, it is an open question whether some crisis countries had sufficient political leadership and institutional capacity to implement such massive and complex structural reforms within a short time. Institutional weaknesses have been the main obstacle to rapid and efficient implementation of reform programs in Indonesia and Thailand.

Though much remains to be done, it is not too early for a critical appraisal of the region's reform efforts. With hindsight, the crisis countries obviously did not have a well-designed road map to guide their financial and corporate restructuring. The reason is clear: with the crisis deepening daily, these countries did not have the luxury of spending months designing an optimal reform program. Nonetheless, there are several lessons to be learned.

Synchronizing Restructuring Efforts. In every crisis country, the restructuring process began with banks. Balance sheets were cleaned up and capital bases strengthened so these banks could take charge of restructuring ailing firms. Unfortunately, this strategy did not work, as banks were ill-prepared to lead the corporate restructuring efforts. Their main priority was to avoid a further deterioration of their assets by becoming more conservative in lending and asset management and sharply scaling back normal inter-

Table 1.3 Fiscal Costs of Recapitalization, Selected Crisis Countries, Mid-October 1999
(percent of 1998 GDP)

Cost	Indonesia	Korea	Malaysia	Thailand
Estimated recapitalization cost	58.3	16.0	10.0	31.9
Funds disbursed	10.6	12.5	4.2	23.9
Expected additional costs	47.7	3.6	5.8	8.0

Source: World Bank (1999a).

Box 1.6 **Trend of Foreign Direct Investment in Crisis Countries**

Foreign direct investment (FDI) has long been an important source of external finance in developing Asia. It also proved to be much more stable than other forms of capital flows during the crisis. In 1998 and 1999, net FDI flows into the five worst-hit countries—Indonesia, Korea, Malaysia, Philippines, and Thailand—slightly increased from the 1997 level of $17.5 billion. However, individual countries fared differently. FDI inflows into Korea were $2.8 billion in 1997, $5.5 billion in 1998, and $8.5 billion in 1999. FDI inflows into Malaysia for the same years were $5.1 billion, $3.7 billion, and $3.8 billion. This difference, in large part, reflected different attitudes by the crisis-affected countries toward the role that FDI should play in corporate and financial reform.

FDI can be important in financial and corporate restructuring. By investing in, or acquiring, distressed companies or banks, foreign investors provide crucial new capital as well as managerial resources. Several countries in the region have made specific efforts to attract FDI, with Korea and Thailand the most prominent. Korea has opened several sectors to foreign investors, including property, securities dealing, and other financial businesses. Restrictions limiting foreign ownership of equity have

been abolished, allowing foreign investors to buy as much as 100 percent of a local firm. The Foreign Investment Promotion Act provides comprehensive legal

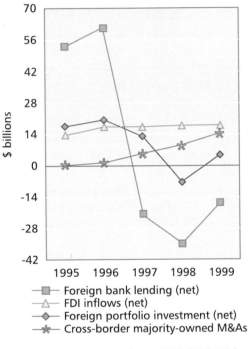

Trend of FDI, Crisis Countries, 1995-1999

- Foreign bank lending (net)
- FDI inflows (net)
- Foreign portfolio investment (net)
- Cross-border majority-owned M&As

Sources: UNCTAD (1999, 2000); IMF (1999c).

protection for foreign investors in Korea. Thailand also allows foreign investors to hold as much as 100 percent equity in domestic banks and finance companies for as long as ten years, while 39 industrial sectors have been opened to increased foreign participation. Majority foreign-owned companies (with the foreign investor holding more than 50 percent of the voting securities of the business) are

now also allowed to distribute their products domestically.

In Malaysia, restrictions on foreign holdings in new export-oriented manufacturing projects have been suspended until 2000 and foreign ownership limits have also been relaxed. Indonesia has just begun implementing new incentives to attract foreign investors, increasing the maximum foreign ownership of banks to 99 percent, while the authorities have provided a clearer legal framework for the conversion of bonds issued locally into equity.

Since the financial crisis, cross-border mergers and acquisitions, as opposed to greenfield investments, have become the most important mode of FDI in the five crisis countries. Cross-border majority-owned mergers and acquisitions reached an annual average value of $12 billion in 1998 and 1999, as compared with $1 billion annually in 1994-1996. Opportunities for cheap acquisitions and a more liberal environment for FDI have attracted foreign investors. In addition to strengthening the rights of foreign investors, the crisis-affected countries have tried to simplify procedures for mergers and acquisitions, revamped their bankruptcy laws, introduced short-term tax measures to facilitate asset transfer, and improved accounting standards to ease asset valuation.

mediary operations. This retrenchment created a vicious circle in which heavily indebted but viable firms could not get credit. This, in turn, led to still more NPLs.

In some countries stricter regulatory and supervisory standards made matters even worse. In Thailand, for instance, banks became even more reluctant to lend as regulatory standards were tightened. This exacerbated the credit crunch, creating more business failures and deepening the recession. Regulatory changes in equity markets worsened the problem. Thailand's stock exchange introduced stringent requirements for new entrants, such as a minimum number of shareholders and minimum profits for several consecutive years, which most SMEs were unable to meet. Simultaneously, access to commercial banks and finance companies was drastically reduced.

Not only did the failure to synchronize the restructuring of banks and corporations worsen the region's recession, but it also left banks extremely fragile. The balance sheets of recapitalized banks could easily deteriorate again, depending on the outcome of corporate workouts. Although identifying all troubled firms and accurately forecasting how many will be able to survive the crisis are difficult, a comprehensive restructuring strategy based on a clear assessment of the corporate and financial sectors would avoid the costs of repeated bank restructuring.

Articulating Methods and Goals. While financial sector restructuring efforts benefited from a clear body of international experience, few precedents were available for corporate restructuring of the scale and type necessary. As a result, the process was confused. Policymakers did not understand why the so-called London approach was deemed appropriate for working out corporate debt, why it was so critical to reduce debt-equity ratios in the short term, or why certain corporate structures were considered superior. For instance, the breakup of the chaebols was deemed desirable, but reformers could not recommend what industrial organization should replace Korea's chaebol-dominated system.

Minimizing Damage to Credit System. A properly functioning credit system is the nerve system of an economy. It contains the most important financial and industrial information of the private sector. Once destroyed, this information is difficult to recreate. Similarly, corporations embody organizational and social capital that is also difficult to recreate quickly. Thus, to the extent possible, it is important to avoid damage to the credit system during bank restructuring and to minimize the erosion of social capital during corporate restructuring. Mergers and acquisitions are preferable to outright bank closure, and workouts are better than outright insolvency.

The crisis countries, however, did not adhere to these principles. Many financial institutions were closed in the early months of the crisis without adequate thought about how this would affect the credit system. Similarly, institutional and supervisory improvements, although well intentioned, further endangered the credit system by making it more difficult for banks to function. The countries did not, for instance, follow reform policies that would encourage mergers by liberalizing domestic laws to make foreign takeovers easier. In several cases, reform efforts undermined the rights of secured creditors.

Considering Local Circumstances. All the crisis countries relied heavily on voluntary, out-of-court settlements for corporate restructuring, the hallmark of the London approach. Given the absence of well-functioning bankruptcy courts, this was perhaps inevitable. Within this framework, however, the government was expected to play the role of mediator, facilitating an orderly resolution, while banks, as creditors, managed the workout. Given their undercapitalization and the heavy burden of NPLs, banks did not play their part, particularly in Indonesia and Thailand. The large role played by foreign-based accounting firms, consulting agencies, and investment banks also complicated matters. Naturally, these firms followed international standards for accountancy and due diligence, which were often more stringent than traditional local standards. The new and tougher criteria made it difficult for the lead banks and corporations to reach agreement on debt workouts. As a result, the London approach had only mixed success, and corporate reform has been slow.

Using Intermediary Institutions. The crisis countries had few intermediary institutions, such as investment banks, to facilitate mergers and acquisitions. Instead commercial banks, which specialized in providing short-term working capital, led the corporate restructuring effort. Not surprisingly, results were disappointing. Instead of evaluating project viability and debt-service capability, commercial banks were more inclined to recover as much of their loans as possible, if necessary by foreclosing on assets clients had pledged as collateral. If they could not recover collateral, the commercial banks kept the NPLs on their books and continued to provide short-term emergency financing to avoid further losses.

Participating in Reform. Beyond these specific lessons for financial and corporate restructuring, broader lessons for reform can be learned. Perhaps the most important is the need for reforms to be "owned" by countries themselves. Only when a country owns a reform program does it act in a cost-effective manner that bears results. Korea stands out as a country whose reform program bore the hallmarks of ownership: committed and strong political leadership, inclusiveness, broad participation, and democratic decisionmaking.

THE NEXT STEPS: SHORT-TERM TASKS

The crisis countries have made significant, if intermittent, progress toward financial and corporate reform. However, there is much more to be done. The biggest risk facing the region is complacency. As markets recover and foreign investors return, the momentum for further reform is weakened. With the growing opposition from vested interests, the risks of backtracking are high.

Slowing or halting the reform process would have serious consequences: it would erode investor confidence, waste the enormous resources already expended, lose an invaluable opportunity to modernize Asia's financial and corporate sectors, and reduce the region's growth potential. The region has much to do, including strengthening the ongoing reforms and improving the governance process.

Strengthen Ongoing Reforms

The focus of the restructuring effort so far has been on resolving NPLs and recapitalizing weak financial

institutions. Little attention, however, has been paid to disposing of those bad assets that were bought by or transferred to AMCs. The short-term reform agenda needs to focus on AMCs and disposing of their assets. It also needs to foster further improvements in the related regulatory environment.

All the crisis economies except Thailand established centralized government-supported AMCs, to which NPLs were transferred. By the end of 1999, two thirds of NPLs in Indonesia had been transferred to its Asset Management Unit. In Korea and Malaysia, the share was 50 percent. However, the proportion of NPLs actually resolved or disposed of is far lower (see table 1.4). In Korea less than 5 percent of NPLs held by the Korea Asset Management Corporation have been resolved, and the share is less than 1 percent in Indonesia and Malaysia. The vast majority of the NPLs are still carried on the government's books, at substantial fiscal cost.

Improving the regulatory framework can speed the resolution of the AMCs' portfolios. The purchase, transfer, management, and sale of assets must be easier. In particular, rules surrounding transfer taxes and recognizing losses from the sale need improvement. A second approach is to increase private sector participation in restructuring. This helps reduce the government's fiscal obligation and ensure that the AMCs are as commercial as possible. At the very least, operations need to be market-driven, efficient, and

Table 1.4 Operations of Asset Management Companies, Selected Crisis Countries, January 2000

Country	NPLs to AMCs		% NPLs disposed of by AMC
	% total	% GDP	
Indonesia	66	35	0.7
Korea	50	20	4.7
Malaysia	50	14	0.1

AMC Asset management company.
NPL Nonperforming loan.

Source: Staff estimates.

transparent. Encouraging direct private participation in AMCs would also be useful. All the AMCs increasingly are employing the expertise of private firms to value assets and develop disposal strategies. Malaysia is considering contracting out a proportion of its nonperforming assets to private management. In 1999, the Korean Asset Management Corporation announced plans to establish joint ventures with foreign investors to dispose of nonperforming assets. Each joint venture has about W300 billion in assets, with the foreign share at 65 percent. However, even with this foreign participation, asset disposal has been extremely slow.

Many aspects of the region's regulatory framework need further improvement. The most crucial is providing mechanisms that give early warning of pending trouble in financial institutions. Laws should require supervisory agencies to provide effective early warning mechanisms and take prompt corrective actions to minimize the risk of financial crisis. For example, when a bank's capital adequacy ratio declines, the bank should automatically fall under greater regulatory scrutiny with tight restrictions on its activities.

More broadly, prudential standards need improvement because they are well below international norms. Bankruptcy and foreclosure laws need to be amended to facilitate seizing debtors' assets and reduce the need to resort to the judicial process. Bank secrecy laws may need loosening to increase financial transparency and discourage the flow of corrupt funds into the region's financial centers. Given that financial and corporate activities are increasingly interrelated, an integrated approach to supervisory functions is needed.

Improve Governance

It is now widely recognized that poor governance was a major weakness in the region's financial and corporate sectors. Symptoms include intricate formal and informal relationships between governments, financial institutions, and corporations; inadequate disclosure requirements; and widespread corruption and favoritism. A major focus of the reform effort has been strengthening governance by improving market discipline and corporate governance, as well as introducing anticorruption and competition policies. Such

reforms take time, however, as their goal is an entirely new corporate framework and culture.

With the assistance of multilateral financial institutions, notably the Asian Development Bank, the IMF, and the World Bank, the crisis countries have focused reform actions on increasing the transparency of economic and financial data, strengthening corporate disclosure requirements, increasing accountability to shareholders, strengthening competition laws, privatizing state-owned enterprises, dismantling state-supported monopolies and cartels, and restructuring opaque corporate relations.

The crisis countries have made significant progress toward improving corporate and financial governance. Rights of minority shareholders and broader stakeholders are better protected, and shareholders, including minority ones, are treated more fairly. Active cooperation between stakeholders and corporations is encouraged. Emphasis has been renewed on the responsibility of the board to give strategic guidance, monitor management effectively, and provide accountability to stakeholders. Disclosure of information, for instance, on a firm's financial status, performance, and ownership structure is now quicker and more accurate. In Korea, firms must provide consolidated financial statements. In Malaysia, individuals are restricted to a maximum of ten directorships in publicly listed companies, and firms are required to provide quarterly financial statements.

Despite this progress, more efforts are needed to establish a modern legal and regulatory framework, reduce the risk of bureaucratic and corruption-prone administrative procedures, reform the ownership structure of large business groups, adopt modern financial management techniques, and reduce corruption.

Corruption is a serious systemic problem in some countries. It can involve either monopolistic "crony capitalist" firms or the rent-seeking bureaucracies that extract bribes, called rents, in return for licensing privileges. Crony capitalist firms are best addressed through a well-designed privatization program. The rent-seeking corruption is more entrenched and more difficult to eradicate, and ill-planned efforts to do so could increase inefficiency. To mitigate these risks, governance reforms should be carefully formulated and implemented. Reforms must take into account a country's individual circumstances—its legal, judiciary, and civil service systems; regulatory standards; corporate governance; and industrial organization—as well as its capacity to implement changes.

SOLVING PROBLEMS: THE LONGER-TERM TASKS

Before the onset of the financial crisis, the region's economies enjoyed strong fiscal positions, and budget surpluses were the norm. When the crisis first hit, fiscal policies were kept tight, but that has changed. All the crisis-affected countries have spent massive fiscal resources on financial restructuring, including buying NPLs, recapitalizing insolvent banks, and protecting depositors and creditors. Public spending also has increased to stimulate economic recovery and provide social safety nets for the poor and vulnerable. Fiscal deficits have risen substantially and public debt has accumulated (see table 1.5 and box 1.7).

Reduce Fiscal Imbalances

Debt accumulation was greater in Indonesia, Korea, and Malaysia, where the financial restructuring was government-led, than in Thailand, which adopted a market-based approach. Indonesia and Thailand, where restructuring is still at a relatively early stage, are likely to suffer large fiscal deficits in 2000 compared with precrisis levels. In Korea, Malaysia, and Philippines, deficits are unlikely to deteriorate further if domestic interest rates remain low and economic recovery continues.

Nonetheless, existing fiscal imbalance must be remedied over the medium term. Otherwise, economic recovery will be stymied as private investment is crowded out and debt-servicing requirements impede the public sector's infrastructure development. Thus, the countries should place high priority on reducing fiscal imbalances as soon as possible. They could generate additional revenues by privatizing nationalized banks and state-owned enterprises, and selling financial assets in the publicly owned AMCs. Attracting more domestic and foreign private investment into the ailing financial and corporate sectors also will help alleviate the fiscal burden. So, too, will more consistent efforts to recover defaulted bank loans through systematic investigations into corporations' uses of such loans.

To ensure equitable distribution of the restructuring burden, costs should be allocated to reflect the division of responsibility for the problem. If a financial institution's problems are due largely to government intervention in directing credit to particular borrowers, then the government should bear a larger part of the costs. If, however, banks' losses are largely due to their own commercial mistakes, bank shareholders and managers should absorb most of the costs.

Table 1.5 Fiscal Balance Before and After the Crisis: Crisis Countries, 1994-2000
(percentage of GDP)

Country	1994	1995	1996	1997	1998	1999	2000
Indonesia	0.4	0.6	0.2	0.0	-3.7	-2.3	-5.0
Korea	0.4	0.3	0.3	-1.5	-4.2	-2.9	-2.8
Malaysia	2.3	0.8	0.7	2.6	-1.5	-3.8	-2.0
Philippines	1.0	0.6	0.3	0.1	-1.8	-3.6	-1.8
Thailand	1.9	3.0	2.4	-0.9	-3.4	-3.0	-3.0

Note: Figures for 1999 and 2000 are staff estimates.

Source: Statistical Appendix.

Box 1.7 Fiscal Deficits, Public Debt, and Development Policies

A history of prudent fiscal policy meant that Asia's developing countries entered the financial crisis with extremely low public debt. The ratios of public debt to GDP in the crisis countries were around 20-30 percent at the end of 1997, compared with an average of 70 percent for Organisation for Economic Co-operation and Development member countries. Since then, however, the size of public debt has surged. Korea's public debt almost tripled from W37 trillion to W94 trillion between 1997 and 1999, even though it remained at a relatively modest 19 percent of GDP. In Thailand, the public debt-to-GDP ratio jumped from 6.3 percent in 1997 to 21 percent at the end of September 1999. Public debt was relatively stable in Malaysia, although at a somewhat higher level of 38 percent at the end of September 1999. By contrast, in Indonesia and Philippines, the debt-to-GDP ratio is expected to reach 95 and 58 percent, respectively, by the end of 2000 and 1999.

Excessive accumulation of public debt can affect financial markets and government's development effort adversely in three ways. First, if the central bank monetizes fiscal deficits, inflationary expectations and market interest rates will increase. Based on a study of 88 developing countries, the International Monetary Fund

Fiscal Balance and Money Supply Growth of Developing Countries, Ranked by Inflation Rates, Various Years (percent)

Economy	Average fiscal balance/GDP	Average money supply (M2) growth
Developing countries: 1983-1989		
28 countries with less than 6% inflation (average 3.2%)	-4.8	9.8
31 countries with 6-15% inflation (average 9.3%)	-5.5	15.4
29 countries with more than 15% inflation (average 84.8%)	-6.9	81.9
Selected DMCs: 1980-1998		
5 countries with less than 6% inflation (average 4.3%)	0.3	16.5
11 countries with 6-15% inflation (average 9.6%)	-5.0	20.8
5 countries with more than 15% inflation (average 37.1%)	-5.8	60.3

DMCs Developing member countries.
Note: Selected DMCs exclude the Central Asian republics and the Pacific DMCs.
Sources: IMF (1990); ADB data.

Fiscal Balance and Development Performance of Selected Economies, 1981-1999 (percent)

	Fiscal balance/GDP	GDP growth rate	Inflation rate
NIEs	0.7	7.1	5.0
India	-6.7	6.0	9.1
Pakistan	-6.8	5.4	8.5
Sri Lanka	-11.2	4.7	11.6
Argentina	-2.3	2.1	414.1
Brazil	-7.3	2.5	602.2
Mexico	-4.8	2.7	45.2

NIEs Newly industrialized economies.
Note: The three Latin American countries cover 1980-1998; their fiscal balance/GDP covers 1980-1997.
Source: ADB data.

concluded that countries with higher fiscal deficits and public debt experienced higher monetary expansion and inflation (1990). Borio and McCauley (1996) also confirmed

the existence of higher interest rates and a crowding-out effect in the bond market.

Second, if the government bond market is not developed (as in Asia's crisis countries), high level of public debt can impair the development of the financial markets. Because Asian bond markets are at their early stages, governments might be tempted to try to force financial institutions to purchase government bonds at higher prices. Such financial repression can restrict the portfolios of financial institutions and distort the market interest rate structure.

Third, government's development effort could be crippled. Interest payments on a large stock of public debt could constrain fiscal expenditure, and prevent governments from focusing on the improvement of public services and investments in physical and social infrastructure. Moreover, a rising interest burden can easily allow public debt to spiral out of control. It was this realization that led the major industrial countries to make fiscal consolidation a priority when their ratios of fiscal deficit to GDP reached 5-10 percent and ratios of public debt to GDP reached 50-60 percent.

Compared with developed countries, the ratios of public debt to GDP in Asian crisis countries are, on average, still low. However, this should not be a reason for complacency. Instead, each government should plan to initiate a fiscal consolidation exercise as quickly as possible.

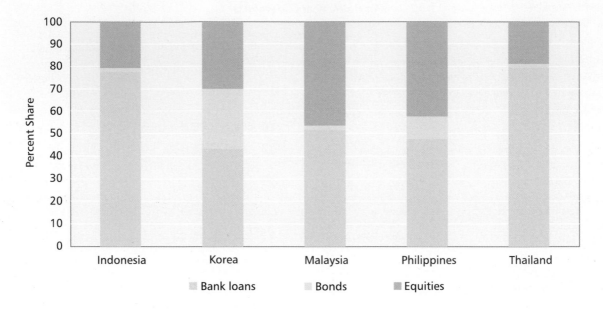

**Figure 1.10 Composition of Financial Assets,
Crisis Countries, 1998**

Sources: Based on data from BLOOMBERG; Monetary authorities' statistics.

Develop Financial Markets

It is generally agreed that one of the major causes of the region's financial crisis was excessive reliance on short-term bank loans from abroad to facilitate long-term investments at home and abroad. Asian finance has traditionally been overwhelmingly bank-based, and that must change (see figure 1.10). An important lesson from the crisis is that it is urgent to develop domestic financial markets that can efficiently allocate domestic savings to long-term projects. Therefore, the crisis countries need to modernize and develop their capital markets, particularly bond markets, and maximize the efficiency with which long-term savings are channeled into profitable industrial and infrastructure projects.

A financial sector development strategy is a useful way to prepare for this kind of fundamental change. The strategy should aim to ensure greater diversification and market orientation in the financial sector by increasing operational efficiency, developing human resources, maximizing synergy between various sub-sectors, and facilitating resource mobilization. It should cover the banking sector, nonbank credit institutions, insurance sector, capital markets, and newer financial institutions such as venture capital entities. Thailand has begun working on a long-term blueprint for the structure of the overall financial sector.

All types of long-term financial markets—equity, bond, and insurance—need to be fostered. However, bond markets deserve particular attention because they have long been neglected, while efforts at developing equity markets began long before the crisis. Bond markets were underdeveloped for several reasons: persistent government surpluses meant that the region's countries had little, if any, outstanding government debt. Therefore, there was no benchmark yield curve of returns on safe government debt, making it difficult to price other bonds. The investor base for bonds was limited; the market infrastructure was inadequate. Moreover, weak corporate governance and underdeveloped regulatory and supervisory arrangements reduced the attractiveness of corporate bonds. As a result, the markets for corporate bonds and asset-backed securities were particularly stunted. According to a 1999 survey by the Asia-Pacific Economic Cooperation Council, outstanding bonds in member countries, excluding Japan and the United States, on average represented only 34 percent of GDP. Once Japan and the United States were included, the average rose to 105 percent.

Given the rudimentary nature of domestic bond markets, a gradual approach is desirable. First, the market for primary government securities issues must be developed. Then a secondary market for these issues should follow, and corporate bond markets will develop. In 1999, Asia-Pacific Economic Cooperation provided guidelines to facilitate the development of domestic bond markets in member countries (see box 1.8).

CONCLUSION

The financial sector was the weakest link in Asian economies. Excessive government intervention, overreliance on banks, and pervasive crony capitalism hampered innovation and distorted incentives. Sustainability of the region's short-term recovery, as well as its long-term economic future, rests largely on how effectively and comprehensively the financial and corporate sectors can be restructured. This will first entail cleaning up from the crisis. Corporate restruc-

---

Box 1.8 Recommendations for Developing Bond Markets

In August 1999, Asia-Pacific Economic Cooperation presented policy recommendations for the development of domestic bond markets, which focused on five key areas: government policies, regulatory framework, market infrastructure, liquidity, and risk management. Government policies were to emphasize these elements: (a) striking a balance between sovereign debt management policy and a strategy for domestic bond market development; (b) developing a comprehensive bond market development strategy; (c) creating a sound legal framework; (d) ensuring a level playing field with consistent tax policies for all financial instruments and market participants; (e) maintaining consistency between the bond market development strategy, fiscal and monetary policies, and the financial sector development strategy; and (f) using a phased approach to the bond market development.

On the regulatory framework, the report emphasized several issues: (a) full, timely, and accurate disclosure of information; (b) objective criteria to differentiate between public offering and private placement and to distinguish sophisticated institutional investors from other investors; (c) good governance principles for institutional investors and contractual savings institutions; (d) clarity in the roles, responsibilities, and objectives of the regulatory authorities; (e) transparency in trading and price reporting; and (f) sound criteria for external credit assessment institutions.

The report made important suggestions on market infrastructure, liquidity, and risk management. To develop market infrastructure, it is essential to ensure clear rules and procedures that can be legally enforced, create an effective regulatory regime and risk-management procedures, and provide relevant information to participants on a timely basis. To ensure the liquidity of domestic bonds, it is crucial to have accurate and reliable benchmark yield curves, transparency in the primary and secondary markets, low transaction costs, diverse groups of market participants, and the gradual creation of derivatives markets.

To promote effective risk management, the report proposed identifying risks of the bond program, maintaining a debt profile, risk sharing between government and private issues, ensuring sound investment and risk management policies by bond investors, preventing issuance through unregulated channels, avoiding overreliance on credit rating, keeping credit rating agency assessments, and keeping credit rating agencies credible.

Source: APEC (1999).

turing, especially, must be accelerated, while nonperforming assets must be disposed of. At the same time, the crisis countries must pay more attention to the foundations of their future financial system. A 21st century financial system requires a different role for government. The public sector can and must play an important role in overcoming coordination failures and setting regulatory standards, but it should not become directly involved in allocating capital. A diverse and largely private financial system within a well-constructed regulatory and supervisory framework allocates resources most efficiently and safely. The region's prosperity depends on how quickly and effectively such a financial system can be created.

Economic Trends and Prospects in Developing Asia

Newly Industrialized Economies

Hong Kong, China

Republic of Korea

Singapore

Taipei,China

Hong Kong, China

The economy of Hong Kong, China has begun to recover from its severest recession in recent decades. It must now focus on meeting new challenges, including stimulating investment, cleaning up the environment, and shifting resources into the information technology industry.

RECENT TRENDS AND PROSPECTS

After contracting by 5.1 percent in 1998, the Hong Kong, China economy grew at 2.9 percent in real terms in 1999. Increased private consumption, higher government spending, and increased exports contributed to this growth. Domestic investment, however, was even weaker than in 1998, a result of high real interest rates and an uncertain business outlook. Prices continued to fall and the composite consumer price index registered a decline of 4 percent in 1999. Fierce price competition, flat rental prices, and a freeze in government fees and most public utility charges contributed to the sustained fall in the consumer price index. Other contributors were weak world commodity prices (except for fuel), a strong US dollar, and deflation in the People's Republic of China (PRC), all of which kept imported inflation at bay.

Hong Kong, China's economic recovery started in the second quarter of 1999, after six consecutive quarters of decline. Increased private consumption and an improved trade balance contributed to the turnaround. The recovery was reinforced by clear signs of economic revival in neighboring economies, which also contributed to a recovery in local asset markets. Total stock market capitalization increased by 77.6 percent during 1999 and the Hang Seng Index reached a postcrisis peak level of around 17,000 in late December 1999, almost 2.5 times the level just before the government's stock market intervention in August 1998.

Recovery in the property market was mainly reflected in the increased volume of spending during the first half of the year. This can be attributed to the announcement of favorable fiscal measures; resumption of land auctions with good results; and relaxation of banks' mortgage policies, including decreased interest rates. The surge, however, was partly reversed by the rise in nominal interest rates in August, following a rise in US rates. Property prices themselves ended up about 50 percent lower than their peak levels before the 1997 crisis.

In external accounts, the merchandise trade deficit continued to narrow and the services surplus continued to expand. Total merchandise exports declined marginally by 0.1 percent in US dollar terms, while total merchandise imports declined by 2.7 percent in 1999, and the trade deficit fell to HK$46.5 billion (US$6 billion) from HK$84.8 billion (US$10.9 billion) in 1998. Estimates indicate that in 1999 the services surplus in current prices was around HK$100.7 billion (US$13 billion), an increase of HK$9.8 billion (US$1.3 billion) over the previous year. The major impetus for the rebound in export performance was re-exports to other Asian countries, especially Indonesia, Japan, Korea, and Singapore, where import demand strengthened as the region's economies revived. However, domestic exports remained sluggish in the face of stiff price competition.

Following the increase in export growth in the PRC in the third quarter, re-exports rose 7 percent and 12 percent, respectively, in the third and final quarters of 1999. The export of services, which suffered severely in 1998, rebounded by 2.6 percent in US dollar terms in 1999. Tourism rebounded, with 11.5 percent more arrivals. Visitors from the PRC and Taipei,China continued to be the most important sources of tourism growth, accounting for almost 50 percent of arrivals. The number of visitors from other Asian countries also increased, especially from Southeast Asia, including Japan, whose tourist numbers had decreased sharply in 1998 because of the financial crisis. However, despite the increased volume of business, total receipts suffered a mild decline as a result of the fall in prices.

Stronger deflationary pressures partly reversed some of the stimulating effects of nominal interest rate cuts, which returned to precrisis levels. Domestic investment, particularly in the private sector, contracted more sharply in 1999 than in 1998, and investment in plants and machinery declined more than investment in building and construction. Completion of some major public projects also contributed to the lack of a compensating rise in public sector investment.

With an uncertain business outlook and high real interest rates, total loan demand continued to be weak. Moreover, the banking sector experienced problem loans, partly because of exposure to some troubled PRC enterprises, such as Guangdong International Trust and Investment Corporation. Largely reflecting a decline in total loans, the ratio of classified loans to total loans rose to 10 percent. This prompted some banks to increase provisions for bad loans, which affected profitability, and to adopt a more cautious lending stance. Nevertheless, banks' asset quality stabilized in the third quarter of 1999 and the sector's capital

Table 2.1 **Major Economic Indicators, Hong Kong, China, 1997-2001**
(percent)

Item	1997	1998	1999	2000	2001
Gross domestic product growth	5.0	-5.1	2.9	5.0	5.5
Gross domestic investment/GDP	34.6	29.7	25.4	27.3	34.0
Gross domestic savings/GDP	31.1	30.2	29.8	30.7	32.0
Inflation rate	5.8	2.8	-4.0	-1.0	3.1
Central government budget	6.6	-1.8	-0.1	-0.5	1.0
Money supply (M2) growth	8.3	11.8	8.1	12.0	15.0
Merchandise exports growth	4.0	-7.5	-0.1	9.1	10.0
Merchandise imports growth	5.1	-11.6	-2.7	10.7	11.0
Service exports growth	0.6	-10.4	2.6	9.1	9.7
Service imports growth	5.4	-2.1	-1.6	6.0	8.1

Sources: Government of Hong Kong Special Administrative Region; staff estimates.

adequacy ratio remained at a healthy level, averaging 20.1 percent.

Reducing unemployment is another challenge for policymakers. Although the unemployment rate stabilized around 6 percent, it was high compared with a precrisis level of 3 percent, and was exacerbated by the continued strong growth of the labor force. For 1999, total employment increased 1.8 percent. However, the labor force rose 3.5 percent because of strong immigration, particularly from the PRC, and an increase in the number of women in the labor force.

Nevertheless, the prospects for employment should improve as economic recovery broadens in 2000. GDP growth is forecast to rise to 5 percent in 2000 and 5.5 percent in 2001. The external sector should continue to improve along with the region's economies. This will be aided, to some extent, by additional tourist revenue from a planned Disney theme park. With more infrastructure projects planned, domestic fixed capital formation will start to increase in the next two years. The conventional measures of real interest rates are expected to peak in mid-2000, with the easing of deflationary pressures. Imports will increase as well, with the visible trade deficit worsening in the coming years.

The prospects of Hong Kong, China as an entrepot for the PRC may wane as the PRC develops its own container and port facilities. However, the projected entry of the PRC into the World Trade Organization in the near future is expected to present new opportunities, including stronger re-exports from the PRC as well as closer trade linkages.

ISSUES IN ECONOMIC MANAGEMENT

A severely contracting economy combined with measures aimed at stimulating spending led to fiscal deficits of 1.8 percent and 0.1 percent of GDP in 1998 and 1999, respectively. A deficit is also expected for 2000. Authorities maintain that the budget will be cyclically balanced, with a surplus expected in 2001. A number of infrastructure projects with total outlay of more than HK$65 billion (US$8.4 billion) are scheduled to start in 2000. Therefore, whether the government can return its budget to a surplus will depend on its success in finding new ways to raise revenues, aside from the natural increase as the economy recovers.

The government has accumulated huge fiscal reserves over the years. Even with the deficits recorded in the last two years, these reserves stood at HK$390 billion (US$50.3 billion) at the end of 1999, and give authorities some latitude in fiscal matters.

High real interest rates have been of greater concern. While nominal interest rates declined for much of 1999 and were well below the peaks reached in 1998, observers have blamed falling prices for pushing real interest rates to their highest levels in more than a decade. Moreover, because the linked exchange rate system forces nominal interest rates to follow closely those in the United States, an anticipated tightening of the US Federal Reserve's monetary policy may keep private investment at its currently subdued levels and hamper the pace of economic recovery.

To some extent, the concern regarding high real interest rates results from how they are typically computed, by adjusting nominal interest rates using actual rates of inflation, rather than the conceptually superior expected rate of inflation. However, the process of deflation is not a downward spiral of prices and production, but rather part of an adjustment process required to make an economy that uses a fixed exchange rate more competitive. Therefore true real interest rates are probably not as high as conventional measures suggest. While prices have been falling, they should cease to do so during the first half of 2000, and investors will take this into account.

Moreover, with the region registering a sustained recovery, business confidence is likely to return to more robust levels. How robust a recovery the economy can stage, however, will depend on how well it can restructure itself to enhance competitiveness as a financial and business center to the PRC, and to the region as a whole.

To facilitate this restructuring, the government has focused its policies not just on macroeconomic management, but also on microeconomic reforms. In particular, the government has taken steps to remove existing barriers to entry and price controls in the telecommunications and banking sectors. Liberalizing the international calls market in January 1999 and implementing mobile phone number portability in March 1999 saw an increased number of suppliers and fierce competition for market shares through better or cheaper services.

Following the completion of the Banking Sector Consultancy Study in December 1998 and considering the views expressed during a public consultation in early 1999, the Hong Kong Monetary Authority developed a coherent package of policy initiatives to reform and further develop the banking sector. Reforms involve deregulating the remaining interest rate rules, relaxing the one-branch policy, implementing a formalized risk-based supervisory approach, simplifying the three-tier licensing system, conducting a full study on deposit protection, and evaluating the feasibility of a credit register for commercial enterprises. The July 1999 announcement allowed foreign banks licensed after 1978 to open as many as three branches. The first phase of interest rate deregulation is scheduled for July 2000, while the review of local bank licensing requirements will be undertaken toward the second half of 2001. Consolidation, in the form of mergers and acquisitions, is also being encouraged to enhance efficiency through exploiting economies of scale, eliminating redundancies, and using joint funding for investments in new technology.

With the advent of the digital age and the rapid global expansion of the Internet, electronic banking offers new products and services, such as multipurpose stored-value cards and banking services via mobile phone or the Internet. However, while these electronic commercial channels offer more convenience, they also pose new risks, such as theft, fraud, or alteration of information by unauthorized access via digital means. Law enforcement is particularly difficult in cases involving cross-border activities. Existing legislation must be amended quickly to provide a prudential supervisory framework for these new financial activities.

In view of the overdependence on the local equity market and banking sector for long-term funding, the Hong Kong Monetary Authority also stepped up its efforts to enhance capital market development. These include developing mortgage-backed securities since 1997 and listing Exchange Fund Notes on the local stock exchange in August 1999. In addition, the merger of the Hong Kong Stock and Futures exchanges and the implementation of the Mandatory Provident Fund will occur in 2000. Thus, the financial sector is expected to expand in 2000-2001, after almost three years of consolidation. Successfully implementing these financial sector reforms will be critical in maintaining Hong Kong, China as a major regional financial center, especially as reforms are also under way in other Asian cities such as Singapore and Shanghai.

POLICY AND DEVELOPMENT ISSUES

The continued relocation of manufacturing industries to the PRC and the slowdown in major service sectors because of the Asian financial turmoil prompted the government to take more initiatives to develop high-value-added and high-tech industries. A string of projects and research funding have emerged. Besides the Science Park currently under construction, other ambitious projects include a HK$13 billion Cyberport and the HK$9.3 billion Silicon Harbor, both to be jointly developed with private sector initiative and involvement. The government's assistance will involve providing research funding and housing subsidies for overseas staff, and granting land at a subsidized rate.

While in the past high-tech industries were considered unduly risky due to their high overhead costs, uncertain demand, and long gestation periods, emphasis on the information technology (IT) industry is being embraced more widely. This is because the IT industry could complement traditional areas of strength, such as finance and trade services. Consequently, banks, property developers, real estate agents, and trading companies are among the first to endorse an IT-based industrial policy.

Development of the IT industry is also being embraced more readily because telecommunications, the basic infrastructure for IT, is well developed and among the best in the world. For example, in terms of telephone lines per household, mobile phones per person, and Internet penetration rates, Hong Kong, China is among the most advanced in the region.

The establishment of the Growth Enterprise Market (GEM) is in line with such industrial development. The strong performance of Internet stocks in the United States, especially on the NASDAQ, provided the incentive for technology ventures to attempt to list in Hong Kong, China. Technology companies dominated the first listings on the GEM in November. Most of these startups were small and medium-size enterprises that lacked the good track record or substantial assets necessary to obtain funds from banks or list on the main board of the stock market. The government set up the Special Finance Scheme for these enterprises in August, and had committed around HK$4.8 billion.

However, the GEM is a more attractive source of funding as it provides a bigger investor base and stronger growth potential. The smaller size of these GEM stock issues, however, will imply higher risk of price fluctuations, and hence of speculation. The announcement that some big US technology stocks may be listed on the GEM in 2000 has further boosted local confidence in this new second board. In addition, some larger local enterprises are setting up subsidiaries to capture this rising wave of positive sentiment. Although the results are not yet clear, the availability of such channels for funding and expansion is a strong incentive for developing companies with strong IT connections.

With hardware manufacturing centered in the PRC, Hong Kong, China's IT industries will need to focus on the design, marketing, and application of the latest technological tools for the production, distribution, and consumption of information. To succeed, a steady supply of highly skilled workers will need to be ensured. This can be achieved through improving and extending tertiary education facilities. While appropriate investment in education is critical, keeping Hong Kong, China attractive for professionals from the PRC and elsewhere will also be important.

To this end, Hong Kong, China needs to improve the overall living environment, which will necessitate a more comprehensive and effective environmental policy. Not only will this help attract the best professionals from around the world, but it is also of vital interest to the local populace. The worsening of various forms of pollution in recent years has generated increasing concern regarding health risks. This has far-reaching implications for rising public health costs as well as lower productivity. The negative impact on tourism serves as a good warning. With the global trend toward greater demand for better environmental standards, it is critical to incorporate environmental issues into any long-term development strategy.

The first significant environmental policy was formed in 1989 with a ten-year plan to fight air, water, noise, and waste pollution. In 1998, the Environmental Impact Assessment Ordinance was implemented to give more legislative power to the Environmental Protection Department. In addition, separate ordinances govern air and water pollution control, noise control, and waste disposal. The authorities have undertaken various forms of control, including requiring licenses and permits for industrial pollution. In 1990, the Hong Kong-Guangdong Environmental Protection Liaison Group was established to facilitate regional pollution control. A joint study of air pollution in the Pearl River Delta was undertaken with the Guangdong authorities and will be completed in 2000. However, most of the problem lies in enforcement, which is hindered by low penalty rates for offenders.

The launching of an air pollution index in 1995 improved public awareness of air pollution levels, and high levels of this index prompted the government to require all diesel-powered taxis to change to liquid petroleum gas by 2005. Improper waste disposal also has worsened as the dumping of household garbage and construction waste has increased, resulting in rising collection and disposal costs for the government. The recycling industry has seen limited success because of high land costs, low profit margins, and the lack of community cooperation.

Eventually the private sector will develop the IT industry, and market forces will shape it. But because of the substantial long-term benefits of an effective environmental protection policy, it is critical that the government spend more resources in enforcement and education to maintain competitiveness as a regional commercial hub and an international city.

Republic of Korea

Economic recovery and financial stabilization in the Republic of Korea (henceforth referred to as Korea) in 1999 were remarkable. Mitigating the adverse impacts of these changes on the fiscal position and labor market, however, is an essential challenge for stable and sustainable economic growth.

RECENT TRENDS AND PROSPECTS

After resorting to a rescue package led by the International Monetary Fund, Korea recovered at a brisk pace in 1999. Aided by ongoing financial and corporate sector restructuring and a favorable export environment, the GDP growth rate reached 10.7 percent. It stood in sharp contrast with –6.7 percent in 1998, and was the highest recorded growth since 1988.

On the production side, the manufacturing sector led the recovery of the economy. On the demand side, the rapid rebounding of private consumption and machinery and equipment investment contributed to the recovery, along with a slower pace of inventory reduction. However, construction continued to contract and net exports slowed economic growth. Owing to the economic recovery, the unemployment rate declined to 4.8 percent by December 1999, after peaking at 8.6 percent in February 1999.

Despite expansionary economic policy and rapid economic recovery, prices were extremely stable. The inflation rate dropped from 7.5 percent in 1998 to 0.8 percent in 1999, the lowest level in recent history. The appreciation of the won has significantly contributed to this price stability.

The financial conditions of the economy have improved dramatically. First, the level of foreign exchange reserves increased rapidly. In 1998 domestic demand abruptly collapsed as interest rates increased and the current account recorded a $41 billion surplus. This surplus greatly contributed to the rapid accumulation of foreign exchange reserves, from less than $10 billion at the end of 1997 to more than $74 billion at the end of 1999. As foreign exchange reserves increased, the exchange rate stabilized to around W1,150 to the dollar by December 1999.

Aided by the appreciation of the Japanese yen and the recovery in Asian markets, export performance improved in 1999. Heavy and chemical industries, particularly electronics, led the export recovery. While exports increased by 10 percent, imports grew more rapidly by 29 percent because of a recovery in domestic demand. This led to the decline in the trade account surplus from $42 billion in 1998 to $29 billion in 1999, or 7 percent of GDP.

In addition to the decline in the trade surplus, the deficit in the nontrade account, including such items as service and interest payments, widened from $1 billion in 1998 to around $4 billion in 1999. Consequently, the current account surplus decreased from $41 billion in 1998 (13 percent of GDP) to $25 billion in 1999 (6 percent of GDP). The capital account showed a surplus of $0.6 billion, despite the repayment of the International Monetary Fund emergency loan of $11 billion. Thus, there was a large net surplus in private sector inflows. Korea had net inflow for nondebt instruments such as foreign direct investment and equity investment in 1999, a likely result of the policy that pushed the large conglomerates (*chaebols*) to reduce their debt-to-equity ratios.

The government maintained the expansionary macroeconomic policies it adopted in mid-1998 to stimulate the economy. The government expenditures in 1999 were initially planned to increase by 5-6 percent from 1998, with the expectation of an overall fiscal deficit of 5 percent of GDP. Actual government expenditures increased 10 percent above the 1998 level, which had already risen by 13.5 percent from 1997. Nevertheless, the rapid recovery and growing tax revenues enabled the government to reduce the fiscal deficit to less than 3 percent of GDP.

To aid economic recovery, the central bank lowered short-term interest rates until May 1999. By then the economy had begun to gather considerable momentum and the central bank decided to halt lowering of interest rates. The call rate was kept below 5 percent for the rest of the year.

Despite the remarkable recovery in 1999, sustainable economic growth for the years to come will require significant economic restructuring, particularly in the financial and corporate sectors. Economic growth in 2000 is projected to be 7.5 percent. Fixed investment will provide the major stimulus, while the contribution of consumption and foreign trade will decline somewhat. Continued economic recovery should provide a favorable environment for business investment. In tandem with continued economic recovery, labor market conditions are expected to tighten slightly. The unemployment rate is projected to fall to 5 percent, down from 6.3 percent in 1999.

Despite strong price stability in 1999, the rapid economic recovery and increased liquidity arising from financial restructuring are likely to trigger inflationary pressure in the second half of 2000. Consequently, somewhat tighter monetary policy will be called for, and short-term interest rates are likely to be increased. However, the monetary authorities will be cautious in

Table 2.2 Major Economic Indicators, Republic of Korea, 1997-2001
(percent)

Item	1997	1998	1999	2000	2001
GDP growth	5.0	-6.7	10.7	7.5	6.0
Gross domestic investment/GDP	34.2	21.2	26.8	28.5	27.2
Gross domestic savings/GDP	32.5	33.9	33.0	30.9	27.9
Inflation rate (consumer price index)	4.5	7.5	0.8	3.2	3.2
Money supply (M2) growth	14.1	27.0	27.3	24.8	21.5
Fiscal balance/GDP	-1.5	-4.2	-2.9	-2.8	-2.6
Merchandise exports growth	6.7	-4.7	10.1	10.0	7.4
Merchandise imports growth	-2.2	-36.2	29.0	23.1	14.3
Current account balance/GDP	-1.7	12.8	6.1	2.4	0.8

Sources: National Statistical Office (1999); Bank of Korea; Korea Development Institute; Ministry of Finance and Economy; staff estimates.

raising short-term interest rates because of concern about adverse consequences of higher rates on the Daewoo crisis and on the liquidity shortages of investment trust companies. On the supply side, nominal wage growth accelerated in 1999, while domestic currency appreciation was minimal. Given these developments, consumer price inflation is projected to accelerate to 3.2 percent in 2000 and 2001.

Exports will continue to grow in 2000 as world economic growth is expected to increase in terms of both output and trade. Import prices will continue to rise more rapidly than export prices because of higher oil prices and the yen appreciation. Therefore, import growth in dollar terms will expand faster than exports and the current account surplus will shrink further.

ISSUES IN ECONOMIC MANAGEMENT

Until the outbreak of the crisis in 1997, the government had long maintained a balanced budget tradition. Operating from this foundation of fiscal prudence, the government could play a pivotal role in helping the economy recover from the crisis. In particular, the government allocated funds for financial restructuring and recapitalization, strengthened social safety nets, and boosted the economy. Because of the government's active involvement in restructuring, stability of the financial system has been restored and the economy is recovering.

The cost of this intervention has increased government debt. The central government debt was less than W50 trillion (around 11 percent of GDP) before the crisis. However, with a budget deficit of around W15 trillion for two consecutive years, government debt nearly doubled to around W94 trillion by the end of 1999. The government also will have to pay interest for W64 trillion in government-guaranteed public bonds issued to underwrite the financial sector restructuring. This will result in interest payments that will amount to 4.5 percent of the consolidated current expenditures from 1999 onward.

Faced with the explosive increase of debt burden, in January 1999 the government announced a medium-term fiscal plan for a balanced budget. According to this plan, the consolidated budget balance is expected to be restored by 2004.

However, fiscal consolidation faces many obstacles. First, the interest payment for the government's own and guaranteed debts will reach W8 trillion to W10 trillion (almost 7 percent of government expenditure) in 2001-2002. Another serious constraint is the sharp increase in the social welfare budget. In particular, the newly enacted Law for Basic Life Protection will substantially reduce the flexibility of government expenditure. This law, which will take effect in October 2000, allows any poor person to claim payments from the government, regardless of ability to work. The deficit in the pension fund for government officials will inevitably increase. According to some projections, this fund will be depleted in 2001, and the deficit will increase substantially. To minimize the subsidy for the fund, reforms need to be instituted promptly to improve the fund management and strike a balance between burden and benefit for subscribers.

Perhaps last, but not least, an important obstacle to fiscal consolidation is the laxity of fiscal discipline. As Korea went through the crisis, its balanced budget tradition was compromised, and it may be difficult to restore. Both policymakers and the public may now take having a budget deficit for granted. Therefore, achieving a strong consensus on the importance of government budget consolidation is critical.

POLICY AND DEVELOPMENT ISSUES

Unemployment, which grew substantially during the crisis, requires new policy initiatives. The unemployment rate jumped from 2.6 percent in 1997 to 6.8 percent in 1998, and peaked at 8.6 percent in February 1999. Although it slowly settled to below 5 percent by the end of 1999, the rate was still high compared with the precrisis level. This can be explained not only by macroeconomic factors such as severe postcrisis recession and massive corporate bankruptcies, but also by structural changes in the labor market.

Indeed, Korea's postcrisis reform package includes measures to improve labor market flexibility while expanding the social safety net. In particular, layoffs due to managerial prerogatives were legally instituted in the new labor law in 1998, while the unemployment insurance system was extended to cover more workers and increase the amount and duration of unemployment benefits. Improved corporate governance and strengthened risk management in the financial sector discourage reckless business expansion and tend to lower potential economic excesses. Furthermore, economic liberalization and opening up the economy will significantly enhance competition in both product and factor markets. In the short run, the move away from a lifetime employment system may exacerbate unemployment, but the long-term effects on economic efficiency and labor market flexibility should be beneficial.

The composition of unemployment changed during 1998-1999 as economic restructuring took place. Despite a continuous decline in the unemployment rate in 1999, long-term displaced workers (those jobless for more than one year) accounted for more than 15 percent of total unemployment, up from 11 percent in 1998. Unskilled production and construction workers with little education also accounted for a substantial number of displaced workers during these two years. Without effective vocational training, these workers will have difficulty re-entering the labor market. The ratio of regular workers to temporary and daily workers, however, changed from 55:45 in the first quarter of 1998 to 47:53 in the fourth quarter of 1999, indicating improved labor market flexibility.

These projections imply that increased structural unemployment must be addressed not only at the active labor policy level, but also at the institutional level. Several policy measures can ease structural unemployment

First, labor market flexibility needs further improvement. Although layoffs were legally instituted in 1998, new and more flexible labor practices may take time to implement fully, as Korea has a long history of lifetime employment. The government should continue to reinforce market principles by strictly enforcing legal standards for disruptive labor practices, including strikes. On an institutional level, adjustable working hours can provide greater employment flexibility and reduce overtime payments. This could cut labor costs and expand employment.

Second, product market competition needs to be promoted to make the factor market more competitive. Comprehensive deregulation was pursued after the crisis by eliminating or relaxing about half of central government regulations. This should be accelerated, focusing on barriers to entry and regulations that limit price competition.

Third, labor force skills need to be enhanced. This is particularly important because growth potential should stem more from productivity growth based on knowledge than factor input expansion. To accomplish this, an improved educational system, stronger vocational training, and expanded investment in technology and innovation are needed. The budget plan for 2000 has allocated a substantially increased amount of fiscal resources for public research, development investment, and venture businesses support.

Finally, the social welfare system needs overhauling to provide an effective safety net for workers while strengthening work incentives. Both the level and duration of unemployment benefits have increased significantly since the crisis. However, they are still far less satisfactory than those of advanced Organisation for Economic Co-operation and Development member countries. Measures to strengthen work incentives for the unemployed have not kept pace with improved unemployment benefits, and the eligibility test for unemployment benefits also needs to be strengthened.

Singapore

Singapore's institutional strengths and flexible economic management enabled it to rebound strongly in 1999 from economic stagnation in the previous year. However, adjustments to the realities of the postcrisis environment will be more challenging and will require further changes in institutional and production structures to retain competitiveness. Long-term prospects for the economy remain bright.

RECENT TRENDS AND PROSPECTS

The economy of Singapore rebounded strongly from a near-stagnant level in 1998 to register GDP growth of 5.4 percent in 1999. The manufacturing sector accounted for much of the growth, reflecting strong external demand for telecommunications equipment, semiconductors, computer peripherals, and computers. The nonelectronic segment of manufacturing also performed well, and chemical output rose sharply, reflecting increased regional demand for industrial chemicals and pharmaceuticals. The construction sector, however, continued to decline, mainly because of a sharp drop in private construction activity. Developers remained cautious because of excess capacity in both residential and nonresidential markets. The service sector also staged a recovery, with increased regional trade flows. Tourist arrivals boosted growth in the transportation and communications sectors, while increased domestic demand led to a sharp rise in the retail and wholesale sectors. The financial services sector also benefited from improved investor sentiment

toward regional equity markets and improved regional demand for insurance and investment advice.

Despite the strong rebound in economic activity and increased investment commitments in the second half of the year, overall growth in fixed investment by both private and public sectors remained below its historical rate before the crisis (see figure 2.1). This was due to insufficient credit expansion and industrial overcapacity. Bank lending, other than for housing, remained weak and lagged behind the recovery in industrial production. Lending for housing rose and property transactions increased, however, as prices remained low and banks offered attractive mortgage financing packages. Fiscal policy provided less of a stimulus to the economy than originally envisaged. The original budget for fiscal year 1999 ending 31 March had predicted a budget deficit of S$5.1 billion (3.4 percent of GDP). However, considerably faster-than-expected revenue growth, combined with lower operating and development expenditure, led to a budget surplus. Although a rise in interbank rates reflected the rise in US interest rates that began in mid-1999, domestic retail rates remained relatively stable throughout the year. Banks did not increase borrowing rates because deposits continued to rise even as lending remained weak.

With the recovery in the domestic economy, labor demand strengthened, and greater employment in the service and manufacturing sectors more than compensated for declines in the construction sector. Job vacancy and recruitment rates increased as well. However, retrenchments remained high, with more than half resulting from relocation of lower-end manufacturing operations to cheaper sites in the region. The rate of unemployment nevertheless decreased to 2.9 percent by the end of 1999, its lowest level since mid-1998.

In response to the sharp depreciation of the region's currencies, in 1998 the government introduced temporary measures to reduce unit business and labor costs and maintain price competitiveness. These included a 10 percent cut in employers' contributions to the Central Provident Fund, a mandatory pension fund; cuts in wages; reductions in government-controlled rentals for commercial and industrial properties; and reductions in government-imposed utility charges for electricity and telecommunications. Because of improved recovery prospects, the government planned to increase employer contributions to the Central Provident Fund to 12 percent in April 2000, and if conditions remain favorable, to 20 percent by 2004. Some smaller companies, however, are not performing well enough to bear the additional costs, and have protested the planned increases. Some observers also are concerned that a tighter labor market will lead to a rise in wage costs.

The Singapore dollar remained broadly stable against the US dollar. It appreciated relative to the currencies of its trading partners in the region, with the exception of Indonesia and Malaysia. While this may adversely affect external competitiveness in the short term, authorities expect that in the long term, developing higher-quality, value-added, and knowledge-based products will improve Singapore's competitiveness.

After declining 0.3 percent in 1998 and another 0.6 percent in the first quarter of 1999, consumer price inflation increased in the second quarter because of higher costs of food, transportation, and communication. Inflation in 1999 was subdued, however, averaging 0.5 percent because of relatively low domestic demand and wage inflation. Reflecting increased activity in the private residential market, residential property prices rose 26 percent from their levels at

Table 2.3 Major Economic Indicators, Singapore, 1997-2001
(percent)

Item	1997	1998	1999	2000	2001
GDP growth	8.0	1.5	5.4	5.9	6.2
Gross domestic investment/GDP	38.7	33.5	32.7	34.2	36.0
Gross domestic savings/GDP	50.4	49.9	51.2	52.0	52.0
Inflation rate (consumer price index)	2.0	-0.3	0.5	1.5	1.5
Money supply (M2) growth	10.3	30.2	8.5	11.6	11.8
Fiscal balance/GDP[a]	9.6	1.6	2.5	3.0	3.3
Merchandise exports growth	-0.2	-12.2	2.6	3.5	5.3
Merchandise imports growth	0.7	-23.2	6.8	7.9	8.8
Current account balance/GDP	15.8	20.9	18.5	17.8	16.0

a. Excludes grants.

Sources: Singapore Department of Statistics (1999); Monetary Authority of Singapore (1999a); IMF (2000); staff estimates.

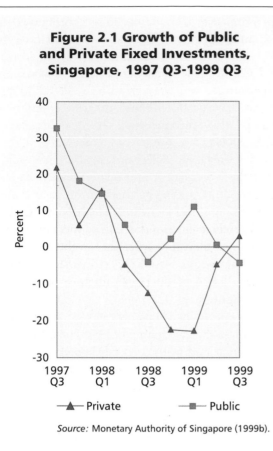

Figure 2.1 Growth of Public and Private Fixed Investments, Singapore, 1997 Q3-1999 Q3

Source: Monetary Authority of Singapore (1999b).

ist arrivals rose, and expanded intraregional trade led to a greater demand for Singapore's shipping services. In addition, financial service exports increased as the recovery in the stock market resulted in more broker services for nonresident investors. Thus, the current account surplus declined only slightly from its 1998 level. However, a smaller deficit on the capital and financial account occurred because of lower net outflows in portfolio investment and higher net inflows of direct investment. Singapore therefore maintained a healthy level of reserves.

GDP growth is expected to accelerate in 2000 as consumption improves. This should reduce excess industrial capacity and provide greater incentives for investment. Increased asset values and the government's decision to partially restore wage cuts imposed in early 1999 will boost private consumption, while fixed investment will increase along with bank lending. This will be facilitated by a decrease in nonperforming loans to the crisis countries as these economies recover. Higher private consumption and fixed investment will allow continued economic expansion and employment generation in 2000-2001. Inflation is likely to increase to 1-2 percent in 2000 because of increased oil prices, wage inflation, and domestic demand, and will remain around this level during 2001. The trade surplus will likely contract further during the next two years as imports will increase more rapidly than exports. Although exports will increase due to stronger trade growth, imports will increase faster because of the import-dependent nature of exports and a higher demand for capital goods. An improvement in the services and income account will partially offset the narrower trade surplus, however, and steady inflows of foreign direct investment will ensure that overall reserves remain at healthy levels. Foreign debt will pose no problems for Singapore during the forecast period.

ISSUES IN ECONOMIC MANAGEMENT

Although restrictions on the use of the Singapore dollar by nonresidents were considerably eased, the government remained cautious toward the internationalization of the Singapore dollar. For instance, despite the removal of the ceiling on foreign ownership of local banks, these banks must retain at least

the end of December 1998. However, they remained about 31 percent lower than their peak levels in the second quarter of 1996. Prices of commercial property, however, continued to decline, as oversupply dampened the market. Boosted by growing optimism about the region's growth prospects, equity prices rose sharply in the first half of 1999, and then leveled off because of trading curbs by brokering houses and interest rate hikes by the US Federal Reserve. Overall equity prices, as measured by the Stock Exchange of Singapore all-share index, rose 74.8 percent in 1999.

The trade surplus narrowed from its record level of 1998. Although strong growth in the region and in the United States increased demand for Singapore's electronic goods, a higher rate of import growth, which resulted from renewed consumer confidence and diminished inventories, more than offset this demand. The service sector surplus, however, increased as tour-

50 percent of residents' deposits so that the Monetary Authority of Singapore can control Singapore dollar transactions. These restrictions were based on concern that a large offshore market in Singapore dollars could destabilize domestic exchange and interest rates. If, however, Singapore is to become a major international financial center, the authorities will likely have to contend with the inevitable internationalization of the Singapore dollar.

POLICY AND DEVELOPMENT ISSUES

Singapore's strong institutions and flexible approach to macroeconomic management have allowed it to emerge quickly from the Asian crisis with few social disruptions. However, adjusting to the realities of the postcrisis environment will be more challenging and will require further changes to institutional and production structures to remain competitive.

The Committee on Singapore's Competitiveness has called for a knowledge-based economy to help improve long-term competitiveness. To this end, the government has been developing an institutional structure that will provide appropriate support. The Ministry of Communications and Information Technology was created, and the existing National Computer Board and the Telecommunications Board of Singapore were merged into the Info-Communications Development Authority. This group was given the task of preparing a master plan to develop the information and communications industry. The government has also initiated measures to provide incentives for entrepreneurs entering high-tech industries, and to train people in skills related to information technology. For example, the government has increased the skills development levy paid by employers to fund approved training courses for lower-paid workers. However, there is no certainty that retraining will enable workers with limited skills and education to qualify for jobs being created in the semiconductor and chemical industries. Although the government's past interventions in industrial development have been beneficial, there is some concern that continued interventions on this scale could impede necessary corporate restructuring as market conditions change.

A sound and well-regulated banking sector helped Singapore weather the Asian crisis. However, many other challenges remain. The domestic banking sector, which is overregulated and characterized by high cost and low liquidity, needs to be improved. To help develop the economy as a regional financial center, the Monetary Authority of Singapore (the de facto central bank) introduced a series of wide-ranging measures in 1998 and 1999 aimed at liberalizing financial markets. These include the merger of the Stock Exchange of Singapore and the Singapore International Monetary Exchange into the Singapore Exchange in December 1999, the first fully integrated financial market in Asia.

The government also liberalized entry into the Singapore Exchange by gradually lifting the restrictions on the number of foreign brokers who can participate and on the value of their trades. In addition, the government is developing a risk-based method of calculating capital requirements for brokers and will allow more Singapore dollar-denominated interest rate derivatives to be traded on the exchange. Beginning in 2001, freely negotiated broker commissions will replace the system of fixed commissions, which authorities expect will lower transaction costs. Bank disclosure rules were strengthened by measures recommended by the Committee on Banking Disclosure in May 1998. The Monetary Authority of Singapore also scrapped the 40 percent ceiling on foreign ownership of local banks and granted licenses to four foreign banking groups, which will allow them to open additional branches and run automatic teller machines off-premises.

These liberalization measures have led to a fundamental change in emphasis from regulation to risk-focused supervision and increased disclosure. The authorities expect this to help reduce risks of contagion, broaden and deepen the capital market, decrease costs, and improve efficiency. This change will also boost Singapore's standing as a regional financial center and its competitiveness in relation to Hong Kong, China.

Taipei,China

A massive earthquake struck Taipei,China in 1999, causing serious damage to infrastructure. Reconstruction work was swift and resulted in only a marginal decline of GDP growth in 1999 compared with government targets. A recovering global economy boosted exports, and better economic growth is projected for 2000.

RECENT TRENDS AND PROSPECTS

Economic performance strengthened in the first half of 1999 as the economy began to recover from a modest growth slowdown following the Asian financial crisis. However, a massive earthquake struck on 21 September 1999, causing considerable damage to the productive capacity of the economy, particularly to physical infrastructure. For example, the microchip makers at the high-tech industrial park in Hsin-Chu City suffered an estimated $320 million in production losses because of power supply interruptions. Despite this setback, real GDP growth in 1999 was 5.7 percent, only marginally lower than the target of 5.8 percent, and more than 1 percent higher than growth in 1998.

Strong performance of the external sector was an important factor in the recovery. The trade balance for 1999 amounted to $15.1 billion, a sharp increase of 46 percent from 1998. While exports declined 9.5 percent in 1998, in 1999 they grew 6.8 percent, led by semiconductors and notebook computer sales. Exports also benefited from the recovery in Asia

and strong import demand from the United States. Merchandise imports grew by 2.8 percent in 1999, in contrast to a 7.4 percent decline in 1998. Machinery and electrical equipment made up the largest share of imports. Japan was the largest source country, accounting for 25.7 percent of total imports.

The growth rate of the industry sector rose to 4.3 percent in 1999 from 2.7 percent in 1998. This was largely propelled by growth in the electronics industry, which benefited from the recovery of the global economy, higher prices, and a boost in Y2K-related demand. Growth in the service sector was modest at 6.3 percent, slightly higher than the previous year. Good weather contributed to the recovery of the agriculture sector from a 6.6 percent decline in 1998 to a 2.9 percent growth in 1999.

Investments grew by 2.1 percent in 1999, less than the 10.4 percent growth the previous year because of a sluggish housing market, fewer large commercial airplane purchases, and a sharp deceleration in the investment growth rate. Consumption expenditure also decelerated, growing by only 4.2 percent in 1999 compared with 7.8 percent in 1998. The only two strong areas of consumption spending in 1999 were transportation and communications, and medical care and health services.

The savings rate has slowly declined for several years, partly reflecting the aging of the population. However, the savings rate still remains high compared with many Asian economies. As a percentage of GDP, nominal gross fixed capital formation declined marginally, from 24.9 percent in 1998 to 24.4 percent in 1999.

The inflation rate was exceptionally low in 1999, essentially because of weak domestic demand. Falling raw material prices contributed to a decline of 4.5 percent in the wholesale price index in 1999. The unemployment rate rose slightly from 2.7 percent in 1998 to 2.9 percent. The labor force grew to 9.7 million, a 1.9 percent increase from 1998. The increase could not be absorbed by the labor market, partly owing to the slow expansion of service sector employment.

Although the amount of income tax collected increased moderately, total tax revenue dropped 6.6 percent in 1999. This resulted partly from less tax income on security transactions due to weak stock market performance. Although nontax revenue posted growth, the reduction in tax revenue caused current revenue to decrease 2.2 percent. Current expenditures were constrained to offset this drop, shrinking by 3.9

percent in 1999, in contrast to growing 9.4 percent in 1998. Monetary policy remained cautious in 1999. The money supply (M2) increased modestly to 9.2 percent from 8.6 percent the previous year.

GDP growth is projected to accelerate slightly, to above 6 percent in 2000 and 2001. Reconstruction of earthquake-damaged structures will provide much of the stimulus; the government pledged nearly NT$100 billion, including infrastructure rebuilding and subsidized loans for new housing. This will further widen the fiscal deficit. Private sector fixed capital formation is also likely to accelerate as build-operate-transfer projects, such as the planned high-speed train, get under way. Export performance is expected to be stronger during 2000 as the Asian region continues to recover, and growth in the United States and other industrial country markets remains buoyant. Prices of industrial raw materials and oil should either remain stable or increase marginally, while exports should be strong, particularly those from the electronics subsector. Increasing government and private investment in plants and equipment will require more imports.

Reflecting stronger aggregate demand, inflation is projected to grow at 1.9 percent in 2000 and 2 percent the next year. There will be little inflationary pressure from external factors, as the import price index is likely to grow moderately during these two years.

Table 2.4 Major Economic Indicators, Taipei,China, 1997-2001
(percent)

Item	1997	1998	1999	2000	2001
GDP growth	6.7	4.6	5.7	6.3	6.2
Gross domestic investment/GDP	24.2	24.9	24.4	24.2	24.5
Gross domestic savings/GDP	26.4	26.0	26.0	26.8	27.2
Inflation rate (consumer price index)	0.9	1.7	0.2	1.9	2.0
Money supply (M2) growth	8.0	8.6	9.2	9.3	9.0
Fiscal balance/GDP	-3.8	-3.3	-4.2	-6.0	-5.8
Merchandise exports growth	5.4	-9.5	6.8	12.5	11.5
Merchandise imports growth	10.1	-7.4	2.8	15.8	13.4
Current account balance/GDP	2.4	1.3	3.0	1.8	1.5

Sources: Wu (1999); staff estimates.

Further recovery of domestic demand is expected to increase the growth rate of goods and services imports to 15.8 percent and 13.4 percent in 2000 and 2001, respectively. Consequently, the current account balance is projected to be $5.7 billion in 2000, and $5.3 billion in 2001.

ISSUES IN ECONOMIC MANAGEMENT

Taipei,China managed its macroeconomy well throughout the Asian crisis, benefiting from its large foreign exchange reserves and minimal foreign debt. The nonperforming loan ratio was low and the capital adequacy ratio of most banks remained above the 8 percent stipulated by the Bank for International Settlements. In addition, a 9.7 percent rate of return on net investment invigorated the financial sector.

The industrial structure was another important factor behind the macroeconomic resilience. Small and medium-size enterprises, which contribute approximately 50 percent of total export revenues, dominate this sector. Since the early 1990s, semiconductor and electronics have replaced the construction industry as the principal engine of growth, providing extra strength and dynamism to the economy. The government also effectively used monetary policy to maintain liquidity and moderate interest rates during the financial crisis.

These export-oriented companies have demonstrated their ability to adjust quickly to a rapidly changing external environment. Government policy should encourage them to maintain their international competitiveness. These corporations need to be increasingly agile, flexible, and pragmatic in reacting to the changing demands of international markets.

POLICY AND DEVELOPMENT ISSUES

Taipei,China is expected to enter the World Trade Organization (WTO) in mid-2000. In preparation, policymakers will reduce tariffs to improve market access. For instance, the average nominal tariff rate of 8.3 percent will be reduced to 7.6 percent upon WTO entry. Government procurement procedures have been streamlined to be compatible with the WTO norms. Nontariff barriers in agriculture were substantially dismantled and the barriers on 18 products

marked for elimination. Entering the WTO should provide manufacturing benefits, but will also probably disrupt the agriculture sector. The economy seems to have lost competitiveness in the agriculture sector, but has gained significant advantage in high-tech and electronics products. Loss of comparative advantage in agriculture should not be seen as negative, but as a stage in the economy's evolution to a fully industrialized status. Therefore, policymakers should not yield to pressure to protect the agriculture sector.

The reconstruction process after the earthquake consumed funds originally intended for stimulating domestic demand and strengthening infrastructure. The construction of the high-speed railway system between Keelum and Kowshon may be delayed. To bridge the investment gap that will ensue from the budget reallocation, the private sector can be called on to support the government. Infrastructure projects initially can be financed by the private sector through build-operate-transfer or build-operate-own projects. Cooperation between the government and the private sector could reduce the government's financial burden, promote private investment, and increase operational efficiency. However, because of lack of experience in these operations, the government and financial institutions are moving slowly.

Since the late 1980s, the traditional sectors of the economy have languished. The economy has developed a dualistic character, with a traditional sector co-existing with a modern high-tech export-oriented group of industries. In the traditional sector, nonperforming loans have increased and profitability and investment have decreased. These industries, particularly the small and medium-size ones, need to be restructured. Their technology is not being upgraded and production modes are inflexible. The government has provided loans for upgrading technology, labor skills, and marketing endeavors. The impact so far, however, has been small because of limited funds. Efforts in this area need to be intensified and more resources committed to assisting small and medium-size enterprises, particularly in the traditional sectors.

WTO membership and the associated financial liberalization are sure to usher in financial internationalization and enhance competition in the domestic financial markets. To increase competitiveness in the banking and financial sectors, the government needs to promote consolidation through mergers and acquisitions. Initial efforts are being made in this direction, but more definitive measures are needed.

Gender differences in earnings persist. The female-to-male earnings ratio averaged 64 percent during 1988-1993 and edged up 67 percent during 1993-1997. Earnings gaps within occupations grew over time. Despite the Labor Standards Law, women do not receive equal pay for work of equal value, and the equal pay law must be better enforced. Employment redistribution can be a viable policy option, because the within-occupation pay inequality generally results from gender segregation across enterprises. Hence, equal pay for equal work within a firm will have little effect on the overall gender earnings gap unless the segregation issue is addressed.

Taipei,China is one of the few developing economies that succeeded in attaining progress with income equality. Although the Gini coefficient (a measure of inequality) began to rise after 1984—increasing from 0.29 that year to 0.32 in 1993—inequality has remained low for the past four decades. Rapid export-oriented growth created a large demand for both low-skilled and highly skilled labor. Brisk and timely development of the agriculture and industry sectors ensured participation of farmers and industrial laborers in the economy, which reduced income inequality. A rapidly growing labor demand resulted in high increases in wages, particularly for young and low-skilled workers. This trend helped narrow wage disparities.

However, since the early 1990s, the rise of a dynamic and skill-oriented export sector has resulted in a widening of differentials as traditional industries have grown more slowly. Upward movement in the stock market during that period favored the wealthier segments of the society and reinforced this trend. Adopting more progressive taxation and restructuring traditional sectors should help stop the trend toward disparities in income and increases in income inequality.

People's Republic of
China and Mongolia

People's Republic
of China

Mongolia

People's Republic of China

Prudent macroeconomic policy aided the People's Republic of China (PRC) in adjusting to the Asian crisis. In 1999, growth slowed slightly and prospects are that a rate lower than the trend in the 1990s can be sustained in the medium term. The challenge will be to continue the reform process of opening the economy, improving efficiency in the state sector, addressing unemployment issues, and developing a legal and regulatory framework essential for efficient functioning of a market economy.

RECENT TRENDS AND PROSPECTS

The economy of the PRC began to decelerate in the fourth quarter of 1998 and continued through the second quarter of 1999. In response, the government cut interest rates in June and announced a fiscal stimulus package in August. These measures were effective, as growth for the year exceeded 7 percent.

Fixed investment grew 5.2 percent in 1999, down from 14 percent in 1998. Private investment, which constitutes about one fourth of total investment in the economy, has been slowing since 1996. The March 1999 constitutional amendment to officially recognize the private sector's role in the economy should improve prospects for private investment. However, the significant excess capacities in many sectors will discourage any large increase in private investment over the medium term.

Consumer demand also remains weak partly because of the increased unemployment from laying off redundant workers from state-owned enterprises (SOEs), and partly because of the uncertainties inherent in reform measures in housing, pension, and other social welfare provisions.

Domestic prices continued to decline because of the weak aggregate demand and the overall deflationary trends in Asia. After falling by 0.8 percent in 1998, the consumer price index declined another 1.4 percent in 1999. The fall in retail prices was even sharper, amounting to 3 percent.

To counteract deflationary trends and maintain robust economic growth, the People's Bank of China lowered interest rates in 1999, reducing the benchmark one-year lending rate for banks from 6.39 to 5.85 percent, and the benchmark one-year deposit rate from 3.78 to 2.25 percent. Simultaneously, the People's Bank of China took measures to stabilize the yuan-dollar exchange rate at around Y8.3 per dollar. Other measures to control the illegal outflow of foreign exchange included (a) strengthening supervision of export receipt remittances, (b) tightening scrutiny of processing trade, (c) curbing offshore renminbi trading, and (d) prohibiting prepayment of foreign currency loans.

With the August fiscal stimulus, the 1999 fiscal deficit increased from Y260 billion (about 3 percent of GDP) in 1998 to Y346 billion (4 percent of GDP). To complement the fiscal stimulus package, a tax was imposed on interest income from bank deposits, to discourage households from saving in banks and to encourage private consumption.

Given the small fiscal deficits and modest public debt, continuing an expansionary fiscal policy to pump-prime the economy in the face of deflationary trends is appropriate. However, the official measure of fiscal deficit underestimates the actual resource imbalance of the government because it does not include the deficit spending of the SOEs, the extrabudgetary government expenditures, and the various subsidies by the state-owned banks. With these items included, the fiscal deficit in 1998 reached 6 percent of GDP. Continued fiscal pump priming to stimulate domestic demand could drain resources away from other needs. Therefore, fiscal stimulus packages to maintain high GDP growth should be used with caution.

Coupled with antipoverty programs, robust growth enabled significant progress in poverty reduction. Much of the economic growth has been pro-poor.

The official estimate of the number of rural poor declined from 42 million (4.6 percent of the rural population) in 1998 to 35 million (4 percent of the rural population) the next year. Between 1978 and 1999, 227 million people were lifted from absolute poverty. The official estimate of poverty has two weaknesses, however. It is based on a very low income criterion of about Y635 annual per capita income ($0.66 per day using purchasing power parity), and does not cover urban areas. According to a World Bank estimate, if the dollar-a-day poverty norm is applied, then in 1997 there were about 208 million rural poor (about 23 percent of the rural population), compared with the official estimate of 50 million (5.4 percent of the rural population). There is no official estimate of the urban poor. However, unofficial estimates indicate that 12 million-15 million (5-6 percent of the urban population) are poor, with per capita income less than Y1,700 (about $1.77 per day using purchasing power parity).

Because of the lack of reliable data, it is difficult to assess the extent of unemployment. Official data do not cover rural areas, which account for 70 percent of the labor force. Unofficial sources indicate that about 150 million, or 30 percent of the rural labor

Table 2.5 Major Economic Indicators, People's Republic of China, 1997-2001
(percent)

Item	1997	1998	1999	2000	2001
GDP growth	8.8	7.8	7.1	6.5	6.0
Gross domestic investment/GDP	38.1	37.8	37.8	37.8	37.3
Gross domestic savings/GDP	41.5	40.9	39.0	37.4	36.4
Inflation rate (consumer price index)	2.8	-0.8	-1.4	1.8	2.0
Money supply (M2) growth	17.3	15.3	14.7	16.0	16.0
Fiscal balance/GDP	-1.8	-3.0	-4.0	-3.0	-3.0
Merchandise exports growth[a]	21.0	0.5	6.0	5.0	5.0
Merchandise imports growth[a]	2.5	-1.5	18.2	10.0	8.0
Current account balance/GDP	3.3	3.1	1.2	-0.4	-0.9
External debt/GDP	14.6	15.2	15.7	16.2	16.7

a. Based on customs data.

Sources: National Bureau of Statistics; staff estimates.

force, are either unemployed or underemployed. Even in urban areas, the official 1999 estimate of 3.1 percent urban unemployment covers only workers registered with the Ministry of Labor and Social Security. It does not include workers who are laid off as *xiagang* workers (those who keep a legal link to their enterprises but receive little pay or benefits) as part of the SOE reforms. Adjusting for these limitations, the urban unemployment rate was about 9.5 percent in 1999.

Largely because of the economic crisis in Asia, export growth was subdued in 1998 and the first half of 1999. Exports increased in the second half of 1999 as growth in the rest of Asia began to accelerate. However, for 1999 as a whole, export growth was a modest 6 percent, while imports grew a robust 18 percent.

Foreign direct investment (FDI) flows reached a high plateau during 1995-1998, and FDI inflow declined in 1999 for the first time since 1990. While FDI commitments declined 18.9 percent, actual FDI inflows went down by 9.7 percent, reflecting concern of foreign investors about weak financial institutions. The impact of this slowdown on the economy was somewhat mitigated in 1998 and 1999 by large fiscal stimulus packages.

Despite the worsening trade balance and the declining capital flows, the external payments situation continued to be comfortable. Both the external debt and the debt-service ratios are low by developing country standards. Foreign exchange reserves were about $155 billion in December 1999 (11 months of import equivalent), slightly more than the total external debt and about nine times the short-term external debt. At less than 10 percent, the external debt-service ratio was well within prudent limits.

In the aftermath of the Asian crisis, some feared an economic downturn in the PRC. Similarities to the crisis-affected countries include indicators of structural vulnerabilities, such as the corporate debt-equity ratio, ratio of nonperforming loans in banks' balance sheets, exposure of the banking sector to the property sector, and growth of bank credit to enterprises. However, macroeconomic indicators—such as inflation, current account balance, short-term capital inflows, share of short-term debt in total external debt, and size of short-term external debt relative to foreign exchange reserves—are much stronger than that of the crisis-affected countries prior to the crisis. Further-

more, capital and exchange rate controls help insulate the economy from external shocks.

Considering both internal and external factors, GDP growth is projected to decline from 7.1 percent in 1999 to about 6 percent by 2001. Most of the slowdown will occur in industry and construction, where growth is expected to decline from 9 percent in 1999 to about 6.5 percent by 2001. The slowing economy and the SOE reforms will cause urban unemployment to increase by about 1 percent to 10.5 percent by 2001. The economic slowdown and increasing unemployment should keep inflation moderate, about 2 percent during 2000-2001. The recovery in the newly industrialized economies should improve export prospects to these countries. Domestic price deflation, continued export tax rebates, and growing import demand in the Asian region will enhance export competitiveness. However, currency devaluation in Southeast Asian economies will make their exports more competitive than the PRC's exports. Import demand will be more moderate, but sufficient to serve the growing need for capital goods. Balancing these factors, the current account is likely to shift from a surplus to a small deficit in 2000 and 2001 (see figure 2.2). Capital inflows are expected to cover this deficit and allow a modest increase in foreign exchange reserves, which stood at $155 billion at the end of 1999. External debt outstanding as a percent of GDP should remain at roughly the same level as in 1999.

ISSUES IN ECONOMIC MANAGEMENT

Because of the rapid growth of the economy, significant expansion of employment opportunities, and impressive achievements in poverty reduction in the last two decades, the population has come to expect ever-improving economic conditions and living standards. However, if high rates of economic growth are not maintained, employment creation may not be sufficient for the increasing redundancy from SOEs and growth of the labor force. The crucial challenge for the government is to ensure that economic growth generates enough jobs to hold the unemployment rate in check.

Under the centrally planned economy, SOEs played a key role in growth and employment generation. Often, these enterprises provided employment

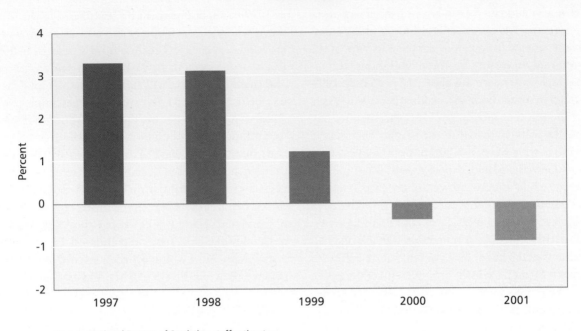

Figure 2.2 Current Account Balance as Percentage of GDP, People's Republic of China, 1997-2001

Source: National Bureau of Statistics; staff estimates.

at the cost of efficient use of resources because the government viewed creating employment as an end in itself, which led to considerable overstaffing and redundant labor. To maintain a reasonable pace of employment generation when enterprises are restructured and redundant labor is retrenched, small and medium-size enterprises and the private sector will have to play a larger role in the economy. Creating an economic environment to facilitate this transformation will require employment-friendly growth to reorient employment strategy in three directions: (a) from large enterprises to small and medium-size enterprises, (b) from industry to the tertiary sector, and (c) from SOEs to small and medium-size enterprises and owner-operated businesses in the private sector.

The Asian crisis exposed weaknesses in the financial and enterprises sectors, both of which need urgent attention from the government. During the March 1999 annual session of the National People's Congress, the constitution was amended to enhance the formal status of the private sector and provide it greater political protection. Building on this initiative, the challenge is to develop a level playing field for the private sector and the public sector. Three developments are needed: a legal framework that sets the rules in a clear and transparent manner; a regulatory framework that reduces restrictions on private businesses; and improved private sector access to financial resources, both from financial institutions and the capital market.

Financial sector reforms and restructuring should focus on recapitalizing and strengthening the banks, and developing a sound capital market that promotes efficient resource allocation and intermediation. This will require

• Balanced development of different segments of the market, products, and services with due consideration to minimizing systemic risk

• Higher governance standards by both regulators and financial institutions

- Stronger legal and regulatory framework to conform to international standards
- Institutional capacities that enforce the legal and regulatory framework.

The government has taken steps in these areas in the last two years. It now needs to make more progress and to effectively implement many of the recent financial sector reforms.

POLICY AND DEVELOPMENT ISSUES

Many of the problems in the financial sector are related to ailing SOEs that account for a large portion of banks' nonperforming loans. Two of the most difficult SOE reform issues are developing alternative methods to provide the social security services traditionally provided by SOEs, and to redeploy redundant workers.

The unemployment situation worsened as a result of the SOE reforms and the consequent breakdown of the social security system that was built around the cradle-to-death employment practices of SOEs. To cope with this, the government established an unemployment insurance scheme in the mid-1980s. This was strengthened in June 1998, with central government raising contributions to the unemployment fund from 1 to 3 percent of the enterprises' total payroll, and requiring the employees to contribute 1 percent. Until 1999, 15.8 million workers were covered by this scheme. The government intends to use the unemployment insurance system not only for expediting SOE reforms, but also for pension fund contributions, medical insurance, and enterprise industrial insurance. The reforms, when fully implemented, should provide a sound basis for enterprise restructuring.

Another important institutional issue is to establish a sound legal framework, essential for efficient functioning of a market economy. During the last two decades, the transition to a market economy has outpaced the development of the legal and regulatory framework. Many of the elements of the legal and regulatory system needed for a market economy to function efficiently are lacking or underdeveloped. The government has set a target to establish a framework for a market economy, and beginning in 1999, a five-year legislative work program will develop and revise important economic laws and the corresponding implementing regulations. The laws covered include company, bankruptcy, trust, antimonopoly and unfair competition, telecommunications, trademark and patents, income and inheritance tax, government procurement, and state assets laws.

Mongolia

Mongolia's transition to a market economy, which began in 1990, has proceeded satisfactorily, and the private sector is now the main producer of goods and services. The immediate challenges are reducing poverty and resolving the public sector imbalances that are the main barriers to growth and promotion of private sector activity.

RECENT TRENDS AND PROSPECTS

In 1999, the economy remained adversely affected by external factors, most notably continued low international prices for Mongolia's main exports of copper, cashmere, and gold and the ongoing economic instability in Russia. The extensive dependence of the country on exports of primary commodities means that even small changes in their international market prices can measurably affect GDP. Real GDP growth reached 3.5 percent in 1999, the same as the previous year, and slightly less than in 1997.

Inflation, which had declined to 6 percent by 1998, increased to 10 percent by end-December 1999. The disruption in Russia—as well as increased world prices for petroleum products and food items, particularly meat products—contributed to the high rate of inflation at the year-end.

The trade balance improved somewhat in 1999. Consequently, the trade deficit declined from 14.5 percent of GDP in 1998 to 9 percent in 1999. The tugrik fell 18.9 percent against the dollar during 1999, compared with 10.9 percent in 1998, which helped

the trade balance. The current account balance also improved in 1999, as the deficit narrowed to 4.7 percent of GDP compared with 11.9 percent in 1998. Gross international reserves increased to 14.3 weeks of import equivalent at the end of 1999, compared with 8.8 weeks of imports the previous year.

Fiscal performance improved slightly during 1999, as the full impact of the mid-1998 revenue measures became effective and additional measures were introduced in mid-1999. In May 1998, the government announced a package of tax and revenue expenditure measures, which included increasing the value-added tax rate from 10 to 13 percent effective September 1998, and increasing petroleum excise tax. These should yield budgetary savings of about 2 percent of GDP per year. Additional revenue-raising measures, adopted by Parliament in May 1999, included a uniform import duty of 5 percent and an excise tax on beer, which were expected to yield revenue equivalent to 1 percent of GDP in 1999.

Partly because of these measures, tax revenues increased to 19 percent of GDP in 1999, compared with 17.5 percent in 1998. However, privatization stalled because of Parliament's resistance, so receipts from the sale of government assets were substantially below expectations. Total revenues and grants therefore declined slightly to 26 percent of GDP in 1999, from 27 percent in 1998. By cutting current expenditures, the government reduced total expenditure to 36 percent of GDP in 1999, compared with 39 percent the previous year. The overall fiscal deficit improved from 11.5 percent of GDP in 1998 to 10 percent. Reducing dependence on external concessional finance can only be achieved through more focused public expenditure and improved revenue performance. The Asian Development Bank's Governance Reform Program Loan, which emphasizes reform in public expenditure management, will help this process.

Annual GDP growth is projected to climb 0.5 percent in 2000 and another 0.5 percent in 2001, emanating from mining, manufacturing, and services. This growth rate could further accelerate if the government's privatization program gathers steam and begins to contribute to economic efficiency.

Fiscal stability is expected to strengthen over the medium term because of the governance reforms supported by multilateral donors. The International Monetary Fund's Enhanced Structural Adjustment Facility program, which was begun in mid-1997 and redefined as a Poverty Reduction and Growth Facility in November 1999, also calls for fiscal reforms. The main fiscal target for the government is to bring down the overall budget deficit so it does not require exceptional financing from concessional foreign sources. This implies reducing the overall deficit from the unsustainable levels of about 11 percent of GDP to less than 4 percent. This would require improved tax administration, decreased current expenditures, and improved public sector efficiency. It would also require focusing on operations in the private sector and on current expenditures to avoid compromising development outlays.

The government is actively trying to increase revenues. Total revenues and grants are forecast to increase and stabilize at about 28 percent of the GDP in 2000-2001. Between 2000 and 2002, receipts from privatization are targeted to contribute 5-6 percent of GDP to government revenues. This represents an ambitious but achievable target. Current expenditures are projected to increase but will be offset by reduced capital expenditure. The ratio of total expenditure to GDP will remain at 36 percent in 2000.

Table 2.6 **Major Economic Indicators, Mongolia, 1997-2001**
(percent)

Item	1997	1998	1999	2000	2001
GDP growth	4.0	3.5	3.5	4.0	4.5
Gross domestic investment/GDP	25.3	27.3	—	—	—
Gross domestic savings/GDP	30.0	28.3	—	—	—
Inflation rate (consumer price index)	36.6	9.8	7.6	5.5	4.3
Money supply (M2) growth	32.5	-1.7	32.1	15.0	15.0
Fiscal balance/GDP	-8.6	-11.5	-10.0	-9.4	-7.7
Merchandise exports growth	16.6	-12.1	2.8	12.8	14.3
Merchandise imports growth	-1.5	9.5	-15.4	8.6	11.8
Current account balance/GDP	1.3	-11.9	-4.7	-9.5	-8.4
Debt service/exports	6.3	6.9	5.0	4.8	5.0

— Not available.

Sources: Bank of Mongolia; National Statistics Office; IMF; staff estimates.

A relatively tight monetary policy is expected to keep inflation in check for the medium term. Growth of broad money (M2) will average 15 percent annually in 2000-2001, which will provide sufficient liquidity while maintaining single-digit inflation. Government borrowing and credit to the public sector from the Bank of Mongolia must be reduced substantially to allow credit to the private sector, and to keep interest rates from increasing because of too much credit demand. Interest rates on deposits will fall in line with inflation rates, but will be kept positive in real terms to provide incentives for domestic savings. With the expected restructuring of the banking sector and improvement in banking practices, the efficiency and financial health of the major banks are expected to improve in the next three years. This could help reduce lending rates to a level more suitable for longer-term investment financing.

Prices of the main export commodities may not recover substantially in the near future, although gold prices have strengthened. The balance of payments remains a challenge, and a depreciating tugrik could contribute to reduced consumer imports. The external current account will maintain a deficit of about 10 percent of GDP in 2000, and decline to 7.5 percent over the medium term. Foreign capital inflows will have to sustain these high external liabilities.

ISSUES IN ECONOMIC MANAGEMENT

Mongolia's heavy dependence on exports of primary commodities that are subject to wide price fluctuations has made the task of macroeconomic stabilization difficult in the 1990s. Copper accounts for 26 percent of Mongolia's exports, and cashmere another 10 percent. Revenues from the copper monopoly Edernet constituted 11.3 percent of government revenues in 1996, the year before international prices fell. This slowed to 10 percent in 1997 and 1.8 percent in 1998, as a sharp decrease in international prices of copper reduced the sector's tax and dividend payments to the government budget. The slump in export earnings also exposed the inherent weaknesses in the banking system, worsening an already difficult situation in the financial sector. As large enterprises faced cash shortages, drawdowns on bank deposits and increased nonperforming loans have severely affected corporate liquidity and profitability. This situation was exacerbated by persistent managerial and governance problems in several big banks, political uncertainty, and inadequate supervision.

The immediate challenge facing the government is to put the financial sector and the fiscal balance back on track. Otherwise, any efforts at reviving sustainable economic activity and employment generation within the private sector could prove difficult. Recognizing this, the government has persevered in its efforts to reform the financial sector and promote fiscal discipline within the public sector.

POLICY AND DEVELOPMENT ISSUES

Since the start of its transition to a market economy, Mongolia has achieved commendable rates in economic growth along with reduction in inflation levels, privatization, and structural reforms in many areas. In the initial years of transition, with high export earnings and inflows of development aid replacing the former subsidies from Moscow, the government continued to help finance the social sector, housing, and heating (about 30 percent of some ministries' budget goes to heating buildings). Public expenditures on health and education still are substantial. Consequently, standards of health and education achievements are high.

However, Mongolia has been facing persistently elevated rates of poverty. The incidence of poverty grew from 15 percent of the population in 1991 to 36 percent in 1996, and since then has remained stable. Simultaneously, the severity of poverty has increased. The increasing depth of poverty indicates that the current development process does not generate sufficient opportunities for viable employment and income. The poor become poorer by depleting their last remaining assets and because of a breakdown of family and social support structures. This pattern reduces the chances for the poor to improve their situation without public assistance. This persistence of poverty, despite continued positive economic growth, is a serious cause for concern.

Various developments since the transition to a market economy may have contributed to this problem. These include (a) lack of sufficient resources to address poverty reduction directly; (b) failure to diversify the economy to generate more sustainable and inclusive growth; (c) externally financed infrastructure projects that tended to use capital-intensive technology with few employment effects; and (d) structural changes in the real economy that evolved more slowly than anticipated.

To combat poverty, the government is working with the Asian Development Bank to

• Generate more employment in the short to medium term, mainly in urban areas, particularly the *aimag* (provincial government) centers where the incidence of poverty is high

• Encourage the private sector to create new employment opportunities

• Improve the social safety net for the very poor who may be beyond the reach of self-help opportunities

• Help deliver needed social services to avoid facing new forms of poverty at a later stage.

The recent growth performance has been creditable, given the structural problems of the economy and the adverse external economic environment. Growth will remain limited until the reform process is further strengthened.

Central Asian Republics

Kazakhstan

Kyrgyz Republic

Tajikistan

Uzbekistan

Kazakhstan

In 1999, the economy began to recover from a deep recession caused by the fall in world commodity prices and the Russian crisis. Nevertheless, to restore sustained economic growth along with macroeconomic stabilization, the government needs to make greater efforts to accelerate enterprise restructuring and alleviate pervasive poverty.

RECENT TRENDS AND PROSPECTS

During 1999, the economy showed signs of recovery from the recession that had been caused by the weak world commodity markets and the Russian crisis that erupted in mid-August 1998. GDP grew by 1.7 percent in 1999, a moderate turnaround compared with a 1.9 percent contraction in 1998. After a continued decline in output during the first half of 1999, the recovery began in the second half. This resulted from a bumper harvest; a rebound in industrial production; an increase in capital investment; and rising world prices for major commodity exports such as oil, gas, and metals.

The agriculture sector grew substantially in 1999, as favorable weather resulted in a good grain harvest. The output of grain totaled 14.3 million tons, more than double the 1998 output. Kazakhstan planned to export at least 3 million tons of grain to neighboring countries such as Turkmenistan and Ukraine. The output of cotton also grew sharply by 54 percent, while production of livestock increased modestly.

Industrial output grew by 2.2 percent in 1999 mainly because of the rebound in production of natural gas and crude oil. In response to rising world prices, the output of gas and oil expanded by 51 percent and 12 percent, respectively. Processing industries, which account for more than half of the overall industrial output, also experienced growth, notably chemicals, metals, and textiles.

Capital investment expanded in 1999 to T277 billion as the government increased development expenditures to stimulate economic recovery. Because of the expansion, construction activities remained strong, while foreign investment continued to flow into the oil and gas subsectors.

Officially, the registered unemployment rate at the end of 1999 was 3.9 percent. However, actual unemployment was much higher because some still officially employed were on forced unpaid leave and many other unemployed persons were not officially registered. Due to mounting unemployment and the reduction in government social expenditures, poverty has risen rapidly.

In 1999, total government revenues accounted for 21.2 percent of GDP while total government expenditures were 24.7 percent, resulting in a budget deficit of 3.5 percent. This deficit was financed by receipts from privatization and by foreign sources. To improve the fiscal situation, the government took measures to strengthen tax collection and administration and rationalize public expenditures. However, the reduction in government expenditures resulted in arrears on payments of public sector wages, pensions, and benefits.

In 1999 monetary policy was designed and implemented to stimulate economic recovery while keeping inflation under control. The refinancing rate was reduced three times during the year, from 25 to 18 percent, and the requirement that exporters must sell 50 percent of their export earnings to the central bank was abolished in November. The rate of inflation was 17.8 percent, compared with 1.9 percent in 1998, largely because of currency devaluation. However,

while inflation increased in 1999, there has been substantial progress in reducing inflation since 1995, even though it has been difficult to sustain a pattern of growth in GDP (see figure 2.3). The national currency, the tenge, depreciated sharply against the dollar after the government floated the currency in April 1999, before stabilizing somewhat in the second half of the year.

The balance-of-payments situation improved, with a sharp reduction in the current account deficit from 5.5 percent of GDP in 1998 to 1.7 percent in 1999. This resulted mainly from the trade surplus of $776 million in 1999—compared with a deficit of $801 million the previous year—because imports declined more sharply than exports. Exports climbed in the second half of 1999 because of the rising world oil price and the effect of the currency devaluation. For the whole year, however, exports decreased by 4.8 percent while imports fell by 28.2 percent.

Foreign direct investment declined in 1999, as investors remained cautious after the Russian crisis.

Figure 2.3 GDP Growth and Inflation Rates, Kazakhstan, 1995-1999

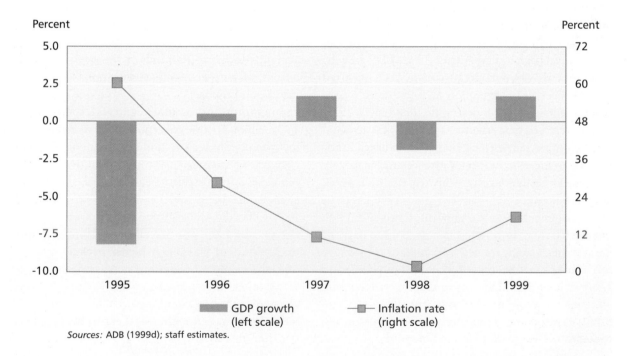

Sources: ADB (1999d); staff estimates.

However, as the first Commonwealth of Independent States country to return to the global capital markets after the Russian crisis, Kazakhstan issued new international bonds totaling $300 million during the period from September to November 1999, the third offering since independence. By the end of 1999, gross international reserves totaled $2 billion (four months of import equivalent). External debt increased in 1999 while the debt-service ratio declined slightly from 26 percent in 1998 to 25 percent in 1999.

The economic outlook for 2000 appears positive. GDP is projected to grow by about 3 percent, driven by a continuing upward trend in revenue from the major export commodities and by economic recovery in Russia. The budget deficit will likely shrink to about 3 percent of GDP, as the government is committed to achieve medium-term sustainability of public finance. The annual rate of inflation is projected to decline to about 13 percent, provided the central bank keeps tight control on credit growth and money supply. The balance-of-payments situation should continue to improve. Exports are expected to grow steadily and inflows of foreign capital should increase.

ISSUES IN ECONOMIC MANAGEMENT

The government has developed an economic program for 2000-2002 aimed at promoting economic growth and achieving macroeconomic stabilization. The program, supported by the International Monetary Fund under a three-year Extended Fund Facility approved in December 1999, focuses on adopting prudent fiscal policies that consolidate public finances, pursuing a tight monetary policy to reduce inflation while maintaining a free-floating exchange rate, and accelerating structural reforms. In the fiscal area, Parliament approved a more prudent government budget for 2000, which requires raising tax revenue, reforming the tax code, strengthening tax and customs administration, and improving public expenditure management.

The central bank will strengthen its supervisory activities to ensure that all banks comply with enhanced prudential requirements. Meanwhile, the central bank will continue to intervene on the currency market to prevent excessive short-term exchange rate fluctuations. The government will maintain efforts to liberalize the trade system, removing the tariffs imposed on its major trading partners in early 1999 and further reducing trade barriers. As part of the structural reform programs, the government will restructure the financial and corporate sectors, accelerate privatization of medium-size and large state-owned enterprises, improve governance, strengthen transparency, develop legal and regulatory frameworks necessary for a market-based economy, and fight corruption. These steps will help improve the quality of public services and promote private sector development.

POLICY AND DEVELOPMENT ISSUES

Despite the positive short-term economic prospects, Kazakhstan needs to take concerted action on many fronts to accelerate economic recovery and realize equitable long-term development. The most important tasks are accelerating enterprise restructuring and strengthening poverty alleviation efforts.

Enterprise restructuring revives the corporate sector and enables private sector development, which are critical for economic growth. An effective and growing corporate sector would increase employment opportunities and thus benefit the poor. While the government has taken initial steps on enterprise restructuring, especially in privatizing state farms, agribusiness, and small and medium-size industrial enterprises, the corporate sector remains weak. Many enterprises have limited operational experience in a market-based economy. Old management remains in control of some privatized enterprises, while the government continues to intervene in operations of privatized or corporatized enterprises. In addition, many state-owned enterprises are experiencing difficulties caused by poor management, inefficient organizational structures, shortcomings in the incentive system, and internationally unacceptable accounting standards. This has resulted in extensive corporate losses and interenterprise arrears. About half of all enterprises were estimated to be unprofitable in 1999. By October 1999, total domestic corporate debts payable amounted to T1.8 trillion, a 25 percent increase over the same period of 1998.

Enterprise restructuring is imperative to develop an efficient corporate sector, and three major actions need to be taken. First, bankruptcy and merger proceedings should be enforced. Strong efforts should be made to formulate the necessary legal and regulatory frameworks for implementing bankruptcy and merger procedures. All nonviable enterprises should be liquidated through bankruptcy to reallocate resources to more efficient producers. Money-losing enterprises that can be salvaged should be merged with efficient ones, to render them profitable by changing their incentives and governance structures. Second, privatization should be accelerated. Whenever possible, the government should sell the remaining state-owned enterprises, especially large ones, in all the nonstrategic sectors. In particular, foreign participation in large companies—both capital and management— should be allowed during privatization. Third, corporate governance should be improved through effective management structures and internationally accepted accounting and auditing standards and manager training programs.

Poverty has climbed because of persistent economic difficulties after attaining independence in 1991, and is now a serious problem. The government indicates that 43 percent of the population lived below the poverty line in 1999. Poverty is also more pervasive in rural areas than in urban ones.

Fighting poverty in the medium term is essential to maintain social stability and public support for the government's macroeconomic stabilization efforts and structural reforms. From a long-term perspective, it is the key objective of development. Strong action needs to be taken to reduce and eventually eliminate poverty. The government planned to develop a national program on poverty reduction by April 2000. Greater efforts are needed in three areas.

First, the government needs to promote pro-poor, sustainable economic growth. Such growth will generate more income and government revenues needed to finance the social safety net. The government should pursue policies that encourage labor-intensive sectors, promote private sector development, and help small enterprises expand. Measures could include orienting public investment toward poor areas, promoting self-employment, providing incentives for job training and retraining, and supporting the poor through microfinance programs.

Second, the government needs to formulate and implement a comprehensive national poverty reduction strategy. An appropriate poverty line should be defined; a reliable database set up; and a comprehensive study undertaken to examine causes, constraints, and opportunities for poverty reduction. The government should also stipulate policies and programs designed for raising the incomes of the poor. Adequate budgetary resources for basic social services and social assistance to the poor should be allocated and the most vulnerable groups targeted. Particular attention should be paid to women, who usually suffer more from poverty, and have limited access to essential social services and assistance.

To formulate and implement the poverty reduction strategy, nongovernment organizations should be encouraged to identify and assist the targeted groups, and the private sector should be permitted to provide basic social services and social assistance to the poor. These efforts should be complemented by continued reforms in the education and health sectors to deliver these services more efficiently, and to strengthen the social security system that provides incentives for self-employment and job training.

Last, efforts should be made to improve governance. Aside from increasing the efficiency of the public sector, good governance also facilitates formulating and implementing pro-poor policies and the poverty reduction strategy. Public administration and expenditure management at both national and local levels must be strengthened to promote pro-poor growth and social development. In particular, strong institutional capacity is needed at the local level, because local governments and communities are primarily responsible for delivering basic public services and providing social assistance to the poor. Meanwhile, the central government must develop the mechanism to closely monitor budgeted social assistance programs. It should also establish effective regulations to ensure the accountability of public funds used for poverty reduction. Strong measures must be undertaken to fight corruption and waste of public resources. These efforts will contribute to effective and efficient delivery of basic public services and successful implementation of targeted antipoverty programs.

Kyrgyz Republic

For the second consecutive year, economic performance in the Kyrgyz Republic was modest. The government must persevere in reforms to push the economy toward more rapid and sustainable growth and higher living standards.

RECENT TRENDS AND PROSPECTS

Real GDP grew by 3.6 percent during 1999, higher than the 2.1 percent in 1998 when the Russian crisis broke out. As in 1998, the agriculture sector produced the best performance, and grew by 8.7 percent. Production of all major crops increased, except for grain and wheat, which decreased slightly. The service sector edged up 1.8 percent. Industrial production declined by 2.4 percent, and gold production at the Kumtor mine also decreased.

The weak fiscal situation continued during 1999. Total government revenue as a percent of GDP increased slightly to 18.1 percent. However, taxes fell short of the planned level, due mostly to the slowdown in imports caused by the steep depreciation of the som. The tax revenue collection relies heavily on industry, and the poor industrial performance also contributed to the shortfall in tax revenue. Nontax revenue and grants remained weak. Total expenditure fell about 1 percent of GDP to 28.3 percent, higher than planned because of unanticipated spending related to a foreign terrorist incursion in the southern province of Osh. The total fiscal deficit remained high, at more than 10 percent of GDP. Because of the weakened fiscal situation, both budget and pension arrears rose steeply.

The money supply (M2) rose at a slightly higher rate in 1999 than in 1998, and inflation more than doubled from 16.8 percent to nearly 40 percent. Inflation had been rising since the fourth quarter of 1998, primarily because of the weakness of the som, caused by a continued lack of public confidence triggered by the Russian crisis of August 1998. During 1999, the som lost another 35 percent of its value to the dollar, after a 32 percent loss between end-August and end-December 1998. Public confidence was further shaken by a major financial fraud involving most of the largest commercial banks. A swift and satisfactory resolution would help restore public confidence in the financial sector and the currency.

Total external trade in 1999 declined by about 25 percent compared with the previous year. Imports declined by nearly 30 percent and exports around 19 percent. Consequently, both trade and current account balances improved, with the latter at 12 percent of GDP, nearly half the deficit of 1998. The savings rate was negative for the second year in a row, while the investment rate was around 12 percent. The resource gap of more than 12 percent of GDP mirrors the current account deficit and reflects a lack of domestic savings in a weak economy. International reserves rose to a level equivalent to more than four months of imports as inflows of concessional assistance exceeded the current account deficit. External debt (public and publicly guaranteed) stood at about $1.3 billion at the end of 1999, an increase of about $150 million from December 1998.

While the economy is capable of growing 4-5 percent per year, the unfavorable domestic and external conditions will likely slow growth to within 2-3 percent in 2000 and 2001. Tighter monetary policy will cut inflation in 2000 by half to about 20 percent, and reduce currency depreciation. If measures designed to enhance revenue and reduce expenditures are followed consistently, the overall fiscal deficit could decrease to about 7.4 percent of GDP. Both imports

and exports are expected to grow moderately, with the current account deficit projected to decrease to 10.5 percent of GDP for 2000. With weak foreign investments, both direct and portfolio, the country will continue to rely on foreign official assistance, mostly on concessional terms, and public and publicly guaranteed debts will accumulate to about $1.5 billion by the end of 2000.

ISSUES IN ECONOMIC MANAGEMENT

While the country made major efforts in reaching agreement with the International Monetary Fund to start the enhanced structural adjustment facility program in 2000, it faces serious challenges in implementing macrostabilization and structural reforms. Besides a continued tight monetary policy, the government must make extra efforts to cut spending while increasing revenue collection. On the revenue side, the focus should continue to be on broadening the tax base and increasing tax compliance for better tax collec-

Figure 2.4 Welfare Status by Geographic Location, Kyrgyz Republic, 1997

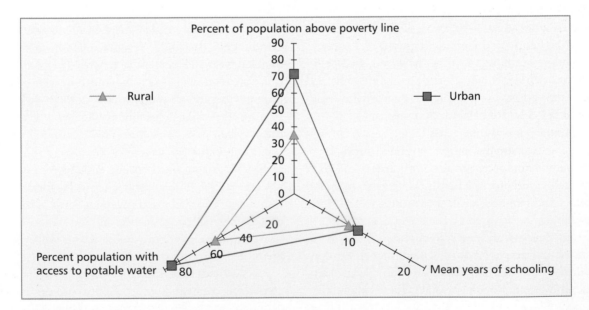

Source: World Bank.

tion. Frequent changes to the tax code and ambiguous interpretation of the tax law discourage business activity and encourage tax evasion. It is essential, therefore, to maintain a stable tax environment. The current system of interpreting the tax code and granting arbitrary exemptions creates more uncertainty, especially among small and medium-size enterprises. It also discourages risk taking by both domestic and foreign entrepreneurs and reduces the incentive to invest. Indirect tax collections have improved, but revenues from direct taxes remain low and below target. Because about one fourth of the working population pays little or no tax, the potential payoff from increased tax efforts is high, particularly regarding direct taxes.

On the expenditure side, efforts should be concentrated on cutting subsidies, especially indirect ones, and shifting expenditures to sectors that are likely to contribute to strong long-term growth. Direct subsidies to state-owned enterprises (SOEs) should be phased out as well as indirect subsidies for gas and electricity consumers. Existing utility tariffs do not reflect full costs and are not designed to absorb shocks such as exchange rate depreciation. Losses by utility companies also contribute to the government's weak fiscal position.

Fiscal management also needs to be improved. In particular, better coordination between the Treasury and the Ministry of Finance is required. Efforts to reorganize the fiscal management system are under way. These include strengthening linkages between the Treasury, the Ministry of Finance, and the National Bank of the Kyrgyz Republic, and they should be monitored for effectiveness.

On the structural side, progress in promoting private sector development has been slow, and privatization of large SOEs continues to lag. Major government efforts, including privatization and restructuring of the SOEs, will be needed to develop the private sector. Changes may be difficult to implement, considering that both the parliamentary and presidential elections occur in 2000.

POLICY AND DEVELOPMENT ISSUES

Historically, the Kyrgyz Republic was one of the poorest regions in the former Soviet Union, and in the five years following independence in 1991 cumulative output fell by about 50 percent. As a result, in 1997 an estimated one half of the population lived below the official poverty line, the equivalent of less than $0.75 per day.

The economic recovery that began in 1996 was robust. However, it has lagged since the Russian currency crisis of August 1998, and real wages are likely still lower than they were in 1992. Due to the depth and severity of poverty, a significant improvement in living standards will require a sustained and broad-based effort by the government and long-term sustained economic growth. The fundamental picture of poverty is unlikely to have changed substantively in the last two years.

Although on national average one in two persons is poor, 80 percent of the poor live in rural areas. The degree of poverty in rural areas has also deteriorated relative to urban areas. While extreme poverty decreased from 19.1 percent of the population in 1996 to 14.8 percent in 1997, most of this resulted from a targeted poverty reduction program in urban areas only. Poverty also appears to affect more women than men.

Realizing that widespread poverty is the main obstacle to improving the welfare of the people, the government has an ongoing national initiative, the Arakat program. The government is waging major efforts to revamp its poverty-fighting strategy and related policies in coordination with major donors, including the Asian Development Bank and the World Bank. It must consider carefully three issues.

First, because poverty is most severe in the rural areas, lifting rural and agriculture development above the current level of subsistence farming must be the core in formulating an effective poverty reduction strategy (see figure 2.4). Some farm households apparently engage in both agricultural and nonagricultural wage labor, which suggests a range of income-generating activities. Policy may need to pay more attention to promoting off-farm employment and secondary (nongrain) food crops, livestock, and horticulture.

Second, policies should aim to increase the quality of life as well as income. Social infrastructure spending needs to be increased, especially in rural areas. About 45 percent of the rural population has no access to potable water versus only 15 percent in urban areas. About 95 percent of those in rural areas still use latrines, compared with 47 percent in urban areas. Centralized systems for heating, water supply, and gas distribution are lacking in rural areas, and the quality and reliability of electric power supply and distribution is much lower than in urban areas.

Third, private sector development efforts should be strengthened. Substantial progress has been made in adopting markets and stimulating the private sector since independence, including price and trade regime liberalization and substantial privatization. By the end of 1997, the private sector accounted for about 65 percent of GDP, the highest private sector share among former Soviet republics. Nevertheless, the government should strengthen its role in creating an environment that encourages private sector growth, and in establishing and enforcing transparent rules and simple procedures. For example, despite decrees and resolutions, small and medium-size enterprises still require 27 clearances to register a business.

The role of the government is still evolving and facing many questions. What are the functions of the government in this era of transition? How can the government optimally participate in building and maintaining a legal and regulatory framework for economic development and poverty reduction? Answers to these questions will guide the government in reorganizing its structure and staffing and making it more suited to meet the long-term challenges of reducing poverty and promoting economic growth.

Tajikistan

The Russian financial crisis, the deterioration in terms of trade, and adverse weather have slowed Tajikistan's economic recovery. Redoubled efforts in privatization and structural reforms, as well as continued commitment to the peace process, are necessary to promote economic growth and prosperity.

RECENT TRENDS AND PROSPECTS

Since its civil war ended in 1997, Tajikistan has made significant progress in creating a stable macroeconomic environment and implementing market-oriented reforms. However, economic growth slowed in 1999 with real GDP growing 3.7 percent (see figure 2.5). This decrease reflects the adverse effects of the Russian financial crisis, the deterioration in Tajikistan's terms of trade, and adverse weather.

Agriculture is a key sector of the economy, contributing 20 percent to GDP and accounting for 60 percent of employment. Agricultural production increased by 3.8 percent in 1999, but production of cotton (the country's most important cash crop) and grain fell by 17.6 and 20 percent, respectively, because of bad weather and limited financing. Industrial production grew 5 percent in 1999, led by aluminum, electricity, and wood and timber. Production of aluminum, the major export, increased 20 percent.

The official unemployment rate was 3.1 percent in 1999, but actual unemployment was close to 30 percent. The official data do not account for unemployment and underemployment in inactive state-owned enterprises and rural areas. Moreover, many of the unemployed have not registered because of the low unemployment benefits.

Budget overruns and weak tax administration widened the budget deficit during the first three quarters of 1999. However, the authorities intensified revenue collection and rationalized expenditures in the fourth quarter. As a result, the deficit fell to 3.1 percent of GDP in 1999 after a 3.8 percent deficit the previous year. The deficit is being financed by concessional borrowing from multilateral lending institutions, privatization proceeds, and an issue of Treasury bills.

The Russian financial crisis damaged Tajikistan's economy. After enjoying more than a year of hard-won stability, the official exchange rate of the Tajik ruble against the dollar depreciated 47.5 percent from August 1998 to August 1999. Since then, however, the exchange rate has remained stable, and will likely depreciate more gradually as the Russian economy improves.

Since June 1997, the authorities have pursued a tight monetary policy to reduce inflation, which fell from 159.8 percent in 1997 to 2.7 percent in 1998. However, the currency devaluation between August 1998 and August 1999 renewed inflationary pressures. Tajikistan faced more shocks in 1999 when prices of key commodities increased. In August, fuel prices rose 50 percent and bread prices 20 percent as the effects of the low grain harvest began to manifest themselves. Administrative price increases in electricity and gasoline also contributed to inflation, which increased to 24 percent in 1999.

Tajikistan continued its liberal trade regime in 1999. In 1998, a uniform tariff of 5 percent was levied on most major imports. In February 1999, Tajikistan joined the customs union of the Commonwealth of Independent States, and raised its average tariff rate to 8 percent. However, the government remains committed to a liberal trade regime and announced that it will apply for World Trade Organization membership, emphasizing that it will not introduce trade policies that violate the organization's policies.

The trade balance faces substantial instability because of the lack of diversity in exports and the volatility in their prices. More than three fourths of export earnings come from cotton and aluminum. In 1998, the trade balance deteriorated sharply when world market prices for both of these products decreased, but recovered in 1999 when the price of aluminum rebounded. Export earnings from aluminum increased 36 percent, although earnings from cotton declined 18 percent as cotton's price continued to fall. The appreciation of the Tajik ruble against the Russian ruble after the Russian crisis caused decreased exports to former Soviet countries in 1999. However, diversifying trading partners since independence cushioned the effects of the crisis. For example, Tajikistan sells cotton and aluminum mostly to countries that were not in the former Soviet Union.

The debt-service burden continues to be heavy. In April 1999, however, Russia agreed to reduce Tajikistan's debt more than 50 percent. Agreements

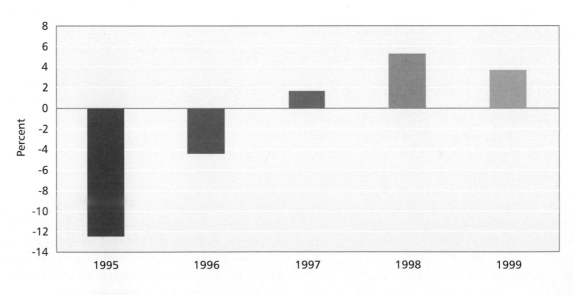

Figure 2.5 Real GDP Growth Rates, Tajikistan, 1995-1999

Source: ADB (2000).

were also signed with Kazakhstan, Kyrgyz Republic, Turkey, and Uzbekistan. The European Union, India, and Pakistan also indicated a willingness to reschedule Tajikistan's debt. Consequently, the foreign debt service fell from $181 million (34.4 percent of exports) in 1996 to $29 million (7.6 percent of exports) in 1999. However, because of the currency depreciation, the debt-to-GDP ratio increased from 91.4 percent in 1998 to 97.2 percent in 1999.

POLICY AND DEVELOPMENT ISSUES

Continued progress in the peace process is the most crucial factor in maintaining a stable macroeconomic environment that will foster economic development and promote investor confidence.

The peace process made significant progress in 1999. The United Tajik Opposition announced in August 1999 that it had completed disarming opposition fighters and integrating them into the Tajik armed forces. The United Tajik Opposition emphasized that it is no longer an armed opposition, but only a political opposition. The Supreme Court subsequently lifted the 1993 ban on opposition parties. Security conditions also improved in much of the country. However, the presidential election in November was criticized by domestic and international observers for irregularities and strained relations between the government and the opposition.

Only 35 percent of recorded GDP is generated in the private sector. However, privatization of small enterprises accelerated in 1999, and in December, the government announced that its privatization program for small enterprises was complete. Moreover, by September 1999, half of state and collective farms had been dismantled, 45 percent of arable land was in private hands, and 63,000 marketable land share certificates were distributed to individual farmers. Privatization of medium and large state-owned enterprises lagged, however, and only seven of 23 cotton gin mills had been sold by October 1999. Problems included unrealistic pricing by the government and delayed payments by buyers. The government has also been slow in restructuring the two largest firms—the electricity monopoly Barki Tajik and the aluminum smelter TADAZ.

The banking sector has performed poorly since 1991 because of weak management skills, directed credits, an inadequate legal and regulatory framework, and a background of political and macroeconomic instability. Consequently, a large proportion of bank loans is nonperforming. Confidence in the banking sector is diminished, which keeps deposits low and severely limits commercial credit expansion. Given the importance of this sector, the authorities are restructuring it.

The first round of restructuring was completed in November 1998, and progress was made in reducing bank staff, improving management practices, and expanding the capital base. In 1999, new prudential regulations reduced the number of banks from 26 to 16, as several weak banks were liquidated or merged with other banks. In April 1999, the National Bank of Tajikistan, the central bank, took over one of the big five banks to liquidate it because of noncompliance with prudential regulations, an action that should set an important example for other banks.

Agricultural finance has been especially constrained in recent years. Financing for the newly privatized "peasant farms" is virtually nonexistent, as the current rural finance system is not designed to accommodate them. Consequently, farmers have been forced either to borrow from moneylenders, enter into forward contracts with suppliers and traders at unfavorable terms, or limit production. The need to develop sustainable rural financial institutions is crucial.

Because of the sharp economic contraction since independence, the government's ability to provide basic social services has been severely strained, and the estimated poverty rate is 83 percent. Although the political and economic situation has stabilized somewhat since 1997, the Russian financial crisis and the deterioration in Tajikistan's terms of trade in 1998 and 1999 have exacerbated fragile living conditions. In the past two years, the country was also hit by major floods that destroyed or damaged infrastructure, homes, and crops. However, the existing social safety net remains inadequate and poorly targeted. With a high incidence of poverty and the government's limited resources, the need to reform and strengthen the social safety net is urgent.

Uzbekistan

GDP growth of 4.4 percent in 1999 was maintained, although international prices for Uzbekistan's primary exports continued to be weak. Major structural reforms to sustain macroeconomic stability and growth are necessary, as well as policy measures to ameliorate the short-term social effects of these reforms.

RECENT TRENDS AND PROSPECTS

Despite the difficult macroeconomic environment and the repercussions from the Russian and Asian economic crises, real GDP grew by 4.4 percent in 1999, the same as the previous year (see figure 2.6). Growth was spurred mainly by agriculture and industry. The agriculture sector did not experience inclement weather as it did during 1996-1998, and hence witnessed an across-the-board increase in output that included cotton, the most important export crop. Agricultural output increased by 5.9 percent in 1999 compared with a 4 percent increase in 1998. However, the soft prices in international commodity markets for cotton and for gold, the other important export commodity, reduced total export earnings.

Industrial production increased by 6.1 percent, and construction services by 3.9 percent, boosting overall economic growth. Growth of the service sector also contributed significantly to real GDP growth, despite the government's policy of restricting imports of consumer goods that in turn constrained private trading. Nevertheless, by opening the service sector

to private initiatives, this sector and nongovernment employment grew rapidly. The fiscal situation continued to improve in 1999 as the government maintained its efforts to reduce the budget deficit. The consolidated budget deficit contracted to 2.2 percent of GDP from 3.4 percent in 1998, reflecting progress in fiscal management.

Despite the tight monetary and fiscal policies maintained by the government, average monthly inflation was 1.9 percent, about 26 percent annually, as in the previous year. The principal cause of inflation was the rapid depreciation of the sum by about 27.3 percent during the year.

The balance of payments remained under pressure in 1999. The Russian crisis, a bad cotton harvest in 1998, and falling world commodity prices contributed to the substantial deterioration in external balances. The government responded by further restricting imports, tightening access to foreign exchange, and increasing foreign borrowing to finance public investments. Although the government continued to restrict the import of consumer goods, the current account deficit widened to 1.3 percent of GDP in 1999 compared with 0.6 percent in 1998. This was mainly attributable to the continued growth in imports, which increased by 10 percent in 1999 after a decline of 25 percent in the previous year.

Despite the deterioration in the current account deficit, gross official reserves stood at $1.2 billion at the end of 1999 (5.8 months of import equivalent), because of the surplus of $342 million in the capital account. This surplus resulted from the presale of gold to a foreign commercial bank for $150 million, and drawdowns on previously contracted debt during the year. Outstanding debt rose to $3.8 billion (25 percent of GDP) at the end of 1999, compared with $3.2 billion (24 percent of GDP) at the end of 1998. The debt-service ratio also rose to 11 percent in 1999, from 9 percent the previous year.

As announced by the government and decreed several times in 1998 and 1999, full liberalization of the foreign trade and exchange regimes is expected to be introduced in 2000, as well as comprehensive structural reforms in agriculture and banking. The govern-

ment expects these changes to improve the growth outlook of the economy. In essence, renewed reform and stabilization efforts—in conjunction with the resulting higher export growth, substantial program lending by international financial institutions, and support from bilateral donors—would ease the foreign exchange constraint. This would allow faster import liberalization as well as a relatively stable exchange rate. Liberalization of the foreign trade and exchange rate regimes will bring upward pressure on inflation and force more rapid restructuring of the corporate and banking sectors.

Significant progress has been made in achieving macroeconomic stabilization, although recent external shocks have placed additional pressure on the economy. While some structural reform measures have been undertaken, much remains to be done. Major reforms in the recent past include increasing the state procurement prices for cotton and wheat by about 50 percent, writing off previous farm debts to the state budget, and rescheduling debts to input suppliers

Figure 2.6 GDP Growth and Gross Domestic Investment Ratio to GDP, Uzbekistan, 1995-1999

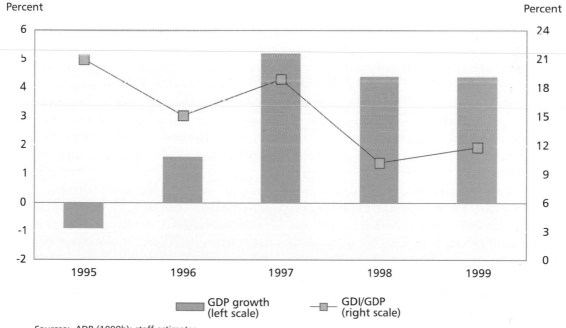

Sources: ADB (1999h); staff estimates.

until 2002. Farmers received a substantial reduction in tax burden, partly because various agricultural taxes were consolidated into a single unified land tax. Other tax relief measures included granting a three-year tax break to newly established private farms and establishing Rural Business Advisory Centers in all the rayons (counties) to provide business advisory and extension services to private farmers.

Prospects for 2000 are mixed. If the planned reforms occur in the foreign exchange and trade regimes, the temporary adverse macroeconomic consequences will likely slow GDP growth in the short run. However, once the relative price and structural adjustments are completed, real GDP is likely to grow steadily until the economy attains its full growth potential. GDP growth is therefore projected to contract to about 3 percent in 2000. The unification of the exchange rate will also lead to a one-time jump in the inflation rate. The fiscal situation is likely to be strained as the slowing of economic growth reduces tax revenues. The government's attempts to develop an effective social safety net—to protect the most vulnerable in society and provide financial assistance to critical industries negatively affected by the reform program—will also strain the fiscal situation. Nevertheless, the government's target budget deficit in the 2000 budget approved by Parliament is 3 percent of GDP. The International Monetary Fund deems this level of budget deficit temporary and sustainable.

Despite the strain on the internal balance, observers expect the external balance to improve somewhat in 2000, and to continue to improve gradually over the medium term. The deficit in the current account is expected to narrow to 1 percent of GDP in 2000 mainly because of the recovery in export growth. Once the reform program is implemented, a steady recovery in exports and an increase in imports should result. These will support much needed technical renovations in the state-owned enterprise sector. Increases in energy and manufactured exports in the medium term, resulting from growing demand in neighboring countries, are projected to boost export growth. Because grain production has improved to levels of near self-sufficiency, grain imports will likely be modest. A surplus on the capital account would suffice to finance the current account deficit. Inflows of foreign direct investment (FDI) and long-term debt

from multilateral and bilateral sources also are expected to increase, given the improved investment climate expected from the reform program.

With the completion of the foreign exchange and trade reforms in 2000 and the relative price adjustments, GDP growth is forecast to increase to 4 percent in 2001, with inflation contained at 20 percent per annum. The deficit in the budget is forecast to widen slightly to 3 percent of GDP in 2001; expenditures will be increased to support the social safety net necessitated by the economic reform program. The current account deficit is also anticipated to increase to 2 percent of GDP in 2001, mainly because of increased imports.

ISSUES IN ECONOMIC MANAGEMENT

The presidential decree of 1 July 1998 stated that Uzbekistan would introduce current account convertibility by the end of 2000. Significant efforts are under way to make this objective a reality. Introduction of current account convertibility would help increase exports and attract greater FDI. It would also stem the capital outflows that have troubled the economy since late 1996. The Partnership and Cooperation Agreement with the European Union of July 1999 was a significant step toward integrating Uzbekistan with the world economy. In an attempt to boost exports, the government cut the profit tax from 35 percent to 30 percent in June 1999. Simultaneously, it allowed payment of value-added tax to be delayed for up to 90 days on imported goods used in the production of exports. However, the multiple exchange rate system continued to restrain export growth and FDI.

The government's privatization program, especially for large-scale enterprises, appears to have encountered difficulties because of limited foreign investor interest. The main problem remains the government's reluctance to offer majority stakes to strategic investors. Other problems are unrealistic price expectations, a difficult investment environment, and falling commodity prices in world markets. The main concern is that, although the management of the corporatized and privatized enterprises is supposed to be autonomous, the ownership patterns and the current regulatory regime are not sufficiently developed to prevent state interference.

Financial sector reforms are being expedited under a $25 million World Bank loan approved in June 1999. The project aims to strengthen corporate governance in commercial banks, improve the supervisory functions of the central bank, and increase the openness of the sector to foreign entry. The key short-term issues for the government include continuing reforms in the financial and corporate sectors, adopting policies to stimulate noninflationary economy growth, and providing a social safety net program to offset the anticipated social costs of liberalizing the foreign exchange and trade regimes.

POLICY AND DEVELOPMENT ISSUES

Long-term growth prospects are promising. Rich natural endowments, the large stock of human capital, and centuries of tradition in commerce and trade bode well for a successful transition to a fast-growing market economy. The realization of this potential is the central development challenge. Creating enough opportunities to reduce unemployment and underemployment and absorb the growth in the labor force is critical. Unless a more robust and sustainable GDP growth rate is attained, it will not be possible to address this issue effectively, and the number of families living below the poverty line will increase. Authorities estimated that in 1998, 23 percent of the population were living below the official poverty line of Sum910 per capita per month which at market exchange rates amounts to less than $5 per month.

The main objectives of the government should be the revival of economic growth and the diversification of the economy. The realization of both objectives hinges on accelerating reforms. An appreciation of this critical aspect is essential. First, while prospects for recovery in international prices of gold and cotton are more optimistic than they have been for several years, the cushion that was provided by attractive commodity export prices in the first few years after independence is no longer available. Higher foreign exchange earnings will depend on larger quantities of commodity exports and new export items. The fallout of the Russian crisis has made it clear that diversification of the export basket has become essential.

Second, cotton and grain yields remain abysmally low by international standards. Increases in production must come from augmented yields, which will require overhauling the incentive structure and, therefore, far-reaching agriculture sector policy reform.

Third, the gradual reform approach has not resulted in large-scale economic disruption, but neither has it yielded high growth or many new employment opportunities. Further, the diversification of the economy remains partial; new fast-growing export sectors have yet to emerge, and the potential of the traditional productive sectors has yet to be fully tapped. To revive growth and diversify the economy, it is imperative to speed up the reform process.

There appear to be some downside risks to the economy over the medium term. First, the Russian economy's recovery has been constrained by continuing political uncertainty, which has further eroded the confidence of private and official creditors. Recent allegations of widespread corruption and misappropriation of public funds could further intensify capital flight and accelerate the decline in FDI. This would in turn reduce the demand for Uzbekistan's exports, because about 45 percent of these exports still go to the former Soviet Union, mainly to Russia. Second, there is always the danger that a continuation of unfavorable world commodity prices for the two major export items, gold and cotton, would lead to a further postponement of the planned foreign exchange and trade reforms.

Southeast Asia

Cambodia

Indonesia

Lao People's
Democratic
Republic

Malaysia

Myanmar

Philippines

Thailand

Viet Nam

Cambodia

Benefiting from favorable weather conditions and an improved political climate, Cambodia experienced higher economic growth in 1999 than in the previous year. Lower inflation, a lower fiscal deficit, and a slightly increased capital account deficit accompanied the improved growth. If the government can maintain the political stability and reform progress achieved in 1999, economic growth of 6-7 percent per year can be expected over the medium term.

RECENT TRENDS AND PROSPECTS

In 1999, real GDP grew by 5 percent. This resulted from a good wet season crop harvest, continued garment export growth, and recovery in tourism. After two years of contraction, agriculture grew in 1999 because of expansion of value added in crops, livestock, and fisheries. Strong growth in manufacturing, particularly textiles, and a rebound in construction activity contributed to double-digit growth in industrial production. A 33 percent increase in tourist arrivals led to moderate growth in services. Both public investment and foreign direct investment declined in 1999 because of the lagged effects of the 1997 political and regional economic crises.

Domestic revenues jumped from 9.2 percent of GDP in 1998 to 11.6 percent in 1999 because a value-added tax was introduced. Current expenditures increased modestly from 9.1 percent of GDP in 1998 to 9.6 percent in 1999. As a result, government savings—current revenues less current expenses—improved from -0.4 percent of GDP in 1998 to 1.7 percent, while capital spending fell from 6.1 percent of GDP in 1998 to 5.5 percent in 1999. This narrowed the overall fiscal deficit from 6.1 percent of GDP in 1998 to 3.7 percent. The National Bank of Cambodia's net claims on the government decreased in 1999, in contrast to the previous year when credit was extended to finance part of the budget deficit.

Average annual inflation fell to 4 percent in 1999 from 14.8 percent in 1998. Broad money (M2) increased by 17.3 percent in 1999. Foreign currency deposits, the main component of quasi-money, rose 31.8 percent in 1999, up from a 0.3 percent hike the previous year. Enhanced political stability also contributed to the growth of deposits. Independent audits of nine commercial banks in 1999, however, indicated that a weak banking sector, characterized by limited credit activity and high cash liquidity, continued to hamper economic development.

Improved 1999 exports of garments, as well as timber, fish products, and rubber, led to strong domestic export growth of about 22 percent. However, because of rapid import growth, the trade deficit widened from 6.8 percent in 1998 to 7.3 percent in 1999, while the current account deficit grew from 8 percent of GDP in 1998 to 8.4 percent. The riel, which had depreciated against the dollar in 1997 and 1998, appreciated by 0.1 percent in 1999.

A return to real GDP growth rates of 6-7 percent is possible in the medium term if political stability and progress in structural reforms are maintained. A critical determinant of long-run agricultural growth will be greater public investment, particularly in rural infrastructure and water resource management. If labor conditions improve, annual increases in US quotas on textile imports from Cambodia will allow moderate growth in garment assembly. However, diversification to other markets and perhaps to other types of basic manufacturing will be necessary to sustain rapid manufacturing growth. Finally, long-term tourism potential, if successfully developed, would stimulate activities in agriculture, industry, and services.

ISSUES IN ECONOMIC MANAGEMENT

On 22 October 1999, the International Monetary Fund approved a three-year, $81.6 million Enhanced Structural Adjustment Facility. The agreement particularly emphasized fiscal reform, because Cambodia's 1998 revenues as a percent of GDP were the lowest of all reporting developing member countries, and spending on social sectors as a percent of GDP was less than both the Lao People's Democratic Republic and Viet Nam. With a goal of raising government revenues to 13 percent of GDP by 2002, the government implemented several revenue-generating measures in 1999, including a value-added tax. Continuing efforts are under way to reduce ad hoc tax exemptions, expand onsite tax audits of large taxpayers, and increase efforts to collect tax arrears. The government is working to increase the capacity and efficiency of the tax and customs departments.

Public expenditure on defense regularly exceeds that on the social sectors. For example, in the 1999 budget, 22 percent was allocated to defense and less than 20 percent for the social sectors. The latter included 8 percent budgeted for education and 5 percent for health. Actual outlays for education—and even more so for health—generally fall short of budgeted levels. This trend to spend less than the

Table 2.7 Major Economic Indicators, Cambodia, 1997-2001
(percent)

Item	1997	1998	1999	2000	2001
GDP growth	2.6	1.3	5.0	6.0	7.0
Gross domestic investment/GDP	14.7	13.4	13.1	13.0	14.0
Gross savings/GDP	5.9	5.4	4.7	4.0	4.0
Inflation rate (consumer price index)	8.0	14.8	4.0	6.0	5.0
Money supply (M2) growth	16.6	15.7	17.3	12.0	12.0
Fiscal balance/GDP[a]	-4.2	-6.1	-3.7	-4.5	-4.0
Merchandise exports growth[b]	81.0	8.3	21.8	11.0	10.0
Merchandise imports growth[c]	5.8	-0.1	20.4	12.0	10.0
Current account balance/GDP[d]	-8.8	-8.0	-8.4	-9.0	-10.0
Debt service/exports	2.5	2.9	2.5	3.0	3.0

a. Cash basis.
b. Domestic exports.
c. Retained imports.
d. Excludes official transfers.

Sources: Ministry of Economy and Finance; National Institute of Statistics; National Bank of Cambodia; staff estimates.

Figure 2.7 Education, Health, and Defense Spending, as Percentage of Total Expenditures Cambodia, 1996-1999

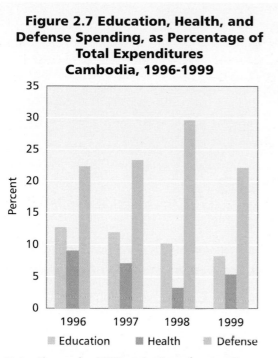

Note: Figures for 1999 are budgeted expenditures.
Source: Ministry of Economy and Finance.

allocated budget seems to have reversed only in the last quarter of 1999.

Defense spending has remained a priority in the past several years. Its share in total expenditure increased while spending on the social sectors declined (figure 2.7). However, defense spending as a percent of GDP fell from 5.7 percent in 1995 to about 4 percent in 1999. The government is further reducing defense spending by demobilizing about 30,000 soldiers during 2000-2003. In addition, various efforts are under way to improve spending on the social sectors, such as decentralizing budget responsibility. These steps should improve the capability to develop human resources.

POLICY AND DEVELOPMENT ISSUES

Insufficient public spending on education and health exacerbates the underdevelopment of human resources. This inhibits economic development and contributes to poverty. The government share of total educational expenditures is about 25 percent. As a result, about 40 percent of the population have never attended school, 32 percent are illiterate, and less than 1 percent has had any training beyond high school. The skills needed to improve administrative, legal, educational, and medical institutions are therefore in short supply, often forcing Cambodia to rely on international experts. The labor force—which has high dependency ratios because of high fertility and an unusually large population with disabilities—also is characterized by low productivity.

Improving the level of education will not be simple, however. Access to basic education varies by geographical region, socioeconomic status, and gender. Distance and an inadequate transportation system are major constraints to school attendance for the rural poor. The high opportunity costs of sending children to school is another major obstacle, because about 80 percent of the population reside in farm households that depend largely on their own child labor. This is particularly true of female labor, resulting in lower enrollments for females than males. The proportion of girls enrolled is about 45 percent in primary school, 40 percent in lower secondary school, and 25 percent in upper secondary school. Basic education suffers from extremely low quality, in part because most instructional materials and many qualified teachers were lost during the Khmer Rouge years. All too often, unqualified, low-paid, and demoralized teachers are confronted with overcrowded and ill-equipped classrooms.

In addition to low levels of education, a poorly functioning health care system results in one of the lowest rates of health service utilization in the world. This, combined with poor water and sanitation coverage, leaves the population debilitated, contributing to low productivity. Stunting is common among children, permanently robbing them of their physical potential. Adults frequently lose days of work because of illnesses for which treatment by a health provider is usually expensive and often unreliable. Self-medication is common. Leading causes of death include malaria, acute respiratory infections, tuberculosis, road accidents, and accidental mine detonations. An HIV/AIDS epidemic looms on the horizon as a threat to future development. Ultimately, to ensure sustainable long-run growth, Cambodia must devote more financial resources to educating its people, and safeguarding their health.

Indonesia

Economic recovery, after nearly two years of recession, is essentially driven by the fiscal stimulus and remains fragile. Progress in structural reforms and an expected increase in export and investment demand will help consolidate this recovery in 2000. The new government is strongly committed to empowering local governments to promote broad-based growth.

RECENT TRENDS AND PROSPECTS

The crisis in Indonesia has bottomed out, and signs of recovery have appeared after nearly two years of financial and economic turmoil. GDP recorded a 0.2 percent increase in 1999, compared with a 13.2 percent contraction the previous year, and the crisis-induced surge in poverty appears to have peaked in early 1999. The recovery, initially underpinned by a rebound in agriculture, gradually spread to other sectors. However, strong growth of agricultural output in the first half of the year faded in the third quarter, and reached only 0.7 percent for the year.

The manufacturing sector expanded by 2.2 percent because of a rebound in the export-oriented oil and gas sector, while the construction sector grew by a modest 1.1 percent. The service sector, however, declined a further 1.5 percent in 1999 because of a contraction in banking and financial services. On the aggregate demand side, the recovery was initially aided by a rise in public spending, reflecting the government's fiscal stimulus to jump-start the economy. Growth of private consumption then led the recovery. Private investment activity, however, continued to contract due to inadequate progress in corporate debt restructuring.

The fragile recovery has not prevented further employment problems. Unemployment increased from 5.5 percent in 1998 to 6.3 percent by August 1999, and underemployment increased from 60 percent in 1998 to 63 percent in 1999. More significantly, although real wages went up in 1999, they remained 20-25 percent below the precrisis levels.

After averaging 58.5 percent in 1998, consumer price inflation came down to 20.5 percent in 1999. On a year-on-year basis, it plummeted to 2 percent at the end of December 1999, compared with 78 percent a year ago. While falling food prices, especially of rice, were the primary cause of declining inflation, the restoration of food distribution channels, the appreciation of the rupiah, and a tight monetary stance also helped. Despite volatility associated with political uncertainties, share prices in Indonesia rebounded because of considerably lower domestic inflation, greater exchange rate stability, and sharply reduced interest rates. Overall equity prices, as measured by the Jakarta Stock Market index, rose by 60 percent

Table 2.8 Major Economic Indicators, Indonesia, 1997-2001
(percent)

Item	1997	1998	1999	2000	2001
GDP growth	4.7	-13.2	0.2	4.0	5.0
Gross domestic investment/GDP	31.8	19.1	11.6	13.0	17.5
Gross national savings/GDP	29.4	23.2	13.2	15.2	18.0
Inflation rate (consumer price index)	6.6	58.5	20.5	6.0	5.0
Money supply (M2) growth	23.2	62.3	11.9	13.0	17.0
Fiscal balance/GDP[a]	0.0	-3.7	-2.3	-5.0	-3.1
Merchandise exports growth	12.2	-10.5	-7.4	8.1	9.0
Merchandise imports growth	4.5	-30.9	-10.8	7.5	14.0
Current account balance/GDP	-2.3	4.1	3.5	2.2	0.5
Debt service/exports[a]	37.8	39.1	34.8	—	—

— Not available.

a. Fiscal year ending 31 March.

Sources: Central Bureau of Statistics; Bank Indonesia (various years); Ministry of Finance; World Bank; staff estimates.

in 1999. Market capitalization climbed to $58 billion at the end of 1999 from $22 billion earlier in the year, still considerably below the precrisis level of $90 billion. The strengthened equity market, however, improved the outlook for the government privatization program and the Indonesian Bank Restructuring Agency's asset recovery effort.

Although market anxiety over structural reforms and political uncertainties continued to influence fluctuations in the rupiah, it strengthened substantially in 1999 and traded around Rp6,800-Rp9,500 per dollar, compared with Rp7,500-Rp17,000 the previous year. The stronger rupiah was in large part attributable to a steady buildup of reserves, high interest rates early in the year, and a tight overall monetary stance. The rupiah ended the year at Rp7,700 per dollar. Despite the appreciation of the nominal exchange rate, the real exchange rate remained around 30 percent below its precrisis level, giving Indonesian exporters a significant comparative advantage over its main regional competitors, Malaysia, Philippines, and Thailand.

The performance of the external sector, however, remained weak. Exports declined by 7.4 percent in 1999, and imports contracted by a further 10.8 per-

cent, led by a decline in imports of capital goods. Despite the large real depreciation of the rupiah and stronger oil export prices, exports remained depressed because of problems associated with high corporate indebtedness and access to credit. The current account surplus, estimated at $4.9 billion in 1999 ($4.1 billion in 1998) was driven mainly by import compression, as in the previous year.

On the capital account, reduced inflows of net official finance were more than offset by lower net outflows of private capital due to loan rescheduling. As a result of the improved current account surplus and a smaller deficit in the capital account, gross foreign reserves increased to $27 billion (six months of import equivalent). At $16 billion, net foreign assets were also well above Bank Indonesia's monetary program floor of $14 billion. Although the debt-to-GDP ratio reached 95 percent (from 93 percent in mid-1998 and 56 percent in mid-1997), the debt-service ratio, after loan rescheduling, is estimated to have decreased to 35 percent in fiscal year 1999/00 (ending 31 March) from 39 percent in the previous fiscal year.

GDP growth should climb gradually in 2000. A moderate rise in investment, increased exports from the nonprimary sectors, and strong agricultural production will lead to a GDP growth rate of around 4 percent in 2000 and 5 percent in 2001. The pace of recovery will, however, be constrained by continued liquidity problems and a massive overhang of corporate debt.

The budget will remain in deficit over the medium term, but will likely decline steadily from a projected 5 percent of GDP in 2000 to 3.1 percent the following year, as private sector activity picks up and outlays on subsidies decline. Imports will increase in 2000 as domestic demand rises, lowering the current account surplus to 2.2 percent, and then to 0.5 percent in 2001. This should, however, be offset by official financial flows and private capital inflows, and the import coverage of reserves will remain at about six months. The debt-to-GDP ratio is expected to gradually fall in 2000 because of declining interest rates, real exchange rate appreciation, and increased IBRA asset recovery. Inflation is likely to exceed the government forecast of 5 percent in 2000 by about 1 percent because of increases in wages and salaries, adjustments in fuel and electricity prices, and tariffs on rice and sugar. Inflation will decline to around 5 percent in 2001 as the domestic supply response improves further and import tariffs decrease.

With greater macroeconomic stability and adequate reserve cover, the exchange rate should remain stable at around Rp7,000-Rp7,500 per dollar in 2000, but will still be vulnerable to swings in market sentiment. However, with a strong increase in reserve growth and exports in 2001, it may drop below Rp7,000 per dollar. The Bank Indonesia Certificates interest rate is likely to fall—from an average of 23 percent in 1999 to 11 percent in 2000 and 10 percent in 2001. These forecasts assume that domestic political conditions in Indonesia will not deteriorate further and that the Asian economies will continue to rebound strongly.

ISSUES IN ECONOMIC MANAGEMENT

The government continued to maintain an expansionary fiscal stance to counteract the economic contraction; the budget for the fiscal year ending 31 March 2000 projected a deficit of 6.8 percent of GDP. However, the realized deficit is provisionally estimated at only 4 percent of GDP, because delays in project implementation will likely cause development expenditures to fall short of their target by nearly 30 percent. The budget deficit was unable to play its envisaged role in stimulating the economy.

The fiscal year 2000 budget covering the nine-month period April-December 2000 projects a deficit of 5 percent of GDP. Although this is smaller than the projected deficit of 6.8 percent the previous year, it reflects negative public savings (current expenditure exceeding domestic revenue) for the second time since the crisis began. Therefore, some development resources will be diverted to support current expenditures.

A major consequence of the crisis has been a sharp rise in public debt. At the end of March 2000, public debt is expected to increase to 95 percent of GDP from only 23 percent at the end of March 1998, a quadrupling in only two years. About 75 percent of the rise in public debt resulted from domestic bond issues to recapitalize banks and repay Bank Indonesia's liquidity support to the banking system after the crisis. Domestic public debt now totals $89 billion compared with $63 billion in external public debt. Outlays on domestic debt payments are projected to increase sharply to Rp42 trillion, more than twice the amount required to service public external debt, representing the interest on government recapitalization bonds.

Together, domestic and external debt-service expenditures make up 41 percent of total current expenditures and 61 percent of total tax revenues, and will drain public resources for the foreseeable future. As the recovery becomes sustainable, the emphasis of public policy must shift from fiscal stimulus to fiscal consolidation, and then to fiscal sustainability. Given the high level of debt and a weak revenue base, achieving this will require more effective and transparent use of resources and reduced borrowing.

Given this public debt scenario, the government faces several urgent imperatives. First, vigorous efforts are needed to speed up domestic resource mobilization through revenue-raising measures, including accelerating asset sales through privatization. Second, although outlay on the petroleum subsidy is projected to decline as the government increases electricity and fuel prices, other timely price adjustments are needed to reduce subsidies while the targeting of social subsidies to the poor needs to be improved. Third, full transparency and accountability in the use of public resources are needed to ensure the greatest possible development effect and to eliminate leakage of funds. Fourth, careful programming of external assistance is required to prevent negative resource transfer.

In 1999, the deceleration of inflation and appreciation of the exchange rate permitted interest rates to drop. The key one-month Bank Indonesia Certificates interest rate declined from around 35 percent in early 1999 to 12.5 percent by the end of 1999, below the precrisis level. Bank lending rates also declined although not nearly as much, but bank lending remained extremely subdued. Due to the massive overhang of corporate sector debt and high levels of nonperforming loans, banks have adopted an extremely cautious approach to new lending, and are strengthening their capital adequacy ratios. Although further declines in inflation allow room for more reduction in interest rates, it is unlikely to be substantial, given risk perceptions and banking sector weakness.

The targets for monetary aggregates, especially net domestic assets and base money, need to be relaxed gradually to support economic recovery. However, this needs to be done cautiously as increases in government salaries and fuel and electricity prices in 2000 could exert inflationary pressures. The government's inflation target of 5 percent could prove difficult to achieve because of these factors.

Of all the crisis countries, Indonesia's financial and corporate problems have been the most acute. Nonperforming loans are estimated at 60-85 percent of all loans and bank recapitalization costs are estimated at a staggering Rp643 trillion (about $89 billion), or 60 percent of GDP. Restructuring efforts got off to a slow start because of political constraints, and it will likely take several years to restore the financial sector to health. The first major step toward recapitalization of private banks was in 1999, when independent audits—of all state banks, nationalized banks, regional banks, and private banks—ranked banks into three categories according to their capital adequacy ratio.

The banks in category C (those with a capital adequacy ratio of less than negative 25 percent) face liquidation, while some banks in category B (those with a ratio of negative 25 percent to less than 4 percent) will be eligible for recapitalization. All category A banks, those with a capital adequacy ratio of 4 percent or higher, are to continue in business. Seven private banks were recapitalized in 1999, and four state-owned banks comprising half of the assets of the banking sector were merged into one and recapitalized. Recapitalization and restructuring of the remaining state-owned banks will complete the first stage of banking sector reforms, and the next stage will involve modernizing regulatory systems and procedures.

Bank recapitalization is being financed by domestic bond issues, with the government and the recapitalized banks exchanging bonds for outstanding shares. The government plans to cover the interest costs of these bonds from the proceeds of privatization and asset sales of IBRA, which include an estimated Rp250 trillion in nonperforming loans transferred by the banking system in the restructuring process. The IBRA, in turn, faces a complex task of selling its assets. Such sales are critical in reducing the public debt. The devastating impact of the crisis on the banking system points to a strong need for developing the capital market to mobilize domestic savings and reduce the corporate sector's excessive reliance on bank borrowing.

To facilitate corporate restructuring, the government set up the Jakarta Initiative Task Force and the Indonesian Debt Restructuring Agency (INDRA). The Jakarta Initiative Task Force provided a platform for corporate debtors to seek voluntary resolution of their debt outside the judicial system, and the INDRA provided forward foreign exchange cover to restructured deals. Despite these initiatives, corporate debt restructuring has been slow. It is essential to improve implementation of the bankruptcy law, which was revised in 1998. Voluntary mechanisms for restructuring corporate debt will have greater appeal if creditors have reasonable expectations of being able to speedily enforce their claims against debtors through legal means, should voluntary methods fail. The government also needs to make greater efforts to address negative perceptions about governance in judicial processes, and to enhance the capacity of the judiciary to implement the bankruptcy law. The slow pace of corporate debt restructuring has impeded economic recovery.

POLICY AND DEVELOPMENT ISSUES

In Indonesia, decades of unaccountable and centralized administration have tended to degrade the quality and efficiency of several public institutions. Strong growth and rising prosperity for years before the crisis gave rise to a false sense of complacency, delaying necessary action on governance reforms. Poor governance was also responsible, in large part, for the magnitude of financial collapse and fiscal distress. Unless governance reform is accelerated and fundamental changes realized, future growth and development will be impeded. Major priorities in improving governance include combating corruption, improving decision-making and administrative structures, and strengthening public institutions.

The government took important steps in 1999 to combat corruption when it passed several new laws. The Clean Government Law requires public officials to declare their assets before assuming their posts and to agree to open their assets to official audit during and after their terms. The Eradication of Criminal Acts of Corruption Law defines corrupt practices that are harmful to the finances or the economy of the state, and establishes the basis for legal prosecution and criminal charges. It also provides for public participation in legal surveillance and the establishment of an independent anticorruption commission for legal enforcement.

New regulations to reform public procurement and project implementation practices are being finalized. While these are important steps, much more remains to be done to promote competition and efficient, transparent, and accountable public administration; encourage citizen participation; and strengthen legal reforms and the role of official oversight agencies. However, institutional change across many sectors could meet significant resistance from vested interests.

Parliament's approval of the Law on Regional Autonomy and the Law on Fiscal Balances earlier in 1999 gave districts and provinces impetus to decentralize. This is intended to improve accountability of the government's decisionmaking process, strengthen participation of beneficiaries, and increase transparency. Implementing the government's wide-ranging decentralization agenda—which includes introducing new systems, structures, and procedures to transfer developmental and administrative functions and fiscal responsibilities to local levels—will pose difficult challenges. Among other things, this implies that many central government agencies will need to make their respective mandates consistent with a decentralized framework. It also implies substantial strengthening of capacity of the public institutions, especially at lower tiers of public administration.

Even before the crisis, poverty was a major concern in Indonesia. The crisis further exacerbated the poverty problem, reversing in a short period gains in social development that were achieved over decades. Even if the surge in poverty proves to be transient, its consequences are not. Moreover, many millions more subsist near the poverty line, and the country has long experienced regional economic disparities that could lead to serious sociopolitical discontent and instability.

Combating poverty remains the foremost development priority, and the new government has given this issue its greatest attention. Decentralization has potential for responding to poverty issues directly and sensitively. It could empower the poor and tap their creative energies, and help build a genuine partnership between government, civil society, and the poor to eradicate poverty. The anticorruption measures of the government will also support poverty reduction, by addressing corruption and inefficiency in public services, including delivery of services to the poor.

Indonesia doubtlessly faces daunting challenges in its path to recovery and sustained growth, and resolution of its problems is likely to take time. However, the arrival of democracy and a government committed to reform have provided new and historic opportunities for the country to confront its problems. It is crucial to seize this window of opportunity now.

Lao People's Democratic Republic

In 1999, the economy experienced moderate expansion accompanied by high monetary growth, rapid inflation, and volatile exchange rates. The outlook is for relatively stable economic growth over the medium term.

RECENT TRENDS AND PROSPECTS

Several factors contributed to sustain economic growth in 1999 at the same rate as 1998. While industry and services grew slowly, agriculture performed well, benefitting from a major government irrigation program. Production of garments, one of the largest export earners, rebounded because of increased penetration in European markets.

The gross investment rate fell as both public and private investment rates weakened. Construction slumped as work wound down on the nearly completed 60-megawatt Nam Leuk and 150-megawatt Huoy Ho hydropower projects. However, an increase in tourist arrivals boosted the service sector, although this was partially offset by weakness in the banking sector.

Fiscal performance improved in 1999 as the drop in public investment reduced the overall fiscal deficit, excluding grants, to 9.3 percent of GDP from nearly 14 percent in the previous year. In contrast to 1998 when bank financing of the budget deficit was required, net bank credit to the government declined in 1999. Revenues recovered from 9.8 percent of GDP

in 1998 to about 11.3 percent because of improvements in both tax and nontax revenue collections. At the same time, the government further compressed current expenditures to 5.5 percent of GDP in 1999, down from 7.1 percent in 1998.

In 1999, rapid money supply growth of approximately 86 percent resulted in an estimated inflation rate of about 87 percent and significant exchange rate depreciation of 40 percent. Although still high, these rates were all lower than the previous year, as the government gradually moved to reduce credit expansion. The government alternated between tightening and easing credit conditions throughout 1999 before settling into a tight monetary stance in the final quarter, which stabilized prices and the exchange rate at the end of the year.

However, because of monetary policy inconsistency, the year was characterized by volatility in the foreign exchange market. Furthermore, because of the government's reluctance to adjust the official exchange rate rapidly in response to changing market conditions, the unofficial exchange rate ranged from more than 40 percent in February and March 1999 to less than

3 percent above the official rate in June 1999. Over-all, confidence in the kip weakened, so banking and other transactions were increasingly carried out in for-eign currencies, which put more pressure on the exchange rate.

The current account balance as a percent of GDP improved modestly in 1999. The trade balance signifi-cantly improved, more than offsetting deterioration in net factor income and private transfers. Foreign direct investment and official development assistance disbursements increased slightly in 1999 relative to 1998. Gross official reserves increased from $112.8 million to $115.9 million.

Prospects are for modest improvement in eco-nomic growth in 2000 and 2001. Agriculture should continue to enjoy moderate growth, helped by continued investment in irrigation. If normal trading relations with the United States are established, this would translate into improved growth in manu-facturing in the near to medium term. Hydropower export earnings are projected to grow by more than 30 percent in 2000 with the start of operations at the

Nam Leuk and Huoy Ho sites. However, foreign di-rect investment likely will stagnate and construction continue to slump in the medium term, partly because of the delay in new hydropower projects resulting from a slowdown in Thai electricity demand.

ISSUES IN ECONOMIC MANAGEMENT

Macroeconomic conditions are intertwined intimately with fiscal management. Figure 2.8 shows the evolu-tion of fiscal revenues and expenditures since 1995. In late 1997, total revenues dropped as the regional crisis lowered trade tax revenues. Furthermore, external financing of the budget decreased because aid flows diminished when donor countries saw the reform effort faltering, particularly in the financial sec-tor. Nevertheless, the government expanded public investment with central bank financing, especially for its irrigation projects.

Using outdated and overvalued exchange rates to calculate import tariffs—thus reducing the tax liability in kip terms—resulted in revenue shortfalls.

Table 2.9 Major Economic Indicators, Lao People's Democratic Republic, 1997-2001
(percent)

Item	1997	1998	1999	2000	2001
GDP growth	6.9	4.0	4.0	4.5	5.0
Gross domestic investment/GDP	26.2	26.1	23.7	24.0	25.0
Gross savings/GDP	9.4	15.5	13.4	13.0	13.0
Inflation rate (consumer price index)[a]	26.6	142.0	86.7	30.0	10.0
Money supply (M2) growth	65.8	113.3	86.3	50.0	30.0
Fiscal balance/GDP[b]	-8.8	-13.9	-9.3	-8.5	-8.0
Merchandise exports growth	-1.2	7.7	2.9	5.0	6.0
Merchandise imports growth	-6.0	-14.7	-2.9	7.0	6.5
Current account balance/GDP[c]	-16.8	-10.6	-10.3	-11.0	-12.0
Debt service/exports	9.0	11.1	12.0	12.5	12.0

Note: Figures for 1999 are preliminary estimates.
a. End of period.
b. On a fiscal year basis ending 30 September; excludes official transfers.
c. Excludes official transfers.

Sources: Bank of Lao PDR; IMF; Ministry of Finance; National Statistical Centre; staff estimates.

Figure 2.8 Fiscal Performance,
Lao People's Democratic Republic, 1995-1999

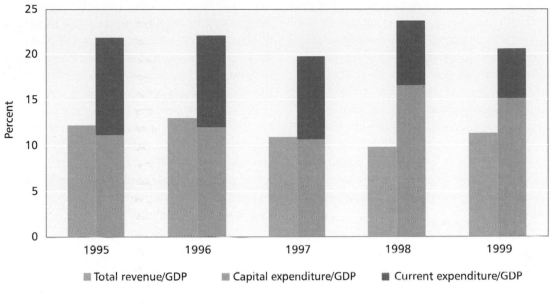

■ Total revenue/GDP   ■ Capital expenditure/GDP   ■ Current expenditure/GDP

Sources: Ministry of Finance; IMF data

The government has since adjusted the exchange rate used for import valuation. Another problem arising from high inflation was erosion in the real value of nominal lump sum commercial income tax payments during the year, although their levels had been fixed at the beginning of the year. As a result of the high inflation and exchange rate depreciation, weaknesses in tax administration were exposed. On the expenditure side, imperfect management often resulted in public investments that were higher than intended. Facing shortfalls in revenues and foreign funding, the government economized on current expenditures, which in 1995 were as high as 10.8 percent of GDP. These have been squeezed over the past several years and continue to be compressed despite recent success in curtailing capital expenditures.

In particular, wages and salaries of government workers have fallen significantly, both as a percentage of GDP (from 5.2 in 1995 to 2.2 in 1999) and in real terms, because nominal wage increases have not kept pace with high inflation during the last two years. In addition, even as public investment accelerated to nearly 17 percent of GDP in 1998, spending on materials and supplies fell from more than 3 percent of GDP in 1995 to less than 2 percent in 1999. These trends can cause problems such as increased absenteeism among government workers, incentives for corruption, and inadequate spending on maintenance, all of which can impair public sector efficiency.

POLICY AND DEVELOPMENT ISSUES

About 40 percent of the population lives below the national poverty line, less than the estimated 45 percent in 1992-1993. The highest incidence of poverty occurs in the north region, although poverty levels in the south and central regions are also significant. Most of the rural poor are subsistence farmers with low productivity and poor market access. Pervasive poverty is also indicated by a low per capita income of $330 in

1998. However, among income groups there is relative equality, as evidenced by a low Gini coefficient (a measure of income inequality) of 0.38.

Wide disparities exist between the richest and poorest quantiles with respect to access to and the quality of public services used. For education, net primary enrollments for the richest quintile are 78 percent compared with 44 percent for the poorest quintile. At secondary levels, the inequities are even greater: net enrollments are 28 percent for the richest and 4 percent for the poorest. Availability of textbooks and access to better-qualified teachers mirror these differences. Student performance rates are lower in the poorest provinces, accompanied by higher dropout rates and lower enrollment rates. Consequently, children from poorer families have little access to skills training and other income-generating opportunities.

Patterns for health care access and quality are similar. Only 8 percent of the poorest quintile use modern health care services, compared with 22 percent of the richest quintile. Similarly, only 8 percent of the poorest quantile as compared with 33 percent of the richest quantile have access to safe water and sanitation, causing more waterborne diseases among the poorest. The cumulative impact of poor access to health care and inadequate sanitation and water services implies a large quality gap in health care between the richest and poorest quintiles.

To address poverty, greater efforts must be made to enhance opportunities for the poor through policies to promote rural economic activities, especially in agriculture. In addition, greater spending on social services by the government is needed to achieve broader coverage and reduce the gap in the utilization of the social services.

Malaysia

Malaysia has made an impressive recovery from economic recession in 1998. Although capital controls enabled the authorities to pursue expansionary fiscal and monetary policies without precipitating capital flight, greater market orientation in several areas will support a more sustainable recovery. Enhancing the skill level of the Malaysian labor force remains a key challenge for improving economic competitiveness and long-term development prospects.

RECENT TRENDS AND PROSPECTS

The economy achieved a robust recovery in 1999, with real GDP expanding by 5.4 percent after having contracted by 7.5 percent in 1998. Stronger economic growth also led to a decline in the rate of unemployment to 3 percent of the labor force in 1999 from 3.2 percent in 1998. Most of the positive signs of economic growth came from greater external demand for manufactured goods and a rise in consumer confidence, as reflected in increased passenger car sales, sales tax receipts, and imports of consumer goods.

All major production sectors, with the exception of construction and mining, recorded higher growth in 1999. The manufacturing sector expanded by 13.6 percent, spearheaded by strong external demand for electronic equipment and components. A significant increase in crude palm oil production pushed agriculture sector growth to 3.8 percent, while increased manufacturing activity and stronger export growth led to a recovery in service subsectors such as transportation, storage, and communications.

Although a large surplus of high-rise commercial buildings and higher-end condominium units continued to depress construction activity, output contraction lessened in 1999. Despite the strong rebound in overall economic activity in 1999, the recovery was uneven, and private investment activity continued to contract because of inadequate credit expansion and excess industrial capacity.

After averaging 5.3 percent in 1998, consumer price inflation decreased steadily during 1999, averaging 2.8 percent. The slowdown reflected continued excess capacity, greater exchange rate stability, and a slower increase in food prices. The strong economic rebound, the relaxation of restrictions on the repatriation of portfolio investment, and the consequent decision of several credit rating agencies to readmit Malaysia to their global benchmark equity indices led to a recovery in share prices. Share prices were, however, somewhat volatile, owing in part to uncertainty over US interest rates and a strengthening yen. Overall equity prices, as measured by the Kuala Lumpur Composite Index, rose by 39 percent in 1999.

Table 2.10 Major Economic Indicators, Malaysia, 1997-2001
(percent)

Item	1997	1998	1999	2000	2001
GDP growth	7.5	-7.5	5.4	6.0	6.1
Gross domestic investment/GDP	42.9	26.7	23.7	24.1	25.0
Gross national savings/GDP	37.3	39.6	37.7	35.4	35.0
Inflation rate (consumer price index)	2.7	5.3	2.8	3.3	3.5
Money supply (M2) growth	18.5	2.7	8.3	12.0	14.5
Fiscal balance/GNP	2.5	-1.9	-4.9	-2.0	0.5
Merchandise exports growth	1.2	-7.5	10.1	8.0	8.0
Merchandise imports growth	1.4	-26.5	10.0	12.6	13.0
Current account balance/GDP	-5.0	12.9	14.0	11.3	8.1
Debt-service ratio	6.5	6.6	6.2	5.3	5.0

Sources: IMF (2000); Bank Negara Malaysia; staff estimates.

The appreciation of the currencies of Malaysia's main trading partners in 1999—following their precipitous declines in the latter half of 1997 and into 1998—left the ringgit relatively undervalued. This, in turn, helped improve the price competitiveness of Malaysian exports. However, any cost advantage from currency undervaluation is likely to be temporary. Countries such as People's Republic of China, India, and Viet Nam, which have a huge cost advantage in relatively unskilled labor, are increasingly moving into producing the lower value-added goods currently exported by Malaysia.

The balance of payments strengthened further in 1999, following a substantial improvement in the trade surplus and higher net inflows of long-term capital. The trade surplus in 1998 was driven by import compression, as imports declined much more sharply than exports (see figure 2.9). The 1999 surplus, however, resulted from a higher initial level of exports as exports and imports expanded at similar rates. Export growth was buoyed by the real depreciation of the ringgit and stronger demand for electronic goods, both within the region and by the United States. Import growth was stimulated by renewed consumer confi-

dence and the need to replenish depleted stocks of raw materials. Imports of capital goods, however, remained subdued because of excess capacity in several production sectors. The significantly larger trade surplus more than offset an increase in the services and transfers deficit and led to a higher current account surplus. Higher net inflows of official long-term capital boosted the capital account. This included a $1 billion global bond issued by the government after a lapse of nine years, and concessional loans from the Japanese government under the New Miyazawa Initiative. Because of these developments, the overall balance of payments was substantially in surplus, and net international reserves increased to $30.9 billion (six months of import equivalent). The external debt position improved in 1999 because of higher repayments and less borrowing by the private sector. Because of the lower incidence of debt and the improved export situation, the debt-service ratio declined to 6.2 percent in 1999 from 6.6 percent the previous year.

GDP growth is likely to accelerate in 2000 as private consumption strengthens, reducing excess industrial capacity and providing more incentives for fixed investment. Purchasing power will recover

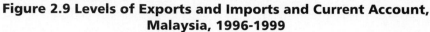

Figure 2.9 Levels of Exports and Imports and Current Account, Malaysia, 1996-1999

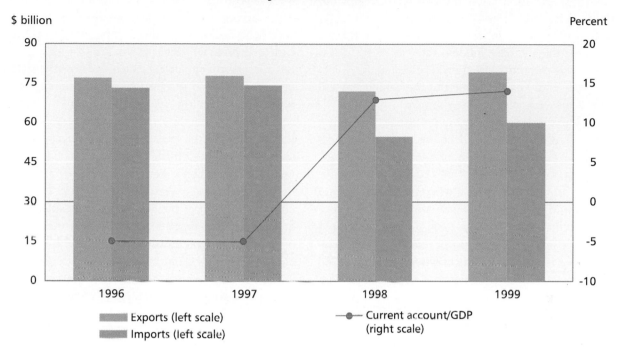

Exports (left scale)
Imports (left scale)
Current account/GDP (right scale)

Sources: IMF (2000); Bank Negara Malaysia.

further as asset values increase and unemployment eases, while fixed investment will pick up because of increased bank lending. These positive trends will, however, be partially offset as public consumption expands more slowly to bring down the level of fiscal deficit. The rate of increase in real GDP growth is likely to moderate in 2001 as the recovery from recession ends. Inflation is likely to pick up slightly because of stronger domestic demand, rising real wages, and a recovery in non-oil commodity prices, but it will remain substantially below its 1998 level. The trade surplus is likely to narrow, as an expected improvement in export performance on the back of stronger world trade growth is offset by faster import growth, because of the import-dependent nature of exports and a higher demand for capital goods. Malaysia's dependence on trade-related service imports and increased outflows of profits and dividend payments will likely widen services and income deficits, in turn causing the current account surplus to narrow. The exter-

nal debt position is expected to remain manageable, and Malaysia should not experience any problems in meeting its debt obligations.

Although stronger economic growth is likely to increase the demand for workers, various factors may limit how much unemployment decreases. These include ongoing restructuring activities in the construction, manufacturing, and financial sectors; the tendency for private companies to employ migrant workers as wage pressures begin to mount; and a loss of competitiveness in labor-intensive, low value-added goods because of increased competition from countries with cheaper unskilled labor.

ISSUES IN ECONOMIC MANAGEMENT

With capital controls in place, the government pursued expansionary fiscal and monetary policies to stimulate the economy in 1999. While expansionary fiscal policies have undoubtedly helped to revive the economy, lower interest rates have been less effective in stimulating loan growth. The central bank's three-month intervention rate—the rate used by banks to fix the base lending rate—reached a low of 5.5 percent in 1999, falling from a high of 11 percent in 1998. Correspondingly, base lending rates declined to less than 7 percent from more than12 percent in July 1998, although total loans extended by the banking system contracted 4 percent during the year.

The ratio of nonperforming loans (NPLs) on a three-month arrears basis decreased only gradually—from 18.9 percent at the end of 1998 to 16.7 percent at the end of December 1999—and corporate debt restructuring proceeded slowly. Hence banks were reluctant to lend for fear of increasing their risk exposure. With domestic demand still subdued, fiscal and monetary policies probably will remain expansionary in the short term to boost private consumption and investment. To encourage investment and loan growth, the government is likely to capitalize on the current low inflation to further reduce interest rates. Loan growth is also likely to increase and NPLs decrease as the economy continues to recover.

The government has, however, made considerable progress in cleaning up the banking sector by NPL purchases and capital injections. Danaharta, the agency set up to purchase and rehabilitate the banking sector's bad debt, acquired around 35 percent of NPLs and began disposing of these assets. Danamodal, the special-purpose organization for recapitalizing and strengthening banks, initially injected RM6.4 billion into ten banks. The amount involved decreased to RM4.6 billion following repayments by five banking institutions. The government also attempted to consolidate the banking sector to create domestic financial institutions that can withstand international competition. This competition is expected to intensify in 2003 when the government liberalizes the sector to conform to its World Trade Organization commitments. The plan initially called for the consolidation of the country's 58 financial institutions by the end of March 2000 into six anchor banks to be selected by the authorities. However, following strong objections to some parts of the plan, the central bank allowed commercial banks to choose their own merger partners—which they have now done—and extended the deadline to December 2000.

Some observers are concerned over the need for greater transparency and a proper balancing of creditor and borrower interests in the voluntary corporate debt workout program. However, notable progress has been achieved in restructuring corporate debt. By the end of September 1999, Malaysia's Corporate Debt Restructuring Committee, which oversees the voluntary program, had received 63 applications for debt restructuring that totalled RM35 billion. Of these, 15 restructuring schemes involving debts of RM12.7 billion were completed or were in various stages of implementation, while a further 15 cases involving debts worth RM3.5 billion were rejected. A program for reforming corporate governance, created in 1998, was enacted. It requires publicly listed companies to file quarterly financial statements, restricts the number of directorships an individual may hold, enhances disclosure requirements for publicly listed companies relating to takeovers and mergers, and requires more stringent listing requirements and capital adequacy ratios for publicly listed financial companies.

During 1999, some of the capital control measures that had been introduced in September 1998 to support economic recovery were significantly relaxed. In February 1999, an exit levy replaced the previous moratorium on the repatriation of portfolio capital. This allowed foreign investors to repatriate the principal and profits upon payment of a graduated levy that varied from 10-30 percent, depending on the duration of investment in Malaysia. In September 1999, a uniform levy of 10 percent on capital gains replaced the graduated levy.

Malaysia has survived the dire predictions made by many analysts when it imposed selective capital controls in September 1998. At a time when international investors had yet to regain confidence in the region, capital controls gave the authorities sufficient flexibility to pursue expansionary fiscal and monetary policies that would stimulate domestic demand without precipitating capital flight. Using capital controls to accelerate corporate and financial sector reforms and replacing the quantitative restrictions on repatriating portfolio investment with an exit levy also helped restore international confidence and reestablish portfolio capital inflows.

In the short term, however, greater market orientation in several areas will help bring about a more robust and sustainable recovery. For instance, setting a minimum loan growth target for banks (as was the policy in 1998 and 1999) is likely to lessen the quality of credit appraisal and jeopardize the asset quality of banks. Loan growth more likely will be stimulated if banks are allowed to set lending rates consistent with underlying risks, rather than the current practice of setting a cap on lending rate using an administratively determined, fixed markup on the base rate.

Reverting to a three-month NPL classification standard and reducing the current six-month disclosure requirement for banks to three months also will strengthen prudential norms and provide a stricter assessment of the banking system's health. This will also reinforce market discipline and be consistent with the direction of current financial sector and corporate sector reforms. Bank exposure limits to certain risky sectors (such as real estate and share transactions) that were relaxed in 1998 must be reviewed to strengthen overall risk management by individual banks. Coping with these issues will reduce the vulnerabilities that characterized the financial sector when the crisis struck in 1997.

POLICY AND DEVELOPMENT ISSUES

In the longer term, the retention of capital controls and the fixed exchange rate probably will increase inefficiency in resource allocation. This, in turn, is likely to have negative implications for economic growth. The number of foreign investment applications has fallen steadily since the imposition of capital controls in September 1998. This suggests continued investor unease over these measures, which has serious implications for a country that wants to shift from producing low-cost, labor-intensive manufactured goods to high-technology, knowledge-based high value-added products.

Malaysia has made impressive gains in increasing the educational levels of its population, especially at the primary and secondary levels. Concern is, however, growing about educational quality considering the shortage of skilled labor for the high-technology and knowledge-based industries that the country hopes to build, and the perceived lack of labor competitiveness compared with most Association of Southeast Asian Nations countries. While the effects of the economic crisis on existing levels of primary and secondary education are believed to be mild, the effect on tertiary education is more severe. The steep rise in the cost of tertiary education abroad has led to increased demand for public tertiary education within Malaysia, both from new school leavers and returning overseas students who cannot afford to complete their studies abroad. Estimates indicate that in 1998 there were 112,000 applications for the 40,222 places available at the country's ten public universities. Under these circumstances, local tertiary education costs have reportedly increased about 30 percent, beyond the reach of many lower middle-income families.

In the initial stages of the crisis, the government decreased its education budget as part of an across-the-board cut of 18 percent in all categories of expenditure to restore international confidence and stabilize the economy. Expenditure cuts in the school construction program in rural areas, teacher training programs, and educational management information systems undoubtedly adversely affected educational access, quality, and efficiency. Following the abandonment of the government's restrictive demand management program in mid-1998, these budget reductions were restored in 1999 and allocations for education were increased in real terms.

However, given the shortage of skilled labor and the bottlenecks in tertiary education, efforts must be redoubled to encourage greater private sector participation in providing higher education and appropriate skills development programs. Private sector employers also need to be involved in providing vocational training. This will not only increase the likelihood that the skills gained by trainees are relevant to employer needs, but would shift the financial burden of providing such courses to employers, away from the public sector. The opportunity cost of not doing so is high, because private provision of education not only increases access to education at little or no cost to the government, but also introduces competition that could improve standards.

Myanmar

Following several years of strong economic performance in the early 1990s, Myanmar's growth rate slowed for the third consecutive year since 1996. Unless necessary structural reforms are undertaken, the economy will continue to depend heavily on ad hoc policies formulated in reaction to random factors such as weather and the changing regional economic environment.

RECENT TRENDS AND DEVELOPMENTS

In the early 1990s GDP increased at the rapid rate of around 8 percent. According to official estimates, GDP growth slowed to 5 percent in 1998. Agriculture output growth declined from 5 percent in 1996 to 2.8 percent in 1998 largely because of droughts, floods, and a shortage of fertilizer and pesticides. The structure of the economy has not changed substantially since the introduction of market-oriented reforms in 1988. It remains largely agrarian, with agriculture accounting for 42 percent of GDP in 1999 and more than 60 percent of the labor force in 1998 (see figure 2.10).

Real growth was about 4.5 percent in 1999. While industry and services maintained approximately the same growth rate as the previous year, growth in agriculture decreased because of bad weather, including drought in the upper part of the country and an untimely monsoon in lower Myanmar. External sector performance remained weak, with trade and current account deficits putting more pressure on the kyat exchange rate.

1999 refers to fiscal year 1999/00, ending 31 March.

The consolidated budget deficit for 1998 amounted to 4.5 percent of GDP. Both revenues and expenditures declined, from 11.5 and 8.9 percent of GDP in 1997 to 8.9 and 7.3 percent in 1998, respectively. The deficit of state-owned enterprises (SOEs) increased in recent years, mainly because exports were valued at the official exchange rate and state sector employees received subsidized rice.

Money supply and domestic credit have both been increasing 30-40 percent annually in recent years. Credit to the private sector has been increasing since 1995. However, it has become difficult for businesses to borrow from commercial banks, which are reluctant to lend in the poor business environment. In April 1999 the central bank lowered its discount rate from 15 to 12 percent, a surprising move given high inflation and negative real interest rates.

Meanwhile, the share of foreign currency deposits in total deposits increased to a little more than 20 percent, twice the level of two years ago, weakening the central bank's control of domestic money supply. Inflation has been high in recent years, largely

**Figure 2.10 Sectoral Share of GDP,
Myanmar, 1993 and 1999**

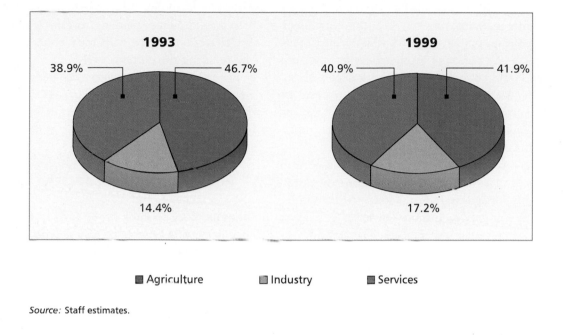

Source: Staff estimates.

because of increasing food prices and excess liquidity resulting from the central bank financing of around 70 percent of the budget deficit. Inflation in Yangon, the capital city, increased to 49 percent in 1998. No data are available for 1999, but inflation likely remained high for three reasons: a tenfold increase in electricity prices effective March 1999, an increase in transportation costs because of higher taxes, and a decline in commodity production.

The foreign exchange market remained highly distorted, with the parallel market rate at around MK350 per dollar, compared with the official rate of about MK6 per dollar. Because of quantitative restrictions and controls on foreign exchange transactions, private traders normally cannot export items such as rice, sugar, rubber, minerals, and gems. Consequently, SOEs are the major players in trading activities. Foreign exchange transactions among nonfinancial firms in the private sector appear to have no restrictions, however.

According to official figures, imports amounted to around $2.6 billion in 1998, while exports were around $1.2 billion, mostly primary products. Border trade with neighboring countries accounted for 30 percent of exports, and the current account, excluding official transfers, registered a deficit of $546 million.

Nevertheless, Myanmar posted a net balance-of-payments surplus of about $64 million in 1998. Foreign exchange reserves were reported to be about $400 million (1.8 months of import equivalent). At the end of March 1998, the total outstanding external debt was $5.6 billion, of which about 90 percent was medium- and long-term debt. At that time Myanmar had arrears totaling about $1.6 billion, of which 70 percent were owed to bilateral sources, 28 percent to private creditors (including suppliers' credit), and the rest to multilateral sources. By the end of March 1999, arrears to multilateral sources were believed to have more than tripled.

ISSUES IN ECONOMIC MANAGEMENT

Given its rich resource base, Myanmar has the economic potential to grow at a high rate. However, the economy remains highly controlled and has yet to adopt sound economic policies to exploit its potential and sustain economic growth. After the initial liberalization of the economy in 1988, which led to a relatively successful period of economic growth, progress stagnated, and persistent structural problems undermined its progress. Unless badly needed reforms are undertaken, the economy will continue to depend heavily on ad hoc policies rather than more carefully considered and far-reaching ones.

Some of the most pressing issues the government needs to address to revive growth are the distortions in the foreign exchange market, the continuing high level of inflation, and the low levels of revenue collection and public expenditure. The central bank needs greater authority and autonomy to control money supply and to determine interest rate policy, so it can help reduce inflation to manageable levels. The current official exchange rate is heavily biased toward import-using SOEs that import at the overvalued exchange rate and sell domestically at market prices. Exchange rate distortions favor a small number of industries at the expense of consumers and most other industries. Unifying the exchange rate would have to go hand in hand with removing price controls and easing restrictions on exports, imports, and foreign exchange transactions. In recent years the economy has begun to integrate with neighboring countries; more open external policies would help improve export performance, given the ongoing economic recovery in the region.

The government continues to strongly support the state sector despite its small contribution to the economy. The private sector transfers many resources to the state sector through taxation and levies, subsidies to SOEs, controlled prices for staples and agricultural and industrial inputs, and the highly overvalued currency. In particular, the large and growing rice subsidy for state employees seems unsustainable. Improving SOEs' performance—and reducing the fiscal deficit—will require restructuring and re-forming SOEs. Economic liberalization would significantly enhance efficiency, and help the development of the nascent private sector. This could shift Myanmar to a higher growth path, and help alleviate poverty.

The fiscal deficit has been reduced, but mainly by reducing public spending to unacceptable levels. Tax collection—along with broadening the tax base and reducing the current level of exemptions—must be improved significantly to resume necessary government spending. Simultaneously, about 70 percent of the fiscal deficit is reportedly financed through central bank credit, an underlying factor contributing to persistently high inflation.

POLICY AND DEVELOPMENT ISSUES

Myanmar does not rank particularly high in its socioeconomic achievements compared with its Southeast Asian neighbors. Although to the extent that social indicators exist, they have improved over the last decades and usually reveal better social conditions than expected, given the low level of per capita income. In 1997, life expectancy stood at 60 years and adult literacy at 84 percent. However, the benefits of economic growth do not seem well distributed. Estimates on poverty are rarely available, and Myanmar does not have an official poverty line. Nevertheless, estimates suggest that at least one in four households could be considered poor, with wide regional and ethnic differences. Infant mortality at 79 per 1,000 births is also slightly higher than the average of 68 per 1,000 births in four other Southeast Asian countries with similar levels of GDP per capita. Child mortality is significantly higher, 113 per 1,000 compared with an average of 77. High levels of malnutrition have been reported among children, reflecting the poverty of many households.

Under these circumstances, it is particularly worrisome that from 1997 to 1998, public expenditure for education fell from 0.93 to 0.64 percent of GDP, and expenditure for health fell from 0.28 to 0.18 percent of GDP. This trend should be reversed to raise the standards of living and to upgrade Myanmar's human resources.

Philippines

Compounded by delays in implementing structural reforms, economic recovery in the Philippines has been slow compared to other crisis-affected countries. Measures to accelerate the implementation of reforms are critical to improve medium-term growth prospects, address the serious poverty problem, and arrest further environmental degradation.

RECENT TRENDS AND PROSPECTS

In 1999, the economy experienced a GDP growth rate of 3.2 percent. Slow growth was primarily due to the anemic performance of the industry sector, which grew only 0.5 percent. Agriculture experienced a strong recovery from the El Niño drought of 1998, and grew by 6.6 percent, the highest rate in decades. Services, which had remained resilient throughout the crisis, grew by 3.9 percent in 1999, based mainly on retail trade growth.

Poor industrial performance resulted from weak consumer demand for nonfood manufactured items, a mild contraction in the construction sector caused by overcapacity, and nonperforming loans (NPLs) that impeded growth in bank financing for new projects. Slow growth in industry has been symptomatic of economic performance in recent years. The industrial share in GDP has shrunk from more than 40 percent two decades ago to around 35 percent in 1998, in contrast to strong industrial growth in neighboring countries such as Malaysia and Thailand.

Despite the slow overall economic recovery, employment in the agriculture sector increased significantly. However, this was almost completely offset by declining employment in industry and rapid growth in the labor force. Consequently, the unemployment rate decreased only slightly and underemployment remained substantial. The investment rate further declined in 1999, following a severe contraction in 1998. Efforts to improve the investment climate by lowering interest rates were countered by a lack of investor confidence in the progress of economic reforms and in the policy framework itself.

Inflation gradually receded, averaging 6.6 percent for the year. The reduction in inflation reflects a strong supply of agriculture products as well as modest domestic demand and a relatively stable exchange rate.

The economic crisis and subsequent efforts to stimulate domestic demand resulted in a larger than planned fiscal imbalance. The fiscal deficit increased to about 3.6 percent of GDP in 1999, nearly double the 1998 level and substantially higher than targeted.

Lower-than-expected tax collections and higher spending were responsible for the increased deficit. The increase in the public debt did not seem to have any crowding-out effect on private borrowing, which remained weak. Despite easing monetary policy and lowering interest rates—the benchmark 91-day Treasury bill rate remained below 9 percent for the last three months of the year—there was no significant increase in bank lending activity. Money supply and credit growth were weak. Domestic credit shrank in the first half of 1999 before recovering slightly in the last six months as the private sector began to recover. Low credit growth in the early months of the year reflected slow economic recovery, low lending spreads, and borrowers' unwillingness to make commitments in a climate of general overcapacity and insufficient demand.

On the external front, the trade and the current account balances turned around sharply in 1999. The trade balance soared from a deficit of $19 million in 1998 to a surplus of more than $4 billion, while the current account surplus widened from $1.3 billion to nearly $6 billion. These surpluses primarily resulted from growth of nearly 20 percent in exports, particularly in electronics and components, which accounted for nearly 60 percent of export revenue. Imports grew slowly, reflecting sluggish domestic demand for both consumer and investment goods. On the capital account, the outflow of short-term private capital continued, although at a lower level than in 1998. However, this was more than offset by a variety of official inflows, including a two-year standby facility from the International Monetary Fund—supported by the Asian Development Bank, Japan, and the World Bank—as well as bond financing on international capital markets. The surplus in the balance of payments resulted in a substantial increase in international reserves to nearly $15 billion, exceeding the precrisis level by more than $2 billion. While the external debt-to-GDP ratio increased to around 65 percent mainly because of the peso's depreciation, the debt-service ratio was a comfortable 13 percent.

The overall macroeconomic situation continued to reflect the adverse effects of the economic crisis. Although the beginnings of a recovery were evident, it has yet to gather full momentum. Unemployment and the number of NPLs continued to be high, and industrial activity, demand for credit, investment

Table 2.11 Major Economic Indicators, Philippines, 1997-2001
(percent)

Item	1997	1998	1999	2000	2001
GDP growth	5.2	-0.5	3.2	3.8	4.3
Gross domestic investment/GDP	24.9	20.4	18.8	19.5	20.0
Gross domestic savings/GDP	19.6	22.3	19.8	20.0	21.0
Inflation rate (consumer price index)	5.9	9.8	6.6	6.5	6.0
Money supply (M3) growth	20.9	7.4	19.3	17.0	18.0
Fiscal balance/GDP	0.1	-1.8	-3.6[a]	-1.8	-2.0
Merchandise exports growth	22.8	16.9	18.8	14.0	14.0
Merchandise imports growth	14.0	-18.8	4.1	14.0	16.0
Current account balance/GDP	-5.3	1.7	9.1[b]	6.3	5.6
Debt-service ratio	11.6	12.7	13.1[c]	14.3	14.5

a. January to September 1999.
b. Projection from Bangko Sentral ng Pilipinas.
c. January to November 1999.

Sources: ADB (1999f); IMF (2000); National Economic and Development Authority; National Statistical Coordination Board; staff estimates.

demand, and foreign private capital inflows were all low. However, inflation has been controlled, interest rates have been lowered, and export demand is strong. The pace of economic reforms, however, has been slow. Concerns include reduced revenue, quality of public expenditures, delayed reforms in the banking and financial sectors, and slow progress in legislation required for capital market reforms and in the privatization program. Many of the pending reforms are close to implementation, and will send positive signals to investors when implemented. The government expects the Securities Act and the Omnibus Power Sector Reform Bill to be passed by the legislature by mid-2000.

In 2000, GDP growth may reach 3.8 percent as the economy continues its moderate recovery, although return of investor confidence is pivotal. For 2001, growth will depend to some extent on weather conditions and their effect on the agriculture sector. Improved growth prospects are contingent on several factors. First, continuing prudent macroeconomic management is required, along with progress in reforms. The government expects that budgetary deficits will continue at least until 2001. These deficits may be necessary to impart the needed boost to the economy in an environment of flagging aggregate demand, and to maintain vital social sector expenditures. However, care must be taken to ensure that financing these deficits does not push up interest rates and crowd out much-needed private investment. Second, strong export growth momentum must continue. However, because the export basket is composed of a narrow range of products—electronics, transport equipment, machinery, garments, and textiles—it is sensitive to shifts in market sentiment and price volatility. Diversification of the export basket and encouraging small and medium-size enterprises in areas where the Philippines has a comparative advantage will help maintain export dynamism, and would ensure future export growth. Finally, a continued favorable regional environment is necessary for recovery.

ISSUES IN ECONOMIC MANAGEMENT

So that recovery can be sustained and growth further accelerated, action on several fronts is necessary. Restoration of investor confidence clearly requires the government's commitment to reform, as well as social consensus for its policies and programs. At the beginning of 1999, changes in various important departments were announced, and the Economic Coordination Council was formed to begin implementing stalled reforms. The business community and the public welcomed a renewed commitment to improving government efficiency, and these changes raised hopes that the stalled reform process will gather speed.

One issue is the size of the budget deficit required to stimulate the economy without causing inflation or a rise in interest rates. In 1999, the deficit exceeded the P100 billion target, but did not affect prices and interest rates. In 2000, the deficit target is much lower, which is appropriate considering the expectations of recovery. Nevertheless, care must be taken to ensure that private sector investment is not discouraged. Should the recovery be delayed, a larger role for public investments may be warranted, particularly to impart further stimulus to the economy and to augment badly needed social expenditures.

Better fiscal management can provide government resources in the short term to fund priority investments without resorting to higher deficits. Investment projects, especially those assisted by donors, have lagged, and this is a critical issue. Better project implementation can improve the productivity of investments and allow efficient use of scarce investable resources. The government has taken initiatives to improve implementation, such as setting up the Presidential Committee on Flagship Programs and Projects. Speedy action is needed to improve project implementation and expenditure monitoring and management, and to increase vitally needed social and infrastructure expenditures.

On the revenue side, measures are being taken to revamp tax administration to improve collections. The government has upgraded the bureaus of internal tax and customs and is considering other administrative measures, such as focusing first on large delinquent taxpayers to improve revenue collections. However, the process has been slow and needs more vigorous efforts.

On the monetary front, the main concern is the number of NPLs in the banking system, currently around 15 percent of total loans. This is much smaller than in other crisis-affected countries, but the con-

Box 2.1 **Dimensions of Poverty**

More than a third of the population of the Philippines—36.7 percent in 1997—is poor. An Asian Development Bank study based on the 1998 Annual Poverty Indicators Survey offers insights into the nature of poverty (see figure 2.11).

• Poverty in the Philippines is predominantly rural. A main cause of rural poverty is low productivity of agricultural employment. The highest incidence of poverty exists among households whose head is employed in the agriculture sector, and is far higher than among those engaged in services or industry.

• Low labor productivity and returns from labor—rather than unemployment—are the main determinants of poverty. More poor are employed than nonpoor, but the wages are not ample to lift them out of poverty. The labor market has a large informal segment capable of keeping wages low.

• Little difference exists in primary school enrollment rates between children of poor and nonpoor households. The net enrollment rates for secondary school, however, show a significant gap between the poor and nonpoor at this level.

• The self-reported rate of sickness is similar for the poor and nonpoor. The poor, however, are more likely to seek treatment at a local public health facility, usually a public rural health clinic, than the nonpoor. The nonpoor more frequently access private medical facilities, private hospitals, and clinics, particularly private clinics. The nearby barangay or village health centers staffed by a midwife or health worker remain underused.

• Compared to the other East Asian countries, population growth in the Philippines is high, which is reflected in higher family size. Average household size among the poor is even higher. While reported awareness of family planning methods is high, contraceptive use is still relatively low, and even lower among poor women. Access to maternal care is low, as evidenced by the low percentage of pregnant women receiving iron and other supplements. These rates are lowest among poor women and those living in certain regions.

• The poor have less access to clean water supply, piped water, and tube wells than the nonpoor, and hence are more likely to use contaminated sources of water such as dug wells. Despite less access to clean water, however, the gap is modest between poor and nonpoor in access to toilets, whether personal or communal.

• The poor have even less access to electricity than to clean water. Nationally, less than half of the poor live in premises connected to a national or cooperative system, while almost 90 percent of the nonpoor have such a connection.

These results have significant policy implications. They confirm that greater rural development is critical to poverty reduction and that raising labor productivity in all sectors, including the informal sector, can be an important step.

In terms of human resource development, while educational policies have been relatively successful at promoting primary education, reforms are needed to increase secondary education among the poor.

In health, as the poor generally access basic public health facilities more often, further improvement in these services would greatly benefit the poor. Additional efforts and reforms are needed to promote the use of the barangay or village health centers. The low contraceptive prevalence rate needs to be increased, and maternal health improved by more pervasive distribution of needed prenatal supplements.

Other services such as providing clean water remain a high priority, particularly for the poor, and in view of the implications for sanitation and hygiene. The large inequity in access to electricity suggests that expanding electricity distribution in rural areas can result in considerable benefits.

Sources: ADB (1999f); NSCB(1998).

tinued increase and persistence is a cause for concern. Faced with stagnant sales volumes, firms are cutting costs, reducing indebtedness, and selling assets. Applications to the Securities and Exchange Commission to suspend debt payments slowed considerably in 1999 from 1998. Nevertheless, the level of NPLs has acted as a drag on the financial system and restrained credit growth. The authorities must continue efforts to stimulate corporate activity and at the same time ensure that loan-loss provisions remain adequate.

The financial crisis and slow economic recovery has exacerbated the problems local government units face in delivering social services. Resources are often inadequate and financial management of these re-

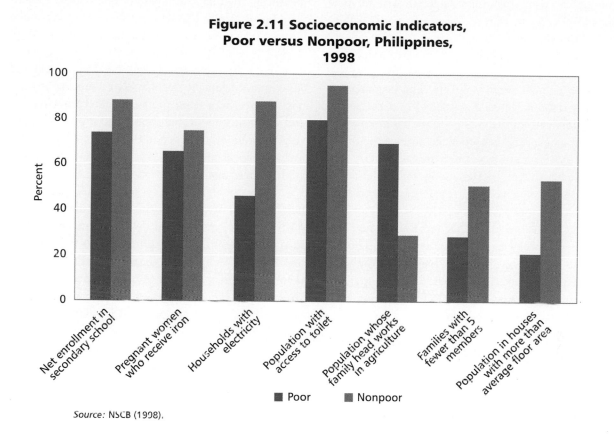

Figure 2.11 Socioeconomic Indicators, Poor versus Nonpoor, Philippines, 1998

Source: NSCB (1998).

sources has been poor. The national government could help by making its transfers to local governments more predictable and basing them on transparent criteria, such as good governance and effective revenue mobilization. Further, the revenue-sharing formula should be broadened to include other parameters, such as the incidence of poverty and levels of education and health. The national government can also organize training for local government units and publicize how the most efficient units have generated local revenue and used their funds efficiently.

POLICY AND DEVELOPMENT ISSUES

The economy faces three structural challenges required to achieve sustained growth: poverty reduction, proper environmental management, and adequate infrastructure. Continuing high poverty shows that the development process has not succeeded, and that large sections of the population, impeded by poverty, are unable to contribute. Environmental protection is essential for sustaining growth and ensuring livelihood for some of the poorest segments of society. Both are major structural constraints to development, and unless tackled urgently, will impede its progress.

Data released by the government indicate that poverty incidence has fallen slowly over the past decades but remains high, particularly in rural areas. Little progress has been made in raising living standards for the poorest of the poor, who are below the subsistence income threshold. Poverty reduction programs have failed to effectively target the needs of these people.

The government considers poverty reduction one of the major planks of its development strategy. However, the Medium Term Philippine Development

Plan has a modest target for reducing the overall incidence of poverty by at most 7 percent in 1997-2004. This is no different from earlier targets, and reflects no major additional emphasis on poverty reduction. As poverty alleviation efforts progress, bringing the remaining poor above the poverty line becomes increasingly difficult. Special measures are necessary to address the needs of the very poor, and far more effort is needed to address this seemingly intractable problem. The government has begun annual poverty surveys, which will help better monitor and delineate the dimensions of poverty and guide efforts to address the needs of the poor (see box 2.1).

Indications are clear that rapid environmental degradation is under way. The annual rate of deforestation, for example, is among the highest in Southeast Asia, and the protected forest area as a percentage of total land area is among the lowest in Southeast Asia. Conservation International, a reputed nongovernment organization, has ranked the Philippines first among 25 countries classified as Priority Biodiversity Hotspots needing urgent attention.

The cost of environmental degradation to the economy is high. Health and productivity losses from air and water pollution in Metro Manila alone have been estimated at about 1 percent of gross national product annually. However, because of difficulties in measuring the full cost of pollution and environmental damage, it is difficult for policymakers to make informed decisions and take appropriate action. More analysis is needed. The government also needs to devote more attention to capacity building of national government agencies that handle environment matters, and to improving their capability for enacting and enforcing environmental regulations. This involves obtaining the cooperation of all stakeholders, including local governments and communities as well as nongovernment organizations.

The Philippines has lagged behind many of its neighbors in physical infrastructure to support the industrialization and general development effort. Poor roads, inadequate port facilities, and unreliable and expensive power have increased costs and reduced economic efficiency. Many of these deficiencies in infrastructure have been addressed in the past few years, but much remains to be done. The Medium Term Philippine Development Plan calls for the private sector to be more involved in accelerating project implementation and restructuring the electricity sector through privatization, which is projected to improve efficiency, and lower costs. Costs of electricity are higher than in neighboring countries, which puts exporters at a disadvantage. A program of specific targets for achieving this objective would be welcome.

Thailand

The Thai economy began to recover in 1999 from the severe recession of 1998. Manufacturing production and the external sector performance improved significantly. In the short term, the immediate challenge continues to be financial sector restructuring. In the medium and long term, industrial restructuring, technological upgrading, and improved education and training will be necessary to consolidate economic recovery and growth.

RECENT TRENDS AND PROSPECTS

After an unprecedented real GDP contraction of 10.4 percent in 1998, the economy began showing positive signs of recovery in the beginning of 1999. Real GDP growth in 1999 was 4.1 percent, led by the manufacturing sector and increased domestic demand boosted through several government stimulus packages. The capacity utilization rate in the manufacturing sector increased to 63 percent from slightly more than 50 percent in 1998. While this was still below normal levels of 70-80 percent, manufacturing was nevertheless the engine of economic recovery, with a growth rate of around 11.3 percent in 1999.

Vehicles and transportation equipment production showed the highest growth rate. New vehicle models boosted domestic demand, and exports expanded as foreign vehicle producers used Thailand as a production center for regional manufacturing. Agriculture showed modest growth of 0.5 percent, with increased production of major crops such as rice, rubber, maize, and cassava partly offset by a sharp decline in farm prices. Domestic demand, which had contracted sharply the previous year, picked up, particularly in the second and third quarters of 1999, and rose to 8.5 percent for the year. Private consumption grew moderately, resulting in part from rising consumer confidence and modestly expanding farm income. Government stimulus measures, which included reducing the value-added tax rate from 10 to 7 percent and cutting taxes on petroleum products, also helped boost private consumption. Tourism continued to grow, with the number of tourists reaching 8.5 million in 1999, a 10.1 percent increase from the previous year. The private investment index declined moderately in 1999, compared with a steep decline in 1998.

The economic crisis resulted in historically high unemployment since mid-1997. Before the crisis, unemployment, including the seasonally inactive labor force, was around 3.6 percent. By 1998, this figure had almost doubled to 6.1 percent of the total labor force, and underemployment had increased significantly. The situation eased somewhat in 1999, as the unemployment rate declined slightly to 5.9 percent. Public programs boosted temporary employment, and the agriculture sector absorbed a significant number of laid-off urban workers who had returned to their provinces. Furthermore, both output and employment growth remain below precrisis growth rates, after falling sharply in 1998 (see figure 2.12).

In 1999, the government maintained the expansionary fiscal stance it adopted in 1998, after the fiscal and monetary targets of the adjustment program of 1997 and early 1998 plunged the country into a deep recession. The government continued to relax its public sector deficit target. Under the Eighth Letter of Intent to the International Monetary Fund in September 1999, the consolidated deficit—including the cost of financial restructuring, estimated at 1.7 percent of GDP—was projected at 7.2 percent of GDP for 1999, compared with 5.5 percent the previous year. During 1999, the government launched two economic stimulus packages, with expenditures of B53 billion and B100 billion, respectively, along with tax and tariff reductions. While the March 1999 package aimed at increasing employment and stimulating private consumption, the August 1999 package focused on tax and tariff measures, equity investment funds,

recovery of the real estate sector, and financing for small and medium-size enterprises.

Despite an easing of monetary policy, the growth rate of money supply continued to slow in 1999, in line with the decrease in commercial bank credits and deposits. At the end of 1999, the increase in money supply (M2) and M2A (including finance and securities companies) was 2.1 percent and 1.3 percent, respectively, compared with 9.5 percent and 6.1 percent at the end of the previous year. With high liquidity in the money market, interest rates dropped to very low levels, with the interbank rate at 1.23 percent, prime rate at 8.25-8.50 percent, and deposit rates at 4.00-4.25 percent in December 1999. However, the credit crunch continued because of the banks' concern with existing levels of nonperforming loans (NPLs), and tightened loan-loss provisioning and capital adequacy requirements. Credit extension by commercial banks posted negative growth throughout the year. Despite progress in debt restructuring, the total amount of NPLs in this financial sector was B2,074 billion, or 38.5 percent of total loans outstanding in December 1999.

Table 2.12 Major Economic Indicators, Thailand, 1997-2001
(percent)

Item	1997	1998	1999	2000	2001
GDP growth	-1.8	-10.4	4.1	4.5	4.6
Gross domestic investment/GDP	33.2	26.1	26.8	30.4	33.0
Gross savings/GDP	32.4	39.3	36.4	36.3	36.0
Inflation rate (consumer price index)	5.6	8.1	0.3	2.5	3.5
Money supply (M2) growth	16.4	9.5	2.1	8.0	12.0
Fiscal balance/GDP[a]	-0.9	-3.4	-3.0	-3.0	—
Merchandise exports growth	3.8	-6.8	7.4	7.0	8.0
Merchandise imports growth	-13.4	-33.8	17.7	16.5	17.0
Current account balance/GDP[b]	-2.1	12.7	9.1	5.5	1.9
Debt service/exports	15.6	20.8	20.4	16.0	—

— Not available.

a. On a fiscal year basis. Covers central government budgetary and nonbudgetary accounts and social security funds, and excludes interest costs of financial sector restructuring.
b. Excludes official transfers.

Sources: Bank of Thailand; Ministry of Finance; National Economic and Social Development Board; National Statistics Office; Bureau of the Budget; Ministry of Commerce; IMF reports; staff estimates.

Figure 2.12 Comparison of GDP and Employment Growth Rates, Thailand, 1995-1999

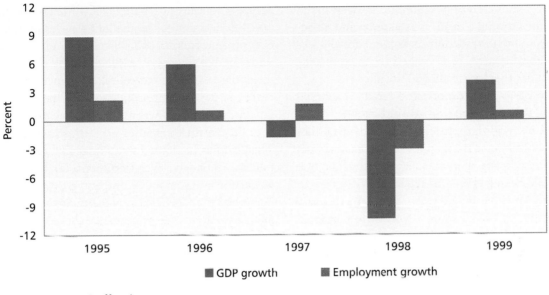

■ GDP growth   ■ Employment growth

Source: Staff estimates.

Following a year of relatively high inflation of 8.1 percent in 1998, the price level was remarkably stable in 1999. Despite upward pressure from rising oil prices in the world market, inflation was contained at 0.3 percent for the year, the lowest level since Thailand started compiling the index more than 50 years ago. The exchange rate and most commodity prices (aside from oil) remained stable, while domestic demand recovery did not generate upward pressure on prices.

While trade and current account surpluses fell slightly in 1999, external sector performance nevertheless improved significantly as export earnings in dollar terms increased by 7.4 percent. Import growth was higher at 17.7 percent, resulting in a decline in the trade surplus from 10.9 percent of GDP in 1998 to 7.2 percent in 1999. The current account surplus fell from 12.7 percent of GDP in 1998 to 9.1 percent in 1999. Meanwhile, despite increased inflows of foreign direct investments, net capital movements registered

a deficit of $6.1 billion, reflecting large private capital outflows as commercial banks continued to repay their external debts, in particular Bangkok International Banking Facility offshore loans. (This organization, established in 1993, allows licensed banks to operate offshore, borrow abroad, and lend to domestic borrowers in foreign currencies.)

Consequently, external debt stood at $75.6 billion in December 1999, down from $86.2 billion at the end of 1998; the share of short-term debt also declined from 27 percent to 19 percent of total external debt during the same period. However, public sector debt as a proportion of total external debt has almost tripled since the crisis began in July 1997, and accounted for 48 percent of total debt. Official international reserves increased to a comfortable level of $34.8 billion (approximately 9 months of import equivalent) in December 1999. This was remarkable because international reserves essentially had been depleted by December 1997. The high level of reserves prompted the government to suspend disbursement of the installment of $3.5 billion due under the $17.2 billion International Monetary Fund standby agreement of August 1997. The exchange rate remained stable at around B37-B39 per dollar in 1999.

To sum up, with the exception of private investment and commercial bank credits, indications of recovery are growing. Private consumption and manufacturing production picked up in particular in the second and third quarter of 1999, and the performance of the external sector steadily improved.

The economy is expected to build on its 1999 performance, growing at a slightly higher rate in 2000 and 2001, but not to return to precrisis growth levels. Capacity utilization in the manufacturing sector should reach normal levels of around 70 percent in the first half of 2000, which should be reflected by a return to positive private investment levels. While the recovery in 1999 was primarily export-driven with additional support from public stimulus measures and tourism, domestic consumption must rise if GDP growth is to continue in 2000-2001. In the financial sector, transfer of bad bank loans to newly established asset management companies (AMCs) is expected to reduce the level of NPLs held by commercial banks by 2001 to around 30 percent of total loans outstanding. However, if these plans are derailed, banks are unlikely to undertake the required volume of new lending to fund a sustained recovery in production and economic growth. As demand catches up and capacity utilization rises, inflation in 2000 is forecast at about 2.5-3 percent. Implementation of the August 1999 fiscal package, along with continued financial restructuring, will keep the consolidated deficit at 6-7 percent of GDP in 2000. If the growth rate of trade continues, the trade surplus will continue to shrink to about 4 percent of GDP in 2000. This will also translate into a decline in the current account surplus to about 5-6 percent of GDP. Gross official reserves are expected to be maintained at the same level in 1999, and external debt and the debt-service ratio are expected to decline further.

ISSUES IN ECONOMIC MANAGEMENT

The biggest immediate challenge is financial restructuring, in particular solving the problem of NPLs, which continue to cripple the financial sector and cause weak credit expansion. If lending does not resume quickly, viable companies that survived the crisis may eventually succumb to sustained liquidity problems. This could cause another wave of business closures and higher unemployment. Many commercial banks have so far been reluctant to restructure problem loans and accept actual losses ("haircuts"). Instead, most have opted for less painful rescheduling such as stretching out the amortization schedule. However, this merely postpones solving the problem. Problem loans will resurface once the extended repayment period is reached, unless additional liquidity is introduced rapidly into the system through foreign capital inflows.

In contrast to other countries in the region, Thailand has not opted for commercial bank recapitalization financed by government. Such a program would encourage moral hazard and put an excessively high burden on taxpayers. Nevertheless, the government has adopted measures since the start of the crisis to help banks cope with the crisis. In addition to the ongoing financial restructuring package launched in August 1998, the government encouraged banks to set up AMCs to deal with NPLs. By separating the management of problem loans from ongoing bank activities, the banks should be able to refocus on new lending, thus helping revive the economy. However, progress has been slow and setting up some AMCs has been put on hold.

During the crisis, private consumption reached its lowest level in the third quarter of 1998. Aided by a series of stimulus measures and tax reductions, it has improved but the trend is volatile. GDP per capita was on the rise after two years of decline, but consumers remained hesitant to resume significant spending. Worries about job security and financial sector stability, a sharp rise in oil prices, and a weaker baht constrained private consumption. Confidence in government policy and the government's commitment to carrying out needed reforms will play a critical role in reestablishing consumer confidence and boosting consumption in the future.

POLICY AND DEVELOPMENT ISSUES

In the medium and long term, industrial upgrading and improvement of productivity will be the main challenges. Increasing local wages have undermined competitiveness in labor-intensive sectors, as have low wages in neighboring countries. In the end, international competitiveness can only be achieved by industrial upgrading. This requires substantial investment in specialized education, research and development, and other knowledge-enhancing measures. This should help the industry sector further develop a high-technology base in computers, electronics, and other technology- and knowledge-intensive products and services.

While the country has done exceptionally well in achieving nearly universal primary education and expanding its secondary school system, quality improvements have not accompanied quantitative achievements. Eighty percent of Thailand's labor force has only a primary education or less. Some 5.5 million persons in the 6- to 19-year-old age group are not in school or another form of training. Educational attainment also varies substantially between urban and rural areas, where participation in education and skills development is strikingly low. Enrollment in higher education focuses on the social sciences and humanities, with science and technology students making up only about 22 percent of total enrollment. Low numbers of qualified faculty and an inadequate budget for university level research and development have impaired the capacity to conduct science and technology research and provide quality graduate education. In addition, vocational and skills training programs have been implemented largely without the active participation of the private sector in planning, design, and execution.

Consequently, concern is growing regarding the mismatch between skills generated by the education and training systems and those required to keep the corporate sector internationally competitive. In particular, the economy needs to move away from labor-intensive production. In recent years, the government has increasingly recognized the importance of human resource development in restoring its long-term competitiveness and ensuring sustainable growth and development. Several policy initiatives address the underlying weaknesses of the educational and training system. The new constitution, approved in 1997, made education free for children up to 12 years old. In addition, the Eighth Plan (1997-2001) outlined priority areas in education and training, including improving quality, relevance, administration, management, and private sector participation.

The National Education Act of 1999 will let the government pursue sweeping education reforms. Essentially, these will cover basic education for all, early childhood education, teachers and teaching methods, educational standards and quality assurance, education management (decentralization), financial management, training and vocational education, and information technology for continued learning.

If Thailand wants to move to higher value-added production, it must also strengthen its domestic capacity for research and development, so it can master new and complex technology that will support growth and development. This would require moving away from a predominantly supply-driven, government-dominated educational system toward a more market-responsive educational system. This system should incorporate private sector participation, education and research programs in science and technology, and market-oriented, specialized training of the active labor force. Specialized and up-to-date education and training will upgrade manufacturing production, but also will improve agricultural production by allowing the use of agricultural biotechnology and environmental technology. Moreover, it is essential to promote private sector collaboration by strengthening links between university and industry. These policy initiatives were incorporated in the Higher Education Development Project approved by the Asian Development Bank in 1999.

Viet Nam

With the loss of reform momentum and the economic slowdown over the last two years, the sustainability of past gains on poverty reduction is at stake. Carrying the process of poverty reduction forward in the coming years will require embarking on a second set of reform measures, one focused on diversifying rural livelihoods.

RECENT TRENDS AND PROSPECTS

In 1999, real GDP growth was estimated at 4.4 percent. This was half the average growth rate during the six-year period from 1992 to the onset of the regional crisis in 1997, an era of high growth driven by first-generation reforms (*doi moi*), booming private consumption, and foreign direct investment (FDI) inflows. The slowdown in growth during 1998-1999 resulted from the impact of the regional crisis, stagnating domestic demand, and loss of reform momentum.

Performance of various sectors in 1999 was mixed. Agriculture sector growth increased to 5 percent from 3 percent the previous year, with a bumper rice crop and growth in fisheries and livestock. The industry and service sectors continued to lag in 1999, with inventory buildup in key manufacturing industries, including cement, steel, coal, and fertilizers. Decreasing domestic demand and eroding competitiveness in vital subsectors slowed industrial growth. The deceleration in the service sector resulted from a slowdown in tourism, real estate services, and transportation, areas that were hit particularly hard by the economic slowdown. Two years of slow growth led to rising unemployment, particularly in the urban areas, and reached an estimated 7.4 percent in 1999.

Investment as a share of GDP has fallen during the last two years, from an estimated 29 percent of GDP in 1998 to 27.2 percent in 1999. This stemmed from lower private investment, less investment by state-owned enterprises (SOEs), and slower FDI inflows. The budgeted increase in public invesment in 1999 to stimulate demand did not materialize. To revive private investment, the government set up a Development Assistance Fund to provide medium- and long-term loans and credit guarantees for investing in productive ventures. FDI declined for the second year in a row, and estimates of the 1999 inflows range from $600 million to $1.4 billion. Before the crisis, two thirds of FDI inflows originated in Asia and hence were vulnerable to weaker regional GDP growth. The decline in FDI continued as investor sentiment remained lukewarm because of uncertainties about the direction and pace of reforms.

The fiscal deficit was about 2 percent of GDP in 1999. The budget deficit was maintained at moderate levels, despite falling revenues, because current expenditures were reduced. The banking system absorbed the bulk of the Treasury bill issuance that accounted for 51 percent of total financing in 1999.

The end-of-year growth rate of retail prices for 1999 was estimated at 0.1 percent compared with 9.2 percent in 1998. A fall in the food price index, weak domestic demand, and a relatively stable exchange rate contributed to price stability. Interest rate ceilings were reduced gradually from around 1.2 percent per month to 0.85 percent. Credit to the government and SOE sector was more restricted than in previous years, while credit to the smaller nonstate sector grew faster. The State Bank of Viet Nam estimated that money supply (M2) grew by 39.1 percent in 1999 compared with 26 percent in 1998, due largely to increased foreign currency deposits from inward remittances. These funds were re-deposited in overseas banks and did not translate into accelerated domestic credit growth. This partly explains why the money supply grew so rapidly in a year of record low inflation.

Exports grew slowly in early 1999 but perked up toward the end of the year, largely because of crude oil and rice exports. Textiles, garments, footwear, and marine products also registered stronger growth than in previous years. Crude oil was exported mainly to the People's Republic of China and Australia, marine products to Japan and other countries in the region, and most of the footwear exports to Europe. A higher volume of exports accounted for most of the increase in export earnings, rather than increased export price.

Overall export growth was 22.3 percent, up from only 1 percent in 1998. Imports showed only a small increase from the previous year, with fewer machinery and consumer goods and more petroleum products, fertilizers, steel, and synthetic fibers. With lower import levels and a resurgence of exports, the current account registered a substantial surplus, in contrast to a large deficit in 1998. Debt remained within manageable limits.

Table 2.13 Major Economic Indicators, Viet Nam, 1997-2001
(percent)

Item	1997	1998	1999	2000	2001
GDP growth	8.2	4.4	4.4	5.0	6.0
Gross domestic investment/GDP	28.3	25.5	19.7	20.8	21.9
Gross savings/GDP	21.8	21.1	22.0	21.6	20.5
Inflation rate (consumer price index)[a]	3.6	9.2	0.1	6.0	7.0
Money supply (M2) growth[b]	25.4	24.6	40.0	25.0	24.0
Fiscal balance/GDP[c]	-1.7	-1.6	-2.0	-1.7	-1.5
Merchandise exports growth	26.5	1.0	22.3	10.0	10.0
Merchandise imports growth	0.8	-2.1	1.2	16.0	17.0
Current account balance/GDP[d]	-6.5	-4.4	2.3	0.8	-1.4
Debt service/exports[e]	11.4	13.2	11.1	12.0	10.9

a. End of period; 1997 data based on retail price index, but since 1998 the CPI has replaced the RPI for estimating inflation.
b. Since 1996 the monetary survey has included 36 nongovernment banks.
c. On cash basis; excludes interest arrears, grants, and onlending.
d. Excludes official transfers.
e. Debt service on debt due/exports of goods and nonfactor services.

Sources: General Statistical Office; Ministry of Finance; State Bank of Viet Nam; staff estimates.

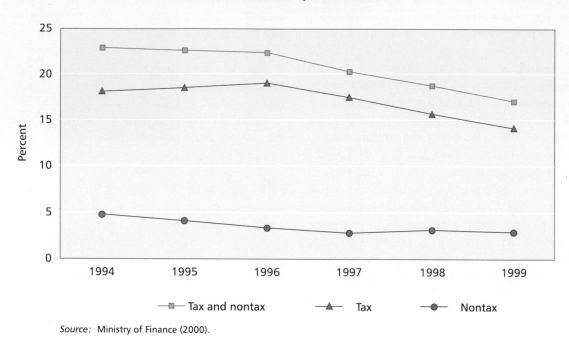

Figure 2.13 Government Revenue as Ratio of GDP, Viet Nam, 1994-1999

Source: Ministry of Finance (2000).

GDP growth is expected to be 5 percent in 2000 and 6 percent in 2001, as the industry and service sectors recover after two years of relatively low growth. Inflation is projected to be 6-7 percent in 2000 and 2001 because of an anticipated increase in prices of agricultural products that reflects the crop destruction caused by floods in 1999, higher prices for petroleum products, and stronger domestic demand. Export growth over the next two years is likely to be around 10 percent, and after a two-year slump, imports should recover in 2000 and grow at 16-17 percent. The current account surplus will probably narrow in 2000 and become a deficit the following year.

ISSUES IN ECONOMIC MANAGEMENT

The downward trend of revenue as a share of GDP over the last few years is a crucial concern (see figure 2.13). The drop largely results from a decline in tax revenue, particularly of corporate income tax and in-

ternational trade tax. Corporate tax revenues declined due to the weak performance of state enterprises and the difficulties the private sector faced in the wake of the Asian crisis and weak domestic demand. Trade tax collections fell because the composition of imports changed, and more recently, the share of imports in GDP fell. The value-added tax, which took effect 1 January 1999, accounted for around 4 percent of GDP in 1999. As in the past few years, the government set lower budgetary targets for revenue as a share of GDP for 2000. To compensate for falling revenues, the government cut back on expenditures, specifically nonwage current expenditures. Considering the budget constraints on necessary nonwage public expenditure, this trend should be reversed.

Opaqueness of budgetary information makes it difficult to assess the fallout in terms of loss in productivity and growth. This has been aggravated by including a budget allocation for contingency to meet revenue shortfalls and other adverse developments.

To improve revenue performance and ensure that priority spending can be maintained without jeopardizing macroeconomic stability, the government must set and achieve revenue targets aligned to its macroeconomic projections. Problems in the design and administration of taxes will have to be addressed with a view to terminating discretionary rates and exemptions. Budgetary information also needs to be made more transparent so that revenue shortfalls can be monitored in terms of productive and nonproductive expenditures. Further, the practice of including a significant allocation for contingency must be reviewed, as it weakens the link between the budget and actual spending.

POLICY AND DEVELOPMENT ISSUES

Rapid economic growth from the early 1990s until the onset of the crisis had a significant impact in reducing poverty. It has also been associated with an increase in inequality, particularly a widening of rural-urban gaps, though Viet Nam has been and remains a relatively egalitarian society. The incidence of poverty, as measured by the headcount ratio, dropped from 58 to 37 percent between 1993 and 1998. During the same period, the depth of poverty measured by the poverty gap declined from 18.5 to 9.5 percent. The incidence of poverty in rural areas is 45 percent compared with 10-15 percent for urban areas, and 90 percent of the poor live in rural areas. In 1993, many people below the poverty line were able to improve their situations enough to cross the line and are now clustered just above it. Therefore, while gains in poverty reduction have been made, they remain quite fragile.

Indicators of inequality for 1993-1998 increased marginally, with the Gini coefficient (a measure of inequality) rising from 0.33 to 0.35. An estimated 96 percent of the increase resulted from widening rural-urban gaps, with differences in growth rates between regions also contributing to the disparity.

Poverty incidence during 1984-1994 declined as a result of high GDP growth rates. In the future, however, GDP growth alone may not suffice to reduce poverty levels. Measures will be needed to improve income distribution, particularly the differentials in the rural-urban income levels. Because most of the poor live in rural areas, it is critical to identify the factors associated with rural poverty, which include geographical factors and household characteristics. The Northern Uplands, Central Highlands, and North Central Coast are the most impoverished regions, with limited natural resources and low agricultural productivity. These three regions have 51 percent of the country's poor, although they contain only 26.8 percent of the population. Poverty among ethnic minorities living in the upland areas is also high.

Rural poverty bears most heavily on those farm households that

- Have small landholdings, often of low quality
- Rely on informal credit with high interest rates
- Have limited access to markets for farm goods
- Lack off-farm employment.

Providing off-farm employment is particularly relevant. This will involve moving away from the capital-intensive pattern of development with limited linkages to the rest of the economy that offers limited employment opportunities. This pattern of development has been perpetuated by a policy of resuscitating SOEs through preferential treatment. The government needs to move decisively to remove both explicit and implicit biases that favor SOEs and discriminate against nonstate enterprises. To make progress in reducing poverty, these distortions must be corrected and policymakers must articulate a time-bound strategy—*doi moi* phase two—for promoting labor-intensive growth.

South Asia

Bangladesh

Bhutan

India

Maldives

Nepal

Pakistan

Sri Lanka

Bangladesh

Macroeconomic stability has been put under severe pressure by the disruptions from flooding in the third quarter of 1998. Signs of vulnerability have emerged both in the domestic and external sectors. Further structural reforms are needed if Bangladesh is to achieve greater economic efficiency, growth, and international competitiveness while reducing poverty.

RECENT TRENDS AND PROSPECTS

In the early 1990s, the government launched a comprehensive set of structural reforms aimed at strengthening fiscal and monetary management, fostering private sector development, and liberalizing the external trade and foreign exchange rate regimes. Such reforms resulted in a relatively stable macroeconomic environment, with improvements in economic growth, savings, and investment. Decreased poverty and improved social indicators accompanied the acceleration in economic growth. Between 1995 and 1999, the GDP growth rate averaged 5 percent compared with 4.7 percent in the preceding five years. The agriculture sector maintained an average growth rate of 3 percent, and the country achieved near self-sufficiency in rice production in those years without flooding. During the same period, growth in the industry sector averaged 6 percent, mainly because of robust manufacturing performance, while the service sector grew at an average of 6 percent. The export sector showed

an average annual growth rate of about 16 percent in dollar terms because of strong trade in garments and knitwear products. Bangladesh succeeded in attracting significant foreign direct investment (FDI), which increased from about $80 million in 1995 to about $400 million per year for 1996 through 1999.

This strong growth trend in GDP was slowed when severe floods hit in the third quarter of 1998, disrupting industrial growth in particular. Nevertheless, with the help of a bumper winter harvest, GDP grew 4.4 percent in 1999. This was better than the immediate postflood estimates of 3.3 percent, though lower than the 5.2 percent growth of 1998. Agriculture and services performed well, overcoming the adverse impact of the flooding. Agriculture grew 3.9 percent, up from 3.2 percent in 1998, because of new higher-yielding varieties, particularly of rice. Moreover, the government helped in postflood rehabilitation by providing seeds, fertilizer, and credits. The service sector maintained steady growth of 5 percent, while growth in the industry sector slipped to 4 per-

1999 refers to fiscal year 1998/99, ending 30 June.

cent from 8.3 percent in 1998. The floods seriously disrupted production of major medium- and large-scale manufacturing enterprises, including ready-made garments for export.

Gross domestic investment increased to 22.5 percent of GDP in 1999, from 21.6 percent the previous year, because of an investment surge in flood-induced reconstruction and rehabilitation. Gross national savings increased to 21.1 percent of GDP compared with 20.4 percent in 1998, mainly because of a surge in remittances from overseas workers.

After double-digit growth for several years, export growth dwindled to 2.8 percent in 1999 from 17.1 percent in 1998. The major setback was in the woven ready-made garments sector, which registered only 4.8 percent growth. While floods adversely affected export shipments and production, the devaluation of Southeast Asian currencies also weakened export competitiveness. This demonstrates how vulnerable the export sector is because of excessive dependence on a single subsector.

Imports grew 6.6 percent in 1999, higher than the preceding two years, because of imports of food grains triggered by the fear of flood losses. As a result, the current account deficit increased to 1.4 percent of

GDP from 1.2 percent the preceding year. Increasing pressure on the balance of payments was reflected by the low level of foreign exchange reserves of $1.5 billion (2.2 months of import equivalent) at the end of 1999. Lower export growth resulted in a slight increase in the debt-service ratio to 12 percent from 11.7 percent the previous year. Currency depreciated slightly, as the annual average exchange rate increased to Tk48.5 per dollar compared with Tk46.3 in 1998. Because of additional spending brought on by the flood —including imports of extra food grains and postflood rehabilitation costs—and a shortfall in current revenue collection resulting from production disruption, a higher budget deficit resulted. Current revenue declined to 9 percent of GDP from 9.7 percent in 1998, while the fiscal deficit increased to 5.3 percent of GDP from 4.2 percent. However, the fiscal losses of Tk15 billion associated with operating state-owned enterprises exposed a serious fiscal management problem. If the fiscal liabilities arising from these losses were considered, the government's fiscal position would be even weaker.

The government pursued an expansionary monetary policy to finance the flood recovery program. Money supply (M2) increased 12.8 percent in 1999

Table 2.14 Major Economic Indicators, Bangladesh, 1997-2001
(percent)

Item	1997	1998	1999	2000	2001
GDP growth	5.4	5.2	4.4	5.0	5.5
Gross domestic investment/GDP	20.8	21.6	22.5	22.8	23.5
Gross national savings/GDP	18.6	20.4	21.1	21.8	22.3
Inflation rate (consumer price index)	2.6	7.0	9.0	6.0	8.0
Money supply (M2) growth	10.8	10.4	12.8	14.0	12.0
Fiscal balance/GDP	-4.5	-4.2	-5.3	-4.2	-5.0
Merchandise exports growth	13.3	17.1	2.8	7.0	12.0
Merchandise imports growth	3.2	5.1	6.6	7.0	7.0
Current account balance/GDP	-2.2	-1.2	-1.4	-1.0	-1.2
Debt service/exports	11.4	11.7	12.0	12.1	12.1

Note: National accounts data are based on 1995/96 base year, are under government review, and not yet officially released.

Sources: Bangladesh Bank; Bangladesh Bureau of Statistics; World Bank; staff estimates.

compared with 10.4 percent the preceding year. The average inflation rate increased to 9 percent from 7 percent in 1998. However, after the new harvest, inflation started falling, reflecting the decline in food prices. In the banking sector some steps were taken to reduce the number of nonperforming loans (NPLs), particularly by removing major defaulters from the directorships of commercial banks. However, NPLs increased to 43 percent of total loans at the end of June 1999, compared with 41 percent six months earlier.

The macroeconomic outlook for 2000 remains positive, with reasonably high GDP growth of 5 percent and inflation limited to 6 percent. The economic growth will continue to be largely dependent on the agriculture sector as in the past few years. Domestic investment and national savings (22.8 percent and 21.8 percent of GDP, respectively) are expected to improve moderately. Two successive bumper harvests should ease the strain on the rural sector, with only moderate price increases expected. The industry sector is expected to recover partly from the setback suffered during the floods. The 2000 budget aims at reversing a flood-related upward trend in the budget deficit by raising revenue 1 percent of GDP to 10 percent, and lowering the budget deficit to 4.2 percent of GDP.

Nevertheless, the historical shortfall in government revenue and increased government borrowing from the banking system reflect the vulnerability of the government's fiscal position. Moreover, growing political turbulence could hurt the investment climate, which in turn could slow industrial growth, including growth in export-oriented establishments. Coupled with a high concentration of export and FDI in certain sectors, the balance of payments is likely to be threatened. Because the taka is overvalued compared with its competitors, any further devaluation in competing Southeast Asian countries, coupled with higher import payments, will pressure Bangladesh to devalue its currency in 2000.

ISSUES IN ECONOMIC MANAGEMENT

Low fiscal effort is a continuing issue. The tax base is narrow and tax compliance low. The share of government revenue is small compared with other countries in the region, and tax elasticity needs to be improved.

The 2000 budget introduced improvements in the tax structure and tax administration. These include automating customs administration, simplifying tax assessment and collection procedures, expanding the value-added tax base to cover 31 new items, and introducing mandatory preshipment inspection. Nevertheless, the fiscal position is likely to deteriorate more unless action is taken to reverse the government's low revenue-generating capacity and poor tax collection record. Government revenue as a percentage of GDP is not likely to exceed 12 percent in the near future. The problem lies primarily in poor tax collection and, in general, poor governance. Unless there is a significant improvement in governance, strict monitoring of the firms assigned to carry out mandatory preshipment inspections—which have yet to be fully implemented—may not be feasible.

On the expenditure side, the budget has faced increasing claims for wages, salaries, and defense expenditure, as well as growing pressure of debt obligations. Increasing government borrowing from the banking system to finance the large budget deficits has contributed to monetary expansion and inflation. The size of the government deficits and the corresponding borrowing requirements, together with the high interest rate on lending, have curtailed or reduced demand for bank credit by the private sector. Coupled with the high proportion of NPLs in the banking system, banks are reluctant to renew credit lines. Unless policies change, growth in the private sector will suffer, including growth in export-oriented industries. The government therefore must reach a political consensus on a national fiscal policy that will ensure increased revenue collection, reduce expenditure on unproductive sectors, and contain the fiscal deficit. Simultaneously, further financial sector and capital market reforms are needed to mobilize domestic resources for enhancing private sector investment.

In the external sector, the balance of payments is likely to deteriorate if export industries and the inflow of FDI are not diversified. Both remain highly dependent on a few products and sectors. Garments compose about 70 percent of total exports, creating vulnerability to unfavorable changes in global demand and supply. In addition, the world demand for garments is growing slowly and markets are extremely competitive. Export diversification is needed, particularly into higher value-added products such as electronics, computers, and higher-quality clothing, where world demand is growing faster. Similarly, the high concentration of FDI in the natural gas and power sectors, about 60 percent, not only has failed to increase foreign exchange reserves, but has also jeopardized the balance of payments. The government is obliged to pay foreign investors under the production-sharing contracts of natural gas and power purchase agreements. The situation will be further aggravated when significant profit repatriation begins. Unless the government considers exporting natural gas to neighboring countries such as India, or diversifying FDI to export-oriented industries, the balance of payments may deteriorate further.

POLICY AND DEVELOPMENT ISSUES

Poverty alleviation will continue to be the central agenda for both the government and external donors. Reducing poverty through accelerated economic and agricultural productivity is the main thrust of the government's Fifth Five-Year Plan (1997-2002). Poverty incidence is targeted to decline from 47.5 percent to 30 percent by 2002, while the annual average GDP growth rate is set at 7 percent, a level necessary to significantly decrease poverty. Halfway through the plan, growth had averaged only 5 percent.

The plan emphasizes the role of the private sector, especially in export-oriented industries, as the main engine for sustainable economic growth and employment opportunities. This will be facilitated by reforms in the financial and capital markets. Because 80 percent of the population still lives in rural areas, self-sufficiency in food grains is emphasized as a route to sustainable poverty reduction. Other measures to tackle poverty are human resource development; promotion of small-scale enterprises through microfinance; participation of local-level institutions in rural development; and good governance.

Prospects for poverty reduction in Bangladesh were set back in 1998 by heavy floods. Progress has been slow despite substantial government effort and resources that included allocating about a fourth of the annual development budget to social infrastructure. Thus, the use of the development budget allocated to the social sectors and social infrastructure needs to be extensively analyzed, and a strategy developed for increasing budget efficiency to reduce poverty in a cost-effective manner.

Microfinance has been extended to a large segment of the rural population. It is time to establish stronger ties between these small-scale enterprises and the formal sector by developing more effective marketing and distribution links with medium- and large-scale industries. Nongovernment institutions organized to assist small-scale industry can play a key role. These links will also enhance the role of the private sector in poverty reduction through generating employment and income for rural small-scale industries, many of which are run by women.

While the government has been actively promoting the private sector's role in the country's development effort, progress in privatizing state-owned enterprises has been slow. The current privatization board, which was established in 1993, lacks full legislative power. The bureaucracy, labor unions, and politicians with vested interest still exert strong resistance to privatization. However, substantial state-owned enterprise losses continue to drain the budget, consuming funds that could otherwise be used for poverty reduction.

The country's annual economic growth target of 7 percent envisaged in the Fifth Five-Year Plan remains unattainable, not because the country lacks economic potential, but because the growth prospects of the economy have been seriously clouded by internecine political conflicts, continuous general strikes (*hartals*) disrupting work, endemic corruption, and the general lack of good governance. Unless the country's political leadership becomes more enlightened and seriously sets itself to the task of addressing these issues, the economy may remain mired in poverty and underdevelopment for years to come.

Bhutan

Economic growth in Bhutan has been strong the past two years. If the government remains committed to the objective of the Eighth Five-Year Plan, including social sector improvements and privatization, continued rapid growth can be continued in 2000 and beyond.

RECENT TRENDS AND PROSPECTS

Economic growth in Bhutan registered 5.8 percent in 1998 and 6 percent in 1999, respectively. Construction activities expanded because of major hydropower and industrial projects. Per capita income grew more slowly as a result of a rapidly expanding population. With a per capita income of $480 in 1997, Bhutan is still one of the poorest countries in the world. While life in much of the country's rugged terrain can be harsh, many of the characteristics of poverty such as hunger, malnutrition, and degraded physical environment found in some parts of South Asia and among people of similar income are not evident.

The government continued to conduct a prudent fiscal policy, with current revenues exceeding current expenditures as they have since 1996. The government receives most of its current revenues as profits from public enterprises and service fees from the ministries, and tax revenues are primarily from enterprise and goods taxes. However, inflows of foreign grants have not been sufficient to cover development expenditures. This led to an overall budget deficit of 2.5 percent of GDP in 1999, in contrast to a 1 percent surplus the previous year. This was due mainly to a major increase in capital expenditures for hydropower projects. Inflation in 1999 was slightly more than the 9 percent recorded the previous year, mainly because food imports from India cost more. Money supply growth slowed from 41.7 percent in 1998 to 21.4 percent because foreign aid slowed and domestic credit declined, particularly to the government. Credit to the private sector increased slightly compared to the previous year.

The dollar value of exports declined 5.9 percent in 1999, compared with a strong growth of 12 percent in 1998, because regional external demand declined. Imports grew 20.5 percent because of import requirements for the large hydropower and industrial projects under construction. The combination of declining exports and rapidly increasing imports resulted in a substantial widening of the trade deficit,

1999 refers to fiscal year 1998/99, ending 30 June.

from 6.4 percent of GDP in 1998 to 15 percent in 1999. The current account deficit also widened from 12 percent of GDP to 25.8 percent. The trade balance with India, Bhutan's main trading partner, also turned from a slight surplus to a deficit of 4.8 percent of GDP. The current account deficit with India deteriorated to almost 19 percent of GDP in 1999 compared with 6.6 percent in 1998.

Capital flows, mostly grants for infrastructure investments, were more than sufficient to cover the current account deficit. This resulted in an overall balance-of-payments surplus of more than 26 percent of GDP in 1999. Consequently, international reserves at the end of the year increased to about $259 million, equivalent to almost 19 months of imports. External debt, all in the form of concessional financing from donor agencies, continued to be small. Total public external debt was less than 30 percent of GDP in 1999 and debt service was about 9 percent of merchandise export earnings. The composition of this debt has been changing, with less nonconvertible currency debt and more convertible currency debt. As the grace periods expire on the concessional debt acquired by Bhutan in the 1980s, the country's external balance will come under increasing pressure because of higher debt-service payments.

Bhutan has concluded two years of its ambitious Eighth Five-Year Plan, and the government has made satisfactory progress in reaching plan targets. It has expanded the physical infrastructure network, including constructing roads and adding to the power supply grid, and has built more schools and added health centers. To fund these projects, the government has relied on international donor support. In the future, there will be greater reliance on domestic resources. In this regard, the preparation for introducing a personal income tax should help broaden the tax base.

Projected GDP growth rate for 2000 is 6 percent, and if the government continues its commitment to the Eighth Plan, Bhutan should continue to experience annual output growth of more than 5.5 percent during 2001 and 2002, the end of the plan period.

ISSUES IN ECONOMIC MANAGEMENT

The government supports the Asian Development Bank's poverty reduction goal, which is consistent with its own objectives. A large housing scheme has been developed for urban dwellers. However, policymakers need to ensure that the program is financially sustainable. To this end, long-term financial mechanisms need to be put in place. Housing subsidies, if provided at all, should be given only to the lowest income groups. Private sector participation should also be encouraged.

Physical and social infrastructure need to be upgraded in various areas. Despite recent improvements in infrastructure development, road transport and power transmission urgently need improvement. In addition, vocational training needs to be strengthened, particularly in technical and semi-skilled occupations in which workers are in short supply.

POLICY AND DEVELOPMENT ISSUES

A major developmental challenge in the years ahead will be the absorption of the excess liquidity that has built up in the financial system, and the use of these funds to underpin private sector growth. The government is strongly committed to the growth of private sector activity. While several institutional, policy, and labor constraints remain, the government has been active in privatizing state-owned firms, promoting institutional and legislative reform, and upgrading domestic skills.

However, industrial policies, particularly with regard to foreign investment, remain ambiguous. While sectoral diversification and privatization have undoubtedly occurred, the industry sector is heavily concentrated on a narrow range of products. It is highly dependent on expatriate labor and is restricted by the small, fragmented domestic market and a narrow range of readily accessible export markets. It is also limited by inadequate and expensive transportation and constrained by national sensitivities concerning resource exploitation—especially in tourism and logging—and by caution regarding foreign investment and foreign labor. The main challenge facing the government is how to realize its commitment to private sector activity in the face of such constraints.

A series of legal and administrative changes are intended to improve government efficiency and increase administrative capacity. Several important bills were passed during the 77th session of the National

Assembly, including the Telecommunications Act, Road Safety and Transport Act, Bankruptcy Act, Immovable and Movable Property Act, and Municipal Act. These bills will strengthen the legal framework for a market-oriented economy and increase the capacity of the central and local government units to manage development on a sustainable basis. Under a new system, the King remains the head of state, but is no longer the head of government. This position now is rotated annually among the six members of the Cabinet of Ministers.

On 11 November 1999, the government released a report aimed at enhancing good governance by promoting efficiency, transparency, and accountability of government administration. Specific recommendations included measures to prevent corruption and abuse of authority. Reorganization of the government administration will be fully implemented by 2002. To further enhance efforts to strengthen government administration through decentralization, a two-year rolling budget will be introduced in 2000, and improved systems for budget planning and monitoring will be introduced. Although the overall external debt position is manageable, the new Department of Aid and Debt Management in the Ministry of Finance will consider all new loans cautiously, in the context of debt-servicing capabilities as well as manpower and skill constraints.

After consolidating and evaluating these measures, the government might consider additional actions to strengthen its planning and development framework to prepare for future development challenges, including reducing poverty and developing the private sector.

India

The recovery is being sustained, and the new government passed several important reform bills at the beginning of its term. However, the unfinished agenda of economic reform remains substantial. In particular, while reforms undertaken so far clearly have helped promote economic growth, progress has been less impressive in developing better social opportunities for the poor.

RECENT TRENDS AND PROSPECTS

The economic recovery that started at the end of 1998 continued in 1999, but at a slightly slower pace because of less growth in agriculture. GDP growth was slightly lower, at around 6 percent, than the 6.8 percent in 1998.

With below normal monsoon in some areas and serious damage from a cyclone that hit the Orissa coast in October 1999, agricultural growth slowed from 1998's strong performance of 7.2 percent to less than 1 percent. However, lower growth in the agriculture sector was partially offset by increased activity in industry and services. Industrial output increased 6.5 percent in contrast to a 4 percent rise the previous year. Double-digit growth in consumer durables, machinery, and cement boosted the sector. Automobiles and steel production also continued to record healthy growth rates. The growth rate of the service sector, which had declined modestly in 1998, bounced back to the previous level of about 8 percent.

1999 refers to fiscal year 1999/00, ending 31 March.

The primary concern of the Reserve Bank of India (RBI) in 1999 was to ensure adequate liquidity for the corporate sector while keeping inflation under control. Under the generally favorable policy environment, characterized by low inflation and a stable Indian rupee, the easing of monetary conditions continued in 1999, with the broad money supply (M3) growing at a comfortable 16 percent. The RBI managed the adverse effect of large government borrowing on interest rates with a blend of auctions, private placement, and open market operations. Sales of bonds to the private sector accounted for 40 percent of total government borrowing.

As the economy recovered in 1999, bank credit and other flows to the commercial sector increased. The RBI cut the cash reserve ratio three times, from 10.5 to 9 percent, and reduced the repurchase and bank rates by 2 percent and 1 percent, respectively. Consequently, bank credit to the commercial sector expanded 11 percent during the first nine months of 1999, compared with 7 percent the previous year.

Nonfood bank credit increased 9.3 percent, in contrast to an increase of 6.2 percent in 1998. The annual inflation rate remained remarkably low during the first half of the year before rising slowly in the second half. Inflation in terms of the wholesale price index was 3.3 percent, compared with 6.9 percent the previous year. The consumer price index for industrial workers also dropped, to 5.3 percent from 12.9 percent in 1998.

The deterioration of the fiscal balances of central and state governments continued, despite the consensus among various levels of government that these imbalances urgently needed correction (see figure 2.14). The combined fiscal deficit reached nearly 10 percent of GDP in 1999, the highest level recorded since 1990. The states' component of the deficit recorded a new high. The gross fiscal deficit of the central government rose to about 5.5 percent of GDP in 1999 from the previous year's 5 percent. The fiscal deficit on states' accounts exceeded 5 percent of GDP. The deterioration in state's finances was not due as much as to a decline in revenues, as in the case of the

central government, but a result primarily of sharp increases in wage expenditures.

The balance-of-payments position remained stable in 1999. Despite the surge in oil prices, the current account deficit was contained below 1.5 percent of GDP because of the solid performance of exports. With the rebound in Asia and recovery in the global economy, exports grew at more than 10 percent in dollar terms after a disappointing 3.9 percent drop in 1998. Manufactured products accounted for 80 percent of exports. Imports also recovered, growing at 9 percent for the year compared with 1998's 0.9 percent growth. The growth of imports was fuelled primarily by the substantial increase in the prices of crude oil and petroleum products, although this was partially offset by a decline in non-oil imports.

Encouraged by the improved economic outlook and increased political stability, foreign investment flowed in strongly, with $3.1 billion during the first nine months of 1999—almost three times as much as the $1.1 billion during the same period in 1998.

Table 2.15 Major Economic Indicators, India, 1997-2001
(percent)

Item	1997	1998	1999	2000	2001
GDP growth[a]	5.0	6.8	5.9	7.0	7.0
Gross domestic investment/GDP	26.2	23.4	22.5	24.0	25.0
Gross domestic savings/GDP	24.7	22.3	21.0	22.0	23.0
Inflation rate (wholesale price index)	4.8	6.9	3.3	4.8	5.0
Money supply (M3) growth	18.0	18.4	16.0	17.0	17.0
Fiscal balance/GDP	-4.8	-5.0	-5.5	-5.0	-4.0
Merchandise exports growth	4.5	-3.9	10.0	4.5	5.0
Merchandise imports growth	4.6	0.9	9.0	7.0	8.0
Current account balance/GDP	-1.3	-1.0	-1.5	-1.8	-1.8
Total debt/GDP[b]	24.7	24.4	23.5	22.3	22.0

Note: All figures are on a fiscal year basis.

a. Based on constant 1993/94 factor cost.

b. At end-March.

Sources: Central Statistical Organization (1999); Reserve Bank of India (1998); Ministry of Finance (2000).

**Figure 2.14 Fiscal Deficit as Percentage of GDP,
India, 1990-1999**

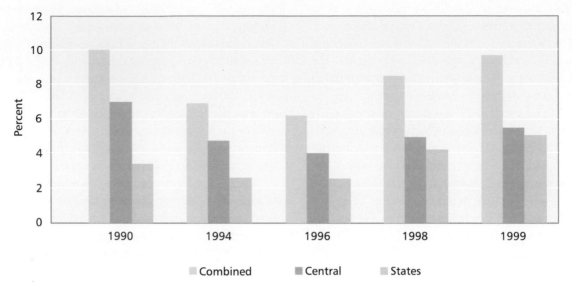

Note: For 1990-1999, positive percentage rates are fiscal deficit.
Source: Reserve Bank of India (various issues).

Portfolio investment turned around significantly, with $1.2 billion of net inflows in 1999 in contrast to $752 million of outflows the previous year. Foreign direct investment inflows fell relative to the previous year, from $1.56 billion to $1.19 billion. However, in a major policy decision in February 2000, the government granted automatic clearance for all foreign direct investment except in a few sensitive sectors. Foreign exchange reserves, except for gold and special drawing rights, were an estimated $32 billion (8 months of import equivalent), an increase of $2.5 billion from the previous year. The pressure on the exchange rate eased considerably, reflecting the revival of the Asian economies and a generally more favorable external environment. Consequently, the Indian rupee depreciated much less than it did the previous year.

With a significant slowdown of economic growth in recent years, concern exists that India may slip again into low growth. It needs to sustain 7-8 percent growth

per year to make significant progress toward reducing poverty. However, with the encouraging outcomes of the election in late 1999, optimism is renewed concerning economic prospects. The new government has a significant majority and a forceful leader with a clear vision to carry out new structural reforms. Simultaneously, a recovery is being sustained, aided by a favorable external environment. Meanwhile, a global technological revolution is helping India benefit from its own "new economy" boom.

The status of public finance remains a serious cause for concern, but the government is addressing the problem via tax reforms and expenditure cuts. With continuing recovery in industrial production and the service sector, the GDP growth rate is projected to increase to 7 percent for 2000 and 2001. The balance of payments is likely to remain stable, with the current account deficit at 1.8 percent of GDP. Exports and imports will both grow more slowly, while the services balance should remain relatively stable. Changes in regulation governing the inflow of foreign direct investment combined with a strong foreign interest in portfolio investment (particularly in technology stocks) is expected to further accelerate the inflow of foreign investment. The RBI will continue its effort to contain inflation at less than 5 percent per year, while providing sufficient credit to the productive sectors of the economy.

ISSUES IN ECONOMIC MANAGEMENT

During its first two months in office, the new government passed the first hurdle in implementing the next phase of reforms. The new insurance bill, which will open the insurance market to the private sector, is a significant first step. Nevertheless, the unfinished agenda of economic reform remains substantial. Reforms that have already begun—reducing protection levels, developing efficient financial and capital markets, and expediting public enterprise reforms—should be completed swiftly, preferably within a defined timeframe. In those areas where reforms have not yet gained momentum, such as fiscal consolidation, labor market, and power sector, it is urgent that these reforms be addressed.

Of particular importance is the need to expand the reform process to state and local governments. Indications are clear that the top levels of the government, as well as the corporate sector, are convinced of the urgency of carrying out economic reforms. However, most state governments and the lower levels of line ministries, which are directly responsible for implementing reforms, are neither fully aware of the urgency of the effort nor equipped to implement them.

Similarly, the capability of the system to put the proposed reform measures into action is also in serious doubt because of institutional weaknesses inherited from the past. The inefficient and oversized bureaucracy and the outdated and nonresponsive legal system are examples. Without efficient administrative and legal systems, the high transaction costs involved in processing the reform agenda will outweigh the potential benefits of reforms. Capacity building and institutional reforms are urgently needed to improve the processing of reforms.

POLICY AND DEVELOPMENT ISSUES

Both the political situation and the external economic environment have been volatile in 1995-1999. However, neither the frequent changes of government nor the financial crisis in East Asia had a lasting impact on the general direction of economic reforms. The consensus on economic reforms not only survived the four changes of government since 1996, but was strengthened through these changes. In terms of external economic environment, the adverse impact of the East Asian economic crisis on India's economy was limited. Sanctions imposed by G7 countries following nuclear tests by India and Pakistan in May 1998 added new uncertainties, but their effect has been marginal.

Although the broad direction of economic reforms has been maintained in recent years, there have been signs of reform fatigue. The initial urge and excitement generated by the reform process abated as the economy recovered from the 1991 crisis. Consequently, the ability of policymakers to make radical changes greatly diminished and special interest groups blocked the progress of reforms on several occasions.

With the slowing of reforms, it became evident that the growth impulses generated by the first generation of reforms had ebbed by the mid-1990s. Industrial growth significantly decelerated and export growth fell. Infrastructure bottlenecks began to hamper the expansion of private sector economic activities. Poverty, illiteracy, and lack of basic health care were aggravated by the worsening environment. The slowdown in GDP growth in 1997-1998 raises a serious question: does the economic slowdown reflect underlying structural impediments that could lead to lower growth if not tackled urgently?

At the core of the reform process lies the reorientation of the government's role to improve efficiency and raise the long-term economic growth potential. Traditionally, the government has controlled private sector activity through various licensing schemes and has produced important goods and services though public sector enterprises. Excessive intervention of government in economic activities was inefficient, however. Therefore, remaining reforms should withdraw unnecessary government interference and refine the role of the state in economic management. Reforms must ensure that the private sector, not the government, is in charge of raising production, creating jobs, and increasing income levels.

Dependence on the private sector and markets does not mean that the government has no role. Reorienting its contribution to the economy is crucial, and government can help create conditions for accelerated growth. For instance, a sound macroeconomic environment—characterized by prudent fiscal policy, an efficient monetary and financial regime, and market-determined exchange rate policies—is essential to attract private investors. International rating agencies issued a warning in 1999 that the fiscal deficit had grown again to unsustainable levels during the past several years. Although there is yet no sign of imminent macroeconomic crisis, lack of fiscal prudence pushed up interest rates. This deters private investment and increases interest costs for government and private firms.

Second, infrastructure bottlenecks are likely to constrain the achievement of a higher growth rate of 7 percent and above. The infrastructure system is overstrained and suffered from underinvestment in the post-reform period. Massive investments will be needed in both public and private sectors to overcome these bottlenecks. A two-pronged approach is required: mobilizing private investment to supplement the public sector effort, and garnering public investment in the many sectors where private investment is difficult to mobilize.

Third, the poor state of human resource development is an even more serious constraint to sustainable development. Clearly, people will not be able to use the new opportunities offered by economic growth if they remain illiterate and lack the basic skills required by modern industries. Creating conditions for accelerated growth is not sufficient unless people are ready to participate in the growth process and use opportunities to integrate with the world market. Large investment in social sectors is therefore essential not only for social development, but also as a precondition for accelerating growth. One important aspect is the role of the states in undertaking remedial actions to rectify the poor social development record. Because

state governments are responsible for social sector investments, fiscal reforms and restructuring at the state level are critical for increasing expenditures on the social sectors, particularly in primary and secondary education and health and sanitation.

Fourth, restructuring public sector enterprises through disinvestment or privatization must be accelerated. One positive development after the 1999 election was the acceptance of the notion of privatization. The ruling coalition advocated privatization in its electoral platform, becoming the first political party to use the word officially. With the dissolution of the Disinvestment Commission at the end of November 1999, the government set up its own committee to provide recommendations and modalities for privatization. This committee will be crucial if the coalition government takes advantage of improving economic conditions and its majority in Parliament to initiate a major drive toward privatizing some state assets.

The economic reforms undertaken have yielded good results, but progress has been less impressive in terms of better social opportunities for the poor. From the beginning of the reform process, the government tried to keep its commitment to traditional poverty alleviation programs that existed before the reforms. These included direct support to the poor by subsidized sale of food grains and kerosene, job-creating public works programs, and a variety of self-employment programs that provided small loans. However, the real issue has been the effectiveness of these programs. Recognizing high costs and minimal impact, the government considered phasing out some antipoverty programs and reallocating part of the savings to improve social services, especially health, education, and family welfare. This shift was motivated by the recognition that a fresh perspective is probably more effective than marginal expansions in traditional schemes.

The government needs to spend more in education and health, but not only because investments in human capital are instrumental for economic growth. While education and better health clearly have value in making people more productive and generating more outputs and incomes, the elimination of illiteracy, ill health, and other deprivations are valuable for their own sake. The adverse effect of persistent illiteracy, for example, goes beyond limited economic opportunities. It constrains a person's freedom and well-being, and has a direct role in the relative deprivation of women in particular. It sustains high mortality and fertility rates. It also contributes to the comparative lack of pressure for social change, and to the weakness of political demand and pressure for effective public attention in fields such as health care.

Maldives

The Maldives continued its strong economic growth in 1999, mainly because of favorable developments in the tourism and fisheries sectors. To continue sustainable economic growth, the country will need to expedite structural reforms, including fiscal consolidation and human resource development.

RECENT TRENDS AND PROSPECTS

During 1996-1998, the Maldives' economy grew by 8-9 percent. This strong performance resulted from favorable developments in transportation, communications, utilities, tourism, fisheries, and manufacturing, particularly garments. For 1999, growth was an estimated 8.5 percent, with tourist arrivals increasing about 10 percent to more than 400,000. Increased growth in tourism continued to facilitate the expansion of construction, the growth of transportation subsectors, and the development of basic infrastructure facilities. Although the fisheries sector remained buoyant, fish export earnings declined because of a fall in fish prices in the international market. Because fish is the principal food item in the Maldives, the increase in fish production favorably affected inflation, with the annual average inflation rate estimated at about 3 percent in 1999.

The fiscal deficit worsened slightly in 1999 to 6 percent of GDP, in contrast to 5.3 percent of GDP the previous year. The deteriorating fiscal position partly resulted from higher expenditures on wages

of public sector employees, which increased about 30 percent on average.

The unemployment rate is low in the Maldives. Estimates suggest that more than 20 percent of the labor force are expatriates and this share is growing. Rapid economic development and the reluctance of Maldivians to work in unskilled occupations have resulted in increased recruiting of expatriate workers to fill these vacancies. Simultaneously, there is a shortage of high-skilled and professional labor. These positions are also being filled by overseas recruitment.

In the external sector, the current account deficit deteriorated further to 10 percent of GDP, compared with about 7 percent in 1998. This was primarily due to increased imports associated with tourism sector investments. The current account deficit, however, was more than offset by private capital inflows, which increased the official reserves to the equivalent of more than four months of imports. External debt as a percent of GDP reached 51.5 percent in 1998 and increased slightly to 52 percent in 1999. The debt-service ratio remained below 4 percent for the past five years except in 1997, when it increased to 7.2 percent because a $15 million loan from the Kuwait Fund for balance-of-payment support was repaid fully. This low level of debt service was possible because most of the debt consisted of concessional foreign assistance.

While the country remains potentially vulnerable to economic shocks because of its dependence on tourism and fishing, the economic outlook for the medium term remains promising. Growth should be around 7 percent in 2000, mainly strengthened by a continued increase in tourist arrivals. Inflation is expected to average about 3 percent in 2000 and beyond, because of a prudent macroeconomic policy stance and favorable external conditions. The current account deficit is expected to fall slightly to 6 percent of GDP in 2000 and 2001 because of strong growth in the tourism and fisheries sectors.

ISSUES IN ECONOMIC MANAGEMENT

Deterioration of the fiscal balance in 1999, coupled with the declining trend in concessional external assistance such as grants, highlights the need to strengthen the government's narrow revenue base. On average, nontax revenue consists of more than half of total revenue, and combined tax receipts from tourism and import duties amounted to 60 percent of tax revenue during 1995-1998. In this regard, tax reform is needed to broaden the tax base and enhance public sector efficiency. The government is preparing to introduce a business profit tax and a property rental value tax to broaden the current tax base, and intends to upgrade the institutional capacity and valuation system of the customs service to improve import duty collections.

The administrative capacity of the government in key agencies also needs improvement. This includes enhancing public sector management, introducing legal and judicial reforms, and restructuring state-owned enterprises. Furthermore, financial sector development is needed to enhance economic efficiency, including promoting competition in the banking sector, increasing the availability of long-term finance, developing capital markets, and strengthening the Maldives Monetary Authority.

POLICY AND DEVELOPMENT ISSUES

Human resource development (HRD) is a high priority, with two distinct goals: to sustain higher economic growth and to address regional disparities between the outer islands and the main urban centers. The dearth of sufficiently skilled workers is a serious obstacle to achieving national development objectives, and continued efforts in HRD will be required to reduce the dependence on expatriate labor and save foreign exchange. Institutional development of the education sector is important to further enhance HRD. An important government strategy is to pool resources; unify the management function; and improve the range, quality, and comprehensiveness of the courses offered at training institutes. This initiative also provides for staff training and institutional development. The HRD strategy should further target quality improvement through curriculum development, expansion of secondary education and distance learning, and skill development through vocational training.

With regard to regional disparities, government estimates indicate that 22 percent of the country's population has a daily income of less than Rf10 ($0.84), and most of them reside in the outer islands. Regional development, including basic social and physical infrastructure and institution-building in the outer islands, is essential for medium- to long-term HRD.

Greater emphasis on HRD, particularly education, is necessary to improve skills in the labor force that are required to help the private sector to become an engine of economic development. To sustain a higher rate of economic growth, these efforts must be complemented by capacity building of government agencies, financial sector reform, and legal and judicial reform.

Nepal

Because of a recovery in agricultural production, the short-term prospects for Nepal's macroeconomy are promising. The new government needs to advance a broad-based reform agenda to sustain this growth. The need to reduce poverty and promote gender equity also raises challenges.

RECENT TRENDS AND PROSPECTS

The macroeconomy was stable in 1999, despite the uncertainty caused by a change in government. Real GDP growth rose to 3.3 percent from 2.3 percent the previous year, led by better performance in the agriculture and industry sectors. However, this growth in production barely exceeded the population growth of 2.4 percent. Consequently, with a per capita GDP of $210, Nepal ranks as among the poorest countries in the region, lower than most of its South Asian neighbors. While the 3.0 percent growth in agriculture fell short of projections in the Agriculture Perspective Plan, which details the agricultural development strategy for two decades, the increase from the previous year's 1 percent growth was promising, considering that poor weather conditions continued to hamper farmers.

Consistent with an economy dominated by subsistence agriculture, the labor force participation rate was high and the unemployment rate low. About 86 percent of the working-age population (aged 15 and above) is economically active, with 73 percent employed in agriculture. The unemployment rate for the country was less than 2 percent, but the rate in urban areas was higher than 7 percent.

Driven by rising food prices, inflation rose to nearly 13 percent in 1999, from 4 percent the previous year. Poor monsoon conditions led to dramatic increases in the prices of food grains and vegetables. Exports of rice also prevented the usual downturn in price after the main harvest, and the food and beverages index rose by 17.3 percent. Inflation from nonfood items, however, was only 4.3 percent, down nearly 1 percent from the previous year. This was due to the stability of key administered prices, notably kerosene, electricity, and diesel. High money growth continued despite slower inflows of foreign assets. Broad money (M2) increased by about 21 percent in 1999, slightly less than the 22 percent the previous year because of the slow inflow of foreign assets.

The budget deficit remained at 6.1 percent of GDP in 1999, despite additional expenses from the

1999 refers to fiscal year 1998/99, ending 15 July.

elections. Preliminary data for 1999 show that domestic revenue collection was substantially lower than the budgeted amount, with actual revenue about 10 percent of GDP, roughly the same as in 1998. The shortfall in revenues was balanced by slower-than-budgeted growth in development expenditures, which rose 9 percent rather than the 26 percent envisaged in the 1999 budget. Even with slower growth, foreign grants and loans financed about 65 percent of development expenditures, compared with 50 percent in the early 1990s, a situation that is unlikely to change in the coming years.

Nepal's current account deficit declined dramatically in 1999 because of strong export growth and a contraction in imports, mainly in aid-related items because of weak investment activity before the elections. Non-aid imports were roughly the same as previous years. While loan disbursements from aid agencies also slowed before the elections, foreign exchange reserves continued to rise. By the end of the year, Nepal had $797 million in foreign exchange reserves (almost seven months of import equivalent). External debt as a percent of GDP rose in 1998, with the inflow of foreign aid reaching 54 percent of GDP. However, because of the concessional nature of this lending, the debt-service ratio for external debt was a manageable 6.1 percent of exports in 1998 (see figure 2.15).

A favorable monsoon season and wider use of fertilizer led to a strong recovery in agriculture during the first quarter of 2000. Production of food grains, particularly rice, and vegetables was expected to be above average, leading to GDP growth of 5-6 percent for the year. Early indicators for the tourism, carpet, and garment industries also suggested strong performance. However, with no large projects upcoming until the end of the year, electricity growth should remain slow. Price performance in 2000 will also benefit from bumper harvests throughout the region. The price of rice, which makes up most of the expenditures in the price index, will probably decline after the harvest. Therefore, Nepal can achieve an inflation target of 5 percent in 2000 (rather than the current 7 percent target) with the support of appropriate monetary policy, despite the high-profile increases in prices of kerosene, diesel, and electricity.

Table 2.16 Major Economic Indicators, Nepal, 1997-2001
(percent)

Item	1997	1998	1999	2000	2001
GDP growth	5.0	2.3	3.3	5.5	5.5
Gross domestic investment/GDP	25.3	20.7	17.3	20.0	22.0
Gross domestic savings/GDP	12.1	9.5	10.6	11.7	11.7
Inflation rate (consumer price index)	7.8	4.0	12.7	5.0	5.0
Money supply (M2) growth	11.9	21.9	20.9	14.0	12.0
Fiscal balance/GDP[a]	-5.1	-6.0	-6.1	-7.1	-7.5
Merchandise exports growth	10.2	11.9	20.3	10.0	12.0
Merchandise imports growth	21.7	-12.4	-10.5	15.0	15.0
Current account balance/GDP	-6.0	-5.5	-3.5	-8.0	-9.5
Debt-service/exports	4.5	6.1	6.5	6.5	6.5

Notes: Data are on a fiscal year basis. Data on savings were derived as a residual.

a. Includes grants.

Sources: Central Bureau of Statistics; Nepal Rastra Bank; staff estimates.

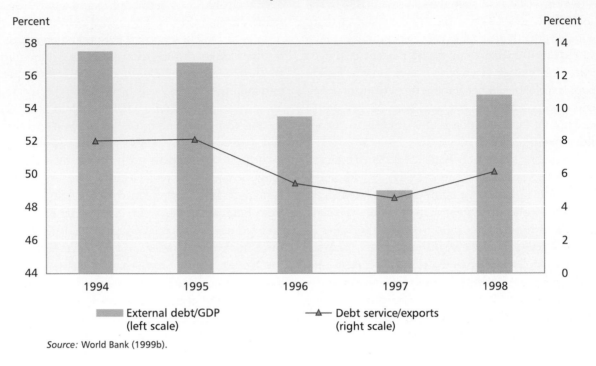

Figure 2.15 External Debt and Debt-Service Ratio, Nepal, 1994-1998

External debt/GDP (left scale)

Debt service/exports (right scale)

Source: World Bank (1999b).

The peg with the Indian rupee provides a useful nominal anchor for the economy, but to sustain it the central bank must reduce the inflation and interest rate differentials with India. A target of 14 percent expansion in broad money (M2) for 2000—with some slowing in 2001—would be consistent with the goal of parity with India, given growth and inflation projections. The central bank needs to liquidate its holdings of Treasury bills, which were acquired through converting the government's overdraft in its budgetary operations. This can help eliminate the negative real interest rates on these instruments and bring the overall interest rate structure in line with India's.

Development expenditures in the 2000 budget are projected to grow by 33 percent. These will be financed mainly by foreign grants, which are projected to increase by 47 percent. Domestic revenue estimates in the current budget are similarly optimistic, with a projected growth rate of 14 percent. Actual revenue performance will hinge on the effective implementa-

tion of the value-added tax. The minimum revenue level for firms covered by the value-added tax was lowered from NRs4.5 million to NRs2 million, and the registration of firms was accelerated to widen the tax base. As in past years, development expenditures probably will bear any shortfalls in domestic revenues and foreign grants. However, preliminary first quarter 2000 figures suggest that the government's ambitious revenue and development expenditure targets are achievable, even with the increase in allowances for civil servants. The fiscal deficit for 2000 is projected to reach 7 percent of GDP and to continue to rise in 2001.

The current account deficit should widen in 2000 as aid-related imports return to their previous levels, particularly if the government succeeds in its ambitious development agenda. Merchandise imports are projected to grow 15 percent, with investment goods expanding faster than consumer goods imports. Export growth should continue to be strong in 2000, but will slow without the grain exports of the previous year. The current account deficit is thus expected to reach about 8 percent of GDP in 2000 and more than 9 percent of GDP in 2001. The debt-service ratio should remain around 6 percent of GDP, as much of this debt is concessional.

ISSUES IN ECONOMIC MANAGEMENT

The government's long-term Agriculture Perspective Plan aims to break this sector's dependence on weather by expanding irrigation facilities, improving the distribution of inputs such as fertilizer, diversifying crops, and expanding rural infrastructure. Under this plan, the monopoly of the state-owned Agricultural Inputs Corporation on the import and distribution of fertilizer has been eliminated, price subsidies on all fertilizers have been removed, and private sector trading in fertilizer is on the rise. In the distribution of food grains, the role of the state-owned Nepal Food Corporation is being altered to promote more private sector activity. The government must continue the momentum for reform in this sector and maintain the progress made by avoiding the political temptation to reintroduce subsidies or state-owned monopolies.

While the newly elected majority government raised expectations of reform, progress has been limited. The increase in value-added tax registrations is promising, but filling key vacancies in this department is needed to improve administration, clear the filing backlog, initiate collection visits, and intensify audit activity. The government also raised prices of kerosene, diesel, and electricity. Despite vocal public protests against these measures and a special parliamentary session called by the opposition to review the price increases, the government has stood firm. However, if the country is to achieve the levels of sustained growth necessary to lift it out of poverty, the government needs to take advantage of its majority position to pursue a broad-based reform agenda, with financial sector reform and civil service reform as the core.

POLICY AND DEVELOPMENT ISSUES

Looking beyond the medium-term macroeconomic issues, the government must consider strategies for reducing poverty and raising women's status. In addition to the equity considerations, the barriers faced by women and the poor limit their ability to provide the basic needs of their families. The system perpetuates itself, as most disadvantaged groups lack the resources to invest in their children's education and health. The people in the poorest regions of the country have the least access to basic health services and the highest rates of infant mortality and child malnutrition.

In Nepal, roughly 42 percent of the total population live in poverty, but the incidence of poverty is only 23 percent in urban areas, compared with 44 percent in rural areas. Geographically, the incidence of poverty in the mid-western and far-western regions greatly exceeds the national average, as does the rate in the mountain districts. Castes with lower social status had higher rates of poverty, as did those without the benefit of education.

One of the chief concerns of the Ninth Five-Year Plan (1998-2002) is poverty reduction, with the objective of reducing poverty incidence by 10 percent by the end of the plan period. However, the breadth of the plan in terms of its targets—covering everything from agricultural production to sports facilities—means the impact on poverty often is lost when the programs are implemented. A more focused plan is needed to provide a comprehensive framework directed toward the primary goal. The government's ongoing review of the Ninth Plan should emphasize the impact on poverty when prioritizing development projects, particularly in view of the emphasis on poverty alleviation by the major donors. In addition, improved information for monitoring the impact of specific projects on poverty is necessary for planning purposes.

Nepal is one of the poorest countries in the world, and its women are among the most disadvantaged. Although there is wide variation across the numerous ethnic groups, the status of women is always lower than that of their male counterparts. Women also lag behind men in access to education, and in ownership and access to assets.

Despite this, women in Nepal have made progress. Women's life expectancy has increased by more than 15 years within the last two decades, although men still live longer on average. The number of women who die in childbirth has decreased, to 539 per 100,000 live births, a vast improvement from the 1980s when the rate was about 50 percent higher. Women are now slightly older when they marry, which has led to a decline in the fertility rate. In education, the gains made by women have been dramatic. Twenty years ago, only 4 percent of the women were literate, and now the rate is 27 percent. For girls, the net enrollment rate has risen to 72 percent for primary school and to 31 percent for lower secondary school. However, men are still more likely to be literate than women, and boys have reached full enrollment in primary school.

Women's economic participation is limited mainly to agricultural production within the household. While the male labor force has been shifting toward manufacturing and services, more than 85 percent of economically active women are in agriculture. Men, however, control the chief inputs to this production: land and real property. These are passed down paternally and a woman's claim to these assets is determined by marriage. It is difficult for women to raise financial capital because they cannot own land, and hence are unlikely to have the necessary collateral. Lower levels of schooling and skills training can prevent women moving from agriculture to other sectors. The preference within households for educating sons and arranging early marriages of daughters reinforces the status quo. Social customs present more hurdles for the women to participate in the economy. In some communities of the southern plains, women are not allowed to mix freely with men.

Nepal's constitution guarantees fundamental rights to all citizens, equal treatment before the law, and equal pay for similar work regardless of gender.

However, these ideals have not been codified in any specific legislation, and the body of family law contains elements that contradict the principle of gender equity. For example, inheritance laws condition a woman's right to parental assets on her age and marital status, and a widow forfeits her claim to her former husband's property if she remarries. The inheritance rights of men, however, are not subject to such conditions. Women have no claims to community property in divorce and spousal support is limited to five years. While the cultural view of women's place in Nepalese society will change slowly over time, the government should work through appropriate legislative reforms toward the principles of gender equity that are espoused in the constitution.

However, legal reforms alone are not enough. For example, prohibitions on violence against women and trafficking in children already exist, but enforcement is often lax. The Ninth Plan proposes to include gender issues in government activities and direct activities to eliminate gender inequalities. Specific action is needed, such as developing women's health programs and ensuring that women do not disproportionately suffer from negative developments such as involuntary resettlement. Improving income-earning capacity is important if women are to become aware of their rights, take advantage of programs offered, and provide feedback for better meeting their needs. Improving conditions for women also will yield important social benefits such as lower population growth and infant mortality, and better health and education for children. Improving women's opportunities helps the families of these women break out of the poverty cycle.

Pakistan

The economy has been slowly recovering since the second half of 1999 because of improved agricultural performance. However, the balance of payments remains fragile and the long economic stagnation hampers the government's efforts to reduce rampant poverty. Medium-term economic prospects depend on political stability, structural reforms, and capital inflows.

RECENT TRENDS AND PROSPECTS

Pakistan faced a challenging year in 1999, with GDP growth declining to 3.1 percent from 4.3 percent in 1998. Following nuclear tests in late May 1998, economic sanctions imposed by G7 countries seriously affected the economy. Economic growth declined steeply as investors lost confidence, private capital flows virtually ceased, and the new official development assistance was suspended. Consequently, Pakistan faced a severe foreign exchange crisis with foreign exchange reserves declining to $415 million in November 1998 (two weeks of import equivalent). To prevent sovereign default, the government adopted short-term emergency policies that included freezing foreign currency deposits held by both residents and nonresidents in domestic banks, adopting a dual exchange rate system, and delaying servicing of foreign debt.

In January 1999, the economic sanctions were partially waived, and international financial institutions subsequently revived their assistance. At a meeting of the Paris Club later that month, the government and bilateral creditors agreed to reschedule official debt worth $3.3 billion. In early July 1999, Pakistan concluded an agreement with the London Club for rescheduling $877.3 million in commercial loans. All these activities helped build up foreign exchange reserves and revive economic growth. By the end of June 1999, foreign reserves reached $1.7 billion (two months of imports).

Both savings and investment rates declined because of slow economic growth and collapse of investors' confidence. Gross domestic investment dropped from 17.1 percent of GDP in 1998 to 14.8 percent in 1999. The decline in investment in manufacturing, construction, and energy sectors offset the rising fixed investment in agriculture, transportation, and telecommunications by the private sector. Poor stock market performance also contributed to the slower growth in investment, although public sector investment increased by 12.6 percent in nominal terms. Gross national saving as percentage of gross national product

1999 refers to fiscal year 1998/99, ending 30 June.

also slowed from 14.2 percent in 1998 to 11.1 percent in 1999.

The fiscal and monetary areas, however, showed encouraging signs. Structural reform measures to reduce the fiscal deficit included: (a) increasing the general sales tax rate from 12.5 to 15 percent, (b) increasing petroleum product tax rates, (c) reducing budgeted current consumption expenditures, and (d) reducing the federal subsidy on wheat. Consequently, the fiscal deficit declined from 6.3 percent of GDP in 1997 to 5.6 percent in 1998, and further to 3.7 percent in 1999. While the customs duty collection declined sharply because of a reduction in tariff rates and negative import growth, an increase in general sales tax revenues helped boost tax collection. Nontax revenue collection also increased. Meanwhile, public expenditures were held in check, and total expenditure as a percent of GDP increased only marginally. Actual development expenditure was 17 percent lower than the budget target for 1999.

Because of tight monetary policy, the growth of broad money (M2) remained at 6.3 percent in 1999, slower than most years in the past decade. The government retired PRs68.4 billion of domestic debt because of a lower fiscal deficit and debt rescheduling. However, because of weakened investors' confidence and the recovery campaign for defaulted loans, credit expansion to the private sector was much slower than the previous year. Tight monetary policy, coupled with prudent fiscal management and slower growth in aggregate demand, helped weaken inflationary pressures. The inflation rate declined to 5.7 percent from 7.8 percent in 1998.

Imports and exports in 1999 contracted by 10.7 percent and 6.7 percent, respectively. The Asian financial crisis adversely affected exports, while government policy measures pursued after the economic sanctions and slow growth in the industry sector contributed to a sharp decrease in imports. In the service sector, workers' remittances and foreign currency account deposits dropped sharply. Overall, the current account deficit was $1.8 billion or 2.7 percent of GDP, the same level as in 1998.

Economic performance in the first half of 2000 exhibited a slow but fragile recovery. While industrial growth remained sluggish because of low investment,

Table 2.17 **Major Economic Indicators, Pakistan, 1997-2001**
(percent)

Item	1997	1998	1999	2000	2001
GDP growth[a]	1.9	4.3	3.1	4.5	5.0
Gross domestic investment/GDP	17.7	17.1	14.8	15.1	15.9
Gross national savings/GNP	11.3	14.2	11.1	12.5	13.0
Inflation rate (consumer price index)	11.8	7.8	5.7	5.0	6.0
Money supply (M2) growth	12.2	14.5	6.3	10.0	9.0
Fiscal balance/GDP	-6.3	-5.6	-3.7	-3.7	-3.5
Merchandise exports growth	-2.6	4.2	-10.7	8.0	9.0
Merchandise imports growth	-6.4	-8.4	-6.7	9.5	9.0
Current account balance/GDP	-5.6	-2.7	-2.7	-2.5	-2.0
Debt-service ratio	24.7	—	—	—	—

— Not available.

a. Based on constant factor cost.

Sources: IMF (2000); State Bank of Pakistan (1999); Government of Pakistan (1999); staff estimates.

an improvement in agriculture sector performance partially offset it. The cotton crop reached 10.5 million bales, about 20 percent higher than the previous year, and the rice crop improved as well. Revenue collection in the first five months was about 20 percent higher than the previous year and slightly above the target level. Because of tight monetary policy and sluggish economic growth, from July to December 1999 the inflation rate remained low at 3.4 percent, in contrast with 6 percent during the same period in 1998.

Despite sustained improvement in trade and current account balances, the balance of payments remained fragile. Export earnings during the first half of 2000 picked up by 7.4 percent, but imports increased significantly by 11.5 percent, mainly because of the sharp rise in world market prices of petroleum products. Consequently, the trade deficit reached $783 million during the first half of 2000, compared with $563 million during the same period the previ-

ous year. The current account deficit narrowed to $1.8 billion in 1999, owing to a substantial reduction in services payments and imports. The foreign exchange reserves stood at $1.5 billion in January 2000 (two months of imports), and the exchange rate remained stable (see figure 2.16).

The medium-term outlook depends critically on political stability and the pace of economic reforms. If the government promptly implements major structural reforms and maintains macroeconomic stability, GDP growth is projected to be 4.5 percent in 2000 and 5 percent in 2001. While industry growth may remain stagnant because of slow investment growth and some structural adjustment measures—such as increases in tax rates and input prices—the agriculture sector could rebound because of increased agricultural investment by the government. Inflation is expected to rise in the second half of 2000 as money supply increases. Because of the expected increase in tax collection, the fiscal

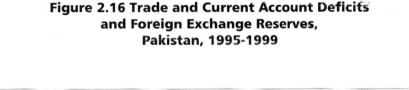

Figure 2.16 Trade and Current Account Deficits and Foreign Exchange Reserves, Pakistan, 1995-1999

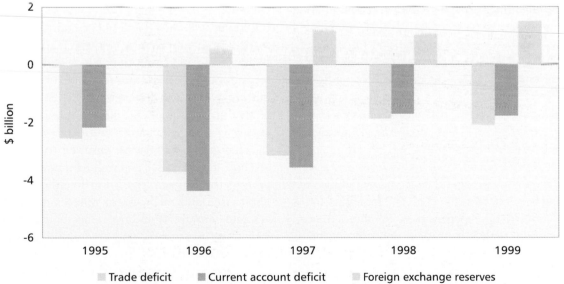

Note: Foreign exchange reserves data are not available for 1995.
Source: State Bank of Pakistan (1999).

deficit is forecast to decline to 3.7 percent of GDP in 2000 and 3.5 percent the next year. Resolving several export issues, such as financing for letters of credit, would maintain robust growth of exports, which are projected to grow by 8 percent in 2000 and 9 percent in 2001. Imports may grow at a slightly higher rate. The current account deficit is projected at 2.5 percent and 2 percent of GDP in 2000 and 2001, respectively.

ISSUES IN ECONOMIC MANAGEMENT

Although Pakistan emerged gradually from the worst phase of the crisis, the economic situation remains fragile. Some of the emergency measures taken over the last two years have long-term adverse implications for economic development. Credibility with official and private creditors was seriously damaged because of freezing foreign currency accounts and delaying servicing of foreign debt. A significant decline in public spending on development programs could also harm the long-term growth potential.

The primary area of concern remains the balance-of-payments position. The traditional sources of capital inflows—foreign aid, short-term commercial lending, and portfolio investments—are expected to weaken in coming years. The deterioration in the terms of trade threatens the ability to achieve the trade deficit target of $1.2 billion in 2000. While the debt rescheduling provides a two-year relief period for debt service, in January 2001 the government will have to resume a substantial repayment of foreign debt. Because foreign aid is the only reliable source of capital inflows, increasing disbursement of foreign aid projects and fulfilling policy reforms promptly are crucial for improving the balance of payments. In particular, export sector issues need to be vigorously addressed, including providing export finance for indirect exporters and small and medium-size enterprises, improving product quality and marketing, and allowing better access to technical information to increase industrial competitiveness. Resolving the ongoing dispute with independent power producers is vital for restructuring the power sector and regaining foreign investors' confidence.

The high interest rates of about 10 percent in real terms discourage private investment. To encourage demand for bank credit from a private sector that is facing a high input cost structure, the nominal average interest rate needs to be reduced at least 3-4 percentage points. This may require a corresponding reduction in deposit rates on the National Savings Scheme. The sustained large budget deficit, financed by government borrowing from financial markets, is the major cause of these high real interest rates. It crowds out financial resources available for lending to the private sector and increases the cost of borrowing. Therefore, reducing the budget deficit is essential.

POLICY AND DEVELOPMENT ISSUES

Pakistan has once again approached a crossroad. The new government faces difficult challenges that include slow economic growth; extremely low private sector confidence; unsustainable domestic and foreign debt obligations; and a rapid rise in the number of the poor, both in rural and urban areas.

The new government urgently needs to undertake fundamental reforms. Aside from speeding up economic growth and structural reforms, Pakistan must address social issues and improve governance, with special attention to social development and protecting poor and vulnerable groups.

Weak governance, both structural and systemic, has contributed to poor economic performance and weak social development. Laws and regulations are inadequately enforced and public control over major institutions is ineffective. Another major cause is politicization and corruption, which weaken the civil service and cause mismanagement of public resources. Furthermore, the government policy has not been effective in vital functions, such as raising fiscal revenues, targeting and implementing programs to assist selected groups or regions, ensuring that public assets are efficiently used and well-maintained, and protecting the citizens' lives and livelihood. Finally, improvised and inconsistent policies contribute to economic instability and unpredictability, discourage long-term investment, and create problems related to lack of transparency.

To address these issues, the following areas need urgent policy attention:

- Implementing transparent public management procedures and regulations to ensure accountability

- Enforcing laws and regulations, particularly those regarding taxation, debt recovery, and human rights
- Undertaking judicial and legal reform to promote social justice, economic development, and investors' confidence
- Enacting public administration reforms, including downsizing the civil service and establishing incentive and control systems based on performance
- Improving corporate governance and speeding up privatization of state-owned enterprises
- Improving public resource management, particularly public expenditure control and debt management
- Decentralizing the government structure and encouraging local governments to adopt policy innovations that improve efficiency.

During the past eight years, the Social Action Program (SAP) has improved social services. SAP was introduced in the early 1990s to expand basic social services, including primary education, basic health, family planning, and rural water supply and sanitation. SAP has increased the primary school participation from 69 to 73 percent, contraceptive use from 14 to 22 percent, access to safe water from 47 to 55 percent of the population, and average life expectancy from 58 to 62.5 years. In its second phase, SAP II continues to emphasize better provision of these basic services as well as population control. These can

be accelerated through decentralizing decisionmaking and project implementation, and rigorously supervising the use of SAP resources.

In the current difficult economic situation, public investment for strengthening and expanding social service delivery under SAP II runs the risk of being reduced. Protection for its funding is necessary, and greater efforts are needed to involve nongovernment organizations in designing and providing social services. An improved policy environment and new mechanisms for government–nongovernment organization cooperation are needed. While nongovernment organizations can contribute much to the social and economic development, they need external assistance to improve institutional capacity, cost effectiveness, accountability, and transparency. Because the poor are adversely affected by drastic structural reforms, strong measures are needed in the short term to protect them.

In the longer term, structural issues affecting the delivery of basic social services and other poverty interventions should be addressed. Given the strong link between poverty and human development, especially in the rural areas, basic social services in education, nutrition, health, and population control need improvement. Participatory integrated rural development programs are needed, including rural infrastructure development, microfinance improvement, and employment generation.

Sri Lanka

Civil conflict in the northeast region of the country contributed to a slowdown of economic growth. Policy reforms are necessary to revive the economy, including fiscal consolidation, public administration and financial sector reform, and private sector development. To sustain growth in the medium term, government policy should also focus on human resource development.

RECENT TRENDS AND PROSPECTS

After achieving real GDP growth of 4.7 percent in 1998, Sri Lanka recorded a lower rate of 4.2 percent in 1999, mainly because of declining industrial output growth. The industry sector's performance improved in the second half of the year, reflecting a gradual improvement in exports. The agriculture sector also performed well, resulting from a higher output of plantation crops.

The national savings-investment gap increased in 1999 compared with the previous year. Domestic investment increased to 27.5 percent of GDP compared with 25.4 percent in 1998, mainly due to aircraft purchases and telecommunications services expansion. Infrastructure development projects, together with housing and small-scale construction projects in rural areas, dominated investment expenditure in 1999. Preliminary data indicate that the ratio of national savings to GDP edged up from 24 percent in 1998 to 25 percent in 1999 because of higher private savings and lower fiscal deficit.

The unemployment rate declined in 1999 due to the increased employment in the tourism sector, strong small business growth, and increased public sector recruitment. The population grew at 1.2 percent annually and reached approximately 19 million at the end of 1999, with about 21 percent below the poverty threshold.

Government revenue increased 12 percent during 1999. A sharp increase in the national security levy and excise tax collections, plus moderate increases in revenues from income taxes and import duty, contributed to the improvement in tax revenue. Total revenue was an estimated 17.6 percent of GDP compared with 17.3 percent in 1998, but it was lower than originally targeted in the 1999 budget. Because of the relatively lower goods and services tax rate and the higher level of exemptions, collections of this tax were lower than the previous year.

Government expenditure increased by 6.3 percent in 1999. Current expenditure is expected to be higher than originally budgeted, largely because of increased salaries and wages and interest payments on domestic debt. However, overall expenditure was 25.6 percent of GDP in 1999, compared with 26.4 percent in 1998. Nonpriority expenditures in the public sector were curtailed and specific borrowing limits imposed on government spending units. Accordingly, the 1999 budget deficit was estimated at 8 percent of GDP, an improvement over 9.2 percent the previous year. Monetary policy in 1999 aimed at maintaining financial market stability, while helping strengthen the declining trend in inflation. The consolidated broad money supply (M2), which includes the operations of the foreign currency banking units, increased by 13.3 percent in 1999. Inflation declined, averaging about 4.7 percent compared with 9.4 percent in 1998, because of improved domestic supply of food items and lower prices of imports.

External sector developments in 1999 reflected the effects of depressed global demand and the decline in commodity prices (see figure 2.17). Exports fell 4.1 percent in 1999 because of weak prices of tea, rubber, textiles, and garments. Imports increased 0.1 percent as import prices—with the exception of oil—went down across the board. Consequently, the trade deficit was $1.3 billion in 1999 compared with $1.1 billion in 1998. Owing to rapid recovery in the tour-

ism sector, the services account significantly improved, registering a surplus of $203 million in 1999 compared with $143 million in 1998. During 1999, tourist arrivals reached 436,400, a 14.5 percent increase from the previous year.

The current account deficit widened to about 2.6 percent of GDP in 1999 and the overall balance of payments registered a deficit of $263 million, down from a surplus of $37 million the previous year. As a result, gross official reserves declined to $1.7 billion at the end of 1999 (3.5 months of import equivalent) from $2 billion at the end of 1998 (4.1 months of imports). External debt was 57 percent of GDP in 1998 and remained at the same level in 1999, but the debt-service ratio increased from 11 percent to 12.7 percent. The Sri Lanka rupee depreciated by 5 percent against the dollar in 1999, trading at SLRe71.5 per dollar at the end of the year.

Real GDP growth is projected at 5 percent and 6 percent in 2000 and 2001, respectively. This higher growth should result from a modest recovery in industrial production, supported by an overall recovery of world trade. Annual average inflation is expected to be around 6.5 percent. However, imported inflation could occur in 2000 following higher oil

Table 2.18 Major Economic Indicators, Sri Lanka, 1997-2001
(percent)

Item	1997	1998	1999	2000	2001
GDP growth	6.3	4.7	4.2	5.0	6.0
Gross domestic investment/GDP	24.4	25.4	27.5	29.0	29.5
Gross national savings/GDP	21.5	24.0	25.0	25.0	26.0
Inflation rate (consumer price index)	9.6	9.4	4.7	6.5	6.5
Money supply (M2) growth	13.8	9.7	13.3	12.5	12.0
Fiscal balance/GDP[a]	-7.9	-9.2	-8.0	-7.6	-5.7
Merchandise exports growth	13.3	3.4	-4.1	10.0	15.0
Merchandise imports growth	7.8	0.4	0.1	14.0	16.0
Current account balance/GDP	-2.6	-1.8	-2.6	-6.8	-3.8
Debt service/exports	13.3	11.0	12.7	12.0	12.0

a. Excludes grants and privatization proceeds.
Sources: Central Bank of Sri Lanka (2000); Ministry of Finance and Planning; IMF; staff estimates.

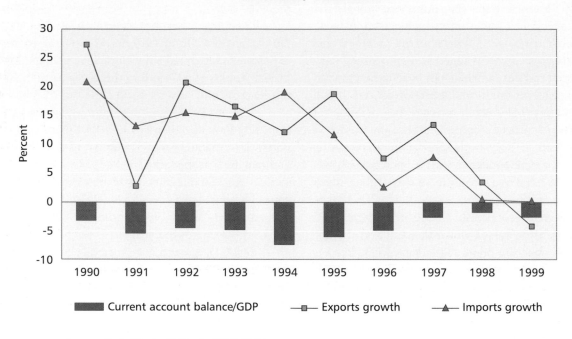

Figure 2.17 Exports, Imports, and Current Account Balance, Sri Lanka, 1990-1999

Current account balance/GDP — Exports growth — Imports growth

Sources: Central Bank of Sri Lanka (1999, 2000).

prices. The ratio of current account deficit to GDP is expected to be 6.8 percent in 2000 and 3.8 percent in 2001. Because of continuing fiscal consolidation efforts, the budget deficit for 2000 should be lower than in 1999. The money supply is expected to grow at 12-13 percent in 2000, providing adequate liquidity to the economy while avoiding inflationary pressure.

ISSUES IN ECONOMIC MANAGEMENT

The government has achieved considerable progress in structural reforms, which include tax reforms and private sector participation in key areas such as gas, telecommunications, and plantations. To sustain higher economic growth, the government should continue structural reform efforts, including fiscal consolidation and reform in public administration and in the financial sector.

The medium-term strategy for fiscal consolidation should include eliminating distortionary taxes,

improving tax administration, restructuring public debt, expanding public enterprise reforms, and reducing defense and security-related expenditures. Public administration reform is also critical to better economic management. The reform agenda should include streamlining government organizations, progressively retrenching or redeploying employees in public institutions and agencies, and ensuring that provincial councils and local governments benefit from a clear delegation of authority. Public administration reform is expected not only to promote private sector development, but also reduce the fiscal deficit.

Although the government has been actively pursuing financial sector reforms to mobilize capital, the role of the domestic capital market remains modest and the development finance institutions are still the major sources of long-term finance. To foster private sector growth in the economy, the government must develop market-based financial institutions and instruments through financial sector reforms.

POLICY AND DEVELOPMENT ISSUES

Traditional agricultural products such as tea and rubber, along with labor-intensive manufacturers, continue to dominate Sri Lankan exports. In the face of modest prospects for these exports and increased competition from regional producers, the government must reorient the existing production structure toward higher value-added activities. To achieve this objective, human resource development is critical.

Sri Lanka has attained remarkable social progress during the past decades. It ranks highest among South Asian countries in human development indicators, and in the middle in socioeconomic indicators. However, human resource development requires strengthening to provide the necessary skills for the current needs of the economy. Major policy initiatives need to focus on building closer links between education and training and the labor markets, improving health care to meet the requirements of a growing aging population, and developing a social security system to help vulnerable and poor groups.

Speedy reforms in the education sector are needed to improve the quality of higher education, especially in technical skills. Policy initiatives should be taken to further involve the private sector in technical education and for raising standards to international levels. Health sector policy needs to address issues relating to the efficiency and effectiveness of the current health service system, especially its financial sustainability and allocation of resources. The quality of private sector services in health care needs appropriate regulatory legislation to equalize standards for the government and private sector health institutions.

Despite sustained commitment to social welfare through various poverty reduction programs such as direct income transfers and subsidies, approximately 21 percent of the country's population are poor. In the short term, the government must ensure that the poor gain access to social services and continue to receive income support through a transfer scheme. In the medium term, the aim is to improve the earnings of the poor through productivity enhancement. In the long term, economic growth will likely be sufficient to absorb an expanded labor force and provide gainful employment for all segments of the society.

Estimates on the country's poverty level do not include the conflict-centered Northeast Province, which has about 2.8 million people, 15 percent of the total population. A considerable portion of them are poor. The government's policy on relief, rehabilitation, and reconstruction in the region aims at providing basic amenities—including education, health, water, and sanitation—to help those affected by the conflict create a physically, economically, and socially sustainable environment for reintegration into productive life. Concerted efforts of the government and donor agencies will be needed to achieve this objective.

The Pacific

Fiji Islands

Papua New Guinea

Cook Islands

Kiribati

Marshall Islands

Federated States
 of Micronesia

Nauru

Samoa

Solomon Islands

Tonga

Tuvalu

Vanuatu

Fiji Islands

After two years of recession, the Fiji Islands economy rebounded strongly in 1999. The medium-term outlook for economic growth is around 3 percent per year. A new administration is addressing the problems of reversing weak employment growth, reinvigorating subdued private investment, improving conditions for the poor, and restructuring the sugar industry.

RECENT TRENDS AND PROSPECTS

After falling about 1.5 percent on average in 1997-1998, the Fiji Islands' real GDP increased an estimated 7.8 percent in 1999 (see figure 2.18). The economic rebound reflected the recovery of the sugar industry from the effects of a prolonged drought. It was further supported by growth in tourism; construction; and gold, clothing, and footwear production.

Sugarcane and raw sugar production increased by 81 percent and 56 percent, respectively. The number of tourist arrivals, stimulated by additional air services from Australia, rose 7.3 percent to a record level of 398,400. Mining production increased 12 percent, clothing and footwear production rose 10 percent as manufacturers took advantage of the extension of a preferential trade agreement with Australia and New Zealand, and construction rose 10 percent.

Simultaneously with the recovery in aggregate production in 1999, the inflation rate dropped to 1.7 percent at the end of the year due to falling prices for domestically produced foods, reduced import duties, and low inflation among major trading partners.

With the Reserve Bank of Fiji maintaining an accommodative monetary policy stance, by September the broad money (M2) supply grew by 3.1 percent because of an increase in net foreign assets. Credit to the private sector increased 6.6 percent by December 1999, stimulated partly by the decrease in the weighted average lending rate to 8.6 percent from 9.3 percent a year earlier. Although credit to the public sector fell, domestic credit rose 2.2 percent. This increase was mostly for personal loans for housing construction and loans to enterprises in the manufacturing and professional service sector. Commercial bank lending to other sectors declined, and confirmed the view that business confidence in general remained low and private fixed investment correspondingly weak (around 4 percent of GDP). Interest rates on savings declined more than lending rates, pushing the interest rate spread above 5.2 percent.

The budget deficit, exclusive of asset sales, was 1.2 percent of GDP in 1999. Operating expenditure was 1 percent above the original budget estimate, largely because of above-budget personnel expenditure and transfer payments. Revenue, however, was almost 10 percent higher than the budget estimate because of the unexpected pace of economic growth. Government debt, which was approximately 80 percent domestic, rose slightly to 39.5 percent of GDP.

The balance of payments was in surplus in 1999, equivalent to 2.6 percent of GDP. The current account surplus narrowed to 0.6 percent of GDP as net investment income and official transfers declined, offsetting improvements in the merchandise trade balance and net services income. The capital account surplus was 1.9 percent of GDP. Foreign exchange reserves rose to F$832 million (US$416 million), or 4.8 months' worth of imports of goods and nonfactor services. During 1999, the Fiji dollar remained stable, consolidating the improved international competitiveness that resulted from the January 1998 devaluation.

The official forecast is that the growth rate will slow to 3.2 percent in 2000 and 2001, and to 2.8 percent in 2002. The administration elected in May 1999 acknowledges that these figures are approximately half

of the rates necessary to reach employment and poverty alleviation targets. The 2000 budget projects an increase in the fiscal deficit to 3.9 percent of GDP. It also includes a 2.3 percent rise in operational expenditure, to be covered by increases in personnel expenditure; transfer payments, including social welfare; and goods and services, particularly maintaining physical infrastructure. Capital expenditure, however, is projected to fall 6 percent. The health and education sectors will benefit the most from the increased expenditure in 2000.

On the revenue side, in August 1999 the government announced removal of the value-added tax from basic food items, water rates, and some educational and medical supplies, to begin in January 2000. The budget itself provides for increased customs and excise duties on tobacco and alcohol, and reduced duties on some foods and second-hand vehicles. Overall, revenue—including grants but excluding asset sales—is projected to drop 2.7 percent, although

Figure 2.18 Real GDP Growth Rates, Fiji Islands, 1995-1999

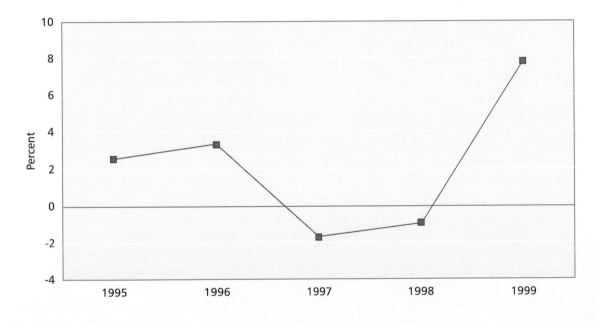

Source: Bureau of Statistics.

revenue from the value-added tax is expected to rise slightly despite a narrower indirect tax base. The 2000 budget projects further strengthening of the balance of payments over the medium term, and plans to relax capital controls further.

ISSUES IN ECONOMIC MANAGEMENT

The 2000 budget presents a gradualist approach to reorienting public expenditure toward social welfare, health, education, and infrastructure, while acknowledging that investment-driven, employment-generating economic growth is central to durable improvements in living standards. Some observers, particularly the business community, had feared a big-spending budget and policy measures that could be unfriendly to the private sector. The main short-term issues will be whether the budget stays on track, and whether wage outcomes will permit low inflation without a restrictive monetary policy.

POLICY AND DEVELOPMENT ISSUES

The Fiji Islands continues to rank high in socioeconomic achievements, but employment growth has been sluggish and concerns are growing over increasing inequality and poverty. In the early 1990s, an estimated 25 percent of households were below the poverty line. Targeted interventions are needed, along with faster, sustainable, and broad-based economic growth, and these will occur only if investor confidence is restored. Such restoration is difficult and requires a coherent, credible, and predictable policy regime. The new administration made a sound beginning with the 2000 budget, but more must be done to elaborate policies, particularly in private sector development, trade, public enterprise reform, and sugar industry restructuring. The latter is still plagued by an unresolved land tenure issue, poor industrial relations, and the long-term prospect of losing preferential access to European markets.

Papua New Guinea

External shocks and economic mismanagement made 1999 a difficult year. However, the economic growth rate surpassed expectations to reach 3.9 percent. Future growth will depend upon maintaining good governance and spreading the benefits of development to the poor.

RECENT TRENDS AND PROSPECTS

During 1997-1998, the economy was hard hit by drought, the effects of the Asian financial crisis, and low commodity prices. A modest growth rate of 2.5 percent was registered in 1998 only because of the recovery of the mining sector, which had earlier suffered from drought-induced water shortages for ore processing. Nonmineral output fell 3.7 percent in 1998.

The 1999 growth rate was 3.9 percent, higher than originally forecast because of improved commodity prices and increased export volumes, particularly from the mineral sector. Signs of intensified macroeconomic instability became apparent in February 1999, when the currency experienced downward pressure during a seasonal downturn in export revenue. The pressure arose primarily from substantial unbudgeted public expenditure in December 1998 and January 1999, and the government's failure to secure anticipated external finance.

The government relied instead on borrowing from the central bank, which exceeded legal limits on occasion. The currency depreciated from K2.094 per dollar at the beginning of 1999 to an historic low of K2.874 on 1 June. It recovered slightly to K2.717 in early August, a 23 percent drop from the level at the beginning of the year. Foreign exchange reserves dropped to a dangerously low level of one month of import cover, while depreciation fueled inflation to an annual rate of 16 percent. In a bid to generate external funds, the government obtained an independent credit rating and attempted a potentially costly Eurobond issue, which proved unsuccessful.

In July 1999, the prime minister lost office. The new administration reviewed the fiscal situation, confirmed its seriousness, and introduced a supplementary budget on 10 August that was endorsed by the International Monetary Fund. Despite limited implementation of a retirement and retrenchment scheme, the number of public servants had risen by almost 3,300 and the wage bill exceeded the budgeted figure by 24 percent. Government arrears had increased to K74 million. In the first half of 1999, the fiscal deficit reached almost 3 percent of GDP and outstanding domestic debt reached about 26 percent of GDP. The supplementary budget provided for cuts to the national government's development expenditure; increased gaming taxes; log export taxes; and excises on petrol, alcoholic beverages, tobacco, and luxury vehicles. The interest-withholding tax on mining and petroleum companies introduced in the original budget was removed. These measures generated a fiscal surplus in the second half of 1999, leaving a total deficit of 1.6 percent of GDP, which was funded by external borrowing.

The fiscal tightening facilitated refocusing of monetary policy toward the credible pursuit of price and exchange rate stability. During the first half of 1999, the monetary authorities adopted an accommodative monetary policy stance. The requirement that commercial banks place 10 percent of their deposits in noninterest-bearing accounts with the central bank was suspended on 31 December 1998, abolished on 12 January 1999, and reintroduced on 15 January. It was then reduced to 5 percent on 16 March, when the minimum liquid assets ratio was introduced. In the second half of the year the new administration tightened monetary policy by raising this ratio to 25 percent. The monetary policy stance is not likely to be eased soon, and this will keep nominal bank lending rates at around 19 percent. The external reserves position remained precarious. Despite an improvement in merchandise exports, import cover was only one month.

The macroeconomic framework of the 2000 budget projects a real GDP growth rate of 4.6 percent, exchange rate stability, a decline in the inflation rate to 13 percent, and a drop in Treasury bill rates from 23.3 to 15 percent. The budget itself provides for a slight increase in the overall deficit to 1.9 percent of GDP, but this reflects mostly a 27 percent rise in development expenditure. Revenue and grants are projected to rise 11.2 percent in nominal terms, to 25.5 percent of GDP, while nominal recurrent expenditure is projected to rise just 1.9 percent, falling to 18.4 percent of GDP and leaving a current

Figure 2.19 Monthly End-of-Period Exchange Rates, Papua New Guinea, January 1996-February 2000

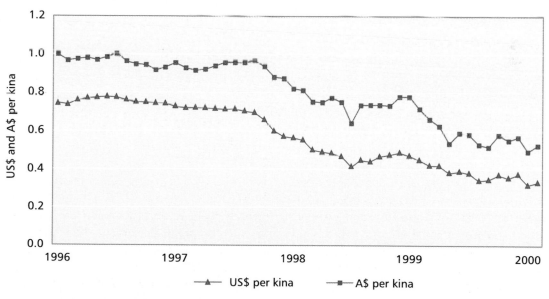

Sources: Oanda website; BLOOMBERG.

surplus. Maintaining aggregate fiscal discipline and meeting interest payments on heavy debt to restore macroeconomic stability will require further reductions in goods and services expenditure.

ISSUES IN ECONOMIC MANAGEMENT

The critical short-term issue is whether the 2000 budget can be implemented successfully. Extraordinary concessional loans of K526 million from the International Monetary Fund and the World Bank were promised in an agreement reached at the end of 1999. An $80 million loan from the Australian government allowed a reduction in domestic debt and a buildup of foreign reserves.

Given these developments, it is realistic to expect continued exchange rate stability (see figure 2.19) a reduced inflation rate, and a relaxed monetary policy that would reduce interest rates. Along with improved governance, these are all necessary conditions for restoring private sector confidence and resuming growth in the nonmineral sector of the economy.

POLICY AND DEVELOPMENT ISSUES

Maintaining good governance is critical, given past experience, particularly considering the disruptive and arbitrary nature of macroeconomic policy in the first half of 1999. Current policy is on the right track, but adhering to policy will require a strong commitment. Government civil servants must have appropriate skills—and salaries must be high enough to attract the best available talent—so fiscal, monetary, and exchange rate policies can be carried out appropriately.

The economy's dualistic nature has resulted in social development that lags behind economic growth. The Human Development Index is the lowest in the Pacific and poverty incidence the highest, with 37 percent of the population below the poverty line. The challenge for government is to encourage economic growth that assists the poor, and to formulate and implement effective poverty interventions. The National Economic and Fiscal Commission, established in 1998, can help by evaluating requests for development assistance by provincial and local governments.

Cook Islands, Kiribati, Marshall Islands, Federated States of Micronesia, Nauru, Samoa, Solomon Islands, Tonga, Tuvalu, and Vanuatu

In 1999, real GDP for the ten smallest Pacific countries increased by a weighted average of almost 1 percent, with the growth rate decelerating in Kiribati, Tuvalu, and Vanuatu and accelerating in the other countries. Inflation rates remained low, and the economic outlook indicates that growth will continue at modest rates.

Economic performance in 1999 improved in the ten smallest Pacific countries as GDP increased by a modest 1 percent. This was an improvement over the previous year when four countries (Cook Islands, Marshall Islands, Federated States of Micronesia, and Samoa) experienced negative growth. Growth outcomes were better in Cook Islands, Marshall Islands, Federated States of Micronesia, Nauru, Samoa, Solomon Islands, and Tonga. In Kiribati and Tuvalu growth slowed, and the Vanuatu economy went into recession. The inflation rates for Cook Islands, Nauru, Tuvalu, and Tonga increased, but decreased in all the other countries for which data were available. The overall balance-of-payments position

in 1999 improved for Solomon Islands, Tonga, and Vanuatu, and deteriorated slightly for Samoa. In the six countries using American, Australian, or New Zealand dollars—Marshall Islands, Kiribati, Nauru, Tuvalu, and Cook Islands—merchandise trade deficits continued to be covered largely by varied combinations of official transfers, overseas investment income, and workers' remittances. Fiscal and monetary policy parameters generally were consistent with macroeconomic stability.

Evidence suggests that human development indicators improved significantly during the 1980s and 1990s. Pacific island economies generally registered declines in infant mortality and increases in life

For Cook Islands, Nauru, Samoa, and Tonga, 1999 refers to fiscal year 1998/99, ending 30 June.
For the Marshall Islands and the Federated States of Micronesia, 1999 refers to fiscal year 1998/99, ending 30 September.
For Kiribati, Solomon Islands, Tuvalu, and Vanuatu, 1999 refers to the calendar year.

expectancy, school attendance, literacy, and per capita income. However, the Solomon Islands and Vanuatu remained low in measures of socioeconomic development, with relatively rapid population growth threatening to erode any gains made. Populations in these two countries had poor access to safe water and health services and high percentages of underweight children less than five years old. Cook Islands, Samoa, Tonga, and Tuvalu ranked higher in socioeconomic measures, and exhibited little poverty. Kiribati, Marshall Islands, Federated States of Micronesia, and Nauru ranked in the middle range of both socioeconomic development and poverty. In all cases—although to varying degrees—smallness, remoteness, geographic fragmentation and dispersion, and economic vulnerability imposed severe development constraints. Vulnerability to natural shocks, including the long-term effects of global warming on sea level, also remained a potentially devastating and largely unpredictable variable in the development equation. Nonetheless, in most cases, governments were committed to improving economic policy and governance, which are crucial but controllable variables. Because of this and an improving international economic environment, the outlook is for modest economic growth in 2000.

COOK ISLANDS

After three years of recession, the Cook Islands economy rebounded in 1999, despite migration and a resultant population decline from 17,400 in 1998 to around 16,000 (see figure 2.20). Real GDP grew by an estimated 2.8 percent, led by tourism, and visitor arrivals, which were up 6.5 percent compared with 1998. Canadians taking advantage of charter flights accounted for approximately one third of the increase in tourists. New flights by Air New Zealand brought additional visitors from Australia and New Zealand, and arrivals from Europe reached a record high. Black pearl production continued to grow, and commercial

Table 2.19 GDP Growth Rates and Inflation Rates, the Pacific, 1998-1999
(percent)

Country	GDP		Inflation	
	1998	1999	1998	1999
Cook Islands[a]	-3.8	2.8	0.8	1.4
Fiji Islands[b]	-1.3	7.8	5.7	1.7
Kiribati[a]	8.3	1.5	4.7	2.0
Marshall Islands[a]	-5.0	0.5	4.0	1.0
Federated States of Micronesia	-0.8	0.3	3.0	—
Nauru	—	—	4.0	6.7
Papua New Guinea	2.5	3.9	13.6	16.0
Samoa	2.6	4.0	2.2	0.3
Solomon Islands[a,b]	-2.2	1.0	12.3	8.0
Tonga[b]	0.1	2.2	3.3	4.4
Tuvalu[a,b]	14.9	3.0	0.8	7.0
Vanuatu[a]	0.2	-2.0	3.9	2.5

— Not available
a. Inflation data refer to the rate in the capital city.
b. GDP data refer to GDP growth at factor cost.

Sources: Country sources; staff estimates.

agricultural production—stimulated by tourism growth—recovered from the drought. Construction activity also increased from the relatively low levels of recent years. Business surveys revealed a substantial rise in business confidence, which was reflected in credit growth in the private sector and increased foreign investment. The inflation rate remained low, rising slightly from 0.8 percent in 1998 to 1.4 percent.

The merchandise trade deficit fell to 46.3 percent of GDP in 1998 as imports declined and pearl exports grew by 66 percent. In 1999, increased pearl exports offset import growth that resulted from the economic recovery, and the trade deficit remained around 46 percent of GDP. Tourism receipts, official transfers, and private remittances substantially covered the trade account imbalance, leaving a current account deficit of approximately 7 percent of GDP. The New Zealand dollar, the currency in circulation, depreciated slightly against the US dollar, almost 8 percent against the Australian dollar, and 10 percent against the yen. It appreciated 5 percent against the euro.

Government finances strengthened in 1999. Operating and overall surpluses were recorded; operating expenditure was kept to the budgeted level and revenues were above expectations. Development expenditure continued to hover around the NZ$10 million level of recent years. The debt-servicing burden eased because of the September 1998 restructuring of the external debt. Interest payments were a modest 12 percent of tax revenue, and the debt stock was equivalent to 78 percent of GDP. The 2000 budget aimed at a balance-on-operating account, with revenue rising 9 percent and operating expenditure 15 percent. Development expenditure was projected to rise to NZ$16 million as the government increased spending on infrastructure assets to support tourism.

Implementation of the budget was disrupted by a period of political instability in the latter half of 1999, caused by poor governance and corrupt government practices. However, a new coalition government took office in November and quickly made a public commitment to continuing the economic and public sector reform process begun in 1996. Six key strategies for improving fiscal governance included minimizing red tape, reducing government involvement in commercial activities, improving the corporate governance

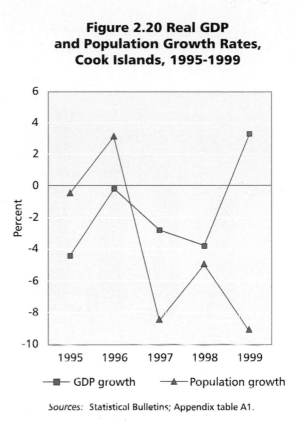

Figure 2.20 Real GDP and Population Growth Rates, Cook Islands, 1995-1999

Sources: Statistical Bulletins; Appendix table A1.

of statutory authorities, restructuring some government corporations to increase efficiency, refocusing the public administration on service delivery, and increasing reliance on local expertise.

Real GDP is forecast to grow by 4.2 percent in 2000. The decline in the resident population attributable to migration to New Zealand is expected to cease. Tourism is again predicted to be a driving force, with tourist arrivals forecast to increase by 6 percent, and production in agriculture and fisheries to rise 6.6 percent.

KIRIBATI

According to revised estimates, real GDP grew by 8.3 percent in 1998 because of recovery in copra production, aid-funded construction projects, and public administration expansion. Gross national product (GNP) was approximately twice the size of GDP because of fishing license fees, net investment income, and

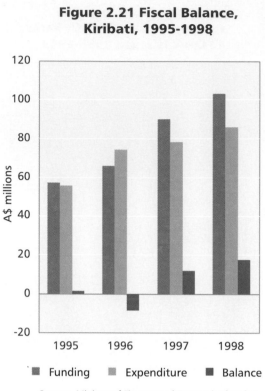

Figure 2.21 Fiscal Balance, Kiribati, 1995-1998

Source: Ministry of Finance and Economic Planning.

percent of GDP were included, the current account position in 1998 was a surplus of 25.9 percent. The capital account in 1998 moved into surplus—10 percent of GDP—because of a rise in capital grants, and the overall balance of A$36 million was 89 percent more than the historically large surplus of 1997. Because of these surpluses and the valuation effects of a depreciated currency denominated by the Australian dollar, official external assets in the Revenue Equalization Reserve Fund (RERF), the Consolidated Fund, and the Development Fund reached A$606 million. External debt was modest at 13.2 percent of GDP, with external debt service equal to 1.4 percent of exports of goods and services. In 1999, however, the merchandise trade and current account balances worsened because of declining exports and fishing license fees, respectively.

The 1999 budget was presented three months into the year, and an overall deficit of 32 percent of GDP was estimated, unlike budget surpluses in the previous years (see figure 2.21). Fishing license fees were projected to fall from A$42.5 million in 1998 to A$12.8 million, while current and development expenditures were estimated to rise 2.7 percent and 39.5 percent, respectively. External concessional loans would finance almost one fourth of the deficit, and the remainder was to be covered by the Consolidated Fund (44 percent) and the RERF (31 percent). The accumulation of reserves during the past two years permits such a budget strategy, but care is needed over the medium to long term if the real per capita value of the RERF is to be maintained.

In the small finance sector, the sole commercial bank, the Bank of Kiribati—jointly owned by the government and the Australian-based Westpac—remains profitable. Like the Kiribati Provident Fund, it holds more than 90 percent of its assets offshore. In August 1999, credit of A$3.1 million to the private sector constituted barely 7 percent of assets, and no credit was extended to the government or public enterprises. Growth of private sector credit is constrained by limited domestic investment opportunities and the inability of the Bank of Kiribati to use land as collateral (the bank is partly foreign-owned, and foreigners are not permitted to own land). The interest rate spread increased slightly to 6 percent. Loans from the Development Bank of Kiribati totaled A$3.8 million at the end of 1998, but further lending was constrained by a

seamen's remittances; GNP grew by 16 percent in 1998 in real terms because fishing license fees were doubled. The next year growth slowed, with GDP increasing an estimated 1-2 percent, primarily because of the Japanese-funded construction of a new wharf at Betio. The real GNP growth rate decelerated as fishing license fees fell because of declining fish stocks associated with changing climatic conditions. The inflation rate fell to around 2 percent, in line with the rate in Australia, the major source of imports. Growth in the money supply was less than 1 percent.

The temporary increase in fishing license fees in 1998 strengthened the external accounts. The current account deficit, exclusive of official grants, fell from 17.9 percent of GDP in 1997 to 3.3 percent in 1998. The strong growth in fishing license fees was reinforced by increases in seamen's remittances, to 11 percent of GDP, and in investment income, to 30 percent. When official grants equivalent to 43 small capital base, and nonperforming loans remained a problem.

Although the government's 1997 Medium Term Strategy presents an agenda of public sector reform and private sector development, little systematic progress had been made by early 1999. The strategies lacked broad support from politicians, officials, and the community at large. These groups must be educated and persuaded before change can occur.

MARSHALL ISLANDS

The Marshall Islands economy is estimated to have grown 0.5 percent in 1999. This modest recovery followed three years of recession (see figure 2.22) caused by cuts in government expenditure and employment under a reform program, and the impact of drought on agriculture and fisheries production. Real GDP remained approximately 25 percent below the 1995 level, and GNP and GNP per capita exceeded GDP figures more than 6 percent because of fishing license fees, which increased significantly in 1998 and remained high in 1999.

The recovery in economic activity in 1999 reflected the direct and indirect effects of aid-funded road works and construction, the private sector construction of a tuna processing factory, and more onshore spending by crews of an expanded foreign fishing fleet. The agriculture sector increased production as it continued to recover from the 1998 drought. Additionally, further planned contractions in public sector activity were forestalled, at least temporarily, by grants from Taipei,China and optimism about re-negotiations regarding the Compact of Free Association. The compact with the United States provides annual block grants that run from 1986-2001, with $40 million per year in the final five years. It also furnishes additional grant assistance to education, health, energy, and communication services; some free US Federal services such as postal and weather services; and unrestricted access for residents to live and work in the United States.

The inflation rate continued its downward trend from almost 10 percent in 1996 to around 1 percent in 1999. Use of the US dollar as domestic currency precludes an independent monetary policy, and the inflation rate tends to track that of the United States,

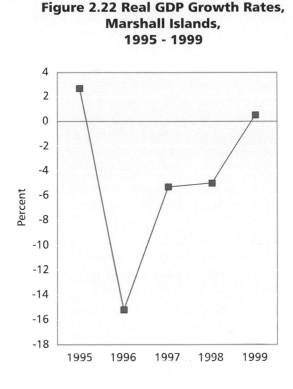

Figure 2.22 Real GDP Growth Rates, Marshall Islands, 1995 - 1999

Source: Appendix table A1.

the major source of imports. During 1995-1998, merchandise imports fell an estimated 24 percent in current prices while exports dropped almost 6 percent. The trade deficit declined, and the current account surplus, including declining official transfers, rose from 1.5 percent of GDP in 1995 to an estimated 22.2 percent in 1998. The capital account remained in deficit after the government ceased borrowing in 1995 and loans were repaid in 1996-1998. Overall, the balance of payments was in deficit throughout these four years. External debt stood at $125 million at the end of 1997, equivalent to 122 percent of GDP, and government holdings of dollar reserves fell to three weeks of merchandise import cover. Balance-of-payments data for 1999 are not available, but the current account surplus likely increased because of grants from Taipei,China.

An absence of timely, reliable, and comprehensive statistical information extends to government finances. However, public finances have been strengthened under the Policy Reform Program. Several ministries have been rationalized, and the number of government employees was reduced 33 percent between late 1995 and March 1999. A 1995 wage freeze remained in place, following a 5 percent pay reduction for salaries higher than $10,400 per year. Subsidies to some state-owned enterprises have been reduced or eliminated, the tariff system has been rationalized, and efforts to strengthen tax and customs administration continued. These measures, combined with a large drop in capital expenditure, moved the overall budget balance into surplus in 1996, 1997, and 1998.

The 1999 budget was passed one month into the fiscal year, before revised estimates for the budget outcomes of the previous year were available. A small deficit of $1 million was budgeted for General Fund accounts, with increased total appropriations to subsidize government agencies. After nine months, it appeared that the deficit would reach $9 million, approximately 9 percent of GDP. Expenditure exceeded the budgeted level, and revenue fell short, in large part because of the March 1999 decision to lower the general import duty from 12 percent to 5 percent. The government, concerned with the November 1999 elections, apparently did not consider the budget implications of this policy and the decision to increase the copra subsidy. Both reversed earlier policy actions under the Policy Reform Program, but did not save the incumbent government, and the new United Democratic Party won office.

Interest in early 2000 centered on whether a new administration would consolidate the gains made under the Policy Reform Program and complete the agenda of reform actions. Public expenditure management is essential. Fiscal discipline may have weakened before the elections, when grants from Taipei,China became available and confidence grew in a successful outcome to Compact funding renegotiations. Whether this optimism proves justified or not, the quality of economic management will be crucial in determining future development outcomes. Other areas requiring attention are public service performance, public enterprise reform, and an improved environment for private sector development. Legislation concerning investment approval, business licensing procedures, issuance of work permits, and improved

security of land leases was being considered. Once passed, and if effectively implemented, the legal framework for increased private sector activity will improve growth prospects.

FEDERATED STATES OF MICRONESIA

The real GDP of the Federated States of Micronesia (FSM) rose an estimated 0.3 percent in 1999. This slight increase in the aggregate level of economic activity ended two years of recession (see figure 2.23), but it was not evenly spread across the four states. The rise in GDP was attributable entirely to an increase in economic activity in Chuuk, where the private sector expanded enough to more than offset a continued decline in government contribution. Real GDP was stagnant in Kosrae and Pohnpei and declined in Yap, although in the latter two states private sector activity increased.

No data are available on the inflation rate, but it tracked the US rate of 2.6 percent, as the US dollar is the currency in circulation and the United States is the dominant source of imports. Commercial banking deposits and loans changed little from the levels since 1993. Deposits dropped and both consumer and commercial loans increased marginally; consumer loans, primarily to public servants, dominated bank portfolios. The loan-to-deposit ratio fell to 43 percent at the end of 1999, as banks continued to invest offshore because of the ongoing lack of domestic commercial lending opportunities. This reflected a specific limitation on mortgage-secured lending caused by laws against land ownership by foreign banks. It also reflected a combination of constraints to private sector development in general, most notably high wage costs, inadequate economic infrastructure, and an incomplete regulatory framework lacking transparency and predictability.

Under the Public Sector Reform Program, easing these and other constraints began through public service downsizing, public enterprise reform, foreign investment legislation, banking deregulation, business support services, and attempts at improving land titling and leasehold arrangements. However, as observed at the national economic summit in September 1999, much policy formulation remains to be done, and implementation must be effective. Regulations, particularly those about attracting foreign investment, must be applied quickly, and must be transparent and nondiscriminatory.

The aid-dependent, public-sector-dominated nature of the FSM economy is well documented. This has altered slightly as reductions in transfer grants under the Compact of Association with the United States forced cutbacks in government expenditure. Staff retrenchment and wage reductions caused national and state government expenditures to fall from 80 percent of GDP in 1993 to 70 percent in 1998, and simultaneously caused a decline in private sector activity, excluding subsistence production.

Historically, this sector evolved largely as a subsidiary goods and services provider to public servants, centering on importing, wholesaling, and retailing, rather than export-oriented agriculture, fisheries, and tourism. The public expenditure reductions contributed substantially to strengthening state government finances, but expenditure remained high by Pacific and international standards, with wages and travel accounting for 85 percent of operating expenditure. Fiscal discipline will be needed to prevent expenditures rising and to allow ongoing reduction in the external debt burden. External debt continued to decline in 1999, reaching 38 percent of GDP, compared with a high of 66 percent in 1993. The debt-service ratio was estimated at 25 percent of exports. Official projections indicated that the country was on track for a debt-to-GDP ratio of 21 percent and a debt-service ratio of just 3 percent by 2002.

The continued reliance of the government on Compact transfers reveals the extent of the long-term economic adjustment that would be required if large aid flows were not continued. These transfers accounted for 47 percent of total government revenue while tax collections provided just 14 percent. Major reform to improve efficiency and effectiveness is required if taxation revenue is to rise without jeopardizing private sector development. This will involve possible replacement of the current gross revenue tax with a value-added tax, greater efficiency in collection, and greater use of service charges and user fees. Revenue sharing between state and national governments was addressed in a July 1999 referendum, which proposed that the national constitution be amended

to divide fishing license revenue equally among the five governments, instead of it all going to the national government. It also suggested allowing 70 percent of tax collections rather than 50 percent to go to the states, but the proposal did not receive the required support of three fourths of voters in at least three states.

The obvious uncertainty confronting FSM governments is the outcome of renegotiations of the US Compact. From an FSM perspective, successful renegotiations will ensure a long-term source of financial support that will ease the pressure for economic restructuring. Micronesians may experience less compulsion to emigrate to Guam, Hawaii, and US mainland in search of employment. If the renegotiations are unsuccessful, provision still exists for grant transfers in 2002 and 2003 at the average level of the 15-year-period from 1986 to 2001. In this event, the government will need to accelerate efforts to design and implement policies that will allow development led by the private sector to flourish.

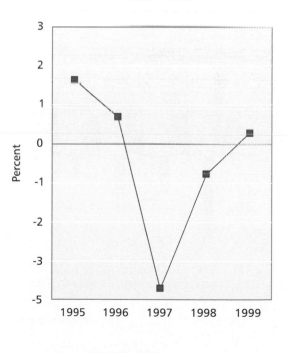

Figure 2.23 Real GDP Growth Rates, Federated States of Micronesia, 1995-1999

Source: Appendix table A1.

NAURU

The factors that caused concern for the economic situation in 1998 continued to be worrisome in 1999. The exhaustion of the phosphate resource, which has provided the main source of income and employment for many years, drew closer. Fiscal planning and discipline continued to be poor, and the financial system was still in a state of collapse. The diminished asset base of the Nauru Phosphate Royalties Trust (NPRT) had not yet been given a reliable value as a basis to assess sustainable consumption levels. Government commitment to an economic and financial reform program weakened noticeably, partly because of an unconditional loan from Taipei,China. In addition, Nauru's international image was tarnished by allegations of involvement in money laundering.

Although there are no national accounts, real GDP probably increased in 1999. Real government expenditure rose 15 percent compared with 1998, the

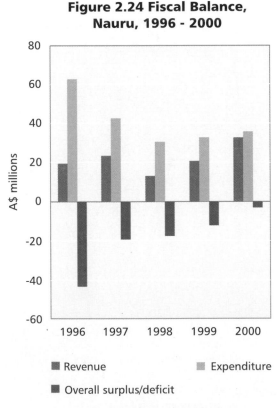

Figure 2.24 Fiscal Balance, Nauru, 1996 - 2000

A\$ millions

Legend:
■ Revenue
■ Expenditure
■ Overall surplus/deficit

Source: Republic of Nauru Annual Accounts.

volume of phosphate exports rose 38 percent, the Japanese-funded construction of Ainabare boat harbor began, and fisheries production for the domestic market increased. About 30 percent (450 people) of the public sector workforce was retrenched beginning in April 1999, but a lump sum payout funded by the Asian Development Bank (ADB)significantly ameliorated the impact on aggregate demand. In addition, the Nauru Phosphate Corporation reportedly hired around 200 casual laborers, and a significant number of retrenched public servants went into coastal fishing and the retail trade. A rise in inflation to 6.7 percent in 1999 corresponded with a rise in economic activity.

The reformist 1999 budget projected an overall surplus, but the actual outcome was officially reported as an A\$12 million deficit (see figure 2.24). The real figure was probably larger, because recorded revenue included A\$4 million in dividend payments from the bankrupt Bank of Nauru, and expenditures did not capture all payments made by government. The deficit was more than covered by external loans, with A\$3.5 million (US\$2.3 million) from the ADB and A\$29 million from Taipei,China. Of the A\$29 million, A\$14 million remained unspent at the end of the year.

Preliminary estimates indicated that at the end of March 1999, the republic's stocks of consolidated domestic and external debt totaled A\$524 million and A\$129 million, respectively. During 1999, NPRT obtained a US\$99 million loan from General Electric Capital to pay dividends to landowners and to refinance and restructure the investments of NPRT, the Nauru Finance Corporation, and the Nauru Superannuation Board. The 2000 budget was presented to Parliament three months into the year. The budget speech clearly identified the country's economic difficulties, gloomy outlook, and necessary courses of action. However, the budget estimates did not represent an adequate attempt to move toward long-term fiscal sustainability. A deficit of A\$3 million was projected, assuming 32 percent growth in nominal domestic revenue, A\$5 million in external grants, and an 8 percent increase in nominal expenditure. The deficit was to be financed with A\$2.7 million in surplus loan funds from 1999, plus A\$7.8 million in proceeds from asset sales, with provision for a net repayment on the foreign loan account of A\$7.6 million. The government intended to sell and lease back Air Nauru's only aircraft, using the proceeds to pay an outstanding loan.

Actual budget outcomes, however, probably will depart significantly from these estimates. Fishing license revenue may not be forthcoming, as legally the National Fisheries and Marine Resources Authority retain it. Dividend income of A$3 million from the Nauru Phosphate Corporation is uncertain, and sale of the aircraft for the expected amount is far from guaranteed. On the expenditure side, overruns can be anticipated because of poor governance and deficiencies in the budget execution system.

For a brief period in 1999, a long-term and difficult reform program was begun. Substantial public service downsizing occurred in an economy where almost all paid jobs were in the public sector. Unfortunately, political instability, substantial and unconditional external loan funds, unwillingness to confront harsh economic realities, combined to stall reform. This process must be revitalized quickly to minimize the harshness of an unavoidable fiscal and economic adjustment.

SAMOA

The growth performance of the Samoan economy exceeded expectations in 1999. After increasing 1.6 percent in 1997 and 2.6 percent in 1998, real GDP in 1999 rose by 4 percent, led by the fisheries and commerce sectors (see figure 2.25), compared with an original budget forecast of 2.5 percent. From 1998 to 1999, value added in fisheries rose 41.8 percent, increasing its share of GDP to 7.4 percent. Value added in the commerce sector rose 29 percent. The construction sector also recorded strong growth, increasing value added by 12.9 percent. The hotels and restaurants sector expanded 4.9 percent, stimulated by almost 9 percent more tourist arrivals. Public administration increased 4.1 percent, but food and beverage manufacturing grew sluggishly, and value added in agriculture and other manufacturing declined.

Employment growth occurred at a modest 2 percent between 1998 and 1999, according to incomplete National Provident Fund figures. Increased employment in public administration, accommodation and restaurants, personal services, and food manufacturing sectors accounted for most formal sector employ-

ment growth, with the rate of female employment growth more than double that of males. Although there was some growth in private sector employment, creating additional job opportunities in that sector remains an ongoing challenge.

A reduction in inflation accompanied the acceleration in output growth in 1999. The average annual rate in June 1999 was 0.8 percent—compared with 5.5 percent in June 1998—and reflected decreased local food prices; low inflation rates in Australia and New Zealand, the major sources of imports; and tariff reductions. Money supply growth was modest: in 1999, the broad money supply increased 10 percent. Increased net foreign assets accounted for 28 percent of this increase, and net domestic assets for the remaining 72 percent.

As the government continued to increase its net deposits with the banking system, credit to the private sector in 1999 increased 16 percent, reaching 27

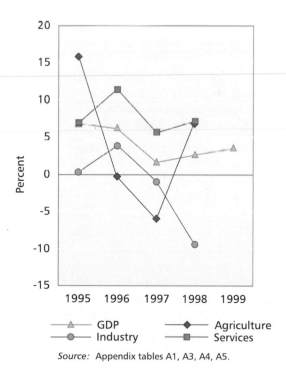

Figure 2.25 Real GDP and Sectoral Growth Rates, Samoa, 1995 - 1999

Source: Appendix tables A1, A3, A4, A5.

percent of GDP compared with 25 percent in 1998. Credit to nonfinancial public enterprises also increased almost fourfold, albeit from a small base. Credit extended to the private sector by nonmonetary financial institutions increased 12 percent. During 1999, the composition of financial institution portfolios with the private sector shifted away from personal and manufacturing sector loans toward loans to the primary sector, construction, trade, transportation and communication, and business and professional services. The weighted average lending rate of commercial banks dropped half a percentage point during early 1999, reducing the interest rate spread to 7.5 percent. The central bank continued to use its own securities as the monetary policy instrument to meet the inflation target of about 2 percent per year.

The balance of payments remained in overall surplus in 1998, equivalent to 3.7 percent of GDP. Net foreign assets rose to ST177.7 million (US$68 million) at the end of the year, or 5.7 months of goods and services imports. The external debt was 74 percent of GDP, of which 69 percent was official government debt. External debt-servicing costs were manageable regarding their demand on revenue from exports of goods, nonfactor services, and private remittances. In the first half of 1999, the balance of payments recorded an overall deficit equivalent to 3.1 percent of GDP, resulting in a decrease in net foreign assets to ST167.2 million (US$64 million), or 4.4 months of goods and services. This reflected a widening in the trade deficit that was primarily attributable to growth in private sector imports, to be expected with the increase in economic activity. During the same period, the nominal exchange rate depreciated 0.3 percent and the real effective exchange rate depreciated 4.4 percent, reflecting the drop in Samoa's inflation rate to below that of its trading partners. This last development reversed the trend of real appreciation that had emerged over 1991-1997 and had threatened a loss of international competitiveness.

Provisional government finance statistics showed that in 1999, for the fourth fiscal year in succession, government ran an overall budget surplus. It was equivalent to 0.5 percent of GDP, a significant improvement over the budgeted deficit of 1.3 percent. Revenue was slightly below the original budget estimate because of a shortfall in tax revenue. However,

current expenditure was also lower, as was externally funded development expenditure because of delays in starting some projects. Because of the surplus, government increased its net deposits in the banking system, further reducing the crowding-out pressure on the private sector.

In 2000, an overall deficit of 5.1 percent of GDP is budgeted. Revenue is projected to rise 8.2 percent, and current expenditure is budgeted to be 6.6 percent higher than in 1999, primarily because of increased spending on education and health and a higher wage bill. A current surplus of 3.4 percent of GDP is projected, and external grants are expected to fall 32.7 percent. Development expenditure will be down 2.1 percent, so external borrowing will increasingly be relied on for funding capital investment projects. This budgetary projection is consistent with Samoa's economic strategy, and the increased official external debt is well within debt-servicing capacity. There will again be a negative domestic borrowing requirement, which will consolidate government's net credit position with the banking system.

The government reaffirmed its commitment to economic reform in its *Partnership for a Prosperous Society: A Statement of Economic Strategy 2000-2001*. This statement emphasizes the importance of ensuring that reform benefits the community as a whole, and includes among its objectives invigorated agriculture and fisheries and a revitalized village economy. Provided the economy is not subject to severe external shocks, the forecast 2000 growth rate of 3-4 percent can be achieved. The government has demonstrated its capacity to deliver a stable macroeconomic environment, and is set to continue to do so through a firm fiscal stance and a sound monetary policy.

In addition, it continues to improve the microeconomic policy environment within which the private sector operates. Several state-owned enterprises were privatized in 1999 and further privatization is planned for 2000. Agriculture, however, continues to pull down the aggregate growth rate. The revival of this sector from the long-term damage caused by the 1994 taro leaf blight is a central medium-term concern. Success in this sector would considerably improve the prospects of increasing the growth rate, and of ensuring that the benefits of growth are more broadly spread.

SOLOMON ISLANDS

After two years of recession, the Solomon Islands economy began to recover in 1999 (see figure 2.26). Real GDP is estimated to have increased around 1 percent, largely because of increased gold and log production, and aid-funded road construction in the capital city. Unfortunately, an insurgency on the island of Guadalcanal prevented a stronger recovery. The government was forced to declare a state of emergency between June and October and 25,000 Malaitans who had settled on the island were displaced. The country's major oil palm producer, Solomon Islands Plantations Limited, closed indefinitely because of the insurgency. Several tourist resorts also closed, cocoa and copra production was disrupted, and market gardening was severely curtailed. Business confidence sank further, diminishing medium-term growth prospects.

The insurgency derailed the expected privatization of Solomon Islands Plantations Limited and threatened the rehabilitation of public finance, which is central to the government's economic and public sector reform program, and where substantial progress had been made. The cost to the budget in lost revenue and increased expenditure on security operations and resettling displaced persons was estimated at SI$30 million ($6 million). However, additional aid from Taipei,China was offered to cover these costs, and actual total recurrent expenditure was kept to just 3 percent above the original budget estimates. Domestic revenue exceeded the budget estimate by 3 percent as revenue collection improved, resulting in a small recurrent surplus. Total domestic public debt at the end of December 1999 had fallen to SI$378 million ($75.6 million), almost 6 percent below the level at the end of 1998. External public debt rose 9 percent to SI$580 million ($116 million), but this was on concessional terms and provided the financial means for the reform program. The government borrowed in external markets to pay off domestic arrears and most foreign arrears, and fund the increase in development expenditure.

The growth rate of the money supply accelerated slightly from 4.8 percent in 1998 to 7 percent in 1999 because of a 16 percent expansion in net foreign assets. Domestic credit declined 2 percent as government continued to reduce its net indebtedness to the

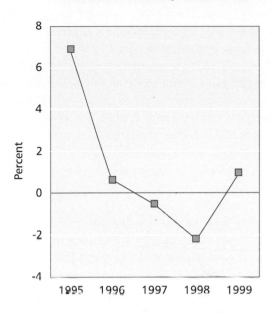

Figure 2.26 Real GDP Growth Rates, Solomon Islands, 1995-1999

Source: Appendix table A1.

banking system, and credit to the private sector expanded a modest 1.3 percent. The government securities market was reactivated in May 1999 following a restructuring of government debt that involved converting frozen Treasury bills into medium-term bonds. Commercial banks invested some of their excess reserves in bills offered at auction, but retained 10 percent of free liquid assets at the end of the year. The interest rate spread remained at 10 percent, with average deposit rates negative in real terms. Monetary policy was tight throughout 1999. The rates on central bank short-term securities and Treasury bills remained unchanged as the emphasis shifted to bills as the main monetary policy instrument.

In 1999 the inflation rate decelerated to 8 percent, from about 12 percent the previous year, because of tight macroeconomic policies and slowed growth in import prices. The impact of the 20 percent devaluation of December 1997 dissipated without generating the price-wage spiral of earlier years. The exchange rate remained relatively stable in 1999, with the Solomon Islands dollar depreciating 2.2 percent and 4.2 percent against the US and Australian dollars, respectively, and appreciating slightly against the New Zealand dollar. The balance-of-payments position strengthened in 1999 because of a 4 percent rise in merchandise export receipts, a 13 percent decline in imports, and an increase in capital receipts attributable to official bilateral and multilateral inflows. The rise in export receipts reflected greater earnings from gold, copra, and log exports, while imports in all categories declined. External reserves amounted to about 3.5 months of import equivalent. This represented a substantial improvement on the two weeks of cover early in the year, but was still less than the five or six months needed.

The government was hopeful that economic growth would accelerate to 3-4 percent in 2000 and inflation would decline to 6-7 percent. This, however, is predicated on an improved international economic environment and, more importantly, on an effective resolution of the social unrest that disrupted primary sector production and depressed investor confidence. Such a resolution will be difficult, and to be durable will require a long-term strategy that addresses the causes of economic inequality between regions and ethnic groups. In the meantime, although the government progressed toward restoring macroeconomic stability and continues to implement its reform program, investor confidence apparently has not revived.

The tax administration and public expenditure management still need work, particularly to improve allocative efficiency. The 2000 budget aims at zero growth in the nominal wage bill, while providing for an overall increase in recurrent expenditure of 10.5 percent, which largely reflects increased spending on health and education. Domestic revenue is projected to rise nearly 8 percent, and a small recurrent surplus is again budgeted. Personal and company income tax rates will be lowered; export duties on palm oil, copra, cocoa, and reef fish removed; and the maximum import tariff rate reduced from 40 to 20 percent. Increased revenue is expected from improved compliance and increased taxes on log exports, alcohol, and tobacco. Deductions allowed for calculating taxable personal income will also be reduced. Development expenditure is projected to increase 58 percent, to be financed

largely by an expected 81 percent increase in external grants. A budget deficit of SI\$71 million (\$14.2 million) is to be financed by external borrowing. These figures are exclusive of Stabex funds (a European Union stabilization system of financial assistance) that total 42 million euros, which could be used to finance government expenditure and establish a trust fund.

TONGA

Following three years of recession and stagnation, the economy rebounded in 1999 (see figure 2.27). Revised national accounts estimates show that real GDP fell 3.7 percent in 1996 and 1.4 percent in 1997, and increased only 0.1 percent in 1998. However, the provisional official estimate is that real GDP grew by 2.2 percent in 1999. This modest growth largely reflected several construction projects, expanded kava manufacturing, and moderate growth in the service sectors: trade, transportation and communications, finance

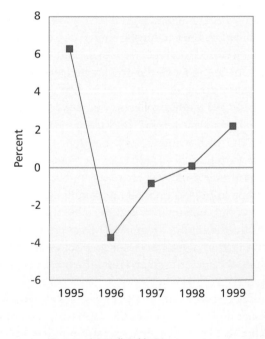

Figure 2.27 Real GDP Growth Rates, Tonga, 1995-1999

Source: Appendix table A1.

and business services. Output in the major productive sector of agriculture, forestry, and fisheries declined for the fourth year in a row, as the effects of drought were compounded by crop damage from Cyclone Cora in December 1998. GDP per capita of the approximately 98,500 population was an estimated T$2,487 ($1,574) at the end of 1999. The inflation rate had edged up to 4.4 percent because of the effects of drought on domestic food prices and currency devaluation.

The balance of payments recorded an overall surplus of 4.2 percent of GDP in 1999, compared with a deficit of 6.4 percent the previous year. Total official foreign reserves rose from 2.5 months of import cover to 3.9 months. The improvement in the balance of payments reflected a reduction in the current account deficit from 10.4 percent of GDP to 1 percent, and a slight increase in the capital account surplus from 4 percent of GDP to 5.3 percent. The change in the current account balance largely was attributable to fewer merchandise imports. Export performance was disappointing, with the principal exports of squash, fish, and root crops all declining, and growth only in vanilla and other agricultural products. Private remittance flows remained buoyant. The nominal and real effective exchange rates depreciated 8.2 percent and 6.7 percent, respectively, during 1999. This was an overdue adjustment after three years of appreciation, and it continued in the beginning of 2000.

Despite an increase in the money supply of nearly 20 percent in 1999 because of an increase of foreign reserve, net domestic credit expanded just 1.6 percent. Lending to public enterprises increased, while credit to the private sector remained stagnant and the government reduced its borrowing. The Reserve Bank maintained a tight monetary policy, but the weakness of its balance sheet continued to constrain the effective use of monetary policy when balance-of-payments pressures developed.

The fiscal situation in 1999 improved over 1998. Official estimates suggested an overall budget surplus of T$2.6 million (US$1.625 million), or approximately 1 percent of GDP, while International Monetary Fund estimates suggested a deficit of T$4.2 million (US$2.674 million), or 1.8 percent of GDP. The overall outcome reflects lower levels of public expenditure than in the original budget estimates, with an increase in the nominal wage bill. In addition, the government's

underlying fiscal capacity as measured by the current balance remained weak. The current deficit in 1999 was T$7.1 million, or 2.9 percent of GDP. The government's total outstanding debt at the end of 1999 was 37.4 percent of GDP, with more than 80 percent consisting of external loans at concessional interest rates.

The wage bill is estimated to rise 4.4 percent, and a smaller overall annual budget surplus of T$0.9 million is projected. These budget estimates, however, are not fully consistent with the stated policy objectives of fiscal tightness, ongoing civil service reform, and improved allocative efficiency, nor are they grounded in a convincing medium-term macroeconomic framework. The budget hopes that growth will accelerate to double-digit figures by 2001, but the source of more rapid growth is unclear. In the early months of 2000, there were signs of a domestic credit expansion. Lending to the private sector rose almost 7 percent, and the government increased borrowing. The budget deficit in 2000 is projected to be T$12.4 million (US$7.75 million), with current expenditure set to grow 9.4 percent and current revenue to rise only 1.7 percent. Debt servicing for 2000 was estimated as a manageable 2.7 percent of GDP.

The 2000 budget contains some significant initiatives, including a new contributory retirement scheme for civil servants and a commitment for tax reform to shift the balance from trade to indirect taxes. Major reforms targeted at enhancing the efficiency of the large and diverse public enterprises sector are desirable. In addition, the economic policy environment needs improvement, as its lack of transparency and predictability seriously discourages domestic and foreign private sector investment. The Industrial Development Incentives Act remains in effect, with all its discretionary provisions. A new Companies Act of 1995 finally became law in April 1999, but was poorly received by the business community and requires immediate amendment. The cumbersome system of granting business, trade, and development licenses also needs reform. This system, combined with ongoing difficulties in obtaining work permits for foreign skilled labor, constitutes a major obstacle to the direct foreign investment needed if Tonga's undoubted development potential—especially in the agriculture, fisheries, and tourism sectors—is to be realized.

TUVALU

A new set of national accounts reveals that the real GDP growth rate in 1998 was 14.9 percent. This rapid growth was led by the government sector, which expanded by almost a third and accounted for one fourth of GDP. In addition, public construction grew by 28.5 percent. This growth reflected the impact of increased public service employment, wages, and physical infrastructure projects on national income. In contrast, agriculture, forestry, and fisheries grew by less than 1 percent. The real GDP growth rate was estimated at 3 percent in 1999, with public administration and public construction again the leading sectors. Official estimates of GNP are not made, but real GNP grew faster than real GDP in 1999 because of rapid growth in fisheries license fees and revenue from passport sales. In addition, the first revenue from leasing Tuvalu's Internet domain address to a foreign company was received, although it was much less than originally anticipated. Income from the Tuvalu Trust Fund

and private remittances remained at the levels of recent years. The inflation rate in 1999 rose to 7 percent from less than 1 percent in 1998 (see figure 2.28). This reflected higher prices in the transport and miscellaneous categories of the consumer price index.

A substantial trade deficit continued to be financed by remittances, investment income, fishing license fees, and official transfers. Net foreign assets, including the Tuvalu Trust Fund, reached A\$90 million at the end of the year (approximately seven years of import cover). An automatic distribution from the trust fund to the Consolidated Investment Fund provided 11.5 percent of the government's total recurrent revenue in 1999. Fishing license fees provided 40 percent and taxation 17 percent, while telecom license fees fell to 4 percent. Because of an unexpected surge in fishing license fees, total recurrent revenue was 30 percent more than the budget estimate. Total operating expenditure was 24 percent below the budgeted level, primarily because of a shortfall in expenditure on goods and services.

Capital expenditure, which for the first time was largely domestically financed, was 32 percent below the approved level. Consequently, instead of a projected budget deficit of approximately 24 percent of GDP, the budget surplus was 9 percent. Such conservative projections of revenue and overestimates of expenditure have been characteristic of Tuvalu government budgets in the 1990s. A new administration introduced the 2000 budget and continued the post-independence tradition of fiscal prudence. It projected a 15 percent increase in revenue, largely attributable to increased distribution of income from the Tuvalu Trust Fund and external grants. Operating expenditure was projected to rise a substantial 72 percent because of increased expenditure on personnel, goods and services, and special items that included contributions to the Falekaupule Trust Fund to finance outer island development projects. This fund was established in late 1999 with ADB loan funds, community contributions, and matching government funds. Capital expenditure is projected to rise the same percentage as operating expenditure, as new government offices are built and outer islands are provided with electricity supplies. The overall budget is officially presented as balanced. In fact, in 2000 Tuvalu will receive ADB concessional loans of A\$1.8 million, and A\$3.2

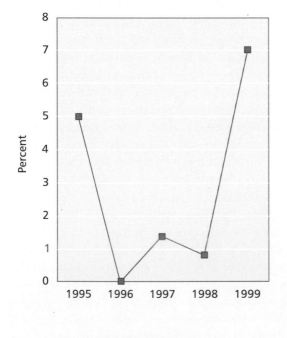

Figure 2.28 Inflation Rates, Tuvalu, 1995-1999

Source: Appendix table A9.

million will come from government's financial reserves in the Consolidated Investment Fund. The total A$5 million matches a planned augmentation of the capital in the Tuvalu Trust Fund.

In 1999, the government began to devolve administrative responsibilities including some expenditure management to Falekaupule, the outer island councils. This was in line with the medium-term development strategy's focus on ensuring greater equality of income distribution between the capital island of Funafuti and the outer islands. The Falekaupule Trust Fund is expected to reach a capital base of A$14.6 million in 2000, and to generate annual development finance of A$590,000 for an outer island population of approximately 5,000, the same number of residents as Funafuti.

The government also began negotiations with Japan for acquiring a multipurpose inter-island vessel to supplement the services of the old existing vessel, and to ease the transport constraint on outer island commercial activity. However, activity in the market economy will continue to be concentrated in Funafuti and will be dominated by the public sector. In 2000, construction of government offices, road reconstruction, slightly increased public service employment, and a 10 percent wage rise for public servants will stimulate private sector activity and significantly accelerate the aggregate economic growth rate. Plans have been announced for accelerating public sector reform through (a) corporatizing inter-island shipping and the Tuvalu Maritime School, (b) commercializing service provision by some ministries, and (c) introducing a performance orientation in the public service and public enterprises. Implementing the reforms can be expected to be a slow process. Meanwhile, private sector development that is not a direct function of public sector expansion remains limited by location, difficulties of access to land, and poor international transport links.

VANUATU

National accounts show that real GDP increased by 0.2 percent in 1998, a year characterized by political instability and disarray in macroeconomic policy. Output of the agriculture, fisheries, and forestry sector grew by 6.9 percent, primarily because of greater copra and kava production. Industry sector output fell 7 percent, while service sector output declined 0.7 percent, largely because of reduced wholesale and retail trade.

In 1999, real GDP fell an estimated 2 percent, despite a 7.6 percent growth in industry sector production from a substantial increase in aid-funded construction (see figure 2.29). Agriculture sector output declined 9.3 percent, with production slowed by a cyclone in February. The government sector reportedly contracted 5 percent, while the overall decline in the service sector was 1.2 percent. Visitor arrivals in the first half of 1999 were lower for various reasons. A Sydney hailstorm grounded the Air Vanuatu aircraft for more than six weeks; a domestic air crash damaged Vanuatu's image; and competition increased from other tourist destinations such as Fiji Islands, New Caledonia, and Tahiti. However, the frequency of flights from Australia increased in comparison with 1998, and the number of visitors began to climb in the latter half of the year.

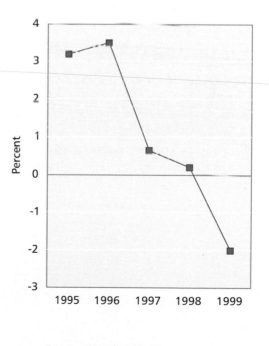

Figure 2.29 Real GDP Growth Rates, Vanuatu, 1995-1999

Source: Appendix table A1.

Along with stagnation in tourism receipts in 1999, cocoa, copra, and kava exports fell from their 1998 levels. However, revenue from beef and timber exports rose as export volumes increased. Import expenditure dropped from the high level of 1998, as tourism and the aggregate level of economic activity fell. The deficit on the current account remained around 8 percent of GDP, and was matched by a capital account surplus from long-term public borrowing, notably disbursement of an ADB program loan. Through 1999, the vatu, which is pegged against a group of currencies, appreciated 0.5 percent against the US dollar and depreciated almost 6 percent against the Australian dollar in both nominal and real terms, as Vanuatu's inflation rate was nearly the same as Australia's. No balance-of-payments pressure was evident, with official foreign reserves at the end of 1999 equivalent to 6.5 months of imports. No significant policy-induced changes in the nominal effective exchange rate were anticipated.

Given the openness of the economy and the pegged exchange rate system, the scope for an independent monetary policy is limited. Up to September 1999 the money supply grew by only 0.3 percent from the corresponding quarter in 1998, entirely because of growth in domestic credit. This growth reflected increased loans to the private sector, particularly for land and house purchases. Net foreign assets fell 1.2 percent. Considerable scope existed for credit expansion, with commercial banks' actual reserve holdings 76 percent higher than the prescribed Statutory Deposit Ratio, which was reintroduced in November 1998. At the end of the third quarter of 1999, the weighted average lending and deposit rates had declined slightly to 12.5 percent and 3.3 percent, respectively, so that the interest spread had widened from 9 to 9.2 percent.

Following an overall budget deficit of 10.3 percent of GDP in 1998, the target outcome in 1999 was a deficit of 5.4 percent of GDP. The actual outcome was estimated to be an overall deficit of 1.2 percent of GDP. This was attributable largely to development expenditure of 39 percent of the budgeted level, which reflected delays in implementing major infrastructure projects. Total expenditure and net lending fell 24 percent from 1998. Revenue and grants reached 95 percent of the budgeted level, despite an economic growth rate well below expectations. The restructuring of the tax system from trade tax to a value-added tax showed encouraging results, with 96 percent of budgeted value-added tax revenue collected.

External concessional loans financed 92 percent of the budget deficit. The total stock of debt stood at Vt9,657.1 million, or 35 percent of GDP, and one fourth was domestic debt. The 2000 budget provided for a balanced recurrent budget, an increase in development expenditure, and an overall deficit of 3 percent of GDP to be financed by external concessional loans. The revenue estimate was a realistic 0.3 percent below the 1999 budget level, while the recurrent expenditure estimate was 2.2 percent below the 1999 level. The latter may prove difficult to achieve unless public service staffing is consistent with budget provisions.

Restoring investor confidence is crucial, and the Foreign Investment Act was amended in April 1999 to be less restrictive of foreign investment. However, a sudden change of government in November 1999 introduced uncertainty into the policy environment. The new prime minister, who headed a coalition of five parties with a slender parliamentary majority, indicated an intention to review the roles of the previous administration and the role of external funding agencies.

As the Century Turns
The Social Challenge in Asia

As the Century Turns
The Social Challenge in Asia

As developing Asia enters the 21st century, it faces an enormous social challenge: to improve the quality of life for around 900 million Asians who still live below the dollar-a-day poverty line. The social challenge, however, goes beyond economic deprivation reflected by an income measure of poverty. It also entails addressing other aspects of human deprivation, such as illiteracy, malnutrition, high incidence of morbidity, poor access to water and sanitation, vulnerability to short-term shocks, and poor governance. Promoting inclusive and sustainable economic growth remains the best path to poverty reduction. Such growth is crucial because it increases demand for the one asset on which the poor depend most—their labor. It is also crucial because the resources for and the political feasibility of anti-poverty programs are greater when incomes and economic opportunities are expanding for all. To achieve such inclusive growth, the Asian economies should promote an overall policy environment that emphasizes openness and market orientation, along with labor market flexibility and prudent macroeconomic management. This policy framework for inclusive growth should be part of an overall national anti-poverty program that includes appropriate investments in human and physical infrastructure, improved governance, and strengthened social safety nets. While Asia's developing countries must accept the burden of responsibility for addressing the region's social challenge, more needs to be done internationally. These international efforts should be directed at improving the global trading environment; increasing the flow of foreign assistance; and providing public goods that have a direct bearing on the welfare of the poor in developing economies, such as research on tropical diseases and agriculture.

Developing Asia enters the new century with an enormous challenge: to improve the quality of life for the hundreds of millions of its citizens who still live in poverty. The magnitude of poverty in the region is staggering. According to the most common international definition of poverty—those who live on less than a dollar a day income measured in purchasing-power-parity dollars—about 900 million people were poor in 1998. That is about twice as many poor people as in the rest of the developing world combined. Using a more generous poverty threshold of two dollars a day, almost two billion people—the majority of Asia's population—are poor.

Asia's social challenge cannot—and should not—be defined by dollar income alone. A broad definition of the quality of human life must include

other aspects of human deprivation: illiteracy, malnutrition, bad health, poor access to water and
sanitation, vulnerability to economic shocks, and lack
of political freedom. In all these dimensions, there is
much to be accomplished. In South Asia, for instance,
50 percent or more of the population is illiterate. In
countries such as Cambodia or Viet Nam, fewer than
half of all households have access to safe drinking
water. Throughout Asia, 2.7 million people die from
diseases related to air pollution every year.

These depressing figures mask a more complex
picture. Parts of Asia have managed spectacular
improvements in quality of life over the past four
decades. Since the 1960s, many countries in the region
have undergone a dramatic economic and social transformation, lifting hundreds of millions of people out
of poverty. Some economies, particularly the newly
industrialized economies (NIEs)—Hong Kong, China;
Republic of Korea (henceforth referred to as Korea);
Singapore, and Taipei,China—telescoped into four
decades the process of social and economic development that took the advanced economies of Western
Europe three centuries to achieve. Abject poverty was
virtually eradicated. Some Southeast Asian economies
also made impressive strides: in Malaysia and
Indonesia, for instance, the incidence of dollar-a-day
poverty during 1975-1995 underwent dramatic
reductions.

Unfortunately, not all parts of Asia shared this
progress. South Asia, in particular, lagged behind. For
instance, the infant mortality rate in South Asia is
77—meaning that 77 babies of every 1,000 die before
their first birthday—and is much higher than the
developing country average of 58. There are also large
differences in progress between ethnic groups and
genders and between rural and urban areas. In general,
women have fared worse than men; minority ethnic
groups have fared worse than majority groups; rural
areas have fared worse than urban areas.

More worrying, there are signs that progress in
reducing poverty has stalled in recent years, and in
some cases has even reversed. In the Central Asian
republics, the collapse of the communist system pre-
saged a massive economic decline, a widespread im-
plosion of the social protection system, and a rise in
poverty. The financial crises of 1997-1998 were a costly
setback for the worst-affected countries in East and

Southeast Asia. Although financial collapse did not
cause poverty rates to soar, as many had feared, poverty
did increase, while improvements in health, education, and nutrition stalled. Even in countries not hit
by crisis—particularly the People's Republic of China
(PRC)—their spectacular progress in poverty
reduction has apparently now faltered. Because of all
these factors combined, there are more people living
in poverty today in Asia than there were in the
mid-1990s.

Addressing this challenge is the main task facing
Asia, but there are reasons for optimism. Policymakers
now have a better understanding of poverty and more
knowledge about which anti-poverty policies work.
Democratic institutions are on the rise, giving the poor
a greater voice in the political process. Greater
participation by the poor, together with broad social
pressures for better governance, makes it more difficult
for governments to remain inattentive. Meanwhile,
global markets continue to offer new opportunities,
and as Asian countries continue the process of liberalization—both internally and externally—these
opportunities become easier to grasp.

The financial crises have shown the region's
vulnerabilities, however, as well as the inadequacy of
its domestic social protection policies. Meanwhile,
ever-less official money is available for development
assistance. Addressing the region's social challenge will
demand creating the right policies and tools to grasp
the new opportunities, while ensuring that no segment
of the society gets left behind. This chapter will
describe Asia's social challenge, explain the reasons it
exists, and then examine policies that can be used to
confront that challenge.

DIMENSIONS OF THE SOCIAL CHALLENGE

The most obvious manifestation of Asia's social
challenge is the number of poor people in the region.
The challenge goes far beyond poverty, however.
Human deprivation can mean poor health, poor
nutrition, and poor education. It can mean living in a
degraded environment, or having few civil liberties
and little opportunity for political participation.

These dimensions do not always move in
tandem. Consider, for instance, Indonesia and the
Philippines. These countries have similar income

levels, but the incidence of poverty in the Philippines is many times higher than it is in Indonesia. Nonetheless, several measures of social well-being, such as the prevalence of malnutrition in children under 5, life expectancy, and adult literacy, suggest that the poor in the Philippines are less deprived than the poor in Indonesia.

Often, however, deprivations reinforce each other. Poor nutritional and health indicators, for instance, make it much more difficult for the poor to earn income. Lack of political and social empowerment renders it unlikely that the poor can influence government allocations of resources for social services, and they allow the nonpoor to more easily capture the benefits of government-directed anti-poverty programs. Thus, the cumulative effect of deprivation adds up to a much worse quality of life than apparent when considering the various dimensions one by one. The social challenge is most acute in countries, or regions within countries, where such a confluence of negative factors occurs. In such cases, in South Asia, for example, making and sustaining progress in eliminating poverty is extremely difficult.

Poverty

The term poverty has many different uses (see box 3.1). A narrow definition is the lack of access to the basic goods and services that constitute a minimally acceptable standard of living. What constitutes a minimally acceptable standard of living is, of course, not fixed, but varies across countries and even over time. In extremely poor countries, poverty might be defined as the lack of access to a subsistence quantity of a staple food product, such as rice. In richer countries, poverty typically is defined as access to higher minimum quantities of a broader set of basic goods and services.

According to the dollar-a-day criterion, the overwhelming majority of Asia's poor live in South Asia. It is striking that while the recent financial and economic crisis in East and Southeast Asia may have added around 10 million more people to the ranks of those living below a dollar-a-day income between 1996 and 1998, the number of dollar-a-day poor in South Asia increased by 17 million over the same period (World Bank 1999b).

The reduction of poverty has been relatively slow in South Asia. India—which accounts for the majority of poor in South Asia—made no visible progress in reducing poverty from 1950 to 1975. As table 3.1 shows, more than half of all Indians lived below its national poverty line in the early 1970s. Since then, however, progress has been made. By the early 1990s, about one in three Indians lived below the national poverty line, although on a dollar-a-day basis almost half of all Indians were still poor in 1994. Poverty is also pervasive in Bangladesh and Nepal. In both countries, the incidence of poverty based on the national poverty lines is even higher than in India. Unfortunately, while the share of people who live on less than a dollar a day has fallen in South Asia in recent years (from 44 to 40 percent from 1990-1998), throughout the 1990s the number of poor has continued to expand along with the growth of the population. In 1998, there were 522 million poor people in South Asia, almost 30 million more than in 1990 (World Bank 1999b).

The PRC has a much lower incidence of poverty than South Asia. In 1998, 213 million people— 17 percent of the population—lived on less than a dollar a day (World Bank 1999b). While the latest studies reveal that poverty reduction has slowed in the last few years, the PRC's record of reducing poverty over the last 20 years has been nothing short of remarkable. Poverty rates fell sharply after liberalizing reforms began in 1978. While 28 percent of the population in 1978 faced income poverty based on the national poverty line, this had shrunk to only 9 percent by 1998.

Other Asian economies making the transition from central planning have not fared nearly as well. In Mongolia, recent estimates suggest that almost 2 million people, 80 percent of the population, live below the dollar-a-day poverty line. In the Central Asian republics and other Asian transition economies, poverty rates are lower—but still significant. Fortunately, the most recent estimates suggest that poverty rates are falling in some cases. Measured in terms of the national poverty line, the incidence of poverty in Viet Nam has fallen from 58 percent in 1993 to 37 percent in 1998 (World Bank 1999b).

Thailand's performance has been more mixed but still impressive. Poverty declined rapidly in the

Box 3.1 **Lexicon of Poverty**

The poverty line is the minimum consumption level required to achieve the minimum acceptable standard of living within a society. This standard may be defined in absolute or relative terms. The absolute poverty line is often defined as the threshold that allows minimum calorie requirements plus a small allowance for nonfood items. A relative poverty line is defined as a function of various income distribution parameters such as the mean or median. For example, a relative poverty line could be defined as 50 percent of the mean income. When consumption falls below this threshold, the person is considered poor.

Because minimum acceptable consumption levels vary across countries and over time, poverty lines also tend to vary across countries and over time. However, differences in the definitions and methodologies used for computing poverty lines tend to vary far more between countries than within the same country over time, especially when the time periods are not too far apart. Thus, it is much easier to assess the changes in poverty in a country over time, than to use national methodologies for international comparisons of poverty.

The dollar-a-day poverty line is the consumption level of one dollar per day, based on 1985/1993 dollars and adjusted for purchasing power parity. This threshold stands as an internationally accepted minimum level of private consumption and seeks to provide a more meaningful comparison of poverty across countries.

Poverty incidence is the proportion of a country's population with income or consumption expenditure below the poverty threshold. The measure may be based on either the national poverty line or the dollar-a-day poverty line. Poverty incidence is also referred to as the headcount index.

The depth of poverty or the income gap ratio is the average amount by which per capita income or the expenditure of poor people falls short of the poverty line, expressed as a proportion of the poverty line.

The intensity of poverty or the poverty gap ratio is the income gap ratio multiplied by the headcount index. This is equivalent to the average amount by which per capita income or the consumption expenditure of the entire population falls short of the poverty line, expressed as a proportion of the poverty line.

The transient poor are those who are poor for a short time, usually because of economic distortions or market imperfections. Those suffering temporary income shortfalls could include farmers whose crops suffered from drought and who had no crop insurance, students in financial trouble because of an imperfectly functioning capital market, and displaced workers who have no unemployment insurance.

The permanent or chronically poor are those who are poor for a long time because they have few assets or skills. The chronically poor earn inadequate incomes even in the best of circumstances with no market distortions.

The Lorenz curve is a curve that represents the cumulative proportion of income that accrues to each cumulative proportion of the population, beginning with the lowest income group. If there were perfect income equality, the Lorenz curve would be a 45-degree line.

An income quintile is one fifth of the population, ranked according to levels of per capita income. The quintile income ratio compares the income earned by the top 20 percent of the population with that of the lowest 20 percent, and is a commonly used measure of inequality. Quintiles are also used in poverty profiles to examine how characteristics such as education may vary between the richest 20 percent and the poorest 20 percent of the population.

The Gini coefficient is a commonly used measure of inequality of income (or consumption expenditure). The Gini coefficient is the area between the Lorenz curve and the 45-degree line, expressed as a percentage of the area under the 45-degree line. With perfect equality, the Gini ratio would equal zero; with perfect inequality, it would equal one. In most countries, Gini coefficients range from a low of 0.3 to a high of 0.7.

1970s, but then rose sharply in the first half of the 1980s. By the mid-1980s, the incidence of dollar-a-day poverty was higher than a decade earlier. Fortunately, the downward trend in poverty incidence resumed after the mid-1980s and continued until the recent financial crisis. Estimates suggest that before the crisis, less than 2 percent of the Thai population lived below the dollar-a-day measure. By contrast, poverty has been more persistent in the Philippines. While dollar-a-day incidence rates came down about

Table 3.1 **Incidence of Poverty Measured by Surveys,
Selected Asian Developing Economies, Selected Years
(percent)**

Subregion and country	Survey year	Headcount index (national poverty line)	Survey year	Headcount index (national poverty line)	Survey year	Headcount index ($1-a-day)
Newly industrialized economies						
Korea, Rep. of	1970	23	1984	5	1998	<1
PRC and Mongolia						
PRC	1978	28	1998	9	1998	17
Mongolia	1991	15	1996	36	1997	80
Central Asian republics						
Kazakhstan	—	—	1996	35	1993	<2
Kyrgyz Republic	—	—	1993	40	1993	19
Southeast Asia						
Indonesia	1976	40	1996	11	1996	8
Malaysia	1970	49	1992	16	1995	4
Philippines	1971	52	1997	38	1994	27
Thailand	1975	32	1992	13	1992	<2
Viet Nam	1993	58	1998	37	—	—
South Asia						
Bangladesh	1973	73	1996	36	—	—
India	1972	52	1994	35	1994	47
Nepal	1979	61	1996	42	1995	50
Pakistan	1975	43	1992	28	1991	12
Sri Lanka	1983	22	1997	21	1994	4

— Not available.

Note: Some years in the earliest survey may refer to midpoint of period covered. Data for $1-a-day poverty are estimated based on most recent surveys.

Sources: ADB data; World Bank (1999c).

8 percentage points from 1985-1995, the number of poor remained roughly constant at around 18 million because of high rates of population growth.

The lowest rates of poverty in developing Asia are in the economically dynamic economies of East and Southeast Asia, especially the NIEs. In the last 40 years, poverty—measured by the dollar-a-day criterion—has been virtually eliminated in Hong Kong, China; Korea; Singapore; and Taipei,China. Southeast Asian economies have not totally eliminated poverty, but—at least until the onset of

the region's financial crisis—had made impressive progress. In Malaysia, the incidence of dollar-a-day poverty fell from 17.4 percent in 1975 to around 4 percent in 1995. Indonesia's record was even more impressive, with the incidence of poverty based on the national poverty line dropping from 40 to 11 percent between the mid-1970s and mid-1990s.

Unfortunately, these dramatic improvements have been stymied by Asia's recent financial crisis. It is clear that the collapsing currencies and dramatic recessions had substantial adverse effects on poverty in the crisis-affected countries. Economic crises hurt the poor through various ways. Most obviously, the contraction in economic activity means that people lose their jobs and household income falls. While the loss of earning opportunities may be uniform across different income groups, given their precarious financial situation, the poor are more vulnerable. Rapid inflation, often the result of a large devaluation, squeezes the purchasing power of earnings. Relative price shifts can severely hurt the poor. Cuts in government spending, because of fiscal austerity programs, can adversely affect health and education services used by the poor.

Some facts are clear from Asia's experience. When the crisis hit, the main adjustment in the labor market was a reduction in earnings rather than a rise in open unemployment. Nevertheless, joblessness did rise—from 2.6 percent in 1997 to 6.8 percent in 1998 in Korea, for example. Workers in some sectors, such as construction, were particularly affected. There was also a big shift from formal to informal employment, particularly as young adults were drafted into family enterprises. In some countries, high inflation hit the poor hard. In Indonesia, for instance, consumer prices jumped nearly 60 percent in 1998, compared with 6.6 percent in the previous year.

It is too soon to gauge exactly the overall impact on poverty. Standard poverty measures are a useful guide to changes in poverty rates over the medium and long term, but they are less useful in the short term, particularly during an economic crisis, for several reasons. First, the surveys on which poverty estimates are based are usually conducted at two- to three-year intervals. Typically, there is a lag of six months to a year or more between the end of data collection (which itself often takes a year to complete) and the time new poverty estimates become available. Second, poverty estimates are very sensitive to the accuracy of the measured price increases. At a time of rapid inflation, as in Indonesia during the recent crisis, mis-estimation is a risk. This is particularly a problem in rural areas, as consumer price data are collected mainly in urban areas. Third, when large changes in relative prices also occur, such as after a big devaluation, people change the composition of their consumption. The basket of goods assumed under the old poverty line may no longer be an accurate reflection of people's minimal consumption, even if it is correctly updated for inflation (Frankenberg, Thomas, and Beegle 1999).

Despite all these caveats, the available numbers do suggest that poverty increased in those countries that were the worst affected by the recent regional economic crisis (see figure 3.1). However, the increases have not been as high as some initially expected. For example, in Indonesia, a forecast prepared by the International Labour Organization in 1998 predicted that poverty incidence would rise to 48 percent by the end of 1998 from a precrisis level of 11 percent (ILO 1998). A study published by the Indonesian Central Bureau of Statistics also forecast that poverty rates based on the national poverty line would reach about 40 percent by mid-1998. Fortunately, the most reliable information available suggests that these dire forecasts have proved inaccurate. Poverty incidence based on the national poverty line increased from 11.3 percent in February 1996 to 16.7 percent in December 1998 (World Bank 1999b). The latest information suggests that in some parts of Indonesia, particularly where a large segment of the population is involved in producing cash crops for exports, household incomes increased rapidly in nominal terms in 1998 (Booth 1999).

Social Indicators

Standard measures of poverty provide information about the material resources available to households, but these are only partial measures of well-being. They do not provide information on critical aspects such as literacy and education, health and nutrition, and the quality of the environment in which people live. As discussed earlier, for a given level of income, the performance of countries on these broader indicators can vary substantially. Some countries are underachievers and others are overachievers in terms of social indicators. For a fuller picture of the quality of life, it is therefore important that social indicators be considered in juxtaposition with the income measures of poverty.

Literacy and Education. Literacy is usually defined as the ability to read and write a simple message. Typically, this is achieved by completing four or five years of primary school. Adult literacy is universal (or nearly

Figure 3.1 Incidence of Poverty based on National Poverty Line, Selected Southeast Asian Countries, 1985-1998

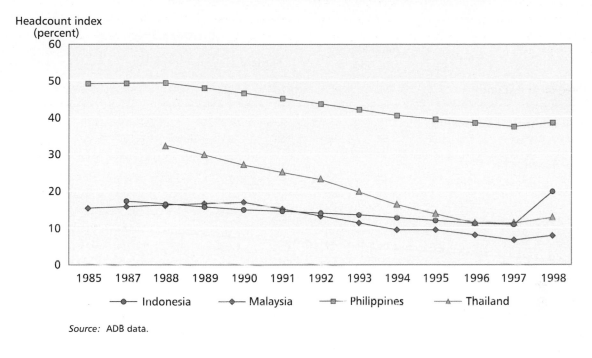

Source: ADB data.

so) in all Central Asian countries and also in Korea, Philippines, Thailand, and Viet Nam. In contrast, the adult literacy rate is around 50 percent in India and lower for the other countries in South Asia (exception for Sri Lanka). It is also low in Cambodia and the Lao People's Democratic Republic (Lao PDR). Mongolia, Sri Lanka, and Viet Nam have relatively high literacy rates, however, and given their low per capita incomes, these are notable achievements.

Raising adult literacy (for ages 15 and up) is a slow process without broad adult literacy programs, which few Asian countries have. Even a sharp and sustained increase in primary school enrollment rates will affect adult literacy rates only after a lag of several years, when those newly enrolled children reach age 15.

Nevertheless, it is encouraging that primary enrollment rates have increased dramatically even among those Asian countries with low rates of adult literacy, such as Bangladesh, India, Lao PDR, and Nepal. Because of the expansion of primary schooling, the dispersion of enrollment rates among Asian economies is much less today than it was a few decades ago (see table 3.2). It is also less than the dispersion in adult literacy rates.

Unfortunately, raising enrollment rates is not a panacea for low literacy levels. Higher enrollment rates reflect neither the ability of schools to retain students long enough to achieve literacy nor the quality of instruction received. In Bangladesh, Nepal, and Pakistan, for example, only about half of all primary school entrants reach grade 5, while Nepal's primary school enrollment ratio is above 100 percent because large numbers of students repeat the early grades. By comparison, about 90 percent of primary school entrants in Indonesia and the PRC reach grade 5. The available information also suggests that the resources invested per student in primary schools are lower in

Table 3.2 Literacy and Enrollment Rates, Selected Asian Developing Economies, Selected Years (percent)

Subregion and country	Adult literacy rate		Gross enrollment rate					
			Primary		Secondary		Tertiary	
	1980	1995	1970	1996	1970	1996	1970	1996
Newly industrialized economies								
Korea, Rep. of	94	98	103	94	42	102	7	60
PRC and Mongolia								
PRC	66	82	91	120	24	71	0	6
Mongolia	72	83	110	89	83	56	6	17
Central Asian republics								
Kazakhstan	—	100	85	98	93	87	34	32
Kyrgyz Republic	—	97	116	104	110	79	16	12
Tajikistan	41	100	—	95	—	78	24	20
Uzbekistan	—	100	81	78	106	94	29	36
Southeast Asia								
Cambodia	—	65	30	109	8	28	2	1
Indonesia	67	84	80	115	16	52	3	11
Lao PDR	42	57	57	111	4	29	0	3
Malaysia	70	84	89	91	34	62	2	11
Myanmar	77	83	88	100	21	35	2	6
Philippines	90	95	108	118	46	79	17	35
Thailand	88	94	81	88	17	57	3	21
Viet Nam	83	94	—	—	—	—	—	—
South Asia								
Bangladesh	30	38	54	84	20	19	2	6
India	41	52	78	101	24	49	5	7
Nepal	19	28	26	105	10	37	2	5
Pakistan	27	38	36	81	13	30	2	4
Sri Lanka	85	90	99	109	47	75	1	5

— Not available.

Notes: Adult literacy rate is the proportion of the population aged 15 years and above who can, with comprehension, read or write, or read and write a simple message. Gross enrollment rate is the ratio of total enrollment, regardless of age, to the population of the age group that officially corresponds to the level of education shown.

Sources: UNESCO (1999); World Bank (1999c).

South Asian schools than elsewhere in Asia (Deolalikar and others 1997). The primary school pupil-teacher ratio was 59 in South Asia in 1992, for example, compared to 23 in Southeast Asia (ADB 1997). While the relationship between pupil-teacher ratios and the quality of education is not a watertight

one, extremely high ratios such as in South Asia usually indicate a low quality of primary education.

The cross-country variation in enrollment rates is greater at higher levels of education. While Bangladesh had a gross secondary enrollment rate of 19 percent in 1996, for example, Korea's enrollment rate exceeded 100 percent. Surprisingly, many of the relatively high-income Southeast Asian economies with high rates of adult literacy and enrollment in primary education do not have particularly high rates of secondary school enrollment.

So far, there is little evidence that the region's economic and financial crisis has dramatically worsened access to education, although it may have affected its quality. Primary school enrollments have not fallen, but evidence indicates that secondary school attendance has suffered, particularly among girls from poor families. Interestingly, in several crisis-affected countries, the crisis has led to higher enrollment at tertiary levels of education. This reflects several factors, particularly the reduction in employment opportunities for young people.

Health and Nutrition. Standards of health and nutrition in Asia have improved substantially over the past four decades. A child born in East and Southeast Asia today can expect to live to about 70, almost 45 percent longer than a child born in 1960. In South Asia, life expectancy has risen from 44 in 1960 to 62 today. This is comparable with life expectancy in the Middle East and North Africa, and is substantially higher than in Sub-Saharan Africa. In Asia, overall life expectancy has risen to an average of 65 years in 1997.

One of the biggest influences on raising life expectancy has been a sharp drop in infant mortality rates. In industrialized countries of the Organisation for Economic Co-operation and Development (OECD), the infant mortality rates are around 6, that is, six infants of every 1,000 die before their first birthday. In Hong Kong, China; Korea; and Singapore, infant mortality rates are similar to those in industrial countries, while in South Asia the infant mortality rate is 77.

These variations reflect differences in nutrition and access to health care, safe water, and sanitation. Standards in all these areas have improved significantly over the past four decades, but in South Asia especially, they remain low compared with the rest of the developing world. Overall calorie consumption per person in South Asia is marginally higher than in Sub-Saharan Africa, but child nutrition is much worse. In 1990, approximately six of ten children in South Asia had stunted growth from malnutrition, compared with four in ten children in Sub-saharan Africa. One in three babies in South Asia is born underweight, compared with one in six in Sub-saharan Africa. In contrast, the incidence of child malnutrition in East and Southeast Asia is almost the lowest in the developing world, and is lower only in Latin America.

Throughout Asia, official measures of access to health care, safe water, and sanitation often are overestimated, and must be interpreted with caution. In general, however, access to all these services is far greater in East and Southeast Asia than in South Asia. On average, more than 90 percent of the population in East and Southeast Asia have access to health care, while national data for South Asia suggest that its corresponding figure is about 75 percent.

Lack of safe water and sanitation is one of the biggest causes of disease in the developing world, and Asia is no exception. In South Asia and some of the transition economies, access to safe water and sanitation is particularly lacking. In countries such as Cambodia, Papua New Guinea, and Viet Nam, less than half of households have access to safe water. Official national estimates from South Asia suggest that about 81 percent of people have access to safe water. Given the region's enormous water pollution problems, however, these access rates are almost certainly overestimated. Access to sanitation facilities is also low: in Cambodia, India, Nepal, Papua New Guinea, and Uzbekistan, less than 30 percent of households have access to sanitation facilities.

Little concrete evidence exists to prove that the recent financial crisis harmed the health and nutrition of people in the crisis-affected countries. Nonetheless, it is highly likely that the poorest and most vulnerable segments suffered some degree of malnutrition. Focus group studies conducted by the Asian Development Bank (ADB) in some of the crisis-affected countries indicated that children from lower income groups were arriving at school without breakfast or lunch (ADB 1999n).

Similarly, there is little evidence to suggest that the crisis significantly worsened the general health level in the affected countries. However, there is evidence that many people shifted from higher-cost, higher-quality private medical services to cheaper, lower-quality public services. This created a "double squeeze" on public health facilities. Demand for their services has increased far beyond normal capacity, while budgetary constraints have forced a reduction in the quantity and quality of services.

Environment. Asia is the world's most polluted and environmentally degraded region (ADB 1997). The range of environmental problems is huge and runs from the pollution of air and water to the degradation of rural land and the congestion of its megacities. Several of the health hazards Asians face can be traced to water pollution, as well as air pollution and inadequate solid waste disposal, which are severe problems in some parts of Asia (see table 3.3).

Of the 2.7 million deaths related to air pollution each year, 1.8 million are caused by indoor pollution in rural areas. This occurs because many poor households, particularly in South Asia, rely overwhelmingly on traditional fuels.

The outdoor air in Asia's cities is among the dirtiest in the world. The level of ambient particulates—smoke particles and dust that are major

Table 3.3 Relative Severity of Environmental Problems, Selected Asian Subregions

Pollutant	PRC	East Asia	Southeast Asia	South Asia	Pacific
Air pollution					
Sulfur dioxide	XX	XXX	XX	X	—
Particulates	XX	—	XX	XXX	—
Lead	X	—	XXX	XX	—
Water pollution					
Suspended solids	XXX	—	XXX	XX	—
Fecal coliforms	XX	—	XXX	XX	XX
Biological oxygen demand	—	—	XXX	XX	—
Nitrates	XX	XX	X	XXX	—
Lead	X	XX	XXX	X	—
Access to water and sanitation					
Lack of access to safe water	X	—	XXX	XXX	XX
Lack of access to sanitation	XXX	—	XX	XXX	XX
Deforestation					
Deforestation rate	XX	—	XXX	XX	—
Land degradation					
Soil erosion	XXX	—	XXX	XXX	—
Waterlogging and salinization	XX	—	XX	XXX	—
Desertification	—	—	—	XXX	—
Imperata spread	—	—	XXX	—	—
Energy consumption					
Annual growth rate	XX	XXX	XXX	XXX	—
Carbon dioxide emissions	XXX	XX	X	X	—

— Not available.

X Moderate but rising.
XX Severe.
XXX Very severe.

Source: ADB (1997).

causes of respiratory diseases—is generally twice the world average, and more than five times as high as in industrial countries and Latin America (ADB 1997).

By virtually every measure, Asia's rivers are far more polluted than those in the rest of the world. More than 90 percent of the wastewater in Asia is discharged directly into streams, open drains, rivers, lakes, and coastal waters without treatment. Asia's rivers typically have four times the world average of suspended solids (the amount of waste suspended in the water) and 20 times the level prevalent in OECD countries (ADB 1997). The levels of suspended solids in Asia's rivers have quadrupled since the late 1970s, while they have remained unchanged or improved in the rest of the world (ADB 1997). Asia's natural resources are also declining rapidly. During the past four decades, Asia has lost half of its forest cover and half its fish stock. Deforestation, which is particularly acute in Southeast Asia but also a serious problem in South Asia and the PRC, is partly responsible for increased desertification, soil erosion, flooding, and loss of biodiversity.

While it is difficult for anyone to fully escape pollution and environmental degradation, various factors suggest that the poor face the brunt of these problems. The poor tend to live in areas that are more prone to environment-related natural disasters, such as flooding and landslides. They are more likely to live near heavily polluting factories, dumps, and hazardous waste sites. Malnutrition and poor health make them more susceptible to infectious diseases. Lower incomes, less education, and less access to health care mean that they are less able to recover once ill, and hence environmental degradation reinforces poverty.

Internal Disparities

National indicators of social and economic well-being mask large disparities among groups within particular countries. The most obvious disparities are those between rich and poor, but disparities occur along other lines, even between members of the same household. Gender, ethnicity, religion, caste, and regional differences can all cause divergences in social and economic well-being.

Income and Wealth Disparities. In general, income inequality is lower in Asia than in other parts of the developing world. For example, Gini indexes—the standard measure of overall income inequality (refer back to box 3.1)—of 0.5 or more are common in Latin America and a few African countries such as South Africa and Kenya. In contrast, the Gini indexes for developing countries in Asia generally fall in the range of 0.3-0.4 and have been fairly stable over time (see table 3.4).

Some notable exceptions exist. In Thailand, for instance, the Gini index reached 0.52 in the early 1990s. While data from the transition economies are generally scanty, some studies suggest that income inequality has risen sharply in countries of the former Soviet Union. In the Kyrgyz Republic, for instance, the Gini index rose from about 0.26 in the 1980s to 0.55 in the 1990s (Kanbur and Lustig 1999).

Despite relatively low income inequality in developing Asia, the inequalities that do exist are troubling because they tend to be closely associated with disparities in other social dimensions, including those related to accumulating human capital. Education differentials, for example, are quite closely related to differentials in income, particularly in South Asia (see table 3.5).

In South Asia, more than 60 percent of the poorest one third of children aged 15-19 do not complete grade 5, compared to about 20 percent in Indonesia and the Philippines (Filmer and Pritchett 1999). In India, where 38 percent of all children do not complete grade 5, the poorest third of the children account for 61 percent of the shortfall, while the richest third accounts for only 4 percent. In the Philippines, where only 13 percent of children fail to complete grade 5, the poorest third account for 72 percent of the children who drop out.

Equally pronounced disparities exist between rich and poor Asians regarding such social indicators as mortality rates, nutritional status, and access to safe water and sanitation. In Indonesia, for example, child mortality rates among the poorest 20 percent of the population are 3.8 times higher than the child mortality rates among the richest 20 percent. Also, 48 percent of Indonesian households from the poorest fifth of the population use river, canal, or surface water for drinking, compared to only 1 percent of the richest

Table 3.4 **Income or Consumption Inequality,
Selected Asian Developing Economies,
Early 1970s, 1980s, and 1990s**

Subregion and country	Gini coefficient			Ratio of H20/L20		
	1970s	1980s	1990s	1970s	1980s	1990s
Newly industrialized economies						
Hong Kong, China	0.41	0.37	0.45	9.0	7.5	10.1
Korea, Rep. of	0.33	0.39	0.34	5.7	8.9	5.7
Singapore	0.41	0.41	0.39	—	7.1	—
Taipei,China	0.28	0.28	0.31	4.2	4.2	5.4
PRC	—	0.32	0.38	—	4.6	6.9
Southeast Asia						
Indonesia	0.31	0.36	0.32	—	5.8	4.7
Malaysia	0.50	0.51	0.48	14.1	15.1	11.7
Philippines	0.49	0.46	0.45	15.0	10.0	—
Thailand	0.43	0.43	0.52	9.8	11.9	15.8
South Asia						
Bangladesh	0.36	0.39	0.28	6.3	6.8	4.1
India	0.30	0.31	0.30	4.5	4.7	4.3
Pakistan	0.30	0.32	0.31	4.3	4.8	4.7
Sri Lanka	0.38	0.42	0.30	6.5	4.7	4.4

— Not available.

Note: The Gini coefficient is based on either income or consumption expenditure, depending on the approach used in each country. The H20 is the share of income of the top 20 percent of the population, and L20 is the share of income of the bottom 20 percent.

Source: Data derived from Deininger and Squire (1996).

fifth. More than seven of every ten people in the poorest fifth of the population use a bush or field as a latrine, compared to only 2 percent among the richest fifth.

Gender Disparities. Gender disparities are among the sharpest internal social disparities in many Asian countries (see table 3.6). In East and Southeast Asian countries, females for the most part fared better than males in terms of social indicators. Women are also better off in Central Asia, although recent develop-ments—including increased women's unemployment rates and reduced access to health care—suggest that women's status is worsening in Central Asia. In contrast, with the exception of Sri Lanka, women are generally worse off than men in South Asian countries.

The level of gender disparity in health and education is greater in South Asia than in any other region in the world (Filmer, King, and Pritchett 1998).

The indicators in table 3.6 point clearly to gender disparity in a number of countries. For example, mortality rates of children less than age 5 are normally lower among girls (for biological reasons). However, mortality of children less than age 5 is substantially higher among girls in South Asian countries, as well as in the PRC. Similarly, malnutrition is normally lower among girls under 5, but in South Asia it is either higher or the same as that of boys.

In South Asia (with the exception of Sri Lanka), school enrollment is substantially lower for girls than boys, and the disparity becomes even more marked at the secondary level. These disparities reflect gender

**Table 3.5 Comparative Index of Completion of Grade Five
for Ages 15-19, by Income Group,
Selected Asian Developing Economies, Selected Years**

Country	Year	Income groups		
		Poorest	Middle	Richest
Bangladesh	1996	45.2	69.8	100
India	1992	40.3	73.4	100
Indonesia	1994	82.0	95.4	100
Kazakhstan	1995	99.5	99.0	100
Nepal	1996	54.6	55.7	100
Pakistan	1990	29.3	61.3	100
Philippines	1993	81.9	97.5	100

Note: The percentage of 15- to 19-year-olds who completed Grade 5 in the richest income group was used as the base for each country, and assigned a value of 100. Rates of the other income groups are expressed as a proportion of the richest group.

Source: Based on Demographic and Health Surveys (DHS) data in Filmer and Pritchett (1999)

bias at the household level, such as a tendency for girls to be withdrawn from or skip school to care for siblings. They also reflect household responses to gender discrimination in labor markets, which lowers private returns to investment in schooling of girls.

Gender disparities exist in other areas. Evidence exists that, particularly in South Asia, girls and women are discriminated against in the allocation of food and other resources within the household (Alderman and others 1995; Deaton 1998). Women and girls are also exposed to greater environmental hazards within the household, such as facing the brunt of indoor air pollution from the use of traditional fuels. In addition, females are exposed to greater risk from violence, including abortion and infanticide of female children, child marriage, child and adult prostitution, domestic violence, and abuse of elderly women (especially widows). Although the quality of women's lives has improved in some areas—increased education levels and paid employment have enhanced intrahousehold power, while modern technologies have reduced

household burdens— the addition of market work to traditional household responsibilities has significantly reduced leisure. In addition, longer life expectancy and fewer siblings have increased women's burden of caring for the elderly.

Women tend to be discriminated against in labor markets in Asia, although the extent of such discrimination and the underlying causes are still the subject of considerable debate. Some formal sector jobs are not open to women, and the wages women receive are usually lower. Women also tend to be laid off before men in times of economic crisis. For example, during the 1997-1998 crisis in Korea, women were laid off much more frequently than men. There are also reports that heightened vulnerability among female employees led to increased levels of sexual harassment (Moon, Lee, and Yoo 1999). Unfortunately, the effect of the gender disparity in layoffs is not visible in gender-specific unemployment rates because many women subsequently withdrew from the labor market (D. Kim 1999).

Table 3.6 **Gender Disparity Indicators, Selected Asian Developing Economies, Selected Years**
(percent)

	Female minus male		Ratio of female to male		
Subregion and country	Probability of dying before age 5 1998	Moderate or severe stunting under age 5 1995	Probability of dying between ages 15 to 60 1997	Secondary school enrollment 1990-1996	Member of nonagricultural labor force 1997
Newly industrialized economies					
Korea, Rep. of	—	—	46	100	67
PRC and Mongolia					
PRC	11	-1	83	90	62
Mongolia	3	1	84	136	96
Central Asian republics					
Kazakhstan	-10	-4	44	101	106
Kyrgyz Republic	-12	—	47	112	101
Tajikistan	-15	—	61	90	69
Uzbekistan	-13	-5	56	88	89
Southeast Asia					
Cambodia	-14	—	87	59	78
Indonesia	-13	-2	78	85	69
Lao PDR	-8	-1	85	61	—
Malaysia	-3	—	61	109	62
Myanmar	-17	-5	83	103	59
Philippines	-11	-3	77	102	79
Thailand	-3	—	56	97	78
Viet Nam	3	<1	73	93	81
South Asia					
Bangladesh	10	1	108	50	36
India	15	<1	95	64	32
Nepal	14	3	115	51	16
Pakistan	-4	—	90	52	25
Sri Lanka	-2	2	64	110	64

— Not available.

Sources: World Bank (1999c); WHO (1999); UNICEF (1999).

Ethnic, Religious, and Caste Disparities. In some Asian countries, sharp differences still exist in income levels and social indicators between ethnic and religious groups and castes. In India in the mid-1980s, for example, the scheduled castes and tribes made up more than one third of the rural poor while accounting for less than one eighth of the rural population. Village surveys have found evidence of caste mobility, but this is mainly among the middle and upper castes. Upward mobility of low castes is rare. One study in Uttar Pradesh found, for example, that despite being targeted for favorable treatment under government programs, the relative position of low-caste *Jatabs* did not change. They still experienced slower per capita income growth, higher and stagnant levels of illiteracy (100 percent of females and 88 percent of males in 1993), virtual exclusion from nonagricultural wage employment, and unaltered land endowments (Lanjouw and Stern 1998).

The situation for ethnic minorities across developing Asia is not much better. In Viet Nam, for example, 53 different ethnic minorities constitute about 12 percent of the population. Social indicators for these groups tend to be lower, and sometimes considerably lower, than those of the dominant groups. The H'mong, for example, experience an infant mortality rate of 106 and a life expectancy of 52.8 years, while the corresponding figures for the majority Kinh population are 38.5 and 67.7, respectively. The differential between the H'mong and the Kinh populations in educational attainments is similarly sharp. In the PRC, the incidence of poverty is at least twice as high among the minorities as in the majority ethnic group.

Regional Disparities. Just as disparities exist between different groups of people, so they also exist between different areas within any single country. These differences are perhaps most stark between rural and urban areas. In most Asian countries, an overwhelming proportion of the poor live in rural areas. In Indonesia, 63 of 100 poor people live in rural areas, while the share is around 80 per 100 in India and Thailand, and nearly 70 per 100 in the Philippines. Because the majority of the population in these countries live in rural areas, it is not surprising that the incidence of rural poverty is higher than urban poverty, sometimes sharply so (see table 3.7)

Access to education, health care, and water and sanitation is generally worse in rural areas. Indoor air pollution is a much more serious problem in rural areas, where there is less access to electricity and other modern fuels. As in the case of poverty incidence, disparities in these other social dimensions can vary greatly across different rural settings. In the late 1980s in the PRC, for example, rural female literacy rates were as low as 11 percent and as high as 75 percent, although annual income per person ranged only from Y400 to Y600 (ADB 1997).

Although the rural-urban differentials in economic well-being are perhaps the most striking, they are not the only geographic disparities. Within Asian countries, sharp differences in social outcomes can be seen across regions, provinces, and states. In India's Bihar state, poverty incidence is 50 percent higher than the national average and more than 12 times higher than in the most prosperous state, Himachal Pradesh. In Pakistan, the incidence of poverty is higher in Pubjab and Baluchistan than in the northwest Frontier Province and Sindh.

Access to social services also varies sharply, but these disparities are often relatively independent of regional income differentials. In India, one of the

Table 3.7 Rural and Urban Population below Poverty Line, Selected Asian Developing Economies, Selected Years (percent)

Subregion and country	Survey year	Rural	Urban
PRC and Mongolia			
PRC	1996	7.9	<2
Mongolia	1995	33.1	38.5
Central Asian republics			
Kazakhstan	1996	39.0	30.0
Kyrgyz Republic	1993	48.1	28.7
Southeast Asia			
Cambodia	1997	40.1	21.1
Indonesia	1990	14.3	16.8
Lao PDR	1993	53.0	24.0
Philippines	1997	51.2	22.5
Thailand	1992	15.5	10.2
Viet Nam	1993	57.2	25.9
South Asia			
Bangladesh	1995, 1996	39.8	14.3
India	1994	36.7	30.5
Nepal	1995, 1996	44.0	23.0
Pakistan	1991	36.9	28.0
Sri Lanka	1990, 1991	38.1	28.4

Note: Multiple survey years refer to several surveys used to derive poverty incidence.

Source: World Bank (1999c).

poorest states, Kerala, has virtually universal primary enrollment rates, while several other states, such as Bihar, Orissa, Rajasthan, and Uttar Pradesh—not all of which are poorer than Kerala—lag 40-60 percent behind national averages (ADB 1997).

Regional disparities may reflect differences in soil fertility, rainfall, or irrigation potential, or development policies biased in favor of industry and against agriculture. In other cases, regional disparities reflect the differential impact of rapidly growing trade opportunities in a global economy. Areas along the PRC's coast, for example, have grown much more rapidly in recent years than interior areas of the country. In the five coastal provinces, average annual growth rates in real per capita income during 1980-1996 were 6.4-9.2 percent in rural areas and 5.5-7.9 percent in urban areas. The corresponding range in the 11 noncoastal provinces was 3.9-7.3 percent in rural areas and 3.6-6.5 percent in urban areas (Gang, Perkins, and Sabin 1997). Incomes in the richest provinces are now two to three times higher than those in the poorest.

Some regional differences also stem from protracted civil disturbances that have hindered infrastructure investments and the delivery of social services. These include Kashmir in India and Pakistan, Tamil-inhabited areas of Sri Lanka, former Khmer Rouge-controlled areas in Cambodia, and Mindanao in the Philippines. In some cases, these conflict-torn areas benefit from special efforts from the national government to improve services, but more often they are simply excluded from the development effort in the rest of the country.

EXPLAINING THE SOCIAL CHALLENGE

The plight of Asia's poor results from a complicated interplay of economic, social, and demographic factors. The lack of economic growth has constricted the development of market opportunities for the poor. A lack of assets—physical assets, financial assets, human and social capital—has meant that even when markets do exist, the poor are unable to take advantage of them. Moreover, the poor are particularly vulnerable to shocks, both economic and environmental. Political and social constraints, including poor governance, gender biases, ethnic and caste bias, all reinforce this

negative spiral, making it more difficult for the voice of the poor to be heard.

Lack of Economic Growth

International experience indicates that when economic growth rates rise, poverty falls. Conversely, where economic growth has been low or negative, poverty rates have typically been more persistent or have increased. The major reason is that economic growth increases the demand for the one asset that the poor have in abundance: their labor. Economic growth also increases the availability of public and private resources that can be used to improve essential services, such as education and health care.

The relationship between economic growth and poverty reduction can be seen both at the regional level and national level. The regions with the fastest economic growth in the 1990s—East and Southeast Asia, including the Pacific, followed by South Asia—are where the largest reductions in the incidence of poverty have taken place (see table 3.8). Conversely, where economic growth has been low or declining in the 1990s, such as Sub-saharan Africa and the transition countries of Eastern Europe and Central Asia, poverty incidence has increased.

Poverty in South Asia remains unacceptably high, largely because of poor prior economic performance in that region. East and Southeast Asia, including the Pacific, experienced average annual per capita growth rates of 5.4 percent between 1965 and 1995, but South Asia's average annual growth rate was around half that.

The same relationship between growth and poverty reduction is clear at the national level. Figure 3.2 shows a linear relationship between poverty reduction and growth rate of GNP per capita, which was derived from 40 developing economies for which data existed in 1970-1992. The poverty incidence was measured by the headcount index, based on the national poverty line. The slope of the relationship was found to be negative and statistically significant, with an elasticity that was close to unity. This meant that income growth had a powerful impact on poverty reduction. The scatter plot for Asian developing economies illustrates this point more vividly (see figure 3.2). PRC, Indonesia, Korea, and

Table 3.8 Changes in Per Capita GNP and Dollar-a-Day Poverty Line, Developing Regions, 1990-1996
(percent)

Developing region	Average annual change in per capita GNP 1990–1996	Population under $1-a-day poverty line		Change in poverty 1990–1996
		1990	1996	
East and Southeast Asia (including the Pacific)	7.9	27.6	14.9	12.7
South Asia	3.5	44.0	40.1	3.9
Middle East and North Africa	0.5	9.3	7.8	1.5
Latin America and the Caribbean	2.0	16.8	15.6	1.2
Sub-saharan Africa	-0.6	47.7	48.5	-0.8
Europe and Central Asia	-5.1	1.6	5.1	-3.5

Note: Per capita GNP is expressed in constant dollar terms. The reduction in poverty is calculated as the difference in the headcount index between 1990 and 1996.

Sources: World Bank (1999b); staff estimates.

Malaysia—all economies that experienced rapid economic growth—were able to reduce the incidence of poverty dramatically. Conversely, slower growth in Nepal and the Philippines meant that poverty reduction was much more limited.

Lack of Assets

One fundamental distinction between the poor and nonpoor is that the poor own and have access to fewer resources, such as human, physical, financial, and social capital. Material well-being, however, depends on assets and the returns to those assets. Some assets such as human and physical capital are individually owned, while others, such as physical infrastructure, are owned by society. Still others, such as social capital, result from social interactions between people, and can have significant influence on the returns to individually owned capital.

Human Capital. Because of generally low literacy levels and poor health and nutritional conditions, the poor lack human capital. Not only does the lack

of human capital cause immediate deprivation, it severely limits productive capacity, and hence earnings potential.

Raising human capital through investment in education can significantly raise earning capacity. Studies suggest that the returns to education can exceed 25 percent for primary education, 15-18 percent for secondary education, and 13-16 percent for tertiary education (Psacharopoulos 1985). Part of these returns may reflect factors other than productivity improvements—such as the role of schooling as a credential-creating device or screening mechanism but it is clear that most of the returns reflect enhanced productivity. Some recent studies that carefully controlled for factors other than productivity found that education positively influences the wage level primarily through its impact on cognitive achievements (Ashenfelter and Krueger 1994; Alderman and others 1996).

The returns to education, however, depend on the context in which they are used. The more dynamic the environment, the greater the returns. A recent study of India found that farmers with a primary

**Figure 3.2 Economic Growth and Poverty Reduction,
Selected Asian Developing Economies, 1970-1992
(percent)**

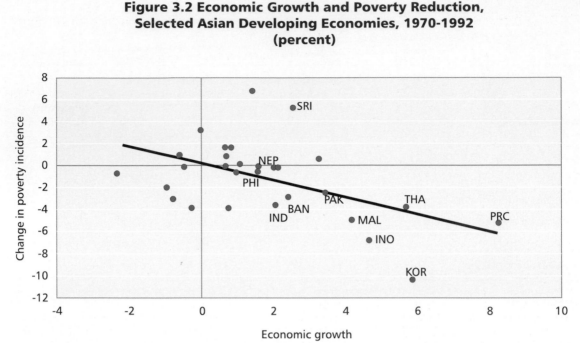

Note: The line shows the inverse relationship between percentage growth in per capita GNP and the percentage change in poverty incidence (based on national poverty lines), and was derived from a regression analysis for approximately 40 developing countries during 1970-1992. Regression parameters for this exercise had the correct sign, significant t-values, and good fit.
Source: Staff estimates.

education were generally more productive than their uneducated counterparts. However, the differences were greatest in more dynamic regions with new seed-fertilizer technology (Foster and Rosenzweig 1996). As education helps in being able to adopt a new technology, the returns to education also increase in such a changing environment.

South Asian countries seem to devote a smaller fraction of total public expenditure to education than the more advanced economies of developing Asia, both historically and currently (see table 3.9). Moreover, the share of public education expenditure devoted to primary education in these South Asian economies is much lower than the extent of poverty in these countries would suggest. Because the largest number and proportion of students from poor households are enrolled in the primary level, any given subsidy is most likely to reach the poor most effectively if it is targeted to that level of education. The Philippines, for example, does not spend as much on

public education as a percentage of GNP as the South Asian countries. A far larger fraction of public expenditure on education is devoted to the primary sector, however. Such prioritizing of primary education helps explain the high rates of adult literacy in the Philippines.

Land and Capital. In most Asian developing countries, poverty is essentially a rural phenomenon. A principal characteristic of the rural poor is that they have little or no land. In India, for instance, households with no land had a poverty incidence of more than 40 percent, while those that cultivated more than eight hectares had less than 10 percent (Dev, Parikh, and Suryanarayana 1994).

Although limited access to land is an important feature of the rural poor, the nature of access to land is not necessarily an indicator of poverty. In the Philippines, for instance, tenancy (rather than ownership) is not significantly related to poverty, although

Table 3.9 Public Expenditure on Education, Selected Asian Developing Economies, Selected Years
(percent)

Subregion and country	Public expenditure on education/ GNP		Public expenditure on education/total government expenditure		Distribution of public expenditure on education, 1995		
	1970	1995	1970	1995	Primary	Secondary	Tertiary
Newly industrialized economies							
Hong Kong, China[a]	2.4	2.9	23	17	27	39	30
Korea, Rep. of [a]	3.4	3.7	21	18	44	39	7
Singapore	3.1	3.0	12	23	—	—	—
PRC	1.2	2.3	4	12	26	25	17
Southeast Asia							
Cambodia	5.8	1.0	24	10	—	—	—
Indonesia	2.6	1.4	—	8	19	57	24
Lao PDR[a]	—	2.4	—	—	42	44	4
Malaysia[a]	4.2	5.3	18	16	39	37	16
Myanmar	3.1	—	18	—	—	—	—
Philippines[a]	2.8	2.2	24	—	64	10	23
Thailand[a]	3.2	4.1	17	20	55	21	16
Viet Nam[a]	—	2.7	—	7	40	20	16
South Asia							
Bangladesh[a]	—	2.3	—	9	44	43	8
India[a]	2.6	3.4	11	12	38	27	15
Nepal[a]	0.6	3.2	7	14	45	18	28
Pakistan	1.7	2.8	4	7	—	—	—
Sri Lanka	4.0	3.0	14	8	12	74	14

— Not available.

Note: The distribution of public expenditure does not add up to 100 due to other education expenditures, such as vocational and specialized training.

a. Data for distribution of public expenditure on education by level refer to year 1992.

Sources: Behrman, Deolalikar, and Soon (1999); UNESCO (2000).

in Bangladesh, the opposite appears to be the case. In India, high-income farmers often lease out land from both large and small landowners. It is also not clear that tenants are slower than owner-operators in adopting modern techniques of farm production.

The rural poor also lack access to other physical and financial assets. In most Asian countries, they often do not own the farm implements that they work with. Without assets to put up as collateral, the poor cannot borrow from formal credit markets. Although informal moneylenders often fill the vacuum created by the absence of a formal credit market, their interest rates are usually higher than those offered by formal credit channels. These high interest rates partly reflect the high costs of administering small loans and the risk associated with higher rates of default.

Many Asian countries have attempted to expand the reach of the formal credit system to address the needs of the poor. However, most formal credit mechanisms, with the exception of those based on cooperative, microcredit-style lending, have had limited success. The high fixed costs of lending, informational problems, and the costs of enforcement in defaults often limit the success of formal credit mechanism in reaching the poor.

Social Capital. While the term social capital is widely used in development parlance, it is seldom precisely defined. A narrow definition includes the social networks or groups that benefit a member, while a broad definition includes all social institutions within which individuals operate, including the legal framework and civil and political liberties. In this discussion, social capital is limited to social organizations, such as networks, norms, and social trusts that facilitate coordination and cooperation among individuals in a society.

Social capital reduces the incentives for opportunistic behavior by individuals and increases trust. Thus it enhances the productivity of individuals and firms by reducing transaction costs, increases the provision of public goods, and helps create an informal safety net in times of economic crisis. In rural societies, for instance, social capital helps promote community enterprises, such as irrigation and the management of common properties. For the poor, social capital in the form of networks and connections is a critical asset in developing economic opportunity and securing access to markets.

Social capital, like human and physical capital, is not uniformly distributed across Asian societies. Ethnic divisions are greater in some societies than others, and the degree of networking and social trusts varies. In Gujarat in India, for instance, violent confrontations between local people and the government over forests management led to economic stagnation. After communities were mobilized and joint forest management programs began, the conflicts declined and land productivity and village incomes rose (Pathan, Arul, and Poffenberger 1993). Finally, while it is clear how social capital works and the contributions it makes to economic development and poverty alleviation, quantitative estimation of these relations is fraught with conceptual and measurement difficulties. It is difficult to gauge precisely how much the poor lack the important resource of social capital.

Infrastructure. Well-developed physical infrastructure is critical to economic development and poverty reduction. Infrastructure—including electric power, roads, irrigation, transportation, and telecommunications systems—is essential for the production, exchange, and distribution of goods and services. Physical infrastructure lowers the cost of production and transactions, complements human capital, and enhances its productivity. Improved access to infrastructure can open up new employment and earning opportunities, for the poor in particular. Access to road and transportation, for instance, allows poor people to explore employment options outside their immediate vicinity. Similarly, having modern infrastructure facilities in rural areas can lead to the growth of small and medium-size industries that can often ensure higher and stable income for the poor.

Physical infrastructure also contributes directly to the improvement of living standards, which in turn enables the poor to use other assets more effectively. The delivery of clean water and safe disposal of solid waste, for instance, reduce the incidence of diseases among the poor, particularly waterborne ones. A fall in morbidity incidence allows a rise in productivity.

Like other assets, physical infrastructure is not distributed evenly throughout the developing Asian region. South Asian countries have, on the average, the most inadequate physical infrastructure in the region (see table 3.10). East and Southeast Asian countries fare better, and Central Asian countries have the best physical infrastructure, a legacy of their Soviet past.

Political and Social Constraints

Inadequate access to capital—physical, human, and financial—helps explain the economic origins of poverty in Asia, but it does not tell the whole story. These economic factors have been compounded by other political and social problems, including poor governance and social discrimination due to gender or ethnicity.

Poor Governance. Poor governance can take many different forms: a lack of accountability for government actions, a lack of voice for the governed, ineffective and partisan executives, political instability and

Table 3.10 **Physical Infrastructure, Selected Asian Developing Economies, Selected Years**

Subregion and country	Paved roads (percentage of total) 1997	Electricity consumption, (kWh per capita) 1996	Irrigated land (percentage of crop land) 1994-1996	Telephones (main lines + mobile) per 1,000 persons 1997
Newly industrialized economies				
Korea, Rep. of	74.0	4,453	60.7	594
PRC and Mongolia				
PRC	—	19	37.0	66
Mongolia	3.4	1,314	6.1	38
Central Asian republics				
Kazakhstan	82.8	2,865	6.9	110
Kyrgyz Republic	91.1	1,479	76.8	76
Tajikistan	82.7	2,292	80.6	38
Uzbekistan	87.3	1,657	81.6	63
Southeast Asia				
Cambodia	7.5	—	4.5	5
Indonesia	46.3	296	15.0	30
Lao PDR	13.8	63	20.3	6
Malaysia	75.1	2,078	4.5	308
Myanmar	12.2	58	15.9	5
Philippines	57.0	405	16.7	47
Thailand	97.5	1,289	23.2	113
Viet Nam	25.1	177	29.6	23
South Asia				
Bangladesh	12.3	97	39.1	3
India	45.7	347	32.0	20
Nepal	41.5	39	30.6	8
Pakistan	58.0	333	80.2	20
Sri Lanka	40.0	203	29.2	23

— Not available.

Sources: UN ESCAP (various years); Statistical Yearbooks (various countries and years).

violence, the absence of the rule of law, or corruption. All have important ramifications for the poor, probably more than any other segment of society.

A government that is not accountable to all segments of society—and does not allow "voice" to its citizens—is likely to be less attentive to the needs of the poor than to other, more powerful, segments of society. As Nobel Laureate Amartya Sen noted (1983), authoritarian regimes that allow little press freedom are the types of regimes in which widespread famines are possible. Ineffective governments are unlikely to make efficient investments in physical and social infrastructure that would benefit the poor, and are also less efficient in delivering the needed social services to the poor.

Governments that are unable to maintain law and order and to control eruptions of political instability and violence are also unlikely to benefit the poor. In recent years, Afghanistan and Cambodia have been subject to such political turmoil. Regional insurrections have also persisted in Sri Lanka and the Philippines for a long time. These political instabilities have undoubtedly adversely affected economic growth, while simultaneously impeding governments' abilities to provide public services to the poor.

Corruption can affect the poor in several ways. It affects them directly, as they are subject to various types of financial extortion by corrupt officials, and because unscrupulous government functionaries often divert funds for social services intended for the poor. Corruption affects them indirectly, by reducing the economy's growth potential. It reduces foreign and domestic investment, decreases the efficiency with which these investments are made, and misallocates resources to rent-seeking activities. All of these can have a powerful negative impact on economic growth.

Gender Bias. There is no doubt that in many societies women often lack access to essential assets and basic social services. In particular, women tend to face greater obstacles than men in attending school, using health services, and participating in the labor market. These problems are particularly serious in South Asia.

Poverty is one reason for the bias, as women often suffer disproportionately from its burden. However, growing evidence suggests that poverty is not the sole source—or even a strong cause—of gender disparities. Tradition, as well as outright discrimination, plays an important role in creating and sustaining these disparities.

In many Asian developing countries, gender bias in the labor market is directly linked to cultural stereotypes of gender roles. The high incidence of unemployment among women is partly due to a cultural perception that considers women's economic role secondary to their reproductive role. The social traditions and customs of the region reinforce this implicit discrimination. In many Asian countries such as Bangladesh, India, and Viet Nam, women's lives are shaped by the patriarchal and patrilineal nature of the social system, where women are subjected to the dictates of their husbands' families.

Another cause of lower female employment rates in the formal sectors is that employing female workers can mean shouldering the additional costs of maternity leave, sick leave, and childcare allowances. Discrimination in labor markets can also be self-perpetuating.

If women face discrimination in employment, parents may invest less in the education of daughters than sons. If employers believe that women quit more often, they will deny them access to training programs, which may in fact cause them to quit.

Gender bias in education is also caused by a combination of economic and social factors. First, the direct costs associated to sending girls to school are higher than for boys, because parents are more reluctant to send daughters to school without proper attire. Second, negative perceptions of girls' academic ability are widespread in many poor developing Asian economies. Third, in some cultures, education beyond the acquisition of literacy can threaten a woman's chance of marriage. Fourth, in poor households, girls generally perform more chores than boys, so the opportunity costs of sending girls to school are high. Finally, a strong perception exists that the economic returns from boys' schooling are greater.

Gender disparities go well beyond labor markets and education. Women also have less access to capital, particularly in the relatively low-interest formal sector. Discrimination in credit markets is one cause, but more important are a lack of collateral and the fact that competing demands on women's time make it difficult for them to travel to large towns where formal lending institutions are located. Fortunately, in many developing countries, microcredit programs, such as the Grameen Bank in Bangladesh, are addressing this problem. Microcredit programs focus on the credit needs of women and use social capital (pressure from a group of fellow borrowers) to ensure loan repayment.

Ethnic, Religious, and Caste Bias. As with gender disparities, ethnic and religious biases stem from economic, social, cultural, and spatial factors. Discrimination may play a role, particularly in labor markets, but it is difficult to find compelling evidence on overt discriminatory practices. The negative spiral of poverty and social constraints are more plausible explanations for the lower levels of education, health, and productivity among ethnic minorities. Poverty and the need for children to work dissuade many ethnic minority households from sending their children to school, as they simply cannot afford the actual and opportunity costs of educating their children.

Social traditions play an important role in perpetuating poverty. If an ethnic minority has a tradition of negative experience with employment opportunities, for example, individuals may reject the idea of investing in human capital. Disadvantaged groups that lack supportive social networks may find it difficult to get access to productive opportunities. Geographical disadvantages often overlap with social disadvantages: many ethnic minority groups live in remote areas, often mountainous. Such locations have few schools and those that exist are difficult to reach. In the plateau area of Bihar, the poorest region of India's poorest state, more than 70 percent of the population are tribal people from traditionally low-caste backgrounds (World Bank 1998). Road density in the plateau area is as low as 6 kilometers per 100 square kilometers, compared with the state average of 21 kilometers and a national average of 46 kilometers. Many areas are inaccessible during the monsoon season, and health facilities are minimal.

Fertility and Dependency

Fertility rates tend to be highest among poorer households (see table 3.11). To some extent, higher fertility among the poor reflects differences in knowledge about and access to contraceptives. Primarily, however, high fertility rates are both a cause and a consequence of poverty. Higher fertility levels among the poor partly reflect a higher demand for children, because children are viewed as potential workers as well as providers of old-age security for parents in the future. Considering that children of the poor tend to receive minimal education and begin work at young ages, the cost of raising additional children is relatively small compared with the benefits they produce. Unfortunately, this behavior results in perpetuating poverty. Fewer investments in children's human capital mean that poor children are denied the income-enhancing opportunities that education brings. Similarly, the more children a family has, the more thinly any physical assets are spread.

Much evidence indicates that poverty incidence tends to rise with family size. In the Philippines, for example, detailed household level data from the 1970s show that only 9 percent of one-person families lived below the poverty line and were considered poor, but the incidence of poverty deepened as households grew larger. Of families with four people, the incidence of poverty was 34 percent; with six people, 52 percent; and with ten or more people, 65 percent (Pernia 1982). Household surveys from India reveal that larger

Table 3.11 Total Fertility Rates by Household Wealth, Selected Asian Developing Economies, 1997

Country	Wealth quintiles					
	Poorest	2	3	4	Richest	Total
Bangladesh	3.8	3.8	3.5	3.1	2.2	3.3
India	4.5	4.3	4.2	3.9	3.4	4.1
Indonesia	3.3	2.9	2.6	2.5	2.0	2.8
Nepal	6.2	5.0	4.7	4.4	2.9	4.6
Pakistan	5.1	5.1	4.9	4.9	4.0	4.9
Philippines	6.5	4.7	3.6	2.9	2.1	3.7
Viet Nam	3.1	2.7	2.2	1.8	1.6	2.3

Note: The total fertility rate represents the number of children that would be born to a woman if she were to live to the end of her child-bearing years and bear children in accordance with current age-specific fertility rates.

Source: World Bank (unpublished DHS data).

families are not only more likely to be poor at any given time but are also more likely to be persistently poor (Gaiha and Deolalikar 1993).

Although fertility rates have fallen throughout Asia in recent decades, fertility remains high in South Asia (particularly in Nepal and Pakistan), in some countries of Southeast Asia (Cambodia, Lao PDR, and Philippines) and Central Asia (Tajikistan and Uzbekistan). These high fertility rates have contributed to a relatively young population, and hence a larger share of young dependents (see table 3.12).

The dynamic and relatively more developed NIEs that have virtually eliminated poverty are now going through a rapid change in demographic structure. Fertility rates have fallen dramatically; the population is aging, and the share of the old people (those 65 years old and above) as a percentage of the total population is increasing.

The shift in the population bulge from young to old has important implications that must be confronted. On one hand, relative pressures for social welfare expenditures on schooling and infant, child, and maternal health will decline as the young dependency ratios drop. On the other hand, relative pressures for an old-age pension and social assistance will increase. There will be a rapid increase in older individuals whose economic vulnerability would be exacerbated by weakening intergenerational ties. Women, who are traditionally more vulnerable, will comprise relatively large shares of the older populations in most countries. Ensuring financial security for the elderly will thus be a challenge to the dynamic East and Southeast Asian economies in the future years (see box 3.2).

Finally, throughout the region, health emphasis will shift from infectious childhood diseases to problems of aging populations, such as heart disease, cancer, and other ailments. Dealing with this change and finding ways to finance the shift may pose substantial challenges for evolving health care systems in developing Asia.

Environmental Deterioration

Several theories explain why Asia's environment has deteriorated so dramatically. According to some, rising populations inevitably put pressure on finite natural resources. Others argue that poverty itself has been the underlying cause of environmental deterioration. Still others regard economic growth as the root cause of a deteriorating environment. More recently, institutional and policy failures have been cited as the basic reason for environmental degradation.

Table 3.12 Fertility and Age Dependency, Selected Asian Developing Economies, 1960 and 1997

Subregion and country	Total fertility rate 1960	Total fertility rate 1997	Young dependency ratio 1997
NIEs			
Korea, Rep. of	6.0	1.7	0.3
PRC and Mongolia			
PRC	5.7	1.9	0.4
Mongolia	6.0	2.6	0.6
Central Asian republics			
Kazakhstan	4.5	2.0	0.5
Kyrgyz Republic	5.1	2.8	0.6
Tajikistan	6.3	3.5	0.8
Uzbekistan	6.3	3.3	0.7
Southeast Asia			
Cambodia	6.3	4.6	0.8
Indonesia	5.5	2.8	0.5
Lao PDR	6.2	5.6	0.8
Malaysia	6.8	3.2	0.6
Myanmar	6.0	2.4	0.5
Philippines	6.9	3.6	0.6
Thailand	6.4	1.7	0.4
Viet Nam	6.1	2.4	0.6
South Asia			
Bangladesh	6.7	3.2	0.7
India	5.9	3.3	0.6
Nepal	5.8	4.4	0.8
Pakistan	6.9	5.0	0.8
Sri Lanka	5.3	2.2	0.4

NIEs - Newly industrialized economies.

Note: The young dependency ratio refers to the ratio of the young population (those younger than 15 years of age) to the working-age population (aged 15-64).

Sources: World Bank (1999c); UNICEF (1999).

Box 3.2 Provisioning for the Aging Population

While Asia's population is young, it is aging rapidly. As fertility rates continue to fall and life expectancy continues to rise, a demographic structure with relatively few young people and a large elderly population will emerge. In the People's Republic of China; Hong Kong, China; Singapore; Sri Lanka; and Taipei,China, those aged 60 or more will make up more than 20 percent of the population by 2050. In these economies, there will be two to five people of working age for every old person. Elsewhere the effect will be similar, but less pronounced. In India, Malaysia, and Thailand, there will be six working-age people per elderly person in the same period. Over time, a rising proportion of the elderly will be extremely old—aged 80 and over (see box figure).

Ensuring financial security for the elderly is an important social challenge for Asia. Traditionally, Asian families have provided for their elderly, but dramatic social changes are weakening filial ties. Increased mobility and migration have meant that fewer children live close to their parents. Simultaneously, women are increasingly taking outside employment and are less able to stay at home to care for the children and the elderly. Lower fertility rates mean that there are fewer siblings to share the task of looking after the elderly.

Pension financing is therefore becoming an increasingly important matter of public policy. Broadly, governments have provided pensions through one of two mechanisms. In the *pay-as-you-go benefit pension system*, most common in industrial countries, today's workers pay for the pensions of today's retirees, usually through a payroll tax. The alternative is a *fully funded mandatory and defined contribution pension system*, whereby individuals must save for their own retirement in specific and regulated pension funds. Under the first system, each pension is usually calculated on the number of years in service and final salary. In the alternative system, the individual's pension depends only on the size and rate of return of accumulated pension contributions. While the Republic of Korea and Taipei,China have recently adopted pay-as-you-go systems, Hong Kong, China; Malaysia; and Singapore have fully funded systems known as provident funds, and Thailand has recently elected to follow this model.

Various factors suggest that Asian countries would do well to avoid the pay-as-you-go schemes. These schemes work well in a rapidly growing economy with a constant number of elderly. If, however, economic growth slackens or the relative number of elderly rises, such systems create a fiscal burden that can reduce government saving and perhaps even lead to a fiscal crisis. In view of Asia's aging populations, public policy should focus on defined contribution schemes where participants receive benefits commensurate to the amounts they contribute and the returns these contributions have earned.

Source: ADB (1997).

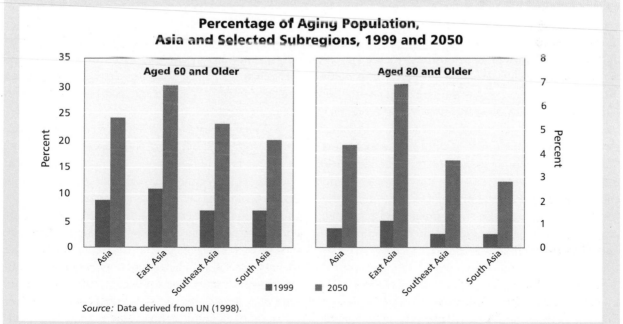

Percentage of Aging Population, Asia and Selected Subregions, 1999 and 2050

Source: Data derived from UN (1998).

A rapidly growing population can stress the environment through deforestation, soil erosion, and damage to local ecosystems. However, how a population behaves is likely to be a bigger factor than the rate at which it is growing. In Sri Lanka and Thailand, population growth rates have fallen rapidly, but environmental degradation has been just as much a problem in these countries than in ones with faster-growing populations. The important factor seems to be whether individuals consider the costs of environmental degradation in decisionmaking. In particular, when property rights to resources are not defined clearly, people are more likely to be unconcerned about degrading them.

Some suggest that the poor are more prone to causing environmental damage through the overuse of resources. Openly accessible natural resources, such as fish, game, water, and firewood, are likely to be exploited more intensely by the poor. While this overuse clearly contributes to environmental degradation, it is caused less by poverty than by market, institutional, and policy failures. Moreover, the poor suffer from environmental degradation that results from the actions of others. Poor people tend to live in areas that are more prone to environmentally related natural disasters such as flooding and landslides, or near heavily polluting factories, dumps, and hazardous waste sites.

Another theory suggests that Asia's rapid economic growth over the past 40 years has been the main cause of its environmental degradation. As agriculture becomes more intensive, resource extraction increases, and as industrialization expands, rates of natural resource depletion rise along with the amount and toxicity of waste. However, as economies become richer, their economic structure eventually moves toward activities that use natural resources less intensively. Greater prosperity also brings an increased environmental awareness and the willingness and capacity to pay for a cleaner environment. Again, the relationship between the environment and economic growth is likely to be heavily influenced by policies and institutions. There is a growing consensus that the main factor in Asia's rapid environmental deterioration has been policy failure (ADB 1997). Environmental policy and problems were neglected for a long time, and when strict pro-environment policies were enacted, they were neither adequately monitored nor enforced. In some cases, policies were applied that hurt the environment rather than helped it (see box 3.3).

Vulnerability to Short-Term Shocks

Standard poverty measures do not reflect the different degrees of risk and vulnerability that households with the same level of expected income may face. One farmer may derive income from rain-fed crops, which are subject to the vagaries of nature, while the other may rely on irrigated crops, whose output is more dependable. Households also differ in their ability to cope with such shocks, as one family might have close, financially secure, relatives in urban areas who can assist in times of need, while another, equally poor household, does not. These differences in vulnerability have serious implications for the welfare of two otherwise identical individuals with the same level of income.

Standard measures of poverty also provide no indication of whether the observed poverty is chronic or transient. In predominantly agricultural societies, variations in weather and other natural factors can cause substantial fluctuations in income from one season to another. Consequently, households can move regularly into and out of poverty. One study of South Indian villages found that only one fifth of households were poor in all the nine years the study covered. Twelve percent were never poor, and the majority moved in and out of poverty (Gaiha and Deolalikar 1993). The distinction between chronic and transient poverty is important, as it has very different policy implications.

Vulnerabilities to transient poverty have several causes and manifestations. Some shocks are natural, as a drought; others are political, such as a civil war; and others are economic, such as a currency crisis. Some shocks, such as a catastrophic illness, are specific to individuals. Others, such as a harvest failure, are common to everyone in the community or the entire village. Still others affect the entire economy, such as a sharp recession. The distinction between various types of shocks is important because they have different policy implications. A shock that affects an entire community obviously cannot be addressed by pooling

Box 3.3 **Improving Environmental Regulation**

Asia has paid heavily for its environmental mismanagement and negligence. Addressing the challenges of today's environmental degradation requires active policies in several areas. First, government policies that exacerbate environmental problems, such as subsidizing the extraction of scarce resources, should be gradually removed. Second, property rights should be clarified. Insecure property rights over land and other natural resources have led people to misuse them or underinvest in their improvement.

Governments also need to promote flexible types of environmental regulation that rely on economic incentives to encourage compliance. Traditionally, environmental protection in Asia was based on a command-and-control system. Common policy tools were licenses, fines, and specific government orders to cease pollution. Governments often imposed a uniform pollution standard across an industry, but monitoring was usually inadequate. The result was a proliferation of unimplemented regulations and a rapidly deteriorating environment.

A more flexible approach would allow industry a much freer hand in setting its own means of compliance based on the cost of the pollution to the polluting entity. Controlling pollution is usually more expensive for older factories with outdated technology and smaller factories that cannot reap the benefits of economies of scale. In India's pulp and paper industry, for instance, the cost of pollution abatement per ton of paper produced decreases by more than 70 percent as mill capacity rises from 10 to 115 tons per day. A flexible system of environmental regulation based on these cost differentials—known as tradable emission permits—would

allow older and smaller plants to reduce their compliance costs by selling to newer or larger factories their permits for a permissible level of pollution.

Under this system, the authorities set an overall level of permissible air or water pollution. The permits divide this level between firms based on norms agreed on by policymakers. As the permissible aggregate level of pollution is lower than the current level, this creates a market in air or water pollution. The permits thereby acquire market value, and firms that wish to expand must either reduce the pollution from their existing factories or buy permits from other factories.

Flexible instruments of environmental regulation include not only these sophisticated tradable emission permits, but also simpler methods, such as imposing charges on polluting inputs rather than on the pollution itself, or providing deposit refund systems to induce producers and consumers of polluting products to return waste for recycling or treatment and safe disposal. Deposit refund systems have an additional advantage of promoting waste collection, which is otherwise a labor-intensive activity.

Fortunately, a growing number of policymakers are showing a willingness to experiment with one of these more flexible approaches. For this to work effectively, however, Asian governments must improve their capacity to implement changes. To accomplish this, first, government involvement in environmental management must shift from top-down management to focused and strategic intervention. Instead of using a huge regulatory bureaucracy employing thousands of environmental inspectors, streamlined environmental ministries must coordinate a decentralized approach and ensure

that environmental impact is considered in all areas of policymaking. At the same time, better environmental management will involve removing issues from the purview of certain government ministries. For example, some Asian countries have begun to move the responsibility for managing protected areas from their forestry departments—which have an acknowledged bias toward timber and extraction—into institutions that focus on preservation.

More generally, central governments will need to devolve responsibility for environmental management to appropriate local and regional levels, and enter partnerships with the private sector, nongovernmental organizations (NGOs), and local communities. The capacities of local governments, the private sector, and NGOs will need to be improved, however. Determining the appropriate level of government for environmental management can be done by considering at which level can effective measures be undertaken. For integrated river basin or watershed management, for instance, institutional arrangements may have to straddle the jurisdictions of several states. For regulating automobile emissions, however, standard setting and enforcement should be at the municipal level.

Civil society needs to be involved more broadly. Environmental impact assessments are an important way that stakeholders can participate at the project level. Greater decentralization and broader participation are prerequisites for Asia's new environment model to work successfully, and the move toward devolution and pluralism in environmental issues would only mirror a broader trend already evident in Asia.

Source: ADB (1997).

resources within the community. Similarly, a large macroeconomic shock requires pooling resources beyond those available within the national borders.

Asian economies have been subject to various major shocks in recent years. Bangladesh and the PRC have experienced serious floods, and Southeast Asia has endured costly droughts. Others have experienced serious epidemics of disease, as Thailand has suffered hugely from HIV/AIDS. Still others have faced political violence and civil disorder, such as Cambodia. Finally, the Asian financial crisis engulfed most of East and Southeast Asia in 1997-1998.

Such economic shocks can be partly mitigated by effective social safety net programs. Although the extent and effectiveness of social safety nets vary between countries, they generally fail to meet the needs of the poor. Many Asian countries experienced years of high economic growth before the onset of the recent financial crisis, and their governments believed that economic growth would be the main form of social safety net, and hence had inadequate formal social safety nets (see box 3.4). In the absence of well-developed formal safety net programs, households in many Asian countries fall back to two strategies during periods of need: family support networks and migration.

Family relationships have undoubtedly been weakened by urbanization and modernization. Nonetheless, the evidence suggests that private transfers are still a significant source of support in times of need. In the PRC, the immediate family is required by law to provide adequate consumption levels, even if family members live in separate households. If necessary, these laws are invoked to compel adult children to care for elderly parents.

According to a survey in Mongolia, families in distress were seven times more likely to receive assistance from friends and relatives than from the government. In the Kyrgyz Republic, about 20 percent of households either give or receive money or goods to or from another household. Such transfers accounted for almost 7 percent of household income in 1996 (ADB 1999j). In India, intergenerational transfers (mostly informal support from children to elderly parents) account for about 1.7 percent of GDP, and amount to more than the aggregate spending on all formal support programs for the elderly.

Migration is a widely used method of coping with difficult times. Urban workers return to rural areas to work in agriculture during periods of economic recession. During the recent financial crisis, for instance, employment shifted significantly from the nonfarm to the farm sector in Korea, Indonesia, and Thailand.

CONFRONTING THE SOCIAL CHALLENGE

As this chapter has shown, Asia's social challenge has several dimensions and numerous causes. Consequently, to be effective, policy responses must be tailored to individual countries' needs and circumstances. These policy responses also should take into account the overall policy environment—both domestic and international.

In the past decade, the domestic and international policy environment has changed enormously. Most countries now have a greater focus on poverty reduction than they did in the past. Democratic institutions are on the rise, and more people recognize the importance of better governance and increased participation by civil society in the various facets of social and economic life. Inspired by the benefits that many East Asian countries reaped from greater economic openness and reliance on market institutions, most countries in the region have taken steps to liberalize their economies. The recent crisis has not set back this trend significantly.

In the international community, there is a greater concern about poverty issues than in the past. The ADB, for example, has declared poverty reduction its over-arching development objective (see box 3.5). Although experience suggest which policies are the most effective policies for alleviating poverty, recent years have seen a steady reduction in the level of resources committed to development assistance (see figure 3.3). The amount of private capital flowing to developing countries has risen dramatically, but this flow has been limited to a dozen or so more advanced developing economies.

Globalization offers new opportunities for economic development and poverty reduction in Asia. Regulatory barriers are falling, and after successive rounds of multilateral trade negotiations, the world trading system is more open than ever before. Average

Box 3.4 The Social Safety Net Systems in Five Crisis-Affected Economies

The Republic of Korea. Compared with other Asian countries, the Republic of Korea (henceforth referred to as Korea) has relatively sophisticated social safety nets, including public assistance programs such as medical aid, veteran relief, and disaster relief. Compared with those of developed countries, however, Korea's social protection levels are rudimentary and limited, and essentially provide only partial protection for formal sector workers.

Since 1995, Korea has had an unemployment benefit scheme. However, by April 1998, it covered only an estimated 22 percent of people who have lost their jobs. Since the onset of the financial crisis, Korea has expanded its unemployment benefit, raising the benefit level gradually from 50 to 70 percent of the minimum wage, and extending the minimum duration of benefits to two months. Also in 1998, the government increased its allocation for social welfare assistance and support by 13 percent to people with no income.

Indonesia. Through a Provident Fund system, lump-sum payments are provided for old age, disability, and survivor benefits. These benefits, however, are limited to firms with more than ten employees or a payroll above Rs1 million ($140) per month. Coverage is gradually being extended to smaller firms and seasonal workers. Indonesia also has a social insurance system that provides medical benefits and work-related injury benefits.

In response to the economic crisis, the government introduced an across-the-board subsidy on food items such as rice, corn, sugar, soybean, wheat flour, soybean meal, and fishmeal at a cost of 0.5-0.7 percent of GDP in 1998. The government also maintains subsidies for petroleum products (particularly,

kerosene and diesel) and electricity, which constitute more than 2 percent of GDP. Other government programs include providing scholarships for needy students, financing essential drugs for rural and urban health centers, providing subsidies for low-cost housing, and expanding rural credit schemes to cover small and medium-size enterprises and rural cooperatives.

Malaysia. Malaysia has two types of social safety net programs: a dual provident fund that provides both lump-sum and periodic payments for old age, disability, death, and medical benefits; and a social insurance system that covers disability and work-related injury benefits.

Recently, the Malaysian government increased public expenditure on major anti-poverty programs to protect the real spending per beneficiary. The programs include the Fund-for-Food program, which provides small-scale loans to the poorest rural areas for income-generating activities, improving water supply, and strengthening welfare programs. The government also expanded safety net programs for those newly vulnerable because of the recent crisis, but who may not be covered by existing programs for the poor. These include urban microcredit programs for hawkers, traders, and entrepreneurs; a fund for small and medium-size industries to increase their competitiveness and viability; skills training for retrenched workers; and preserving priority long-term development investments in education and health.

Philippines. The Philippines' social insurance system covers benefits for old age, disability, death, and medical care. Contributions are compulsory for all private employees, whether permanent or provisional, who are

not more than 60 years old. A separate system covers government employees.

To promote food security, the government has begun to subsidize essential staples—such as rice and oil—for the poorest households in the poorest villages. Public employment programs are another major social safety net. The country has introduced two types of public works schemes: the Food-for-Work scheme, set up in 1987; and the Cash-for-Work scheme, set up in 1990. For the latter, the wage rate was set about 25 percent higher than agricultural market wages.

Thailand. In Thailand, old age, disability, death, and medical benefits are provided through a limited social insurance system that covers firms with ten or more employees. Currently, the pension system covers only 10 percent of the labor force.

In response to the financial crisis, the Thai government initiated temporary labor-intensive civil works programs in construction and infrastructure. It also established two investment funds. The Social Investment Fund will provide support for community activities, including community development programs and small credit schemes; and the Urban Development Loan Fund will support labor-intensive investments by municipalities. The Thai government is also strengthening its social spending programs by expanding its scholarship and loan programs to minimize student dropouts, protecting operational budgets for teacher training and instructional materials, reallocating resources toward health programs for the poor, and redeploying health staff to rural areas. To protect urban low-income workers, a subsidy for urban bus and rail fares will be maintained.

Box 3.5 The Poverty Reduction Strategy of the Asian Development Bank

The Asian Development Bank (ADB) has recently declared poverty reduction to be its overarching goal. Other strategic concerns, such as human development, sound environmental management, improvement of women's status, and economic growth, will also be earnestly pursued, but in such a way as to maximize their contribution to poverty reduction, where possible.

The three pillars of the new poverty reduction strategy are fostering sustainable economic growth that benefits the poor, promoting social development, and encouraging good governance. The ADB's next task is to translate the broad thrust of its Poverty Reduction Strategy into comprehensive country-specific action plans. Those will prioritize the three strategic pillars according to country circumstances, the ADB's cross-country experience in poverty reduction, and the changing global environment facing developing member countries.

In the past, the ADB has financed the region's urgent need for physical infrastructure—such as electricity, roads, irrigation systems, school buildings, and health centers—with an emphasis on boosting economic growth. It later expanded its focus to include human development, gender equity, and environmental protection.

Future ADB investments will address the region's poor more directly. In transportation, the aim will be to reduce transport costs between rural areas and growth centers. In communications, the ADB will harness information technology to enhance the poor's market access. The ADB will also invest more to provide the poor

access to essential services, including electricity, water supply and sanitation. Access to basic education and primary health care will increase the poor's chance of earning income, and providing social safety nets will reduce the indebtedness that entraps many poor in a vicious circle.

A critical element of ADB's poverty reduction strategy is governance. Good governance, as well as sound macroeconomic management, is essential for participatory, pro-poor policies. It ensures the transparent use of public funds, encourages growth of the private sector, promotes effective delivery of public services, and helps establish the rule of law. Actions on governance must proceed at two levels. At the national level, public administration and expenditure management will be strengthened to promote growth and social development that helps the poor. At the same time, responsibility for providing public services will be moved to the lowest appropriate level of government. The ADB's long-term objective is to empower the poor and develop institutional arrangements that foster participation and accountability at the local level. Henceforth, the emphasis will be on the client, particularly community-based organizations, people's organizations, and cooperatives.

In implementing its poverty reduction strategy, the ADB will work closely with member governments, nongovernmental organizations and other members of civil society, as well as the donor community. The ADB will also undertake poverty analyses of individual countries to ascertain the most effective policies and institutions to fight poverty. These

analyses will be discussed at high-level forums where governments, community-based organizations, the private sector, and the donor community will be represented. These forums will produce country operational strategies that will form the basis for programs. These programs, in turn, will be implemented through partnership agreements, which will include mechanisms for reviewing performance and which will link performance to the allocation of funds.

To make antipoverty operations effective, the ADB will introduce new instruments or find new ways of using existing ones. For example, there will be greater use of longer-term sector development programs, where front-end support for policy change and capacity building will pave the way for financing for productive investment. Slow-disbursing policy-based lending in support of national poverty reduction programs will also be considered, with a view to ensuring that such programs are effective and correctly targeted. Moreover, the ADB will take initiatives to lend directly to local governments, promote social investment funds, and support nongovernmental organizations with proven track records for helping the poor.

The ADB will help introduce effective poverty monitoring system in the developing member countries. The ADB will also help borrowing countries improve their capacity to generate timely and reliable data, as well as develop indicators that can be easily used. In monitoring progress toward the agreed targets, the ADB will also assist borrowing governments in refining their respective policies and programs for poverty reduction. In the process, the ADB will become more accountable for its own actions.

Source: ADB (1999i).

tariff rates in industrial countries have fallen to 3-4 percent (although some of the products that poorer developing countries would like to export are still covered by high tariffs, quotas, and other nontariff barriers). There are fewer restrictions on foreign direct investment, although the movement of labor across borders is still restricted. With the expected launching of the new Millennium Round, the world trading and investment climate is likely to be further liberalized.

Developing countries also have much better access to knowledge and information than they had in the past. With communications costs falling rapidly, the cost of transferring knowledge is tumbling. The unfolding biotechnology revolution in agriculture has the potential to radically transform agricultural production and processing.

Expanded trade, financial, and information flows have brought new technologies and markets and new sources of finance. However, globalization may sometimes cause instability. The destabilizing effects

of premature liberalization on short-term capital flows can be large, as Asia's recent experience illustrates. Today's international economic environment is one that offers great promise, but that must also be treated with caution.

Within these fast-changing domestic and international policy environments are common elements that should influence every country's anti-poverty strategy. They include an overall policy regime that promotes inclusive economic growth; investments in human capital, infrastructure, and microfinance; improved governance and civil society participation in decisionmaking; effective social safety nets; and targeted redistributive policies.

Promoting Inclusive Growth

Rapid, sustainable, and inclusive economic growth is the major component of a strategy for addressing Asia's social challenge. Growth is crucial because it increases

Figure 3.3 Official Development Assistance from OECD Countries, 1992 and 1997

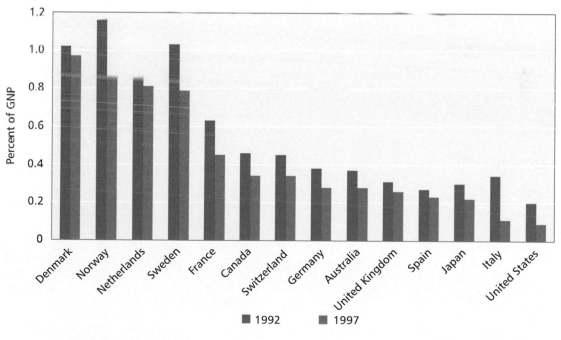

Source: World Bank (1999c).

the demand for labor, the asset on which the poor depend. It is also crucial because the resources for anti-poverty programs and the political feasibility of spending money on the poor are greater when incomes and economic opportunities are expanding for all.

Economic growth has benefited the poor even when based on an initially unequal distribution of income. Brazil and Mexico have had unequal income distributions, but any income growth has been better for the poor than none (Fields 1995). If growth rates are high enough, the poor can benefit even if inequality rises. In Sri Lanka and Thailand in 1970, average income per head was roughly equal, although Thailand had greater inequality (see table 3.13). Over the next two decades, Thailand's income inequality increased, while Sri Lanka's fell, but Thailand's economic growth rate was far higher than Sri Lanka's. Therefore, the poorest 20 percent of the Thai population had an income that was 45 percent higher than the corresponding group in Sri Lanka.

Had Thailand been able to generate the same growth rate while maintaining its initial level of inequality, the poorest 20 percent would have benefited far more, and their incomes would have been around 28 percent higher. Had Thailand somehow combined its rapid growth with a decline in income inequality similar to what Sri Lanka achieved by 1990, the poorest 20 percent of Thais would have had an income 122 percent higher than it actually was.

This highlights two important questions. What can Asia's developing economies do to accelerate economic growth? And what mechanisms will ensure that this growth benefits the poor, either in proportion or more than proportionally to the rest of the population? In other words, what types of policies will encourage inclusive growth? The answer involves an overall policy regime that emphasizes economic openness and market orientation, and is characterized by prudent macroeconomic management, appropriate investments in human and physical infrastructure, improvements in governance, increased decentralization, and the active participation of the poor in decisions that affect their lives.

Openness and Market Orientation. It is difficult to overemphasize the importance of using market incentives and outward orientation to achieve inclusive economic growth. Following the Second World War, many developing countries adopted a development strategy based on industrialization led by import substitution. High tariff rates and quantitative restrictions on imports were used to conserve foreign

Table 3.13 Growth and Income Inequality, Sri Lanka and Thailand, 1970 and 1990

Country and indicator	1970	1990	Country and indicator	1970	1990
Sri Lanka			**Thailand**		
GDP per capita ($)	180	470	GDP per capita ($)	200	1,520
Income inequality (Gini coefficient)	0.38	0.30	Income inequality (Gini coefficient)	0.43	0.49
Income share of poorest 20 percent (percent)	6.9	8.9	Income share of poorest 20 percent (percent)	5.1	4.0
Income share of poorest 20 percent ($/capita)	12	42	Income share of poorest 20 percent ($/capita)	10	61

Source: Deininger and Squire (1996).

exchange and shield new domestic industries from well-established foreign competition. The costs of "essential" imports were kept artificially low by over-valued exchange rates. Simultaneously, a complex code of industrial licensing was used to allocate resources in the protected domestic market. This strategy—followed most closely by India and other South Asian economies—aimed at accelerating industrialization and poverty reduction. Unfortunately, it generally failed to achieve either objective.

Instead, it created an industrial structure characterized by large barriers to entry—both foreign and domestic—with narrow ownership. It also created an economic structure that penalized agriculture, where most of Asia's poor work. The protection of domestic industries raised the price of manufactured inputs to agriculture, while overvalued exchange rates reduced the domestic currency value of agricultural exports. Other measures, such as export taxes, food price controls, and public investment programs biased toward industry, also hurt the agriculture sector. Not surprisingly, the result was low growth and stagnant productivity in agriculture, and an inefficient industry sector that was not conducive to creating growth or employment.

In contrast, the more dynamic developing economies of East and Southeast Asia did not penalize the traded goods sectors, nor did they attempt to supplant market forces so pervasively. Given the relative abundance of unskilled and semi-skilled labor, openness to trade and reliance on market forces encouraged the production and exports of goods that were intensive in unskilled and semi-skilled labor (see box 3.6). This in turn led to employment opportunities for the poor and reductions in poverty.

A strong inverse relationship exists between openness to trade and growth in poverty incidence in developing Asia (see figure 3.4). The relationship was derived from 40 developing countries for which relevant data existed for the period 1970-1992. The poverty incidence was measured by the headcount index based on the national poverty line, and openness by trade share as a percentage of GDP. The slope of the relationship was found to be negative and statistically significant, with a high (yet less than one) elasticity. This suggests that openness exerts a significant influence on poverty reduction.

Should market-oriented policies be limited to product markets only? Labor markets are often viewed as inherently different from product markets. They influence the terms of employment, such as wages and employment conditions, which affect the quality of life of workers and their families. Driven by such concerns, most governments regulate labor markets by establishing the role of unions, setting minimum wages, providing unemployment insurance, and regulating employment contracts (ADB 1997). The extent and nature of these regulations differ across countries. In general, the more dynamic East and Southeast Asian economies have had significantly fewer labor market regulations than South Asian economies.

Are labor-market interventions always in the best interest of workers? In South Asia, labor market regulations have generally worked against workers by creating an inflexible market—that is, a labor market that is unresponsive to economic circumstances and changes. Over the years, India adopted a number of laws that protect trade union rights, guarantee a minimum wage, and prevent layoffs, with the laudable intention of protecting the welfare of workers. Many observers believe, however, that the legislation has made the economy less flexible and has harmed the interests of labor. Judging exactly how these regulations affect employment levels is difficult, but firm-level statistics suggest that the larger firms that are subject to these regulations have responded by reducing their levels of employment, while employment has increased in smaller firms.

It does not follow that any system that tries to protect workers' employment will be unsuccessful. Consider Japan, which has a system of lifetime employment for part of its workforce. Superficially, such a system may seem to generate the same type of inefficiencies witnessed in India, but the Japanese system appears to have worked rather well for a long time. The simple reason is that this system of lifetime employment maintains its flexibility through wage and bonus packages that allow firms to cut pay during downswings (ADB 1997). It is equally simplistic to blame powerful unions for labor market rigidities, while the nature of the collective bargaining process is much more important. In India, collective bargaining occurs at the level of industry in the organized sector, but in most of the dynamic East and Southeast Asian

Box 3.6 **Openness and Poverty**

To what extent does the structure of a country's exports depend on the composition of its resources? This may seem an arcane issue of international trade, but it is important in increasing market opportunities for the poor in developing countries.

According to the Heckscher-Ohlin theory of trade, the composition of a country's resources affects the structure of its exports. Countries with relatively abundant unskilled labor tend to export goods intensive in unskilled labor, while those with more abundant supplies of skilled labor export skill-intensive products. Poor countries, which generally have large supplies of unskilled labor, benefit from trade because market opportunities increase for their abundant unskilled labor.

A recent study using data from 111 countries examined the impact of countries' relative supplies of land and labor resources on the structure of exports. The composition of between one and two thirds of exports can be explained by countries' relative supplies of resources. In particular, countries with a larger proportion of unskilled labor tend to have more primary exports than manufactured goods, and within the manufacturing sector, more labor-intensive than skill-intensive manufactured goods. This fits the Heckscher-Ohlin theory, and helps explain why developing countries tend to export labor-intensive products to developed countries in return for imports of skill-intensive products.

Thus, economies in South Asia, which have relatively small supplies of skilled labor and few natural resources, export more labor-intensive goods than East and Southeast Asia. The more dynamic economies of East and Southeast Asia have more educated work forces, with an export structure heavily tilted toward skill-intensive goods.

South Asian economies have been among the most closed in the world. Consequently, export levels of countries in South Asia have been minuscule compared to East and Southeast Asia. In 1996, total merchandise exports of South Asian economies were less than the exports of Thailand alone. Had these economies been more open, they likely would have been able to generate many more employment opportunities for their large pool of unskilled labor.

Source: Wood and Mayer (1999).

---

economies, it occurs at the factory level. This means that factory-specific productivity growth and wages are not linked in the Indian case, in contrast to East and Southeast Asian economies.

The contrasting experiences of South Asia and the more dynamic economies of East and Southeast Asia suggest that developing economies will not be able to realize the potential benefits of the large pools of employable labor unless their labor markets are flexible. Workers must have the opportunity and incentives to shift between jobs and sectors as the economy's structure changes. If workers are unemployed or underemployed because they lack skills, because the minimum wage is too high, or because wage increases significantly outstrip productivity gains, this will limit the potential for rapid economic growth and poverty reduction (ADB 1997).

Governments can do many important things in the labor market, including protecting the vulnerable, such as female and child workers (see box 3.7). In some cases, unfettered market activity may lead to undesirable health and safety conditions at work, which governments can act against. They can also help create an industrial relations environment in which workers and enterprises are partners in shared development. Governments also have a role in educating and training the disadvantaged to match the skills and knowledge of workers with the demands of employers.

Macroeconomic Stability. While openness and market-oriented policies form the foundations on which inclusive growth is built, it is important that these policies operate in the context of a stable macroeconomic environment. Manageable levels of internal and external debt, the absence of high and volatile inflation, and the avoidance of serious misalignments in exchange rates are all important

Figure 3.4 Openness and Poverty Reduction, Selected Asian Developing Economies, 1970-1992 (percent)

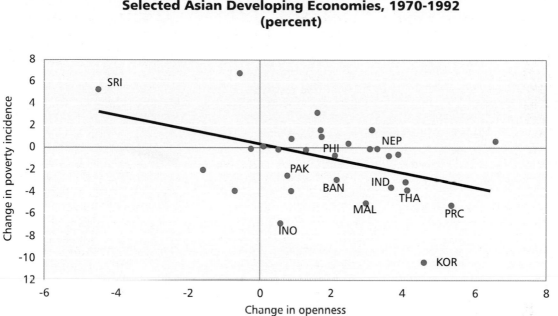

Note: The line shows the inverse relationship between percentage growth of openness (as measured by the trade to GDP ratio) and the percentage change in poverty incidence (based on national poverty lines), and was derived from a regression analysis for approximately 40 developing countries during 1970-1992. The regression parameters for this exercise had the correct sign, significant t-values and good fit.

Source: Staff estimates.

factors in creating an environment conducive for efficient, growth-oriented investment and saving decisions. They are also important for avoiding macroeconomic crisis.

Large public deficits, in particular, must be avoided. If deficits are financed by the creation of money, this will put upward pressure on prices. High inflation reduces the real income of those whose wages are slow to adjust, leads to distortions in relative prices, and interferes with the ability of markets to allocate resources efficiently. The poor are hurt, in particular, because they hold more of their assets in cash than the nonpoor. If large public deficits are financed through government borrowing, domestic private investment can be crowded out as interest rates rise. If the borrowing is externally financed, a balance of payments crisis could occur if an economy's export earnings falter.

Traditionally, Asian countries have avoided the profligate fiscal policies that led to the high rates of inflation and unsustainable current account deficits that were common in other parts of the developing world in previous decades (particularly in Latin America and Africa). Nonetheless, Asia has not been immune to the macroeconomic instability resulting from weaknesses in banking systems and financial regulation—weaknesses that can be exposed by an unsustainable exchange rate regime and a lack of prudential controls on short-term capital flows.

Economists have yet to reach a consensus on which type of exchange rate regime makes developing countries less vulnerable to external shocks, although fixed but adjustable exchange rate pegs have become widely discredited in the wake of crises in Asia, Latin America, and Russia. The remaining divergence of opinion rests on whether currency boards, or even

Box 3.7 **What Can be Done About Child Labor?**

The question of child labor stirs powerful emotions, for obvious reasons. Child labor often implies gross exploitation, where children are employed in harmful occupations, as field workers using dangerous pesticides, as prostitutes, or perhaps as abused domestic servants. From an economic standpoint, it almost always represents a waste of human potential. Children who work are unable to get an education and acquire marketable skills. Unfortunately, child labor is also hard to eradicate.

The fundamental cause of child labor is abject poverty. Parents usually know that more schooling would improve their child's skills, bringing higher income later in life. But abject poverty means that parents cannot afford to take their children out of the labor market. There is a cruel conflict between the short-term economic interests of the parent and the long-term interests of the child.

This conflict will not end until the problem of poverty is addressed. A simple ban on child labor will not help (though governments should obviously try to eliminate the worst forms of child labor, such as those that involve sexual abuse). Enforcing an outright ban on child labor would be extremely difficult in many poor countries. Laws that decree compulsory schooling through primary school are already unenforced among poorer segments of society in many developing countries.

Nor will the imposition of trade sanctions against countries that employ child labor help. In fact, trade sanctions would worsen the situation, because by reducing export opportunities for the poorest countries, trade sanctions will simply force children into worse forms of employment.

The only long-term route to eliminating child labor is economic growth and poverty reduction. However, effectively designed economic incentives can affect parents' and employers' behavior in the interim. One approach is to provide financial incentives to poor parents to keep their children in school. These stipends must be relatively close to the child's potential earnings. In many countries, the stipend paid to keep girls, especially teenagers, in school must be higher than for boys.

In Mexico, a pioneering program called *Progresa* that pays parents to keep their children—particularly daughters—in school has had considerable success. Since its inception on 8 August 1997, Progresa has raised school attendance of children through educational grants, which are given out to children of beneficiary families who are between the third and ninth grades. During the school year beginning in 1998, Progresa gave educational grants to 1.7 million boys and girls. In the next school year, which began in August 1999, the number of children receiving grants is expected to increase to 2.2 million boys and girls (SEDESOL 1999). Progresa also successfully narrowed the gender gap

in education by giving girls at the secondary level slightly higher grants than boys. This is to compensate for the fact that girls tend to drop out of school at a younger age than boys.

However, such schemes require substantial public investment. In fiscally constrained poor countries, the resources are difficult to mobilize. One economically sensible—although politically challenging—option would be to reduce the money spent subsidizing tertiary education, which tends to benefit the rich elite.

An alternative approach is private collaboration between employers and the child who is employed. In Bangladesh, for instance, garment manufacturers—in collaboration with nongovernmental organizations—have established school facilities for working children.

Evidence suggests that working children have considerably lower educational attainments than nonworking children. However, even an inferior education is better than no education at all. It is also better than the malnutrition that could result from a sizeable drop in the family's income.

Moreover, it is worth noting that in some poor countries the choice between school and work is irrelevant, because access to effective schooling facilities is not available. In many parts of rural India, for instance, there are no functioning schools. Parents, quite rationally, view a child's early entry into the labor market as more beneficial than time wasted in a school with permanently absent or chronically ill-qualified teachers.

dollarization, are superior to flexible exchange rates in terms of avoiding crises and in terms of facilitating adjustment during a crisis. Opening up an economy to short-term capital flows is viewed as a bad idea when domestic banking and financial systems are weak, and supervisory and regulatory standards are lacking.

In summary, prudent macroeconomic management provides a strong underpinning to efforts aimed at promoting inclusive growth in an economy. Numerous studies confirm that economies that have adopted open trade policies and practiced prudent macroeconomic management have grown more rapidly than those that did not. Moreover, following prudent macroeconomic policies enables economies to better handle crises emanating from economic shocks. If previous budget surpluses exist, an economy affected by a systemic financial and banking crisis is able to recapitalize its banking system.

Investing in Human and Physical Infrastructure, Rural Development, and Microcredit

Investment plays a central role in adding to the resource base for economic activity and in providing people better life opportunities. This section considers four types of investment: in human capital, in physical infrastructure, in rural development, and in microcredit.

Human Capital. Most governments are active as both financiers and providers of social services. The financing and provision of these services can be made more effective, however. One way is to recognize synergies that exist between various investments in human capital. Investments in education, particularly girls' schooling, for example, simultaneously promote improvements in health, nutrition, and family planning as girls enter reproductive ages (see box 3.8). Investments in family planning that enable wider spacing of births and reductions in fertility are associated with improvements in maternal and child health, nutrition, and education. Reductions in fertility free up both household and government resources, and facilitate a shift in human capital investments away from quantity and toward higher quality. Investments in health and nutrition improve the productivity of

children in school, and support fertility declines by reducing levels of child mortality. These synergies suggest that an integrated approach to investments in human capital is required.

Because public resources are limited provision of social services must be targeted to those areas where the divergence between private and social returns are greatest, and to those people who cannot afford these services on their own. In the health sector, public finance should focus on public health interventions targeted at combating communicable diseases and infections carried by water and food through such relatively inexpensive health interventions as health education, immunizations, and screening. HIV/AIDS, in particular, deserves special attention, especially in countries such as Cambodia, India, Lao PDR, Myanmar, and Thailand, which have among the most serious HIV epidemics in the world. In the education sector, there is scope for reallocating public finances toward primary education and away from higher education.

Investing in human capital is not just an issue of allocating more public resources to the appropriate types of health interventions or levels of education. It also requires a fundamental change in the institutional setting, including the incentive structures under which social services such as health and education operate.

A growing body of evidence from around the developing world shows that nongovernment providers, including the private sector, deliver social services more effectively than the government (see box 3.9). This suggests that governments would do well to remove the explicit and implicit restrictions—such as regulatory barriers, stringent financial requirements, and stricter standards—from private and nongovernment provision of health and education services. These constraints often mean that government and nongovernment providers of social services are not operating on a level playing field. The opportunity cost of these restrictions is high, because the presence of nongovernment providers in the health and education sectors not only improves household access to schooling and health opportunities at little or no cost to the government, but also introduces competition, thereby raising the quality of services.

The studies that show superior performance of nongovernment providers of social services, especially

Box 3.8 **Mother's Schooling Always Helps Children's Education**

Numerous studies for developing countries have found a positive association between maternal and child schooling. This relationship is surprisingly robust even when considering family characteristics, such as income and paternal schooling.

One explanation is that mothers help their children at home, complementing the education received at school, and better-educated mothers are better able to teach their children. An alternative explanation is that women, perhaps because of maternal altruism, prefer to allocate more resources to children than their husbands do. A better-educated woman is more likely to have employment outside the household, which in turn likely increases her control over the allocation of family resources, and she chooses to devote more resources to her children's education.

These two explanations have important but different implications for development policies. If the first is correct, then maternal education will have a direct and immediate impact on children's education, regardless of outside employment opportunities for women. However,

if the second explanation is correct, then women's education will lead to better education of children only if labor market opportunities exist for women. In many poor countries, such outside female employment opportunities are limited, and designing specific program interventions to create such opportunities is not easy. Until such opportunities can be created, if the second explanation is correct, in those countries with little job opportunity for women, female education will not help improve children's education.

What is the situation in India? A recent study drew a large household data set from rural India covering 15 years when the Green Revolution took place. The study found that the education of farmers played an important role in the adoption and efficient use of this new seed-fertilizer technology. However, the farmers are generally male, and as women did not usually participate in farm management, the education of wives did not affect the use of the new technology. Similarly, rural India offered few employment opportunities for educated wives outside the household. As female education neither expanded income

opportunities outside the household nor contributed to increased farm incomes, it could be considered a waste of resources.

However, the demand for literate wives in rural India increased after the advent of the Green Revolution. The study concluded that this increase in demand was apparently a "derived demand." Educated wives had an advantage over uneducated women in educating children, and spent more time on such activities as helping children with homework. For farmers coming from areas with technical change, where high-yielding variety seeds were introduced, education had a pecuniary value, because only educated people could successfully use the new technologies. Therefore, the demand increased for educated wives who could improve educational outcomes for children.

The evidence from rural India suggests that even if women do not have any labor market opportunities, they can make a direct contribution to improving children's education. However, if outside employment opportunities exist for women, education may have even more effect on educational outcomes of the children.

Source: Behrman and others (1999).

---

in education, also help explain why government provision seems to be lacking. One reason for the differences between public and private schools, for instance, is that headmasters in private schools typically have greater control over school-level decisions that influence student outcomes, such as selecting teachers, textbooks, and curriculum (Jimenez and Lockheed 1995). When coupled with the fact that headmasters in private schools are ultimately accountable to students' parents, they have every

incentive to control school-level decisions in a way compatible with parents' interests.

Reforming the incentive structures of government providers of social services so that they become more responsive to the needs of the people they are meant to serve is likely to lead to large payoffs. One way to achieve this is decentralizing decisionmaking and finance to local levels. Decentralization is by no means a panacea, however. Simply decentralizing finances to lower levels of government may exacerbate

Box 3.9 Are Private Schools Better than Public Schools?

While virtually all developing economies in Asia have made impressive strides in expanding the coverage of education, particularly at the primary level, many problems remain even in areas where schooling is available. High rates of dropout; grade repetition; and low learning outcomes, even among those who complete schooling cycles, remain serious issues. One of the factors responsible is the relative lack of attention policymakers devote to education quality. Schools with inadequately trained teachers and limited supplies of textbooks and other teaching materials are, unfortunately, only too common across Asia's developing economies.

Although channeling greater public resources toward public schools is part of the solution, a growing number of experts believe that it is also important to make major changes in the institutional setting under which public schooling is currently delivered. In particular, an increasing body of research finds that private schools are more efficient, and suggests that it is not only better resources that account for this differential. Some experts argue that because private schools enjoy relatively high degrees of autonomy in management and are ultimately accountable to parents who pay the school fees, they are more responsive to the needs of their pupils. In contrast, public schools are characterized by a lack of managerial autonomy: typically, they must make decisions in accordance with strict guidelines set by ministries of education. They also rely on government funding, which is usually not linked to performance, and are largely unaccountable to parents.

Because these arguments potentially have dramatic implications for the management of public schools, it is important to evaluate them rigorously. Fewer dropouts or higher test scores in private schools do not necessarily indicate a deficiency in the management of public schools, even if the two operate with similar per student costs. If students with better abilities or from families able to provide a more conducive atmosphere for studying choose private schools, then those schools could seem more efficient even if the educational services at the two schools were identical. A careful comparison of public and private schools, while taking into account the effects of innate student ability and the possibility of nonrandom selection across school types, was made in a study for a district in Uttar Pradesh state in Northern India.

The results suggest that students with a higher likelihood of performing better systematically choose to attend private schools. Thus, a raw comparison of test scores across public and private schools could be misleading. However, not all of the difference in scores was attributable to student and family characteristics. Between 10 to 19 percent of higher student scores at a fully private school can be attributed to school influences. Moreover, the superior performance of private schools cannot be attributed to larger expenditure outlays. While capital expenditures across public and private schools are similar, private schools have annual recurrent expenditures that are less than half those of public schools. Private schools achieve superior cost effectiveness partly by paying teachers less than the high government-prescribed salaries, and by having higher pupil-teacher ratios than public schools.

The study concludes that greater school-level autonomy in decisionmaking, aimed at giving school administrators more freedom in hiring, remuneration, and pedagogical decisions, may align the incentives of schools and teachers in ways that make them more responsive to their students. Similarly, removing constraints on entry into private schools—an important problem in many countries—would lead to gains in efficiency because private schools perform better. It would also be fairer, because if children from better-off households select into superior private schools, more public money could be targeted toward the poor.

Source: Kingdon (1996).

existing inequities, or may simply shift "the same old problems" to levels even less capable of resolving them. Nonetheless, if the capacity of local governments can be improved, then decentralization is a promising route toward more effective delivery of social services.

Infrastructure. Infrastructure investments have an important role to play in confronting Asia's social challenges. As described earlier, infrastructure investments enhance quality of life directly, in addition to contributing to inclusive economic growth.

Despite this, private markets do not provide enough infrastructure investments. This may be because they are "non-rival" goods, which means that consumption by one user does not reduce the supply for others. A road, for instance, can be used by a hundred people as easily as by one. These are also "non-excludable" goods, meaning it is difficult to prevent those who have not paid for the service from reaping its benefits. Investments in flood control in a low area, for instance, benefit everybody who lives there, regardless of who paid for the flood control. Infrastructure investments such as laying underground water pipes or electric cables can also involve substantial fixed costs, which can make it cheaper for one provider to serve a market than for two or more. In such cases, a natural monopoly exists, and some governments have been wary of allowing the private sector to provide the infrastructure in question.

Because of these specific characteristics, investments in infrastructure in developing Asian economies have been undertaken mostly by state-owned entities. However, for several reasons it is neither possible nor desirable for governments to continue to be involved in the area of infrastructure services as deeply as they have been. The need for infrastructure services is so great in the region that governments do not have the necessary resources for financing, and government operation and management of infrastructure services has often been highly inefficient. Services have typically been provided at well below supply cost, making it virtually impossible to apply sound commercial principles to operations. Subsidized infrastructure, in turn, encourages wasteful usage and contributes to serious fiscal imbalances. It does not, however, benefit the poor. Evidence from around the developing world shows that infrastructure subsidies, especially those applied through price subsidies, benefit the nonpoor much more than the poor.

The economic and technological characteristics of many types of infrastructure allow them to be provided extremely efficiently by the private sector. Rural roadways, for example, are likely to be underprovided by private markets, but that is not necessarily the case for long-distance telecommunication services.

Given their different infrastructure requirements, Asia's developing economies need an effective public-private partnership in infrastructure provision. Such a partnership would emphasize applying commercial principles to the operation of infrastructure services, and foster competition by appropriately regulating the private sector providers of infrastructure. It would also ensure that user fees are not only recoverable, but also set fairly.

Local governments and communities would be brought into the decisionmaking process of infrastructure provision. Growing evidence shows that participatory approaches to delivering infrastructure have improved performance and quality of the infrastructure provided and the impact on the poor. When an ADB-financed high-speed toll road in the PRC was designed to include roads connecting the expressway to poor counties in Hebei, only after the intended beneficiaries—the poor—were involved in the decisionmaking process did it become clear the project would only help them if village access roads were added (ADB 1998a). Another study of 121 rural water supply projects in 49 countries found that 68 percent of the projects that enjoyed a high level of beneficiary participation were successful, compared to only 12 percent among those with low beneficiary involvement (Isham, Narayan, and Pritchett 1995).

Agriculture and Rural Development. Despite Asia's progress in alleviating poverty and overcoming other social challenges over the last four decades, deprivation remains overwhelmingly a rural problem. More than three fourths of the people below the poverty line in Asia live in rural areas, and are mostly employed in or dependent on agriculture. Clearly, in the battle against poverty and related social challenges, the transformation of the rural economy—and its integration with the modern sector—is crucial.

The transformation of the rural economy would require liberalization of markets to allow greater internal and external competition. In the past, many governments in developing Asia, in particular in South Asia, pursued an inward-oriented strategy of development. This strategy adopted a structure of trade protection and an exchange rate regime that offered negative protection to agriculture. However, in recent years, most Asian economies have adopted a more neutral policy stance that attempts to correct the anti-agricultural bias in trade and exchange rates, and to dismantle the various state interventions such as input and credit subsidies and price and marketing support. The impact of these market liberalization policies has been positive, and often dramatic, as in the PRC.

Liberalization of markets alone will not transform the rural economy. Governments must play a more active role in providing the critical public goods, such as agricultural research, extension services, and rural infrastructure. In rural areas, providing the right type of infrastructure can go a long way toward expanding the market opportunities available to the rural poor by raising farm productivity and providing new opportunities for nonfarm employment. One study of rural districts in India found that the combined impact of services provided by rural roadways and modern irrigation projects positively affected agricultural yields and the ability of farmers to access markets (World Bank 1994). One unanticipated benefit of rural roads was to lower banks' costs of operating in the rural areas, which, in turn, facilitated the expansion of rural credit and enabled farmers to borrow to purchase productivity-improving fertilizer. Similarly, infrastructure services related to transportation, telecommunications, and power at the village level had been a key ingredient of the PRC's success in promoting rural enterprises, which now account for more than a third of national output and about a fifth of the labor force.

Microcredit. The poor, especially the rural poor, lack access to credit. Outside agencies (banks or governments) lack the local information that allows them to easily identify good credit risks. When information on creditworthiness is lacking, the cost of monitoring numerous small loans is high, and banks must demand collateral from borrowers. This effectively excludes the poor.

Governments can improve access to credit for the poorest by subsidizing credit and by fostering specific market-oriented financial services targeted at the poor.

The effectiveness of subsidized credit is questionable. In the Integrated Rural Development Program, a large credit program in India, for example, wealthier borrowers succeeded in capturing most of the credit subsidies intended for the poor, while

underpriced credit encouraged the inefficient use of capital (Bardhan 1996a). By 1986, repayment rates had fallen to 41 percent, and the program had become a costly and poorly targeted transfer program (Morduch 1999a).

The alternative is to improve credit markets. One way would be to provide the poor with collateral. This could be done by giving poor people a lump-sum transfer (or even a ration card) to be used as collateral. The collateral will provide a strong incentive for repayment that is absent with unsecured loans. Another option is to overcome the monitoring problems cited above through peer-monitoring loans. Asian countries, particularly Bangladesh, have pioneered these efforts, and the first and most famous program of this type was the Grameen Bank in Bangladesh.

The Grameen Bank lends money to the landless poor, and especially to impoverished women. It started commercial operations in 1983, and by 1998, had amassed approximately $100 million in equity and $275 million in outstanding loan portfolio. It has lent more than $2 billion to 2.3 million low-income borrowers in rural Bangladesh, of which 94 percent are women, spread across 37,000 villages. Loan recovery rate has been a high 98 percent, especially impressive when compared with a rate of approximately 25 percent for the country's commercial and agricultural development banks.

The Grameen Bank's business strategy is based on the voluntary formation of small groups of about five individuals to provide mutual, morally binding group guarantees in lieu of the collateral required by conventional banks. If any member of the group defaults, all are cut off from new lending until the outstanding debt is repaid. In this way, the social capital in closely-knit communities is mobilized to monitor the actions of borrowers, press them to repay loans, and impose sanctions against those who do not. Other microcredit institutions modeled after Grameen Bank serve an additional 2 million clients in Bangladesh.

Similar group-based lending programs have been implemented in more than 45 countries. One controversial question about microcredit programs, however, is whether they can make a permanent dent on poverty. Several studies have concluded that households with Grameen Bank credit saw significant improvements in welfare. Not only did the borrowers have higher income and consumption, but they also managed to provide better schooling for their children, especially girls, and had a higher use of contraceptives and lower rate of fertility. However, other authors have found methodological faults with those studies, and found no impact on income and consumption. What is not controversial, however, is that the Grameen credit had indeed reduced consumption variability, which has an important bearing on the welfare of the poor.

Questions have also been raised about the financial viability of the Grameen program, which is heavily dependent on subsidies from the government and donors. There appears to be a critical tradeoff between profitability and subsidies. Bolivia's BancoSol and Indonesia's Bank Rakyat Indonesia (Morduch 1999a, b) both earn profit, but mainly by serving richer clients as well as the poor. If a microcredit program serves only the poor, then financial sustainability is likely to remain a problem. Microcredit is not a magic wand that will transform the poor into dynamic entrepreneurs, but it does play an important function in smoothing poor people's consumption and safeguarding them from the worst consequences of poverty.

Improving Governance and Participation

More than anything else, Asia's success in overcoming its social challenge will depend on the quality of its governance. Governance encompasses not only the institutional arrangements through which governments are chosen and replaced, but also the ability of those in power to formulate appropriate policies and implement them effectively. It also includes the manner and extent to which ordinary people are able to voice their opinions and affect the decisions that influence their lives.

Democracy and Civil Liberties. With rising incomes, education, and awareness of other more inclusive systems of government, demand will increase in Asia for more democratic forms of government and the civil liberties that go with it. What impact will this have on Asia's social challenge? Greater civil and political liberties—the freedom to express oneself; the freedom

to form and join organizations, political, or otherwise; and the freedom of the press—will directly improve the well-being of Asians. The connections between democracy and the various forms of deprivation, including poverty, are complex. Some of the most spectacular achievements in poverty reduction have taken place in East and Southeast Asian countries under regimes that are not necessarily democratic. Conversely, India—a democracy since it gained independence—has a less impressive record in poverty reduction.

It appears that democracy, with its characteristics of transparency, accountability, and consensus formation, can avoid some of the worst forms of rent seeking and predation associated with many authoritarian regimes. At the same time, democracy can be stymied with political deadlock and the lengthy and cumbersome process of consensus building, and can be hijacked by special interest groups. On balance, however, it is difficult to argue that less democracy is better for economic growth and poverty reduction. The fact that some authoritarian regimes have been able to generate growth and translate it into large and tangible improvements in the lives of the poor must be balanced with the performance of other authoritarian regimes, where rulers have used their power to steal national wealth and carry out unproductive investments. Authoritarian regimes are associated with both the best and worst of performances in economic growth and poverty reduction.

Nonetheless, democracies clearly vary in their performance in poverty reduction. Part of this variation depends on the participation of the poor in the political decisionmaking process. The level of decentralization and the quality of civil society and its legal and judicial institutions all affect how much democracy promotes poverty reduction. The legal and judicial system safeguards citizens, the poor included, from an abuse of power by the state or other agents. The rule of law—in the form of enforced contracts and clear property rights—is associated with higher level of economic growth (Barro 1996).

Decentralization. The demand for greater democracy is mirrored by calls for greater decentralization in political, fiscal, and administrative matters. Decentralization holds much promise. Greater local control over decisionmaking may improve the delivery of various social and infrastructure services. Local involvement can provide incentives and information for improving the quality and cost-effectiveness of programs. However, there is no guarantee that decentralization will lead to superior outcomes, especially for disadvantaged peoples and regions.

In particular, there is a danger that decentralized settings may exacerbate existing inequities across households and regions. For example, poorer regions with a low tax base may not be able to raise adequate revenues if finance is decentralized. There is also a danger that landlords and other local elites may more effectively dominate local politics than national politics. Gender disparity may be a problem under decentralization, because available evidence suggests that it has a strong local component (Filmer, King, and Pritchett 1998). In the absence of central controls, women and girls may have less than equal access to basic services such as education and health care. While the dangers are very real, the benefits from decentralization designed and executed appropriately are too great to ignore, however.

Tendencies toward worsening inequities and power capture by local elites need to be dealt with head on. Decentralization requires an effective mechanism for transferring resources from relatively wealthy localities to relatively poor ones. However, the transfer of resources should be based on hard-budget constraints. Local governments must retain a real resource stake in the activities and services they are providing. It is difficult to involve communities in the management of social services if they are not also providing a substantial share of funding. At the same time, public subsidies (whether from the national level or local) should take the form of demand-side finance rather than supply-side finance. For example, in the case of schools, subsidies could follow students rather than schools through a system of vouchers.

In combating the capture of power by local elites, it is important to institute regular public meetings at the local level, such as in the village or municipal town. In these meetings, major items of expenditure could be publicly discussed and accounted for. In parts of India there is, for example, a growing movement calling for a Freedom of Information Act.

With respect to the issue of gender and caste disparities, some experiments in India with the relatively new *panchayati raj* councils—elected village and urban councils with control over a wide range of social and developmental activities—suggest some possible solutions. In particular, the law requires that a third of the elected council members be women. In addition, the scheduled castes and tribes must be represented on councils in proportion to their share in the population. While traditional patterns of discrimination are difficult to break and women council members may still be manipulated by men in regions where gender disparity is high, the evidence suggests that women are increasingly becoming conscious of their rights and are beginning to act more independently.

Enhanced Participation. A key aspect of decentralization is the emphasis on introducing local knowledge and local sensitivities into decisionmaking. For this to take place effectively, local people must participate in the decisions that are intended to influence their lives. However, mobilizing such participation is not easy and requires nurturing the institutions of civil society.

Civil society organizations have various advantages. They can often substitute for corrupt and ineffective governments in delivering needed services to the poor. Given their knowledge of the locality, civil society organizations or nongovernmental organizations (NGOs) are able to distinguish between the "deserving" and the "undeserving," and may have less corruption. NGOs can also serve an essential role in the political process, promoting empowerment among the poor and lobbying governments to change policies and to direct more resources to eradicate poverty. Because poor people have relatively little political power, their needs tend to be neglected when the location of roads, schools, and health facilities is decided.

Nonetheless, it is not clear that civil society organizations always live up to this promise. Most of these organizations offer high-quality services, but some do not. Some suffer from inadequate community participation and poor accountability. Some NGOs and governments have long histories of mutual mistrust. Others act in isolation, setting up their own fiefdoms. One evaluation of an anti-poverty program in the Philippines implemented by a large NGO found that only about one third of the program's beneficiaries were poor. More surprisingly, about one third of the beneficiaries had incomes ranging from three to more than 20 times the official poverty line (Balisacan 1997). Even the evidence on corruption among NGOs is unclear.

It is difficult to generalize about how much NGOs contribute to poverty reduction. In some countries and in some sectors, they have done excellent jobs; while in other countries and other sectors, they have not. Overall, they offer a new institutional arrangement for providing public goods, and have been a positive force in improving governance. Individually, each organization must be considered in terms of its own merit and past performance.

Social Safety Nets

The recent financial crisis has emphasized that not even the most dynamic Asian economies, let alone the poor ones, had an adequate system of safety nets. As this chapter has shown, formal social assistance coverage is relatively low; these countries instead rely heavily on informal family-based networks. Consequently, there is considerable debate within the region about whether to extend formal safety nets, and how to do so.

These formal programs include unemployment insurance, old-age pension and social assistance, public works and social funds, health insurance and crop insurance, and other agriculture stabilization measures.

Unemployment Insurance. Unemployment insurance programs are intended to cushion against such labor market risks as job loss, disability, and ill health. In most Asian developing economies, these programs, when they exist, cover only a small portion of the labor force in the formal sector. The main argument against introducing broader unemployment insurance programs is that they add to labor costs and may lead to the erosion of international competitiveness and to sluggish employment growth. In addition, high labor costs in the formal sector encourage growth of the informal sector.

Although the richer developing economies of Asia do have the financial and administrative capacity to introduce a more comprehensive system of unemployment insurance, it is not feasible for poorer economies. More appropriate and feasible actions for these countries include means-tested social assistance and public works programs. Thailand, for instance, has a system that aims to alleviate poverty among the unemployed by providing limited transfers—in the form of flat benefits—to those close to the poverty line.

Old-Age Pension and Assistance. In poorer Asian developing economies, only a small portion of the labor force receives formal pensions. In most countries, the extended family is the principal source of old-age support. Given that governments in most poorer Asian developing economies are faced with worsening budget problems, it is highly unlikely that the state will be able to bear the full burden of the elderly. Primary responsibility lies with the family. However, the higher-income Asian developing economies need to pay greater attention to the needs of the elderly and must introduce more comprehensive old-age pension and other social assistance programs such as health care. The design and financing mechanisms for these pension systems, however, need careful review.

Over the long run, issues such as pension fund governance (improving the transparency and efficiency of pension fund management), integration of public and private retirement income provisions, establishment of financial and pension regulatory regimes, and expansion of capital markets for private and institutional investors should be integral elements of a comprehensive pension reform agenda. Raising public support and awareness of the implications of demographic scenarios are also crucial in facilitating the reform process.

Social Assistance and Welfare Programs. Social assistance and welfare programs provide support to those who do not earn an income sufficient to provide for minimum consumption needs. Pure cash transfers are rare in developing countries, except in times of dire crisis. Most of these programs are in-kind transfers targeted at specific objectives: schooling, health, or nutrition. Some are common even in the poorer Asian developing economies.

The design and administration of these programs are fraught with many difficulties. The government should finance these programs, but that does not necessarily mean it should be involved in their actual provision. Often excessive government involvement in the design, financing, and implementation of social assistance programs is highly inefficient. For example, the food stamp program in Sri Lanka, where the government is not involved in distribution, is more efficient than in India, where the government is involved. The use of NGOs in the distribution process can be useful.

To ensure that the provision of such subsidies is fiscally sustainable, and to minimize distortions in consumption and production, only those goods that are normally consumed by low-income households (such as coarse rice, brown sugar, or generic medicines) should be subsidized. Such subsidies have been successfully implemented in Indonesia and the Philippines using *regional targeting*, where only the poorest villages receive the subsidy; and *commodity-specific targeting*, where only low-quality foods are subsidized.

Social Funds and Public Works Programs.

Social funds are agencies funded by national governments and donors that provide temporary employment for the poor. They have dual objectives: to transfer income to the poor and to improve infrastructure. Social funds operate at local levels, sometimes through NGOs, usually to improve local infrastructure such as schools, hospitals, and roads. Public works programs are also designed to provide short-term employment to the poor during economic difficulties and to develop local infrastructure. However, public works programs operate on an ad-hoc basis without a permanent governing structure and regular funding.

The important attraction of public works program has been their self-targeting nature. As the work is arduous and the wage level is below the market wage level for unskilled laborers, the public works usually attract only the poor. Experiences in India and Bangladesh suggest that these programs play an important part in risk management for the poor and the vulnerable. However, the infrastructure these programs build is often unplanned, and inefficiently located or designed. These disadvantages can be avoided with more local participation and involvement by civil society. Nevertheless, even when the

infrastructures built are unplanned, the very existence of these public works programs increases the bargaining power of poor workers, especially those in the rural labor markets.

Crop Insurance.

Crop insurance pools the risks that farmers face from various natural disasters. The rationale for government-supported crop insurance is that it encourages the farmer to pursue high-return, high-risk investments. However, crop insurance is rare in developing countries, and has been fraught with problems. Farmers, however, can take other measures that can largely redress the need for crop insurance, such as diversifying crops and crop varieties and offering a portion of household labor to off-farm employment. Many governments have also adopted floor prices for agricultural products that act as a form of insurance.

These measures are the main forms of social safety net provision that developing economies in Asia need to consider. Some of these measures already exist in rudimentary form in some countries. At issue are what new measures should be introduced and how fast, and how far the existing ones should be expanded. No single answer applies to all Asian developing economies, however. In devising an appropriate safety net program, each country must consider the nature of risks its poor face, as well as the financial and administrative capacity of the government and the nature and extent of private safety nets.

Redistributing Assets, Affirmative Actions, and Targeting

This section considers additional methods of helping the poor directly: asset redistribution, particularly land reform; and affirmative action. Both offer radical potential methods to improve the situation of the poorest, but considerable controversy surrounds both the political feasibility as well as the economic efficiency of these approaches. Finally, the advantages and difficulties of targeted transfers and social programs are explored.

Land Reform.

Land reform includes both land redistribution and tenancy reforms. Land redistribution can mean giving land from those who own more than a legal limit to those with less or no land, or granting ownership rights to those who are currently cultivating the land. Tenancy reform can include both changes in the share of output received by the tenant and the provision of greater tenurial security. Policies relating to land consolidation, land titling, land reclamation, and reforestation—which often have a strong effect on growth and equity—are sometimes included under the rubric of land reform. However, this section does not address those issues.

There are two main arguments in favor of land reform: equity and efficiency. The equity argument suggests that a fairer distribution of land or improved terms of contract in tenancy in favor of the tenant would lead to better income distribution, and so reduce poverty. The efficiency argument suggests that land distribution or improved tenancy contracts leads to greater economic productivity, which in turn will help reduce poverty.

The argument that land reform increases productivity assumes that large farms are less productive than small farms. In traditional agriculture (as distinct from plantation agriculture), small farms have lower labor costs than large farms, as much of the labor in a small farm is mobilized from within the family. Some empirical evidence supports this argument: in Punjab, Pakistan, for example, the productivity of the largest farms measured by value added per unit of land was less than 40 percent of that in the second smallest size group (Banerjee 1999). In Malaysia, the corresponding ratio was 67 percent.

In addition to purely economic arguments, redistributive land reform has often been advocated on grounds of political economy. Land reform often helps change the local political structure, replacing the traditional dominance of the landlord with a structure that is more equitable and diffused. In a traditional rural economy, one of the motives for large landholdings stems from the disproportionate political power they confer. In such an environment, land reform gives the poor a voice, and creates an environment in which the rich are less able to capture the benefits of government projects intended for the poor. Local labor and products markets might also function better when landlords are not in a position to dominate them.

The main argument for tenancy reform is that share tenants are presumed to be less efficient than the owner-farmers because tenants have less incentive to work hard on the rented land because part of the output is taken by the landlord. The larger the share of the tenant's output, the greater his incentive to work. However, there are other ways to overcome the disincentive effect of sharecropping, including direct monitoring of the tenant's effort (when the landlords are present) or sharing costs of inputs. In addition, share tenancy provides some risk-sharing advantages that are not available to fixed rental contracts or owner cultivation. The empirical evidence on farm productivity does not suggest that sharecropping is inefficient (Rashid and Quibria 1995). Many of the observed differences in productivity across farms under different types of tenurial arrangement may, for instance, also be due to unobserved differences in land quality.

In most Asian countries, the experience with tenancy reform has not been good. One exception seems to be West Bengal, India, where a tenancy reform program called Operation Barga was introduced in 1977. It raised the share of output received by the tenant from 50 to 70 percent (Banerjee, Gertler, and Ghatak 1998). By 1982, the reform covered about one half of the state's sharecroppers, who account for about half of the total cropped area. Over the next decade, West Bengal achieved a breakthrough in agricultural production. One estimate suggests that more than a third of West Bengal's production growth from 1981-1992 resulted from this tenancy reform. However, other analyses of tenancy reform in India have not found any positive effect on productivity.

Despite its putative economic benefits, there are major political constraints on land reform. Most significantly, land redistribution has been associated with the termination of colonial rule or political upheavals. The much-discussed land reform in Korea and Taipei,China was imposed by outside forces. Very few successful land reform efforts have been launched in democracies and in peacetime. Given these limitations, one option is to undertake market-based land reform. Voluntary land reform with full compensation, as in Zimbabwe and the Philippines, is very expensive, however, and implies that little land will be redistributed. Additionally, the worst land is usually sold to the state, and if the beneficiaries pay the cost of compensation over time, their net asset situation is not much improved.

Unless accompanied by other measures, land redistribution or tenancy reforms may not yield the full productivity benefits of land reform. Land reform should ideally be accompanied by programs that attempt to deliver some of the services landlords provide to small farmers. Landlords are often the main source of credit and other inputs, including farming advice. Land reform may reduce or eliminate access to these inputs, and unless governments make up for this loss by providing support in such areas as research, credit and extension, crop insurance, and emergency income assistance (such as food-for-work programs), the impact on productive efficiency remains uncertain.

In sum, there are economies in Asia, notably Korea and Taipei,China, where early land reform programs may have had a positive impact on efficiency and growth. However, it is not a prerequisite for reducing poverty. Countries such as Indonesia, Malaysia, and Thailand, with little or no land reform, grew briskly and saw rapid reductions in poverty. Nor is land reform necessarily an efficient tool of poverty reduction, as it often imposes heavy financial, bureaucratic, and political demands. A government that is strong enough to implement a coercive land reform program should be able to impose and enforce the necessary taxes to produce a more equitable distribution of income and wealth.

Affirmative Action. Many developing Asian countries have adopted various types of affirmative action policies to address different types of social discrimination arising from ethnic, gender, caste, and religious diversities. In India, for example, tribal people are eligible for special development assistance under the Tribal Sub-Plan, jointly funded and administered by the central and state governments (World Bank 1998). Malaysia has made extensive use of affirmative action to address problems of economic disparity between Malays, Indians, and Chinese. The New Economic Policy, introduced under the Second Malaysia Plan in 1973, sought to reduce poverty as well as differences in economic conditions among racial groups by expanding primary education and health care and

eliminating differences in employment and asset ownership. It was extremely successful: between 1973 and 1987, poverty among Malays fell from 55 to 21 percent, among Chinese from 20 to 4 percent, and among Indians from 28 to 9 percent (Ahuja and others 1997).

Affirmative action programs have often been criticized on grounds of inefficiency. However, such criticism has little or no empirical support, and the Malaysian experience suggests that affirmative action policies do not harm economic growth. Until the recent financial crisis, Malaysia was one of the fastest growing economies in the region. Similarly, evidence from the advanced countries, such as the United States, suggests that affirmative actions had minimal adverse impact on efficiency (although other undesirable consequences are possible, such as increased social tensions between the favored group and the others).

Affirmative action can also be used to close gender disparities. Bangladesh, for instance, has introduced various programs including special seats for women in Parliament, quotas in the civil service, and scholarships for girls in school. Microcredit programs targeted at women can reduce gender disparities in access to financial resources, and subsidies to health services that benefit primarily women (such as family planning services) can be effective. So, too, can legal changes.

In recent years, many Asian developing countries adopted legislative measures that aim at redefining women's roles and granting them equal status with men. These include equal employment and equal pay laws, as well as statutory provision of maternity leave and state-funded childcare.

The most critical element for the success of affirmative action measures is the commitment of the government. The countries that have succeeded, such as Malaysia, have been deeply committed to the goal. Finally, policy efforts in developing Asia in the past were focused mostly on *preferential affirmative action*: measures that give preference to the discriminated group by setting a different threshold of expectations or by lowering standards of evaluation. However, the more effective means of circumventing social discrimination is *developmental affirmative action*: measures that contribute directly to enhance the performance of the discriminated group so it can compete on equal footing (Loury 1999).

Targeting. The idea of targeting social protection programs toward the most needy recipients is appealing, as social assistance is cheaper if it goes only to those who most need it. Taxpayers are more likely to support programs they know are not diverted to undeserving beneficiaries. In practice, however, targeting can be expensive and ineffective. The administrative costs of ensuring that a social program is narrowly targeted can be high (Gelbach and Pritchett 1997; van de Walle 1998). The introduction of targeted assistance can induce people to change their behavior to qualify—for instance, by altering their work patterns so they can be considered poor. Under certain conditions, it can also undermine the political support for transfers: sometimes voters support a social program if and only if they personally benefit. Useful targeting efforts must avoid these pitfalls.

The most accurate and expensive method of targeting is formal means testing. This usually involves administering a questionnaire or conducting an interview about the potential recipient's job status, earnings, education, and assets. Cost considerations ensure that means testing is generally only applicable to those employed in the formal sector where employment and earnings information can easily be validated. In Asia, formal means testing is confined to relatively developed countries, such as Korea.

Informal means testing—usually the preparation of lists of the poor by village leaders—is common in Indonesia, Thailand, and Viet Nam. "Proxy" or "indicator" targeting bases eligibility on easily verifiable characteristics closely related to poverty, such as race, number of children, gender of household head, or location of residence. Malaysia, for instance, has relied on racial targeting for decades, while PRC, Indonesia, and Viet Nam have extensively used geographical indicators. Although systematic evaluations of these systems are rare, the available information suggests that they are not very accurate.

Self-targeting is another low-cost option that is widely used in food-for-work and public works programs. Setting the wage well below the local market wage for unskilled labor ensures that it is only the very poor who are attracted to such programs. Similarly, confining food subsidies to items such as coarse grains, which are consumed primarily by the poor, is another form of self-targeting.

CONCLUSIONS

Developing Asia ended the 20th century with much to be proud of. In the early 1970s, more than half the region was poor, only two out of five adults were literate, and the average Asian could expect to live just 48 years. Today the share of poor people is down to almost one fourth, 70 percent of adults are literate, and life expectancy is up to 65 years. Yet, as the discussion in this chapter has shown, developing Asia still faces an enormous social challenge. There are huge differentials in human well-being between countries, between regions, and between social groups. Two-thirds of the developing world's poor still live in Asia.

As the region enters the 21st century, it faces a fast-changing global and domestic environment. Three broad trends—globalization, information technology, and democratization—are changing the environment Asia faces.

This new globalizing world offers ever-greater markets for trade and foreign investment. As the recent crises so dramatically showed, however, greater integration also increases economic vulnerabilities. Similarly, the explosion of information technology can be a potentially powerful tool in Asia's efforts at poverty reduction—although it could also generate greater social inequalities both across and within nations. Democracy and pluralism bring huge potential benefits, but also carry risks. Asian countries are enjoying rapid growth in democratic participation, and there has been a phenomenal rise in the prominence of civil society organizations. This offers the potential for better, more accountable governance, but also increases the difficulty of creating consensus in favor of difficult policies within the parameters of electoral politics.

In this new global and national context, what needs to be accomplished to meet the social challenge in Asia? Promoting economic growth remains the best path to poverty reduction. If developing Asia can continue with its historical trend in economic growth—and if there is no substantial increase in inequality—it will be largely free of poverty by 2025 (ADB 1997). According to a recent World Bank estimate, if Asia can maintain its historical growth trend, it will be able to more than achieve the International Development Goal of the OECD countries: to reduce by at least one half the number of people living under the dollar-a-day poverty line by 2015, relative to 1990. To have a large impact on poverty reduction, it must be inclusive growth—growth that the poor and disadvantaged share in. The strategy to address the social challenge in Asia, of which promoting inclusive economic growth must remain a critical element, needs to concentrate on the following policy priorities:

Openness and market orientation: East Asian countries' success in economic and social transformation is based on market orientation and economic openness. This strategy enabled them to exploit new economic possibilities in international economy, while imposing policy discipline. In today's integrated global economy, it is essential that the strategy of openness and market orientation be supported by prudent macroeconomic policies. Maintaining stable and manageable levels of debt, inflation, and exchange rates is a crucial factor in creating an environment conducive to inclusive growth. Moreover, by practicing prudent macroeconomic management, economies will be better equipped to handle crisis emanating from economic shocks.

Investing in human resources: Investment in human resource development, particularly education, health care, and nutrition, must be an essential component of Asia's anti-poverty strategy. Not only do such investments directly improve Asians' quality of life, but they also boost economic growth.

Investing in physical infrastructure: Asia needs massive investment in physical infrastructure. Not only does better infrastructure raise the productivity of labor, but it also has a direct bearing on human well-being. Providing basic water sanitation services to urban slum communities and rural villages, electricity, or a better mass transportation system can all significantly improve the quality of life and productivity of the poor.

Improving governance: Asia's economies need better governance. Democracy, political and civil liberties, and participation are desirable objectives in themselves, but they are also crucial for effective 21st century economies. Good governance requires adopting a policy framework that is responsive to the needs of the people. It also means efficient and equitable public expenditure management that results in appropriate investments in human resources, physical infrastructure, and social protection. Good governance also leads to efficient decentralization and increased local management of public resources.

Strengthening social protection: The protection from the possibility of being suddenly rendered poor is equally important as measures to help the poor out of poverty. Asia needs a more effective social safety net. The recent financial crisis dramatically highlighted the inadequacies of today's system. All Asian developing economies need to develop fiscally prudent programs that effectively supplement private safety nets.

While Asia's developing economies must accept the burden of responsibility for addressing the region's social challenge, more can, and must, be done internationally to address the scourge of poverty and social deprivation. In particular, there must be an effort toward:

Improving the global trading environment: While the global trading environment has improved over the years, there are still too many areas important to poor countries, particularly textiles and agriculture, where rich-country markets remain encumbered by many trade restrictions. The use of anti-dumping measures by advanced countries and the specter of protectionism in the guise of labor and environment measures do not help inspire confidence in poor countries about the fairness of the global trading system. Part of this frustration was manifested in the eventual breakdown of the Seattle Ministerial Meeting, which underscored a lack of agreement between the developing and advanced countries.

Increasing the flow of foreign assistance: The flow of foreign economic assistance from the advanced to the developing world has steadily declined since the early

1990s, despite the fact that most industrial economies are now in much better fiscal shape than at any time in recent history. Certainly, not all aid has been used effectively. With improved governance in developing countries, however, there is every likelihood that aid can, and should, make a substantial difference.

Providing international public goods: The international community can make major contributions toward global poverty reduction by providing important international public goods that are currently not being provided. Medical research in advanced countries, for instance, neglects research on tropical diseases because it is mainly poor people who live in these tropical areas. As a result, a sad paradox emerges, with only 10 percent of the $50 billion-$60 billion spent worldwide on medical research expended on diseases that afflict 90 percent of the world's population (WHO 1999). Similarly, global agricultural research pays scant attention to tropical crops or how advances in biotechnology can be used in transforming the farming system of the rural poor in developing economies. More emphasis on, and greater funds for, these global public goods would have a dramatic impact on reducing poverty and improving well-being in developing countries.

If national governments and the international community work together to implement these policies, each will reinforce the other. Consequently, the scourge of poverty and abject human deprivation in Asia—and elsewhere—could be reduced dramatically, and quickly.

Selected
Bibliography

Selected Bibliography

Acemoglu, Daron and Robert Shimer. 1999. "Efficient Unemployment Insurance." *Journal of Political Economy* 107(4): 893-928.

ADB (Asian Development Bank). 1997. *Emerging Asia: Changes and Challenges.* Manila.

_____. 1998a. "Special Issue on Participation." *ADB Review.* 30(2): 1-31.

_____. 1998b. *Key Indicators of Developing Asian and Pacific Countries 1998.* Volume XXIX. Manila: Published by Oxford University Press for the Asian Development Bank.

_____. 1998c. *Asian Development Outlook 1998.* Manila.

_____. 1999a. "ADB Basic Statistics: Developing Member Countries." Manila.

_____. 1999b. *Asian Development Outlook 1999 Update.* Manila.

_____. 1999c. *Country Assistance Plan: Sri Lanka (2000-2002).* Manila.

_____. 1999d. "Country Economic Review on Kazakhstan." Manila.

_____. 1999e. "Country Economic Review on Kyrgyz Republic." Manila.

_____. 1999f. "Country Economic Review on the Philippines." Manila.

_____. 1999g. "Country Economic Review on Nepal." Manila.

_____. 1999h. "Country Economic Review on Uzbekistan." Manila.

_____. 1999i. "Fighting Poverty in Asia and the Pacific: The Poverty Reduction Strategy of the Asian Development Bank." Draft (15 October). Manila.

_____. 1999j. "Framework for Operations on Social Protection." Manila.

_____. 1999k. *Key Indicators of Developing Asian and Pacific Countries 1999.* Volume XXIX. Manila. Published by Oxford University Press for the Asian Development Bank.

_____. 1999l. "Policy for the Health Sector." Manila.

_____. 1999m. "Poverty Incidence in the Asian and Pacific Region: Data Situation and Measurement Issues." EDRC Briefing Note No. 17. Manila: Published by Oxford University Press for the Asian Development Bank.

_____. 1999n. "Social Consequences of the Financial Crisis in Asia: The Deeper Crisis." EDRC Briefing Note No. 16. Manila.

_____. 1999o. "Strategies for Reducing Poverty: A Report Based on Consultations in Selected Developing Member Countries of the Asian Development Bank." Mimeo (24 May). Manila.

_____. 1999p. "Urban Sector Strategy." Manila.

_____. 2000. "Country Economic Review on Tajikistan." Manila.

Ahluwalia, Montek S. 1996. "Comment on 'Inequality, Poverty, and Growth: Where Do We Stand?' by Albert Fishlow." In Michael Bruno and Boris

Pleskovic, eds., *Annual World Bank Conference on Development Economics 1995*, pp. 40-45. Washington, DC: World Bank.

Ahuja, Vinod, Benu Bidani, Francisco Ferreira, and Michael Walton. 1997. *Everyone's Miracle? Revisiting Poverty and Inequality in East Asia.* Washington, DC: World Bank.

Alderman, H., P.A. Chiappori, L. Haddad, J. Hoddinott, and R. Kanbur. 1995. "Unitary versus Collective Models of the Household: Is it Time to Shift the Burden of Proof?" *The World Bank Research Observer* 10(1): 1-20.

Alderman, H., J. Behrman, D. Ross, and R. Sabot. 1996. "The Return to Endogenous Human Capital: Pakistan's Rural Labor Market." *Oxford Bulletin of Economics and Statistics* 58(1): 29-55.

Alesina, Alberto and Dani Rodrik. 1994. "Distributive Politics and Economic Growth." *The Quarterly Journal of Economics* 109(2): 465-90.

Alesina, A., R. Baqir, and W. Easterly. 1997. "Public Goods and Ethnic Divisions." Unpublished mimeo. World Bank, Washington, DC.

APEC (Asia-Pacific Economic Cooperation). 1999. "Compendium of Sound Practices: Guidelines to Facilitate the Development of Domestic Bond Markets in APEC Member Economies." Report prepared by APEC Collaborative Initiative on Development of Domestic Bond Markets (August). Hong Kong.

Ashenfelter, O. and A. Krueger. 1994. "Estimate of the Economic Return to Schooling from a New Sample of Twins." *The American Economic Review* 84(5): 1157-73.

Balisacan, Arsenio M. 1994. "Urban Poverty in the Philippines: Nature, Causes and Policy Measures." *Asian Development Review* 12(1): 117-52.

_____. 1997. "Comment on 'Political Economy of Alleviating Poverty: Theory and Experience' by Timothy Besley." In Michael Bruno and Boris Pleskovic, eds., *Annual World Bank Conference on Development Economics 1996*, pp. 135-38. Washington, DC: World Bank.

Baliño, T.J.T., Charles Enoch, Anne-Marie Gulde, Carl-Johan Lindgren, Marc Quintyn, and Leslie Teo. 1999. "Financial Sector Crisis and Restructuring: Lessons from Asia." Advance copy (September). Washington, DC: International Monetary Fund.

Ballard, Charles L. and Don Fullerton. 1992. "Distortionary Taxes and the Provision of Public Goods." *Journal of Economic Perspectives* 6(3): 117-31.

Banerjee, Abhijit V. 1999. "Land Reforms: Prospects and Strategies." Mimeo. Massachusetts Institute of Technology, Department of Economics, Cambridge, MA.

Banerjee, Abhijit, Paul Gertler, and Maitreesh Ghatak. 1998. "Empowerment and Efficiency: The Economics of Agrarian Reform." Mimeo. Massachusetts Institute of Technology, Department of Economics, Cambridge, MA.

Bank of America. 1999, "Banking Reform in Asia: Comparative Rankings of Progress Made," *Asian Financial Outlook*, Issue No. 25 (August).

Bank Indonesia. Various years. *Indonesian Financial Statistics.* Jakarta.

Bank Negara Malaysia. (Online). Available. http://www.bnm.gov.my.

Barclays. 2000. *Barclays Economic Review* (First Quarter 2000). United Kingdom.

Bardhan, Pranab. 1996a. "Efficiency, Equity and Poverty Alleviation: Policy Issues in Less Developed Countries." *The Economic Journal* 106(3): 1344-55.

_____. 1996b. "Research on Poverty and Development Twenty Years after Redistribution with Growth". In Michael Bruno and Boris Pleskovic, eds., *Annual World Bank Conference on Development Economics 1995*, pp. 59-72. Washington, DC: World Bank.

Barro, Robert. 1996. "Democracy: A Recipe for Growth?" In M.G. Quibria and J. Malcolm Dowling, eds., *Current Issues in Economic Development: An Asian Perspective*, pp. 67-106. Hong Kong: Oxford University Press.

Basu, Kaushik. 1995. "Rural Credit and Interlinkage: Implications for Rural Poverty, Agrarian Efficiency, and Public Policy." In M.G. Quibria, ed., *Critical Issues in Asian Development: Theories, Experiences and Policies*, pp. 108-26. Hong Kong: Oxford University Press.

_____. 1998. "Child Labor: Cause, Consequence and Cure, with Remarks on International Labor Standards." Mimeo (30 March). Cornell University, Department of Economics, New York.

Basu, K., G. Fields, and S. Debgupta. 1998. "Retrench-
ment, Labor Laws and Government Policy:
An Analysis with Special Reference to India."
Mimeo. Cornell University, Department of
Economics, New York.

Behrman, Jere R. 1993. "Investing in Human
Resources." *Economic and Social Progress in Latin
America*. Washington, DC: Inter-American
Development Bank.

_____. 1996. "The Impact of Health and Nutrition
on Education." *The World Bank Research Observer* 11(1): 23-38.

Behrman, Jere R. and James C. Knowles. 1998. "Popu-
lation and Reproductive Health: An Economic
Framework for Policy Evaluation." *Population and
Development Review* 24(4): 697-737.

_____. 1999a. "Household Income and Child
Schooling in Vietnam." *The World Bank Economic Review* 13(2): 211-56.

_____. 1999b. "The Demand for Health Insurance in
Vietnam." Unpublished mimeo. University of
Pennsylvania, Department of Economics,
Philadelphia, PA.

Behrman, Jere R., Anil B. Deolalikar, and Lee-Ying
Soon. 1999. "The Role of Education Decen-
tralization in Promoting Effective Schooling in
Selected DMCs." Paper prepared for the Asian
Development Bank study on "Financing Human
Resource Development in Asia." Manila.

Behrman, Jere R., Andrew D. Foster, Mark R.
Rosenzweig, and Prem Vashista. 1999. "Women's
Schooling, Home Teaching, and Economic
Growth." *Journal of Political Economy* 10(4):
682-714.

Besley, Timothy. 1997. "Political Economy of Allevi-
ating Poverty: Theory and Institutions."
In Michael Bruno and Boris Pleskovic, eds.,
*Annual World Bank Conference on Development
Economics 1996*, pp.117-34. Washington, DC:
World Bank.

Binswanger, Hans P. and Mark R. Rosenzweig. 1993.
"Wealth, Weather Risk and the Composition and
Profitability of Agricultural Investments." *The
Economic Journal* 103 (January): 56-78.

Booth, Anne. 1999. "The Social Impact of the Asian
Crisis: What Do We Know Two Years On?" *Asian
Pacific Economic Literature* 13(2): 16-29.

Borio, Claudio E. V. and Robert N. McCauley. 1996.
"The Economics of Recent Bond Yield Volatili-
ties," Basle: Bank for International Settlements.

Bourguignon, François. 1996. "Comment on 'Inequality, Poverty, and Growth: Where Do We Stand?'
by Albert Fishlow." In Michael Bruno and Boris
Pleskovic, eds., *Annual World Bank Conference
on Development Economics 1995*, pp 46-49. Washington, DC: World Bank.

Bourguignon, François and Christian Morrisson. 1990.
"Income Distribution, Development and Foreign
Trade: A Cross-Sectional Analysis." *European
Economic Review* 34(6): 1113-32.

Bray, Mark. 1996. "Counting the Full Cost: Parental
and Community Financing of Education in East
Asia." Washington, DC: World Bank.

Brooks, Douglas H. and Myo Thant. 1998. *Social Sector Issues in Transitional Economies of Asia*. Hong
Kong: Oxford University Press.

Bruno, Michael, Lyn Squire, and Martin Ravallion.
1995. "Equity and Growth in Developing
Countries: Old and New Perspectives." Policy
Research Working Paper No. 1563. World Bank,
Development Research Group, Washing-
ton, DC.

Burnside, Craig and David Dollar. 1997. "Aid, Policies, and Growth." Policy Research Working Paper No. 1777. World Bank, Development
Research Group, Washington, DC.

_____. 1998. "Aid, the Incentive Regime, and Poverty
Reduction." Policy Research Working Paper
No. 1937. World Bank, Development Research
Group, Washington, DC.

Central Bank of Sri Lanka. 1999. *Annual Report 1998*.
Colombo.

_____. 2000. *Sri Lanka Economy in 1999 and Medium-
Term Prospects* (February). Colombo.

Central Statistical Organization. 2000. "National
Income, Consumption Expenditure, Saving, and
Capital Formation, 1997-98." New Delhi
(February).

Chenery, Hollis, Montek S. Ahluwalia, Clive Bell, John
H. Duloy, and Richard Jolly. 1974. *Redistribution
with Growth*. New York: Oxford University Press.

Claessens, Stijn, Simeon Djankov, and Larry Lang.
1998. "East Asian Corporates: Growth, Financing and Risks over the Last Decade." World
Bank (October).

Clarke, George. 1995. "More Evidence on Income Distribution and Growth." *Journal of Development Economics* 47(2): 403-27.

Collier, Paul. 1999. "The Political Economy of Ethnicity." In Boris Pleskovic and Joseph E. Stiglitz, eds., *Annual World Bank Conference on Development Economics 1998*, pp. 387-99. Washington, DC: World Bank.

Consensus Economics, Inc. 2000. "Foreign Exchange Consensus Forecasts." United Kingdom (14 February).

Cox, Donald and Emmanuel Jimenez. 1995. "Private Transfers and the Effectiveness of Public Income Redistribution in the Philippines." In Dominique van de Walle and Kimberly Nead, eds., *Public Spending and the Poor: Theory and Evidence*. Baltimore, MD: The Johns Hopkins University Press.

Cox, Donald, James Fetzer, and Emmanuel Jimenez. 1995. "Private Safety Nets Through Inter-Household Transfers." Mimeo. Boston College, Department of Economics, Boston, MA.

Datt, Gaurav and Martin Ravallion. 1992. "Growth and Poverty in Rural India." World Bank, Policy Research Department, Washington, DC.

de Hann, Arjan and Michael Lipton. 1999. "Poverty in Emerging Asia: Progress, Setbacks and Logjams." *Asian Development Review* 16(2): 135-76.

Deaton, Angus. 1998. *The Analysis of Household Surveys*. Baltimore, MD: The Johns Hopkins University Press.

Deininger, Klaus and Lyn Squire. 1996. "Measuring Income Inequality: A New Database." *The World Bank Economic Review* 10(3): 565-91.

———. 1998. "New Ways of Looking at Old Issues: Inequality and Growth." *Journal of Development Economics* 57(2): 259-87.

Deolalikar, Anil B. 1988. "Nutrition and Labor Productivity in Agriculture: Wage Equation and Farm Production Estimates for Rural India." *The Review of Economics and Statistics* 70(3): 406-14.

Deolalikar, Anil, Rana Hasan, Haider Khan, and M.G. Quibria. 1997. "Competitiveness and Human Resource Development in Asia." *Asian Development Review* 15(2): 131-63.

Deutsche Bank. 1999. "Is Asia's Recovery Sustainable?" *Global Emerging Markets* 2(3), May.

Dev, S. M., K. Parikh, and M.H. Suryanarayana. 1994. "India." In M.G. Quibria, ed., *Rural Poverty in Developing Asia*, pp. 191-354. Manila: Asian Development Bank.

Easterly, W. and R. Levine. 1997. "Africa's Growth Tragedy: Policies and Ethnic Divisions." *Quarterly Journal of Economics* 112(4): 1203-50.

Edwards, Michael and David Hulme. 1995. *Non-Governmental Organizations—Performance and Accountability: Beyond the Magic Bullet*. London: Earthscan Publications.

Feldstein, Martin. 1995. "Tax Avoidance and the Deadweight Loss of the Income Tax." NBER Working Paper No. 5055. Cambridge, MA: National Bureau of Economic Research.

Fields, Gary. 1995. "Income Distribution in Developing Countries: Conceptual, Data and Policy Issues in Broad-Based Growth." In M.G. Quibria, ed., *Critical Issues in Asian Development: Theories, Experiences and Policies*, pp. 75-107. Hong Kong: Oxford University Press.

Filmer, Deon, Elizabeth King, and Lant Pritchett. 1998. "Gender Disparity in South Asia: Comparisons between and within Countries." Mimeo (January). World Bank, Washington, DC.

Filmer, Deon and Lant Pritchett. 1999. "The Effect of Household Wealth on Educational Attainment: Evidence from 35 Countries." *Population and Development Review* 25(1):85-120.

Finsterbusch, K. and W. van Wicklin. 1987. "The Contribution of Beneficiary Participation to Development Project Effectiveness." *Public Administration and Development* 7:1-23.

Fishlow, Albert. 1996. "Inequality, Poverty, and Growth: Where Do We Stand?" In Michael Bruno and Boris Pleskovic, eds., *Annual World Bank Conference on Development Economics 1995*, pp 25-39. Washington, DC: World Bank.

Foster, Andrew and Mark Rosenzweig. 1996. "Technical Change and Human Capital Returns and Investments: Evidence from the Green Revolution." *The American Economic Review* 86(4): 931-53.

Frankenberg, Elizabeth, Duncan Thomas, and Kathleen Beegle. 1999. "The Real Costs of Indonesia's Economic Crisis: Preliminary Findings from the Indonesia Family Life Surveys." Working Paper Series No. 99-04. Santa Monica, CA: RAND.

Gaiha, Raghav and Anil Deolalikar. 1993. "Persistent, Expected and Innate Poverty: Estimates for Semi-arid Rural South India, 1975-1984." *Cambridge Journal of Economics* 17 (December): 409-21.

Gang, Fan, Dwight Perkins, and Lora Sabin. 1997. "People's Republic of China: Economic Performance and Prospects." *Asian Development Review* 15(2): 43-85.

Gelbach, Jonah B. and Lant H. Pritchett. 1997. "More for the Poor is Less for the Poor: The Politics of Targeting." Draft (July). World Bank, Development Research Group, Washington, DC.

Government of Pakistan. 1999. *Economic Survey 1998-99.* Islamabad.

Hoff, Karla. 1997. "Comment on 'Political Economy of Alleviating Poverty: Theory and Institutions' by Timothy Besley." In Michael Bruno and Boris Pleskovic, eds., *Annual World Bank Conference on Development Economics 1996*, pp. 139-44. Washington, DC: World Bank.

Hoff, Karla and Andrew Lyon. 1995. "Non-Leaky Buckets: Optimal Redistributive Taxation and Agency Costs." *Journal of Public Economics* 58(3): 365-90.

Horowitz, Donald L. 1999. "Structure and Strategy in Ethnic Conflict." In Boris Pleskovic and Joseph E. Stiglitz, eds., *Annual World Bank Conference on Development Economics 1998*, pp. 345-70 . Washington, DC: World Bank.

IDB (Inter-American Development Bank). 1999. "Social Protection for the Poor: A Special Report." Draft (July). Inter-American Development Bank, Washington, DC.

IIE (Institute for International Economics). 1999. Economic Policy Briefs No. 99-6 (June). (Also Online) Available. http://www.iie.com.

ILO (International Labour Organization). 1996. *Child Labor: Targeting the Intolerable.* Geneva: International Labour Organization.

_____. 1998. *Employment Challenges of the Indonesian Economic Crisis.* Jakarta: International Labour Organization and United Nations Development Programme.

IMF (International Monetary Fund). 1990. *World Economic Outlook 1990* (May). Washington, DC.

_____. 1998a. *World Economic Outlook 1998* (May). Washington, DC.

_____. 1998b. *World Economic Outlook 1998* (October). Washington, DC.

_____. 1999a. *Direction of Trade Statistics Quarterly.* Washington, DC.

_____. 1999b. *World Economic Outlook 1999* (May). Washington, DC.

_____. 1999c. *World Economic Outlook 1999* (October). Washington, DC.

_____. 2000. *International Financial Statistics* (January). Washington, DC.

Isham, Jonathan, Deepa Narayan, and Lant Pritchett. 1995. "Does Participation Improve Performance? Establishing Causality with Subjective Data." *The World Bank Economic Review* 9(2): 175-200.

J.P. Morgan. 1990. "Reform Progress in Asia's Crisis Economies." Asian Financial Markets (July). Singapore.

_____.1999. "The Budgetary Legacy of the Asian Crisis." Asian Financial Markets (Fourth Quarter), Singapore.

Jamison, Dean T. 1986. "Child Malnutrition and School Performance in China." *Journal of Development Economics* 20(2): 299-310.

Jayaraman, Rajshri and Peter Lanjouw. 1999. "The Evolution of Poverty and Inequality in Indian Villages." *The World Bank Research Observer* 14(1): 1-30.

Jejeebhoy, Shireen J. 1996. "Adolescent Sexual and Reproductive Behavior: A Review of the Evidence from India." ICRW Working Paper No. 3. Washington, DC: International Center for Research on Women.

Jimenez, Emmanuel and Marlaine Lockheed. 1995. *Public and Private Secondary Education in Developing Countries: A Comparative Study.* Washington, DC: World Bank.

Kanbur, Ravi and Nora Lustig. 1999. "Why is Inequality Back on the Agenda?" Paper prepared for the Annual World Bank Conference on Development Economics (28-30 April). Mimeo. Cornell University, Department of Economics, New York.

Khandker, Shahidur R. 1996. "Grameen Bank: Impact, Costs, and Program Sustainability." *Asian Development Review* 14(1): 97-130.

Kikeri, Sunita, John Nellis, and Mary Shirley. 1994. "Privatization: Lessons from Market Economies." *The World Bank Research Observer* 9(2): 241-72.

Kim, Dae Il. 1999. "The Impact of the Asian Financial and Economic Crisis on the Labor Market of the Republic of Korea." Mimeo (March). Seoul National University, Department of Economies. Seoul.

Kim, Yun-Hwan. 1999. "Creating Long-term Mortgage-Backed Bond Markets in Asian Developing Economies – A Postcrisis Reform Agenda." EDRC Briefing Note No.18. Manila: Asian Development Bank.

Kingdon, Geeta. 1996. "The Quality and Efficiency of Private and Public Education: A Case Study of Urban India." *Oxford Bulletin of Economics and Statistics* 58(1): 57-82.

Knowles, James C., Ernesto M. Pernia, and Mary Racelis. 1999. "Social Consequences of the Financial Crisis in Asia." Economic Staff Paper No. 60 (November). Asian Development Bank, Economics and Development Resource Center, Manila.

Kremer, Michael R. 1995. 'Research on Schooling: What We Know and What We Don't: A Comment on Hanushek." *World Bank Research Observer* 10(2): 247-54.

Kumar, Rajiv. 1999. "Economic Development and Prospects for Developing Asian Economies," Paper presented at the Twelfth Workshop on Asian Economic Outlook (23 November), Asian Development Bank, Manila.

Lanjouw, Peter and Nicholas Stern. 1998. *Economic Development in Palanpur over Five Decades.* Oxford: Clarendon Press.

Lieberman, Sandy. 1999. "Indonesia's Health Strategy Before and After the Crisis." Mimeo (August). World Bank, Jakarta.

Lipton, Michael and Martin Ravallion. 1995. "Poverty and Policy." In Jere Behrman and T.N. Srinivasan, eds., *Handbook of Development Economics*, vol. 3B, pp. 2551-657. Amsterdam: North Holland.

Lipton, Michael. 1996. "Comment on 'Research on Poverty and Development Twenty Years after *Redistribution with Growth*,' by Pranab Bardhan." In Michael Bruno and Boris Pleskovic, eds., *Annual World Bank Conference on Development Economics 1995*, pp. 73-80. Washington, DC: World Bank.

Loury, Glenn C. 1999. "Social Exclusion and Ethnic Groups: The Challenge to Economics." Paper prepared for the Annual World Bank Conference on Development Economics (28-30 April), World Bank, Washington, DC.

Mauro, Paulo. 1995. "Corruption and Growth." *The Quarterly Journal of Economics* 110(3): 681-712.

Mijares, T.A. and L.C. Belarmino. 1973. "Some Notes on the Sources of Income Disparities among Philippine Families." *Journal of Philippine Statistics* (September).

Ministry of Finance. 1999. *Monthly Statistics of Exports and Imports, Taiwan Area, the Republic of China* (December). Department of Statistics.

Ministry of Finance. 2000. *Economic Survey 1999/00* (March). New Delhi.

Monetary Authority of Singapore. 1999a. *Quarterly Bulletin* (December). Singapore.

_____. 1999b. *Monthly Statistical Bulletin* (September). Singapore.

Moock, Peter and Joanne Leslie. 1986. "Childhood Malnutrition and Schooling in the Terai Region of Nepal." *Journal of Development Economics* 20(1): 33-52.

Moon, Hyungpyo, Hyehoon Lee, and Gyeongjoon Yoo. 1999. "Social Impact of the Financial Crisis in Korea." Report prepared for the Finalization Conference, "Assessing the Social Impact of the Financial Crisis in Selected Asian Developing Economies" (17-18 June), Asian Development Bank, Manila.

Morduch, Jonathan. 1999a. "The Grameen Bank: A Financial Reckoning." Mimeo (May). Princeton University, New Jersey.

_____. 1999b. "The Microfinance Promise." *Journal of Economic Literature* 4(37): 1569-614.

Narayan, D. 1995. "The Contribution of People's Participation: Evidence from 121 Rural Water Supply Projects." Environmentally Sustainable Development (ESD) Occasional Paper Series No. 1. Washington, DC: World Bank.

National Economic and Development Authority of the Philippines. (Online). Available. http://www.neda.gov.ph.

National Statistical Committee of the Kyrgyz Republic. 2000. Latest Economic and Financial Data (Online). Available. http://nsc.bishkek.su.

NSCB (National Statistical Coordination Board) of the Philippines. (Online). Available. http://www. nscb.gov.ph.

_____. 1998. "Annual Poverty Indicators Survey 1998." Manila.

National Statistical Office. 1999. *Korea Statistical Yearbook 1999*. Vol. 46. Seoul.

OECD (Organisation for Economic Co-operation and Development). 1999. *OECD Economic Outlook*. Paris: OECD.

Pathan, R., N. Arul, and M. Poffenberger. 1993. "Forest Protection Committees in Gujarat—Joint Management Initiatives." Reference Paper No. 8. Prepared for Sustainable Forest Management Conference, sponsored by the Ford Foundation, Delhi, India.

Pernia, E.M. 1982. "Micro-level Implications of Population Growth." In A. Herrin, V.P. Paqueo, and E.M. Pernia, eds., *Essays on the Economics of Fertility, Population Growth and Public Intervention in a Developing Country: The Philippines*. Quezon City: University of the Philippines School of Economics.

Pernia, E. and M.G. Quibria. 1999. "Poverty in Developing Countries." In E.S. Mills and P.C. Cheshire, eds., *Handbook of Regional and Urban Economics*, Volume 3, Part III, Chap.45. Netherlands: Elsevier Science Publishers BV.

Perotti, Roberto. 1993. "Political Equilibrium, Income Distribution, and Growth." *The Review of Economic Studies* 60 (4): 755-76.

Persson, Torsten and Guido Tabellini. 1994. "Is Inequality Harmful for Growth?" *The American Economic Review* 84(3): 600-21.

Pitt, Mark and S.R. Khandker. 1996. "Household and Intrahousehold Impacts of the Grameen Bank and Similar Targeted Credit Programs in Bangladesh." Discussion Paper No. 320. Washington, DC: World Bank.

_____. 1998. "The Impact of Group-Based Credit Programs on Poor Households in Bangladesh: Does the Gender of Participants Matter?" *Journal of Political Economy* 106(5): 958-96.

Poppele, Jessica, Sudarno Sumarto, and Lant Pritchett. 1999. "Social Impacts of the Indonesian Crisis: New Data and Policy Implications." Mimeo (May). SMERU (Social Monitoring and Early Response Unit), Jakarta.

Prescott, Nicholas. 1998. "Choices in Financing Health Care and Old Age Security." Proceedings of a Conference (8 November), sponsored by the Institute of Policy Studies, Singapore, and the World Bank, Washington, DC.

Prud'homme, Remy. 1995. "The Dangers of Decentralization." *The World Bank Research Observer* 10(2): 201-20.

Psacharopoulos, George. 1985. "Returns to Education: A Further International Update and Implications." *Journal of Human Resources* 20: 583-97.

_____. 1994. "Returns to Investment in Education: A Global Update." *World Development* 22(9): 1325-43.

Quibria, M.G. 1995. "Gender and Poverty: Issues and Policies with Special Reference to Asian Developing Countries." *Journal of Economic Surveys* 9(4): 373-411.

_____. ed. 1996. *Rural Poverty in Developing Asia*. Manila: Asian Development Bank.

_____. 1999. "Comment on Leading Issues in Microfinance." Mimeo. Asian Development Bank, Manila.

Ranis, Gustav. 1996. "Comment on 'Inequality, Poverty, and Growth: Where Do We Stand?' by Albert Fishlow." In Michael Bruno and Boris Pleskovic, eds., *Annual World Bank Conference on Development Economics 1995*, pp. 50-55. Washington, DC: World Bank.

Rashid, Salim and M.G. Quibria. 1995. "Is Land Reform Passe: With Special Reference to Asian Agriculture." In M.G. Quibria, ed., *Critical Issues in Asian Development: Theories, Experiences and Policies*, pp. 127-59. Hong Kong: Oxford University Press.

Ravallion, Martin. 1996. "Issues in Measuring and Modeling Poverty." *The Economic Journal* 106(3): 1328-43.

_____. 1999a. "Is More Targeting Consistent with Less Spending?" Draft paper (February). World Bank, Development Research Group, Washington, DC.

_____. 1999b. "Monitoring Targeting Performance when Decentralized Allocations to the Poor are Unobserved." Draft paper. World Bank, Development Research Group, Washington, DC.

Reserve Bank of India. *Report of Currency and Finance, 1996-1997 and 1997-1998.* Mumbai.

———. 1999. *1998-1999 Finances of State Governments.* Mumbai.

———. Various years. *Annual Report.* Mumbai.

Reyes, Celia M., R.G. Manasan, A.C. Orbeta, and G.G. de Guzman. 1999. "Social Impact of the Regional Financial Crisis in the Philippines." Mimeo. Final report of a study prepared for the Asian Development Bank, Manila.

Rosegrant, Mark W. and Peter B.R. Hazell. 1999. "The Transformation of the Rural Economy in Asia." Paper prepared for the Asian Development Bank "Study of Rural Asia," Manila.

Rosenzweig, Mark and H. P. Binswanger. 1993. "Wealth, Weather Risk and the Composition and Profitability of Agricultural Investments." *The Economic Journal* 103(416): 56-78.

Rosenzweig, Mark and Kenneth Wolpin. 1993. "Credit Market Constraints, Consumption Smoothing, and the Accumulation of Durable Assets in Low-Income Countries: Investments in Bullocks in India." *Journal of Political Economy* 101(2): 223-41.

Saadah, Fadia and Meno Pradhan. 1999. "Indonesia Health Sector Analysis Based on the 1995, 1997 and 1998 SUSENAS." Mimeo. World Bank, Washington, DC.

Saadah, Fadia, Hugh Waters, and Peter Heywood. 1999. "Indonesia, Undernutrition in Young Children." Watching Brief Issue No. 1, World Bank, East Asia and Pacific Region, Washington, DC.

Sathar, Zeba A. and John B. Casterline. 1998. "The Onset of Fertility Transition in Pakistan." *Population and Development Review* 24(4): 773-96.

SEDESOL (Secretaria de Desarrollo Social). 1999. "Program for Education, Health and Nutrition (Progresa)." (Online). Available (19 November). http://www.sedesol.gob.mx.

Sen, Amartya. 1981. *Poverty and Famines: An Essay on Entitlement and Deprivation.* Oxford: Clarendon Press.

———. 1983. "Development: Which Way Now?" *The Economic Journal* 93 (December): 745-62.

———. 1985. *Commodities and Capabilities.* Amsterdam: North Holland.

Singapore Department of Statistics. 1999. *Economic Survey of Singapore, 3rd Quarter of 1999.* Singapore.

Siregar, Reza Y. 1998. "Economic Development and Prospects for Developing Asian Economies," Paper presented at the Eleventh Workshop on Asian Economic Outlook (27 November), Asian Development Bank, Manila.

State Bank of Pakistan. 1999. *Annual Report 1998-1999.* Karachi.

Strauss, John. 1986. "Does Better Nutrition Raise Farm Productivity?" *Journal of Political Economy* 94(2): 297-320.

Strauss, John and Duncan Thomas. 1998. "Health, Nutrition, and Economic Development." *Journal of Economic Literature* 36(2): 766-817.

Streeten, Paul, S.J. Burki, M. Haq, N. Hicks, and F. Stewart. 1981. *First Things First: Meeting Basic Needs in Developing Countries.* New York: Oxford University Press.

Stiglitz, J. 1999. "Back to Basics: Policies and Strategies for Enhanced Growth and Equity in Post-Crisis East Asia." Washington, DC: World Bank.

Tan, H. and G. Batra. 1997. "Technology and Firm Size-Wage Differentials in Colombia, Mexico, and Taiwan (China)." *The World Bank Economic Review* 11(1): 59-83.

Tanzi, Vito. 1996. "Fiscal Federalism and Decentralization: A Review of Some Efficiency and Macroeconomic Aspects". In Michael Bruno and Boris Pleskovic, eds., *Annual World Bank Conference on Development Economics 1995,* pp.295-316. Washington, DC: World Bank.

The Brookings Institution. (Online). Available. http://www.brookings.org.

UN (United Nations). 1998. *World Population Prospects (The 1998 Revision).* Electronic database. New York.

UN ESCAP (United Nations Economic and Social Commission for Asia and the Pacific). Various years. *Statistical Yearbook for Asia and the Pacific.* Bangkok: UN ESCAP.

UNCTAD (United Nations Conference on Trade and Development). 1999. *World Investment Report 1999: Foreign Direct Investment and the Challenge of Development.* New York: UNCTAD.

_____. 2000. UNCTAD Press Release. (Online). Available. http://www.unctad.org.

UNDP (United Nations Development Programme). 1998. *Human Development Report 1998*. New York: UNDP.

UNESCO (United Nations Educational, Scientific and Cultural Organization). 1999. *Statistical Yearbook 1999*. France: Imprimerie Jean Lamour, Maxeville.

_____. 2000. "Public Expenditure on Education." (Online). Available (18 January). http://unescostat.unesco.org.

UNICEF (United Nations Children's Fund). 1999. *The State of the World's Children 1999*. New York: United Nations Children's Fund.

United States Bureau of Labor and Statistics Data. (Online). Available. http://stats.bls.gov.

van de Walle, Dominique. 1998. "Targeting Revisited." *The World Bank Research Observer* 13(2): 147-70.

Wallich, Christine. 1999. "Role of the Private Sector in Poverty Reduction." Speech delivered at the seminar on "Poverty Reduction: What's New and What's Different," 32nd Annual Meeting of the Asian Development Bank (29 April), Manila.

WHO (World Health Organization). 1999. *The World Health Report 1999: Making a Difference*. Geneva: World Health Organization.

Wood, Adrian and Jörg Mayer. 1999. "South Asia's Export Structure in a Comparative Perspective." IDS Working Paper No. 91. University of Sussex: Institute of Development Studies.

World Bank. 1992. *World Development Report 1992: Development and the Environment*. New York: Oxford University Press.

_____. 1994. *World Development Report 1994: Infrastructure for Development*. New York: Oxford University Press.

_____. 1995. *World Tables Diskette 1995*. Washington, DC: World Bank.

_____. 1996a. *Poverty Reduction and the World Bank: Progress and Challenges in the 1990s*. Washington, DC: World Bank.

_____. 1996b. "China: Issues and Options in Health Financing." Report No. 15278-CHA. World Bank, China and Mongolia Department, Human Development Department, Washington, DC.

_____. 1997a. *World Development Report 1997*. New York: Oxford University Press.

_____. 1997b. "Ensuring Old-Age Security in China." In a Press Release (22 September) prepared for the Annual Meeting Seminar Program on "Household Security in China: Health and Pensions," World Bank, Hong Kong.

_____. 1998. "Water and Work for India's Poorest Rural Region." Project Brief (October). World Bank, Washington, DC.

_____. 1999a. "Global Economic Prospects and the Developing Countries 2000." (Online). Available. http://www.worldbank.org.

_____. 1999b. "Poverty Trends and Voices of the Poor." Mimeo (29 September). World Bank, Poverty Reduction and Economic Management, Human Development Networks, Washington, DC.

_____. 1999c. *World Development Indicators 1999*. Washington, DC: World Bank.

_____. 1999d. *World Development Report 1998/99: Knowledge for Development*. Washington, DC: World Bank.

World Resources Institute. 1996. *World Resources 1996-1997: A Guide to Global Environment*. Electronic database. New York: Oxford University Press.

Yaron, Jacob, Benjamin McDonald, and Stephanie Charitonenko. 1998. "Promoting Efficient Rural Financial Intermediation." *The World Bank Research Observer* 13 (2): 147-70.

Statistical
Appendix

Statistical Notes

The Statistical Appendix presents selected economic indicators for the 37 developing member countries of the Asian Development Bank (ADB) in a total of 23 tables. These are presented by account: production and demand sectors of the national income accounts, consumer price index, money supply, components of the balance of payments, external debt and debt service, exchange rate, and the budget of the central government. These tables contain the time series information from 1994 to 1999. Except for policy variables, such as the exchange rate and the financial account of the central government, the tables give projections for 2000 and 2001. The table on foreign direct investment shows data from 1993 to 1998 (the latest year for which data are available). The following sections describe the source, scope, and conceptual definition of the data in each table.

Historical data are derived mostly from official sources; updated statistical publications; other secondary publications; and working papers and other internal documents of the ADB, the World Bank, the International Monetary Fund (IMF), and the United Nations. Some of the preliminary data for 1999 are ADB staff estimates calculated from quarterly or monthly data available for the year. Projections for 2000 and 2001 are staff estimates.

Despite limitations arising from differences in statistical methodology, definition, coverage, and practice, efforts were made to standardize the data. The aim is to allow comparability of data over time and across the countries, and to ensure consistency across

accounts. Data-splicing and data-rebasing techniques were also used to fill in data gaps.

Data in these tables refer to either calendar year or fiscal year. For Cook Islands, India, Marshall Islands, Federated States of Micronesia, Myanmar, Nauru, Nepal, Pakistan, Samoa, and Tonga, all data are on a fiscal year basis. However, for Bangladesh, Bhutan and Maldives, some data refer to calendar year and some to fiscal year. For the rest of the countries, data on national accounts, consumer price index, monetary accounts, and balance of payments are reported for the calendar year. Government finances for all countries are reported on a fiscal year basis.

Regional averages or totals for the countries and for each of the six subregions are incorporated in ten of the 23 tables. These tables include growth rate of gross domestic product (GDP), growth rate of per capita GDP, changes in consumer price index, growth rate of merchandise exports and imports, trade balance, direction of exports current account balance, current account balance as a percentage of GDP, and foreign direct investment. Averages are computed as simple, weighted arithmetic means using the contemporaneous GDP values in current US dollars as weights. Because of reliability concerns, data for Myanmar are excluded from the computation of averages or totals.

Tables A1, A2, A3, A4, A5, and A6: Growth and Structure of Production. The definitions used in these tables relating to output growth and production are generally based on the United Nations System of National Accounts. Table A1 shows annual growth rates of GDP valued either at constant market prices or at constant factor costs. Most countries use the constant market prices valuation. The exceptions are Bhutan, Fiji Islands, India, Mongolia, Pakistan, Sri Lanka, Solomon Islands, Tonga, and Tuvalu, which use GDP at constant factor cost. For Papua New Guinea the growth rate is based on GDP at constant purchaser's value.

Table A2 presents the growth rate figures for per capita real GDP. Per capita real GDP is obtained by dividing GDP at constant market prices by population. With the exception of India, countries that used constant factor costs in table A1 employ constant market prices to compute per capita real GDP. The switch to market prices creates a residual between GDP growth, per capita GDP growth, and population growth.

Tables A3, A4, and A5 present the annual growth rates of real gross value added in agriculture, industry, and services, respectively. The agriculture sector includes agricultural crops, livestock, poultry, fisheries, and forestry. Mining and quarrying, manufacturing, construction, and utilities fall under the industry sector. The service sector comprises transportation and communications, trade, banking and finance, real estate, public administration, and other services. The sectoral growth rates are consistently defined with the reported GDP values in table A1. Adding-up restrictions are imposed where numerical discrepancies are noted or where reclassifications of the sectors are implemented.

Table A6 shows the sectoral shares of GDP based on constant market prices. For Cook Islands, Fiji Islands, India, Lao People's Democratic Republic (Lao PDR), Mongolia, Nepal, Pakistan, Sri Lanka, and Tonga, the sectoral shares of GDP are based on constant factor costs. For Bhutan, the shares are based on gross value added at current factor cost.

Tables A7 and A8: Saving and Investment. Gross national savings or gross domestic savings are computed as the difference between gross national product (GNP) or GDP, and total consumption expenditure. For some countries, gross savings data are obtained from official sources. Gross savings may differ from either gross national savings or gross domestic savings by being derived from the consolidated income and outlay account, and include private transfers recorded in the balance of payments. Gross domestic investment is calculated as the sum of gross fixed capital formation and changes in stocks. For the Pacific economies—except the Fiji Islands, where reliable estimates of consumption expenditures are not available—gross domestic savings are computed as the sum of gross domestic investment and current account balance minus the sum of net factor income from abroad and net transfers.

Table A7 gives the ratio of gross domestic savings to GDP as obtained from official sources. For India, Maldives, and Pakistan, the ratio of gross national savings to GNP is used, for Cambodia, Thailand, and Viet Nam, the ratio of gross savings to GDP is used; and for Malaysia and Sri Lanka, the ratio of gross national savings to GDP is used. Table A8 presents the ratio of gross domestic investment to GDP, except for the Maldives, which uses the ratio of gross domestic investment to GNP. All figures used in computing the ratios in tables A7 and A8 are in current market prices.

Table A9: Consumer Prices. This table presents the annual inflation rate based on the consumer price index, as obtained from official local sources. For countries for which data are not available locally, data were obtained from the IMF. For most of the countries, the reported inflation rates are period averages. For the Central Asian republics and Viet Nam, the end-of-period consumer price index is used for calculating inflation rates. For Hong Kong, China, the inflation rate is based on the composite consumer price index, while for India, it is based on the wholesale price index.

Table A10: Growth of Money Supply. This table tracks the annual percentage change in money supply as represented by M2. M2 is defined as the sum of M1 and quasi-money, where M1 denotes currency in circulation plus demand deposits, and quasi-money is time and savings deposits plus foreign currency deposits. For India and the Philippines, the M3 is used as the measure of liquidity. All data for M2 are obtained from country sources, except for Fiji Islands, Papua New

Guinea, Samoa, and Vanuatu, which are taken from the ADB's *Key Indicators of Developing Asian and Pacific Countries* and the IMF's *International Financial Statistics* (IMF 2000).

Tables A11 and A13: Growth Rate of Merchandise Exports and Imports. Historical data for 1994-1998 and some preliminary estimates for 1999 on merchandise exports and imports are taken from the balance-of-payments accounts, except for Cook Islands data, which are taken from the external trade account. These figures are on a free-on-board basis, except for India and the Lao PDR, for which import data are on a cost, insurance, and freight basis. Export and import statistics are reported in calendar years except for India, Marshall Islands, Federated States of Micronesia, Myanmar, Nepal, Pakistan, and Tonga, which use fiscal year figures. For Cambodia, export data refer to domestic exports only, while import data refer to retained imports only. Retained imports are total imports net of re-exports, but include project aid imports and an estimate of unrecorded imports. Data for People's Republic of China (PRC), Republic of Korea, Malaysia, Mongolia, and Thailand are derived from IMF documents.

Table A12: Direction of Exports. For each country, the table indicates the percentage share of that economy's exports going to each of the major trading partners (other developing member countries, Australia and New Zealand, Japan, United States, and European Union). With the exception of Taipei,China, for which data are obtained directly from local sources, data are from the IMF's *Direction of Trade Statistics Quarterly* (IMF 1999a).

Tables A14, A15, and A16: Balance of Payments. The balance of trade is the difference between merchandise exports and merchandise imports. The current account balance is the sum of the balance of trade, net trade in services and factor income, and net unrequited transfers. In the case of Cambodia, India, Lao PDR, Thailand, and Viet Nam, official transfers are excluded from the current account balance. Data reported for PRC, Republic of Korea, and Malaysia are taken from the IMF's *International Financial Statistics* (IMF 2000) or IMF staff country reports. The balance-of-payments data for the rest of the countries are from local sources.

Table A17: Foreign Direct Investment. The United Nations Conference on Trade and Development's *World Investment Report 1999* (UNCTAD 1999) provides data on gross foreign direct investment flows for 1993-1998. Direct investment capital refers to equity capital, reinvested earnings, and other capital associated with the transactions of enterprises.

Tables A18 and A19: External Debt. For most countries, external debt outstanding includes long-term debt, short-term debt, and IMF credit. Principal repayments and interest payments on long-term debt and IMF credit, and interest payments on short-term debt are lumped together in the debt-service payment. For Viet Nam, external debt data exclude debts in nonconvertible currencies. For Mongolia, medium- and long-term debt include payment on Council for Mutual Economic Assistance debts, but exclude unresolved claims of former council members. The debt-service ratio is defined as debt-service payments expressed as a percentage of total exports of goods and services. For Cambodia, the debt-service ratio is calculated as a percentage of domestic exports and services only. For Viet Nam, debt-service ratio is debt service or debt due as a ratio of exports of goods and nonfactor services. For most countries, data are collected from official country sources. World Bank data are used for PRC, Malaysia, and Maldives.

Table A20: Foreign Exchange Rates. The exchange rate quoted is the annual average exchange rate of local currencies of the countries to the US dollar. The IMF's *International Financial Statistics* (IMF 2000) is the source for basic data for Bangladesh; India; Indonesia; Republic of Korea; Malaysia; Mongolia; Pakistan; Philippines; Singapore; and Taipei,China. For all other countries, the sources are official country publications.

Tables A21, A22, and A23: Government Finance. These tables account for only central government finance on a fiscal year basis. Government expenditure includes both current and capital expenditures. Likewise, total revenue includes current revenue and capital receipts. In most countries, the overall budget surplus or deficit is the balance between government revenue and expenditure, excluding grants. In Bhutan, Republic of Korea, Kyrgyz Republic, Marshall Islands,

Federated States of Micronesia, Nepal, Pakistan, Tajikistan, and Vanuatu, the overall fiscal balance includes grants. For India, the overall balance excludes borrowing and other liabilities, while for Uzbekistan it includes net lending and budgetary funds. For Kazakhstan, the fiscal balance includes grants, but excludes privatization receipts. Figures for Sri Lanka exclude not only grants, but also privatization proceeds. For Pakistan, the fiscal balance includes consolidated federal and provincial accounts. All ratios are reported as a percentage of GDP in current market prices. Data are from official country sources.

Table A1 **Growth Rate of GDP**
(percent per year)

Economy	1994	1995	1996	1997	1998	1999	2000	2001
Newly industrialized economies	7.7	7.5	6.3	5.7	-1.9	7.0	6.5	6.0
Hong Kong, China	5.4	3.9	4.5	5.0	-5.1	2.9	5.0	5.5
Korea, Rep. of	8.3	8.9	6.8	5.0	-6.7	10.7	7.5	6.0
Singapore	11.2	8.4	7.5	8.0	1.5	5.4	5.9	6.2
Taipei,China	7.1	6.4	6.1	6.7	4.6	5.7	6.3	6.2
People's Rep. of China and Mongolia	12.7	10.5	9.6	8.7	7.8	7.1	6.5	6.0
China, People's Rep. of	12.7	10.5	9.6	8.8	7.8	7.1	6.5	6.0
Mongolia	2.3	6.3	2.4	4.0	3.5	3.5	4.0	4.5
Central Asian republics	-10.4	-5.6	1.1	3.3	0.8	2.8	3.0	3.6
Kazakhstan	-12.6	-8.2	0.5	1.7	-1.9	1.7	3.0	3.3
Kyrgyz Republic	-20.1	-5.4	7.1	9.9	2.1	3.6	2.5	3.2
Tajikistan	-18.9	-12.5	-4.4	1.7	5.3	3.7	4.0	5.0
Uzbekistan	-4.2	-0.9	1.6	5.2	4.4	4.4	3.0	4.0
Southeast Asia	7.8	8.2	7.4	3.7	-7.5	3.2	4.6	5.0
Cambodia	3.9	6.7	5.5	2.6	1.3	5.0	6.0	7.0
Indonesia	7.5	8.2	7.8	4.7	-13.2	0.2	4.0	5.0
Lao People's Democratic Rep.	8.1	7.0	6.9	6.9	4.0	4.0	4.5	5.0
Malaysia	9.2	9.8	10.0	7.5	-7.5	5.4	6.0	6.1
Myanmar	7.5	6.9	6.4	5.7	5.0	4.5	—	—
Philippines	4.4	4.7	5.8	5.2	-0.5	3.2	3.8	4.3
Thailand	9.0	8.9	5.9	-1.8	-10.4	4.1	4.5	4.6
Viet Nam	8.8	9.5	9.3	8.2	4.4	4.4	5.0	6.0
South Asia	7.0	6.9	6.9	4.7	6.2	5.5	6.4	6.6
Bangladesh	4.2	4.4	5.0	5.4	5.2	4.4	5.0	5.5
Bhutan	6.4	7.5	6.0	7.3	5.8	6.0	6.0	5.5
India	7.8	7.6	7.5	5.0	6.8	5.9	7.0	7.0
Maldives	6.6	7.2	7.9	9.1	9.1	8.5	7.0	7.0
Nepal	8.2	3.5	5.3	5.0	2.3	3.3	5.5	5.5
Pakistan	3.9	5.1	5.0	1.2	3.3	3.9	3.8	5.2
Sri Lanka	5.6	5.5	3.8	6.3	4.7	4.2	5.0	6.0
Pacific DMCs	3.0	0.3	3.0	-3.2	1.2	4.4	—	—
Cook Islands	3.9	-4.4	-0.2	-2.8	-3.8	2.8	4.2	—
Fiji Islands	5.1	2.6	3.3	-1.8	-1.3	7.8	3.2	3.2
Kiribati	7.7	3.4	6.3	2.3	8.3	1.5	—	—
Marshall Islands	2.8	2.7	-15.2	-5.3	-5.0	0.5	—	—
Micronesia, Federated States of	-1.8	1.6	0.7	-4.2	-0.8	0.3	—	—
Nauru	—	—	—	—	—	—	—	—
Papua New Guinea	2.2	-1.6	3.5	-4.6	2.5	3.9	4.6	—
Samoa	-7.8	6.8	6.1	1.6	2.6	4.0	4.0	—
Solomon Islands	5.1	6.8	0.6	-0.5	-2.2	1.0	3.5	—
Tonga	10.0	6.3	-3.7	-1.4	0.1	2.2	—	—
Tuvalu	10.3	-5.0	10.3	3.5	14.9	3.0	—	—
Vanuatu	2.6	3.2	3.5	0.6	0.2	-2.0	—	—
Average	8.7	8.3	7.5	6.0	2.3	6.2	6.2	6.0

— Not available.

Table A2 Growth Rate of Per Capita GDP
(percent per year)

Economy	1994	1995	1996	1997	1998	1999	2000	2001	Per Capita GNP (US$) 1998
Newly industrialized economies	6.4	6.2	5.0	4.3	-3.4	5.6	5.0	4.7	
Hong Kong, China	3.1	1.9	1.9	1.9	-7.8	0.6	2.7	3.4	23,670
Korea, Rep. of	7.2	7.8	5.7	4.0	-7.6	9.6	6.4	5.0	7,970
Singapore	9.0	6.4	5.5	5.9	-1.0	3.7	3.5	3.5	30,060
Taipei,China	6.2	5.5	5.3	5.8	3.5	4.6	5.1	5.4	12,850
People's Rep. of China and Mongolia	11.4	9.4	8.4	7.7	6.8	6.1	5.4	4.9	
China, People's Rep. of	11.4	9.4	8.4	7.7	6.8	6.1	5.4	4.9	750
Mongolia	1.0	4.5	0.8	1.2	2.5	2.2	2.7	3.2	400
Central Asian republics	-10.8	-5.5	0.9	3.3	—	—	—	—	
Kazakhstan	—	—	—	—	—	—	—	—	1,310
Kyrgyz Republic	-18.9	-7.8	6.8	9.5	0.7	—	—	—	350
Tajikistan	-19.8	-14.3	-5.9	0.1	—	—	—	—	350
Uzbekistan	-6.0	-3.1	-0.2	3.4	2.2	2.4	—	—	870
Southeast Asia	6.0	6.6	5.6	2.0	-8.9	1.5	2.9	3.4	
Cambodia	1.4	4.1	2.9	0.1	-1.2	2.4	—	—	280
Indonesia	5.8	6.5	6.0	3.1	-14.4	1.3	2.5	—	680
Lao People's Democratic Rep.	5.4	6.9	4.3	4.3	1.4	1.5	—	—	330
Malaysia	6.7	7.4	7.6	5.2	-9.2	3.0	3.7	3.8	3,600
Myanmar	5.5	5.0	4.5	3.7	3.1	—	—	—	—
Philippines	2.0	2.2	3.4	2.8	-2.7	1.0	1.6	2.1	1,050
Thailand	7.6	8.2	4.8	-2.9	-11.2	3.1	3.5	3.8	2,200
Viet Nam	6.6	7.4	7.3	6.2	2.7	2.5	3.1	4.0	330
South Asia	4.9	4.9	2.4	2.8	4.7	3.7	4.5	4.9	
Bangladesh	2.3	2.6	3.5	3.5	3.4	2.5	3.1	3.6	350
Bhutan	3.2	4.3	3.0	4.2	2.7	2.9	—	—	—
India	5.7	5.4	2.3	3.3	5.5	4.2	5.3	5.3	430
Maldives	3.8	5.2	5.2	6.0	5.5	4.5	3.5	—	1,230
Nepal	5.1	0.2	3.1	2.2	0.2	0.9	3.0	3.0	210
Pakistan	1.4	3.8	2.5	-1.2	0.9	1.5	0.3	3.0	480
Sri Lanka	4.2	4.0	2.6	4.9	3.5	3.0	3.8	4.8	810
Pacific DMCs	1.4	-1.6	1.3	-4.6	-1.0	—	—	—	
Cook Islands	3.4	-5.8	-1.7	6.2	1.1	14.4	—	—	—
Fiji Islands	4.1	1.4	2.5	-2.4	-4.7	1.9	6.6	—	2,110
Kiribati	6.2	1.9	6.3	1.5	1.5	—	—	—	1,180
Marshall Islands	-0.4	-0.9	-18.0	-8.1	-8.1	—	—	—	1,540
Micronesia, Federated States of	-3.1	0.3	-0.6	-5.5	-4.8	—	—	—	1,800
Nauru	—	—	—	—	—	—	—	—	—
Papua New Guinea	0.2	-3.6	1.5	-6.4	0.6	2.9	3.6	—	890
Samoa	—	4.9	5.5	1.0	—	—	—	—	1,020
Solomon Islands	2.4	2.8	-3.1	—	—	—	—	—	750
Tonga	10.7	6.0	-4.0	-1.8	-0.2	1.8	—	—	1,690
Tuvalu	8.9	-6.2	8.9	2.2	13.6	1.8	—	—	—
Vanuatu	-0.2	0.6	0.8	—	—	—	—	—	1,270
Average	7.0	6.7	5.6	4.6	1.0	4.9	4.8	4.6	

Table A3 **Growth Rate of Value-Added in Agriculture**
(percent per year)

Economy	1994	1995	1996	1997	1998	1999	2000	2001
Newly industrialized economies								
Hong Kong, China	—	—	—	—	—	—	—	—
Korea, Rep. of	0.2	6.6	3.3	4.6	-6.6	4.7	—	—
Singapore	5.7	8.0	6.0	-5.8	-5.7	4.9	1.6	1.5
Taipei,China	3.3	5.5	-0.3	-1.5	-6.6	3.1	-1.3	-2.4
People's Rep. of China and Mongolia								
China, People's Rep. of	4.0	5.0	5.1	3.5	3.5	2.8	3.0	3.0
Mongolia	2.7	4.2	4.4	4.3	7.0	—	—	—
Central Asian republics								
Kazakhstan	-21.0	-24.4	-5.0	1.9	-18.9	28.9	-6.5	2.0
Kyrgyz Republic	-8.6	-2.0	15.2	12.3	2.9	8.7	—	—
Tajikistan	—	—	—	6.5	—	3.8	—	—
Uzbekistan	-3.4	2.0	-7.3	5.8	4.0	5.9	—	—
Southeast Asia								
Cambodia	2.3	7.5	2.2	-0.1	-1.2	2.4	4.2	—
Indonesia	0.6	4.4	3.1	1.0	0.8	0.7	3.0	3.5
Lao People's Democratic Rep.	8.3	3.1	2.8	7.0	3.7	3.2	—	—
Malaysia	-1.9	-2.5	4.5	0.4	-4.5	3.8	4.2	—
Myanmar	5.9	4.8	5.0	3.7	2.8	2.5	—	—
Philippines	2.6	0.8	3.8	2.9	-6.6	6.6	3.0	—
Thailand	4.7	3.5	3.8	-0.5	-0.3	0.5	1.5	2.0
Viet Nam	3.3	4.8	4.4	4.3	2.8	5.0	3.5	3.5
South Asia								
Bangladesh	0.3	-1.0	3.4	6.1	3.2	3.9	3.2	4.0
Bhutan	3.9	4.0	6.4	3.1	3.5	—	—	—
India	5.4	0.2	9.6	-1.9	7.2	0.8	—	—
Maldives	2.6	1.6	1.9	2.3	6.2	6.5	6.5	6.5
Nepal	7.6	-0.3	4.4	4.1	1.0	3.0	4.3	4.0
Pakistan	5.2	6.6	11.7	0.1	3.8	0.4	4.8	4.1
Sri Lanka	3.3	3.3	-4.6	3.0	2.5	4.8	2.9	3.0
Pacific DMCs								
Cook Islands	5.4	-2.5	4.3	12.2	-4.6	—	—	—
Fiji Islands	11.0	-3.2	1.9	-12.5	-10.4	—	—	—
Kiribati	7.0	-11.9	4.7	—	—	—	—	—
Marshall Islands	24.2	-3.9	-20.9	1.2	—	—	—	—
Micronesia, Federated States of	—	—	—	—	—	—	—	—
Nauru	—	—	—	—	—	—	—	—
Papua New Guinea	9.8	-7.7	2.2	-1.2	-8.8	—	—	—
Samoa	-22.6	15.8	-0.3	-5.9	7.0	—	—	—
Solomon Islands	6.2	7.7	-4.3	—	—	—	—	—
Tonga	13.3	12.1	-9.2	-3.0	-2.1	-0.9	—	—
Tuvalu	0.6	0.6	-16.2	5.8	0.7	—	—	—
Vanuatu	2.2	6.4	—	—	6.9	-9.3	—	—

Table A4 Growth Rate of Value-Added in Industry
(percent per year)

Economy	1994	1995	1996	1997	1998	1999	2000	2001
Newly industrialized economies								
Hong Kong, China	—	—	—	—	—	—	—	—
Korea, Rep. of	9.1	10.3	7.0	5.4	-7.5	13.0	—	—
Singapore	13.3	9.5	7.2	7.3	0.9	4.4	4.9	5.0
Taipei,China	2.6	2.6	4.2	6.1	2.7	4.5	6.5	6.3
People's Rep. of China and Mongolia								
China, People's Rep. of	18.4	13.9	12.1	10.8	9.2	8.5	7.5	6.5
Mongolia	2.1	14.6	0.5	-7.0	7.2	—	—	—
Central Asian republics								
Kazakhstan	-24.7	-14.9	-3.5	5.0	6.0	2.2	4.0	4.0
Kyrgyz Republic	-37.3	-12.3	2.6	19.8	-1.8	-2.4	—	—
Tajikistan	—	—	—	-2.8	—	5.0	—	—
Uzbekistan	-6.6	-5.6	1.7	2.2	2.3	6.1	—	—
Southeast Asia								
Cambodia	4.2	20.2	11.7	31.8	9.2	12.9	11.8	—
Indonesia	11.2	10.4	10.7	5.2	-15.1	1.7	6.0	6.6
Lao People's Democratic Rep.	10.7	13.1	17.3	8.1	8.5	10.5	—	—
Malaysia	10.9	14.9	14.4	7.9	-11.0	8.5	1.5	—
Myanmar	10.3	12.7	10.7	8.9	6.6	6.0	—	—
Philippines	5.8	6.7	6.4	6.1	-1.9	0.5	4.0	—
Thailand	10.1	10.2	7.1	-2.7	-13.6	8.3	6.8	6.5
Viet Nam	13.4	13.6	14.5	12.6	8.3	7.0	7.4	8.8
South Asia								
Bangladesh	7.8	8.4	5.3	5.8	8.3	4.0	7.5	7.0
Bhutan	13.9	17.0	8.4	3.8	7.3	—	—	—
India	9.3	12.2	5.2	5.0	3.7	6.2	—	—
Maldives	6.3	8.6	9.0	18.7	15.3	5.0	5.0	5.0
Nepal	9.0	4.0	8.3	6.4	0.2	5.7	6.6	6.9
Pakistan	4.5	4.9	5.4	0.6	6.8	3.8	4.8	4.8
Sri Lanka	8.1	7.8	5.6	7.7	5.9	4.6	5.5	7.3
Pacific DMCs								
Cook Islands	5.4	-15.9	-5.0	6.4	-6.2	—	—	—
Fiji Islands	3.9	1.8	6.1	-0.9	-4.3	—	—	—
Kiribati	14.3	0.6	-4.1	—	—	—	—	—
Marshall Islands	14.7	18.7	-32.6	-6.1	—	—	—	—
Micronesia, Federated States of	—	—	—	—	—	—	—	—
Nauru	—	—	—	—	—	—	—	—
Papua New Guinea	-3.6	4.1	4.1	-14.8	18.6	—	—	—
Samoa	-3.2	0.3	3.8	-1.0	-9.4	—	—	—
Solomon Islands	10.2	34.1	32.0	—	—	—	—	—
Tonga	12.6	3.6	4.3	-8.1	-5.7	9.3	—	—
Tuvalu	4.8	-13.1	85.6	4.0	21.5	—	—	—
Vanuatu	7.3	6.4	—	—	-7.0	7.6	—	—

Table A5 Growth Rate of Value-Added in Services
(percent per year)

Economy	1994	1995	1996	1997	1998	1999	2000	2001
Newly industrialized economies								
Hong Kong, China	—	—	—	—	—	—	—	—
Korea, Rep. of	9.7	9.9	7.5	6.5	-4.7	9.8	—	—
Singapore	10.4	8.1	7.9	8.7	1.8	5.4	5.8	5.8
Taipei,China	10.4	8.9	7.8	7.4	6.2	6.3	6.5	6.5
People's Rep. of China and Mongolia								
China, People's Rep. of	9.6	8.4	7.9	8.2	7.7	6.9	7.0	7.0
Mongolia	2.0	0.2	-4.1	9.2	-2.6	—	—	—
Central Asian republics								
Kazakhstan	0.2	-1.3	3.2	0.9	0.4	-1.7	3.0	3.0
Kyrgyz Republic	-17.1	-4.4	-0.2	0.6	3.9	1.8	—	—
Tajikistan	—	—	—	—	—	—	—	—
Uzbekistan	-3.7	-0.5	5.0	5.9	—	—	—	—
Southeast Asia								
Cambodia	-0.2	4.2	4.8	-5.1	0.3	2.6	4.0	—
Indonesia	7.1	7.6	6.8	5.6	-16.2	-1.5	2.3	3.9
Lao People's Democratic Rep.	5.5	10.2	8.5	7.5	4.8	7.9	—	—
Malaysia	9.8	9.6	8.9	11.1	-1.1	2.3	2.5	—
Myanmar	8.3	7.3	6.5	6.6	6.7	6.0	—	—
Philippines	4.2	5.0	6.4	5.5	3.5	3.9	4.5	—
Thailand	8.9	8.9	5.3	-1.1	-9.4	1.4	3.0	3.4
Viet Nam	9.6	9.8	8.8	7.1	2.4	2.0	3.9	4.9
South Asia								
Bangladesh	5.8	6.9	6.5	4.8	4.5	5.0	7.0	5.5
Bhutan	5.2	7.1	5.0	13.5	8.2	—	—	—
India	8.5	9.8	1.1	9.0	8.3	8.0	—	—
Maldives	8.1	8.7	9.5	8.9	8.3	10.0	7.7	7.7
Nepal	7.7	6.0	5.8	4.6	5.8	3.9	5.8	5.7
Pakistan	4.3	4.7	5.0	3.6	3.2	4.1	4.2	5.9
Sri Lanka	5.1	4.9	6.0	7.1	5.1	3.8	5.7	6.6
Pacific DMCs								
Cook Islands	3.8	-3.6	-0.8	-7.4	-3.4	—	—	—
Fiji Islands	3.5	5.2	2.4	1.8	-1.8	—	—	—
Kiribati	11.3	0.7	8.7	—	—	—	—	—
Marshall Islands	-1.0	2.6	-10.7	-7.4	—	—	—	—
Micronesia, Federated States of	—	—	—	—	—	—	—	—
Nauru	—	—	—	—	—	—	—	—
Papua New Guinea	1.4	-3.7	2.7	5.5	-6.1	—	—	—
Samoa	11.0	6.9	11.4	5.7	7.1	—	—	—
Solomon Islands	2.9	-0.2	-2.2	—	—	—	—	—
Tonga	6.9	2.5	-1.1	1.8	3.2	2.7	—	—
Tuvalu	14.7	-4.8	2.6	2.7	16.0	—	—	—
Vanuatu	1.7	1.4	—	—	-0.7	-1.2	—	—

Table A6 **Sectoral Share of GDP**
(percent)

Economy	Agriculture			Industry			Services		
	1970	1980	1999	1970	1980	1999	1970	1980	1999
Newly industrialized economies									
Hong Kong, China	—	—	—	—	—	—	—	—	—
Korea, Rep. of	29.8	14.2	6.1	23.8	37.8	47.4	46.4	48.1	46.5
Singapore	2.2	1.1	0.1	36.4	38.8	32.2	61.4	60.0	67.7
Taipei,China	—	7.9	2.6	—	46.0	34.5	—	46.1	62.9
People's Rep. of China and Mongolia									
China, People's Rep. of	42.2	25.6	15.8	44.6	51.7	56.3	13.2	22.7	27.9
Mongolia	33.1	17.4	—	26.3	33.3	—	40.6	49.3	—
Central Asian republics									
Kazakhstan	—	—	13.9	—	—	35.7	—	—	50.4
Kyrgyz Republic	—	—	53.8	—	—	18.3	—	—	27.8
Tajikistan	—	—		—	—				
Uzbekistan	—	—	—	—	—	—	—	—	—
Southeast Asia									
Cambodia	—	—	37.4	—	—	22.1	—	—	35.5
Indonesia	35.0	24.4	17.4	28.0	41.3	42.8	37.0	34.3	39.8
Lao People's Democratic Rep.	—	—	51.2	—	—	22.9	—	—	25.9
Malaysia	—	22.9	8.9	—	35.8	42.8	—	41.3	48.4
Myanmar	49.5	47.9	41.9	12.0	12.3	17.2	38.5	39.8	41.0
Philippines	28.2	23.5	20.0	33.7	40.5	34.5	38.1	36.0	45.5
Thailand	30.2	20.2	10.2	25.7	30.1	42.9	44.1	49.7	46.9
Viet Nam	—	42.7	23.9	—	26.3	34.7	—	31.0	41.4
South Asia									
Bangladesh	—	49.4	31.6	—	14.8	19.3	—	35.8	49.1
Bhutan	—	56.7	—	—	12.2	—	—	31.1	—
India	44.5	38.1	25.5	23.9	25.9	27.3	31.6	36.0	47.2
Maldives	—	—	17.3	—	—	17.5	—	—	65.3
Nepal	—	61.8	40.6	—	11.9	19.2	—	26.3	40.2
Pakistan	40.1	30.6	24.5	19.6	25.6	26.7	40.3	43.8	48.7
Sri Lanka	30.7	26.6	21.4	27.1	27.2	27.2	42.2	46.2	51.4
Pacific DMCs									
Cook Islands	—	—	—	—	—	—	—	—	—
Fiji Islands	30.2	22.5	—	23.1	21.7	—	46.7	55.8	—
Kiribati	—	—	—	—	—	—	—	—	—
Marshall Islands	—	—	—	—	—	—	—	—	—
Micronesia, Federated States of	—	—	—	—	—	—	—	—	—
Nauru	—	—	—	—	—	—	—	—	—
Papua New Guinea	—	—	—	—	—	—	—	—	—
Samoa	—	—	—	—	—	—	—	—	—
Solomon Islands	—	52.5	—	—	10.0	—	—	37.4	—
Tonga	—	47.6	35.4	—	11.0	12.7	—	41.4	51.9
Tuvalu	—	—	—	—	—	—	—	—	—
Vanuatu	—	—	—	—	—	—	—	—	—

Table A7 Gross Domestic Savings
(percentage of GDP)

Economy	1994	1995	1996	1997	1998	1999	2000	2001
Newly industrialized economies								
Hong Kong, China	33.1	30.5	30.7	31.1	30.2	29.8	30.7	32.0
Korea, Rep. of	35.5	35.4	33.5	32.5	33.9	33.0	30.9	27.9
Singapore	47.3	49.5	49.3	50.4	49.9	51.2	52.0	52.0
Taipei,China	25.8	25.6	26.6	26.4	26.0	26.0	26.8	27.2
People's Rep. of China and Mongolia								
China, People's Rep. of	42.6	41.1	40.5	41.5	40.9	39.0	37.4	36.4
Mongolia	16.1	21.8	17.7	30.0	28.3	—	—	—
Central Asian republics								
Kazakhstan	14.0	17.4	8.2	8.9	8.1	—	—	—
Kyrgyz Republic	2.7	5.5	—	—	—	—	—	—
Tajikistan	—	—	—	—	—	—	—	—
Uzbekistan	7.8	20.4	7.9	14.9	9.9	10.5	11.0	11.5
Southeast Asia								
Cambodia	—	—	—	5.9	5.4	4.7	4.0	4.0
Indonesia	29.4	28.6	27.3	29.4	23.2	13.2	15.2	18.0
Lao People's Democratic Rep.	—	11.5	12.4	9.4	15.5	13.4	13.0	13.0
Malaysia	39.6	39.7	42.9	37.3	39.6	37.7	35.4	35.0
Myanmar	11.7	13.4	11.5	11.9	10.6	—	—	—
Philippines	19.0	17.5	18.5	19.6	22.3	19.8	20.0	21.0
Thailand	34.6	33.4	33.6	32.4	39.3	36.4	36.3	36.0
Viet Nam	17.5	16.1	17.8	21.8	21.1	22.0	21.6	20.5
South Asia								
Bangladesh	14.2	13.9	13.1	18.6	20.4	21.1	21.8	22.3
Bhutan	45.0	48.7	38.3	38.8	37.9	—	—	—
India	24.2	24.1	23.3	24.7	22.3	21.0	22.0	23.0
Maldives	33.1	41.4	43.5	—	—	—	—	—
Nepal	16.1	16.3	13.8	12.1	9.5	10.6	11.7	11.7
Pakistan	16.7	15.7	14.4	13.1	16.1	15.1	14.7	15.6
Sri Lanka	19.1	19.5	19.0	21.5	24.0	25.0	25.0	26.0
Pacific DMCs								
Cook Islands	—	—	—	—	—	—	—	—
Fiji Islands	12.4	12.9	14.7	13.2	7.5	—	—	—
Kiribati	—	—	—	—	—	—	—	—
Marshall Islands	—	—	—	—	—	—	—	—
Micronesia, Federated States of	—	—	—	—	—	—	—	—
Nauru	—	—	—	—	—	—	—	—
Papua New Guinea	25.1	28.9	32.1	23.0	28.3	29.3	34.4	—
Samoa	—	—	—	—	—	—	—	—
Solomon Islands	—	—	—	—	—	—	—	—
Tonga	—	—	—	—	—	—	—	—
Tuvalu	—	—	—	—	—	—	—	—
Vanuatu	23.1	26.1	—	—	—	—	—	—

Table A8 **Gross Domestic Investment**
(percentage of GDP)

Economy	1994	1995	1996	1997	1988	1999	2000	2001
Newly industrialized economies								
Hong Kong, China	31.9	34.8	32.1	34.6	29.7	25.4	27.3	34.0
Korea, Rep. of	36.5	37.2	37.9	34.2	21.2	26.8	28.5	27.2
Singapore	33.5	34.5	37.0	38.7	33.5	32.7	34.2	36.0
Taipei,China	23.9	23.7	23.2	24.2	24.9	24.4	24.2	24.5
People's Rep. of China and Mongolia								
China, People's Rep. of	41.2	40.8	39.6	38.1	37.8	37.8	37.8	37.3
Mongolia	22.0	26.4	22.4	25.3	27.3	—	—	—
Central Asian republics								
Kazakhstan	22.6	20.5	11.8	12.9	14.9	—	—	—
Kyrgyz Republic	9.0	18.3	25.2	15.8	15.4	11.7	10.0	10.1
Tajikistan	—	—	—	—	—	—	—	—
Uzbekistan	5.7	20.9	15.1	18.9	10.2	11.8	12.0	13.5
Southeast Asia								
Cambodia	12.2	12.9	15.2	14.7	13.4	13.1	13.0	14.0
Indonesia	31.1	31.9	30.7	31.8	19.1	11.6	13.0	17.5
Lao People's Democratic Rep.	—	24.5	29.0	26.2	26.1	23.7	24.0	25.0
Malaysia	41.2	43.6	41.5	42.9	26.7	23.7	24.1	25.0
Myanmar	12.4	14.2	12.3	12.6	11.1	—	—	—
Philippines	23.5	21.6	23.0	24.9	20.4	18.8	19.5	20.0
Thailand	40.2	41.4	41.7	33.2	26.1	26.8	30.4	33.0
Viet Nam	25.5	27.1	28.1	28.3	25.5	19.7	20.8	21.9
South Asia								
Bangladesh	19.0	20.0	20.8	20.8	21.6	22.5	22.8	23.5
Bhutan	54.9	53.5	48.0	48.1	47.3	—	—	—
India	22.9	25.6	21.9	26.2	23.4	22.5	24.0	25.0
Maldives	37.5	47.5	52.7	—	—	—	—	—
Nepal	22.4	25.2	27.3	25.3	20.7	17.3	20.0	22.0
Pakistan	19.4	18.4	18.8	17.7	17.1	14.8	15.1	15.9
Sri Lanka	27.0	25.7	24.2	24.4	25.4	27.5	29.0	29.5
Pacific DMCs								
Cook Islands	—	—	—	—	—	—	—	—
Fiji Islands	13.9	13.1	11.0	12.5	12.0	—	—	—
Kiribati	—	—	—	—	—	—	—	—
Marshall Islands	—	—	—	—	—	—	—	—
Micronesia, Federated States of	—	—	—	—	—	—	—	—
Nauru	—	—	—	—	—	—	—	—
Papua New Guinea	16.3	19.4	27.9	27.1	30.3	29.4	42.0	—
Samoa	—	—	—	—	—	—	—	—
Solomon Islands	—	—	—	—	—	—	—	—
Tonga	17.5	13.7	—	—	—	—	—	—
Tuvalu	67.6	68.0	56.2	—	—	—	—	—
Vanuatu	28.8	32.7	—	—	—	—	—	—

Table A9 **Changes in Consumer Prices**
(percent per year)

Economy	1994	1995	1996	1997	1998	1999	2000	2001
Newly industrialized economies	5.8	4.7	4.3	3.5	3.9	-0.4	1.8	2.6
Hong Kong, China	8.8	9.0	6.3	5.8	2.8	-4.0	-1.0	3.1
Korea, Rep. of	6.2	4.5	4.9	4.5	7.5	0.8	3.2	3.2
Singapore	3.1	1.7	1.4	2.0	-0.3	0.5	1.5	1.5
Taipei,China	4.1	3.7	3.1	0.9	1.7	0.2	1.9	2.0
People's Rep. of China and Mongolia	24.2	17.2	8.4	2.8	-0.8	-1.4	1.8	2.0
China, People's Rep. of	24.1	17.1	8.3	2.8	-0.8	-1.4	1.8	2.0
Mongolia	87.5	56.8	57.5	36.6	9.8	7.6	5.5	4.3
Central Asian republics	1,086.4	122.8	42.4	21.4	11.4	21.9	15.1	10.7
Kazakhstan	1,156.8	60.4	28.6	11.3	1.9	17.8	13.0	5.5
Kyrgyz Republic	62.1	32.1	34.8	13.0	16.8	39.9	—	—
Tajikistan	1.1	2,131.9	40.6	159.8	2.7	24.0	15.0	10.0
Uzbekistan	1,281.4	116.9	64.3	27.6	26.1	26.0	20.0	20.0
Southeast Asia	6.9	7.3	6.6	5.5	21.3	7.4	4.7	4.6
Cambodia	-0.8	8.1	7.2	8.0	14.8	4.0	6.0	5.0
Indonesia	8.5	9.4	7.9	6.6	58.5	20.5	6.0	5.0
Lao People's Democratic Rep.	6.8	25.7	7.3	26.6	142.0	86.7	30.0	10.0
Malaysia	3.7	3.4	3.5	2.7	5.3	2.8	3.3	3.5
Myanmar	24.1	31.5	20.0	34.0	49.0	—	—	—
Philippines	9.0	8.0	9.0	5.9	9.8	6.6	6.5	6.0
Thailand	5.1	5.8	5.9	5.6	8.1	0.3	2.5	3.5
Viet Nam	14.4	12.7	4.5	3.6	9.2	0.1	6.0	7.0
South Asia	8.3	10.9	6.7	5.6	7.1	4.1	5.0	5.4
Bangladesh	3.3	8.9	6.6	2.6	7.0	9.0	6.0	8.0
Bhutan	5.9	8.2	9.3	7.4	9.0	9.2	—	—
India	8.4	10.9	5.7	4.8	6.9	3.3	4.8	5.0
Maldives	3.4	5.3	6.2	7.6	-2.2	3.0	3.0	3.0
Nepal	8.9	7.6	8.1	7.8	4.0	12.7	5.0	5.0
Pakistan	11.2	13.0	10.8	11.8	7.8	5.7	5.0	6.0
Sri Lanka	8.4	7.7	15.9	9.6	9.4	4.7	6.5	6.5
Pacific DMCs	2.9	11.6	8.6	3.9	9.9	10.4	—	—
Cook Islands	2.7	0.9	-0.6	-0.4	0.8	1.4	—	—
Fiji Islands	0.6	2.2	3.1	3.4	5.7	1.7	—	—
Kiribati	5.3	3.6	-1.5	2.2	4.7	2.0	—	—
Marshall Islands	5.7	8.3	9.8	4.7	4.0	1.0	—	—
Micronesia, Federated States of	4.0	4.0	4.0	3.0	3.0	—	—	—
Nauru	—	1.7	4.0	6.1	4.0	6.7	—	—
Papua New Guinea	2.9	17.3	11.6	3.9	13.6	16.0	13.0	—
Samoa	12.1	-2.9	5.4	6.8	2.2	0.3	2.0	2.0
Solomon Islands	13.3	9.6	11.8	8.1	12.3	8.0	6.5	—
Tonga	1.1	1.4	3.0	2.3	3.3	4.4	—	—
Tuvalu	1.4	5.0	0.0	1.4	0.8	7.0	—	—
Vanuatu	2.3	2.2	0.9	2.8	3.9	2.5	—	—
Average	19.6	10.7	6.8	4.3	5.5	1.6	3.0	3.3

Table A10 **Changes in Money Supply (M2)**
(percent per year)

Economy	1994	1995	1996	1997	1998	1999	2000	2001
Newly industrialized economies								
Hong Kong, China	12.9	14.6	10.9	8.3	11.8	8.1	12.0	15.0
Korea, Rep. of	18.7	15.6	15.8	14.1	27.0	27.3	24.8	21.5
Singapore	14.4	8.5	9.8	10.3	30.2	8.5	11.6	11.8
Taipei,China	15.1	9.4	9.1	8.0	8.6	9.2	9.3	9.0
People's Rep. of China and Mongolia								
China, People's Rep. of	34.5	29.5	25.3	17.3	15.3	14.7	16.0	16.0
Mongolia	78.3	33.1	20.9	32.5	-1.7	32.1	15.0	15.0
Central Asian republics								
Kazakhstan	596.6	106.1	16.5	21.6	-18.7	76.6	—	—
Kyrgyz Republic	117.8	78.2	21.3	25.4	17.2	18.5	—	—
Tajikistan	159.4	—	93.2	110.7	30.7		—	—
Uzbekistan	680.0	158.1	113.7	36.0	28.0	31.5	32.0	28.0
Southeast Asia								
Cambodia	34.9	44.3	40.4	16.6	15.7	17.3	12.0	12.0
Indonesia	20.2	27.6	29.6	23.2	62.3	11.9	13.0	17.0
Lao People's Democratic Rep.	31.9	16.4	26.7	65.8	113.3	86.3	50.0	30.0
Malaysia	14.7	24.0	20.9	18.5	2.7	8.3	12.0	14.5
Myanmar	34.0	40.4	38.9	29.0	36.4	—	—	—
Philippines	26.8	25.2	15.8	20.5	7.1	15.0	15.0	—
Thailand	12.9	17.0	12.6	16.4	9.5	2.1	8.0	12.0
Viet Nam	27.8	22.6	22.7	25.4	24.6	30.0	25.0	24.0
South Asia								
Bangladesh	18.6	13.0	8.3	10.8	10.4	12.8	14.0	12.0
Bhutan	21.5	29.9	30.4	30.9	41.7	21.4	—	—
India	22.3	13.7	15.2	18.0	18.4	16.0	17.0	17.0
Maldives	24.2	15.6	26.0	23.1	22.8	3.6	—	—
Nepal	19.6	16.1	14.4	11.9	21.9	20.9	14.0	12.0
Pakistan	18.1	17.2	13.8	12.2	14.5	6.3	10.0	9.0
Sri Lanka	19.7	19.2	10.8	13.8	9.7	13.3	12.5	12.0
Pacific DMCs								
Cook Islands	—	—	6.9	15.6	18.5	9.5	—	—
Fiji Islands	2.7	4.3	0.9	-8.7	-0.3	3.1	—	—
Kiribati	—	—	—	—	—	—	—	—
Marshall Islands	—	—	—	—	—	—	—	—
Micronesia, Federated States of	—	—	—	—	—	—	—	—
Nauru	—	—	—	—	—	—	—	—
Papua New Guinea	-1.3	13.7	30.7	7.7	2.5	5.1	—	—
Samoa	13.0	21.8	5.1	13.2	—	9.1	—	—
Solomon Islands	24.1	9.9	15.7	6.3	4.8	7.0	—	—
Tonga	8.8	17.1	2.8	14.1	2.4	19.9	—	—
Tuvalu	—	—	—	—	—	—	—	—
Vanuatu	2.9	13.3	10.1	-0.4	4.6	—	—	—

Table A11 **Growth Rate of Merchandise Exports**
(percent per year)

Economy	1994	1995	1996	1997	1998	1999	2000	2001
Newly industrialized economies	15.0	20.8	4.6	4.0	-8.3	4.5	8.9	8.7
Hong Kong, China	11.9	14.8	4.0	4.0	-7.5	-0.1	9.1	10.0
Korea, Rep. of	15.7	31.2	4.3	6.7	-4.7	10.1	10.0	7.4
Singapore	25.8	21.0	6.4	-0.2	-12.2	2.6	3.5	5.3
Taipei,China	9.4	20.0	3.8	5.4	-9.5	6.8	12.5	11.5
People's Rep. of China and Mongolia	35.4	24.9	17.8	20.9	0.6	6.0	5.0	5.0
China, People's Rep. of	35.6	24.9	17.9	20.9	0.6	6.0	5.0	5.0
Mongolia	0.3	32.3	-11.6	16.6	-12.1	2.8	12.8	14.3
Central Asian republics	-1.9	37.9	13.2	7.6	-17.8	-6.3	—	—
Kazakhstan	-8.4	57.2	21.8	9.7	-16.3	-4.8	9.5	6.9
Kyrgyz Republic	0.1	20.3	29.9	18.8	-7.2	-19.1	6.9	7.9
Tajikistan	22.6	39.4	-1.2	-3.1	-21.4	9.4	—	—
Uzbekistan	2.2	18.2	1.7	4.5	-21.8	-10.0	8.5	8.0
Southeast Asia	19.3	24.0	5.9	7.6	-4.8	6.4	8.8	-9.4
Cambodia	158.0	2.4	10.1	81.0	8.3	21.8	11.0	10.0
Indonesia	9.9	18.0	5.8	12.2	-10.5	-7.4	8.1	9.0
Lao People's Democratic Republic	24.9	4.1	2.5	-1.2	7.7	2.9	5.0	6.0
Malaysia	23.1	26.1	7.1	1.2	-7.5	10.1	8.0	8.0
Myanmar	31.8	1.9	-0.4	8.7	24.4	—	—	—
Philippines	18.5	29.4	17.7	22.8	16.9	18.8	14.0	14.0
Thailand	22.1	24.8	-1.9	3.8	-6.8	7.4	7.0	8.0
Viet Nam	35.8	28.2	41.0	26.5	1.0	22.3	10.0	10.0
South Asia	21.3	20.2	5.5	4.8	-0.1	4.6	5.5	7.2
Bangladesh	6.3	37.1	11.8	13.3	17.1	2.8	7.0	12.0
Bhutan	-4.1	10.3	39.6	1.7	12.0	-5.9	—	—
India	18.4	20.3	4.2	4.5	-3.9	10.0	4.5	5.0
Maldives	43.1	12.7	-6.0	15.9	3.2	-7.0	—	—
Nepal	3.6	-9.7	1.9	10.2	11.9	20.3	10.0	12.0
Pakistan	-1.4	16.1	7.1	-2.6	4.2	-10.7	8.0	9.0
Sri Lanka	12.0	18.6	7.6	13.3	3.4	-4.1	10.0	15.0
Pacific DMCs	7.9	1.9	-1.6	-14.3	-19.9	0.7	—	—
Cook Islands	6.8	10.4	-31.0	-10.3	14.0	—	—	—
Fiji Islands	31.8	6.1	23.3	-18.9	-26.6	26.5	—	—
Kiribati	50.9	43.0	-26.0	17.3	-5.5	—	—	—
Marshall Islands	129.6	23.1	-12.2	28.4	-16.3	—	—	—
Micronesia, Federated States of	135.9	-26.1	-34.7	3.1	-3.0	—	—	—
Nauru	—	—	—	—	—	—	—	—
Papua New Guinea	2.5	0.4	-5.6	-15.1	-20.1	10.1	-5.0	—
Samoa	-45.3	149.1	15.1	44.3	39.5	—	—	—
Solomon Islands	11.3	17.1	-3.5	-3.1	-9.3	—	—	—
Tonga	34.7	6.4	-25.7	-18.6	-17.2	4.0	—	—
Tuvalu	10.5	4.3	9.8	-2.0	-84.8	—	—	—
Vanuatu	10.1	13.2	6.4	17.0	-4.4	—	—	—
Average	18.5	22.1	6.8	7.4	-5.0	6.4	7.6	3.7

Table A12 Direction of Exports
(percent share)

To / From	DMCs 1985	DMCs 1998	Japan 1985	Japan 1998	US 1985	US 1998	EU 1985	EU 1998	Australia/ New Zealand 1985	Australia/ New Zealand 1998	Others 1985	Others 1998
Newly industrialized economies												
Hong Kong, China	35.6	41.6	4.2	5.3	30.8	23.4	11.8	—	2.3	1.5	15.3	28.2
Korea, Rep. of	12.9	30.2	15.0	9.3	35.6	17.4	10.4	—	1.3	2.3	24.7	40.9
Singapore	36.7	41.5	9.4	6.6	21.2	19.9	10.1	—	4.4	3.2	18.1	28.8
Taipei,China	15.6	36.7	11.3	8.4	15.5	26.6	5.5	17.8	2.4	1.7	49.7	8.9
People's Rep. of China and Mongolia												
China, People's Rep. of	38.2	31.5	22.3	16.2	8.5	20.7	7.8	—	0.8	1.4	22.5	30.2
Mongolia	3.1	—	11.2	—	5.5	—	20.5	—	0.0	—	59.6	—
Central Asian republics												
Kazakhstan		16.6	—	2.2	—	3.3	—	—	—	0.1	—	77.8
Kyrgyz Republic	—	29.0	—	0.1	—	1.5	—	—	—	—	—	69.4
Tajikistan	—	57.2	—	—	—	5.2	—	—	—	—	—	37.6
Uzbekistan	—	28.2	—	1.6	—	1.3	—	—	—	—	—	68.9
Southeast Asia												
Cambodia	67.9	—	7.0	—	—	—	13.2	—	0.0	—	11.9	—
Indonesia	17.2	31.1	46.2	17.6	21.7	15.8	6.0	—	1.2	4.1	7.6	31.4
Lao People's Democratic Rep.	71.9	—	6.6	—	2.7	—	0.5	—	5.5	—	12.7	—
Malaysia	38.1	37.4	24.6	10.5	12.8	21.6	13.6	—	1.9	2.6	9.1	27.9
Myanmar	47.1	44.5	8.4	6.7	0.8	13.2	8.4	—	0.0	0.7	35.4	34.9
Philippines	19.5	20.2	19.0	14.4	35.9	34.4	13.8	—	2.1	0.6	9.7	30.4
Thailand	27.1	27.3	13.4	13.7	19.7	22.3	17.8	—	1.9	2.0	20.1	34.6
Viet Nam	50.4	19.8	17.4	18.1	—	6.2	6.2	—	2.2	5.7	23.8	50.2
South Asia												
Bangladesh	14.5	6.8	7.2	1.7	18.1	35.8	13.0	—	1.8	0.5	45.5	55.2
Bhutan			—	—	—	—	—	—	—	—	—	—
India	8.9	19.5	11.1	5.1	18.9	20.9	16.7	—	1.4	1.3	43.0	53.1
Maldives	50.8	—	10.1	—	24.3		4.0	—	—	—	10.9	—
Nepal	41.4	—	0.7	—	35.3	—	20.3	—	0.1	—	2.3	—
Pakistan	16.0	18.8	11.3	3.4	10.0	21.6	20.9	—	1.1	1.7	40.6	54.5
Sri Lanka	11.2	7.6	5.1	4.7	22.3	38.4	17.9	—	1.7	1.3	41.9	48.0
Pacific DMCs												
Cook Islands	—	—	—	—	—	—	—	—	—	—	—	—
Fiji Islands	22.5	11.0	3.0	4.7	4.9	16.3	31.0	—	18.2	38.3	20.4	29.7
Kiribati	7.2	—	4.3	—	0.0	—	44.5	—	0.5	—	43.5	—
Nauru	—	—	—	—	—	—	—	—	—	—	—	—
Marshall Islands	—	—	—	—	—	—	—	—	—	—	—	—
Micronesia, Federated States of	—	—	—	—	—	—	—	—	—	—	—	—
Papua New Guinea	9.9	13.1	22.1	13.1	4.0	5.6	46.5	—	12.0	20.6	5.6	47.7
Samoa	0.3	2.0	0.9	0.1	59.4	29.0	5.8	—	29.7	56.5	3.9	12.5
Solomon Islands	11.1	44.0	52.1	30.2	2.4	1.8	26.3	—	3.2	2.4	5.0	21.6
Tonga	5.9	—	0.2	—	3.2	—	0.5	—	83.1	—	7.1	—
Tuvalu	—	—	—	—	—	—	—	—	—	—	—	—
Vanuatu	1.4	—	6.7	—	0.0	—	25.4	—	1.6	—	65.0	—
DMCs	25.6	33.7	16.5	10.2	26.3	21.4	10.7	2.0	2.1	2.1	18.8	30.7

Table A13 Growth Rate of Merchandise Imports
(percent per year)

Economy	1994	1995	1996	1997	1998	1999	2000	2001
Newly industrialized economies	17.4	22.9	5.2	3.1	-19.3	6.5	14.1	11.9
Hong Kong, China	16.7	19.1	3.0	5.1	-11.6	-2.7	10.7	11.0
Korea, Rep. of	22.6	31.9	12.3	-2.2	-36.2	29.0	23.1	14.3
Singapore	19.8	21.7	5.4	0.7	-23.2	6.8	7.9	8.8
Taipei,China	10.4	21.2	-0.1	10.1	-7.4	2.8	15.8	13.4
People's Rep. of China and Mongolia	10.3	15.6	19.4	8.3	-1.5	18.1	9.8	8.0
China, People's Rep. of	10.4	15.5	19.5	8.3	-1.5	18.3	9.8	8.0
Mongolia	-1.1	32.0	8.2	-1.5	9.5	-15.4	8.6	11.8
Central Asian republics	-15.2	24.3	24.5	-0.3	-13.1	-20.7	—	—
Kazakhstan	-18.3	28.1	23.0	8.3	-8.4	-28.2	9.3	7.9
Kyrgyz Republic	-4.6	24.6	47.5	-17.5	17.0	-29.4	7.5	4.6
Tajikistan	7.4	22.2	-6.2	3.0	-9.7	-5.1	—	—
Uzbekistan	-16.3	18.8	31.0	-11.2	-25.2	10.0	8.2	8.5
Southeast Asia	21.7	29.5	6.1	-0.7	-26.4	4.7	13.3	-5.8
Cambodia	78.4	16.4	20.3	5.8	-0.1	20.4	12.0	10.0
Indonesia	13.9	26.6	8.1	4.5	-30.9	-10.8	7.5	14.0
Lao People's Democratic Rep.	30.6	4.4	17.1	-6.0	-14.7	-2.9	7.0	6.5
Malaysia	28.1	29.9	1.6	1.4	-26.5	10.0	12.6	13.0
Myanmar	14.3	23.0	6.3	15.3	14.7	—	—	—
Philippines	21.2	23.7	20.8	14.0	-18.8	4.1	14.0	16.0
Thailand	18.4	31.9	0.6	-13.4	-33.8	17.7	16.5	17.0
Viet Nam	48.5	43.8	38.9	0.8	-2.1	1.2	16.0	17.0
South Asia	38.7	21.6	10.5	3.3	-0.4	5.1	7.7	8.8
Bangladesh	2.9	39.2	17.9	3.2	5.1	6.6	7.0	7.0
Bhutan	-25.7	4.6	14.1	18.4	3.7	20.5	—	—
India	34.3	21.6	9.1	4.6	0.9	9.0	7.0	8.0
Maldives	9.7	20.9	12.6	15.6	1.5	13.5	—	—
Nepal	21.9	21.7	5.8	21.7	-12.4	-10.5	15.0	15.0
Pakistan	-13.6	18.5	16.7	-6.4	-8.4	-6.7	9.5	9.0
Sri Lanka	18.9	11.4	2.4	7.8	0.4	0.1	14.0	16.0
Pacific DMCs	11.4	0.4	10.4	-1.5	-24.0	-16.1	—	—
Cook Islands	-14.0	-0.4	-10.7	10.5	-20.8	—	—	—
Fiji Islands	10.2	5.8	10.3	-2.5	-25.3	13.9	—	—
Kiribati	-8.3	33.4	0.9	2.6	-14.4	—	—	—
Marshall Islands	11.1	8.5	-0.9	-15.8	-9.3	—	—	—
Micronesia, Federated States of	16.6	-22.2	-26.8	-6.7	-2.4	—	—	—
Nauru	—	—	—	—	—	—	—	—
Papua New Guinea	17.2	-4.5	19.3	-2.0	-30.2	10.4	15.2	—
Samoa	-22.0	15.2	7.3	0.6	3.1	—	—	—
Solomon Islands	3.9	8.6	-1.9	22.6	-13.4	-13.0	—	—
Tonga	10.3	35.4	-9.9	-18.7	-8.3	-13.1	—	—
Tuvalu	11.9	6.4	9.8	28.8	18.6	—	—	—
Vanuatu	13.4	6.4	2.5	-2.6	-3.5	—	—	—
Average	18.2	23.3	7.6	2.9	-16.2	9.1	12.4	7.5

Table A14 Balance of Trade
($ million)

Economy	1994	1995	1996	1997	1998	1999	2000	2001
Newly industrialized economies	-582	-9,826	-13,550	-9,300	55,674	48,814	27,370	11,536
Hong Kong, China	-10,923	-19,594	-18,352	-21,121	-10,946	-5,994	-9,417	-12,351
Korea, Rep. of	-2,860	-4,444	-14,965	-3,179	41,627	28,716	16,290	7,576
Singapore	1,354	977	2,224	1,118	14,677	11,039	6,928	3,436
Taipei,China	11,847	13,235	17,543	13,882	10,316	15,053	13,569	12,875
People's Rep. of China and Mongolia	7,294	18,057	19,463	40,260	43,483	29,080	22,597	18,309
China, People's Rep. of	7,290	18,050	19,550	40,270	43,600	29,100	22,600	18,300
Mongolia	4	7	-87	-10	-117	-20	-3	9
Central Asian republics	-918	-166	-1,309	-428	-944	669	165	133
Kazakhstan	-920	-223	-335	-276	-801	776	233	187
Kyrgyz Republic	-86	-122	-252	-15	-171	-60	-68	-54
Tajikistan	-127	-59	-16	-64	-145	-53	—	—
Uzbekistan	215	238	-706	-73	172	6	—	—
Southeast Asia	-9,381	-21,017	-22,679	-5,042	45,469	51,339	47,911	36,098
Cambodia	-255	-333	-428	-231	-186	-216	-212	—
Indonesia	7,901	6,533	5,948	10,074	18,429	18,174	19,817	20,070
Lao People's Democratic Rep.	-264	-276	-369	-331	-212	-186	-206	-221
Malaysia	1,577	-104	3,826	3,726	17,521	19,345	18,138	16,217
Myanmar	-571	-896	-1,016	-1,233	-1,315	—	—	—
Philippines	-7,850	-8,944	-11,342	-11,121	-19	4,316	4,920	—
Thailand	-8,730	-14,652	-16,148	-4,626	12,231	8,928	5,007	391
Viet Nam	-1,190	-2,345	-3,150	-1,300	-981	978	447	-359
South Asia	-15,070	-18,862	-23,215	-23,222	-22,985	-24,737	-27,502	-30,930
Bangladesh	-1,657	-2,361	-2,999	-2,703	-2,313	-2,661	-2,848	-2,764
Bhutan	-30	-27	-13	-32	-25	-50	—	—
India	-9,049	-11,359	-13,980	-14,657	-16,477	-17,622	-19,786	-22,535
Maldives	-120	-151	-186	-214	-216	-262	—	—
Nepal	-656	-922	-990	-1,246	-995	-753	-893	-1,044
Pakistan	-2,000	-2,537	-3,704	-3,145	-1,867	-2,085	-2,396	-2,612
Sri Lanka	-1,558	-1,504	-1,344	-1,225	-1,092	-1,294	-1,660	-1,976
Pacific DMCs	737	793	451	-14	111	492	—	—
Cook Islands	-45	-44	-40	-45	-35	—	—	—
Fiji Islands	-223	-235	-191	-292	-225	-207	—	—
Kiribati	-21	-28	-30	-33	-27	—	—	—
Marshall Islands	-50	-51	-53	-36	-34	—	—	—
Micronesia, Federated States of	-94	-76	-59	-52	-51	—	—	—
Nauru	—	—	—	—	—	—	—	—
Papua New Guinea	1,339	1,410	1,015	663	679	743	472	—
Western Samoa	-77	-83	-89	-85	-76	—	—	—
Solomon Islands	2	14	11	-28	-18	—	—	—
Tonga	-38	-57	-54	-56	-53	-44	—	—
Tuvalu	-7	-7	-8	-6	-7	—	—	—
Vanuatu	-50	-51	-51	-44	-42	—	—	—
Total	-17,920	-31,021	-40,839	2,254	120,808	105,657	70,461	35,145

Table A15 Balance of Payments on Current Account
($ million)

Economy	1994	1995	1996	1997	1998	1999	2000	2001
Newly industrialized economies	14,031	11,402	2,427	13,917	61,873	49,827	33,594	24,762
Hong Kong, China	—	—	—	—	—	—	—	—
Korea, Rep. of	-3,867	-8,507	-23,006	-8,167	40,823	25,500	11,800	4,500
Singapore	11,400	14,435	14,510	15,033	17,613	16,133	16,058	14,933
Taipei,China	6,498	5,474	10,923	7,051	3,437	8,694	5,736	5,329
People's Rep. of China and Mongolia	7,625	1,575	7,166	29,682	29,199	11,962	-4,423	-10,700
China, People's Rep. of	7,657	1,617	7,280	29,717	29,324	12,000	-4,400	-10,700
Mongolia	-32	-42	-114	-35	-125	-38	-23	—
Central Asian republics	-1,040	-860	-2,233	-1,586	-1,770	-668	-371	-365
Kazakhstan	-905	-517	-751	-804	-1,248	-269	-218	-218
Kyrgyz Republic	-84	-235	-425	-139	-323	-168	-154	-148
Tajikistan	-171	-89	-77	-60	-113	-29	—	—
Uzbekistan	120	-20	-980	-584	-86	-202	—	—
Southeast Asia	-20,232	-35,215	-34,737	-20,142	26,870	33,512	22,886	3,044
Cambodia	-367	-444	-546	-268	-219	-249	-301	—
Indonesia	-2,960	-6,760	-7,801	-5,001	4,097	4,904	3,819	936
Lao People's Democratic Rep.	-221	-233	-307	-293	-137	-147	—	—
Malaysia	-4,521	-8,700	-4,900	-5,000	9,200	11,050	11,801	—
Myanmar	-53	-244	-305	-350	-447	—	—	—
Philippines	-2,950	-3,304	-3,953	-4,345	1,290	6,000	—	—
Thailand	-7,862	-13,248	-14,380	-3,130	14,261	11,300	7,307	2,591
Viet Nam	-1,298	-2,282	-2,545	-1,756	-1,175	654	260	-484
South Asia	-6,559	-9,914	-12,045	-7,515	-10,216	-2,814	-3,254	-2,595
Bangladesh	-89	-664	-1,291	-534	-253	-394	—	—
Bhutan	-40	-34	-37	-56	-47	-102	—	—
India	-3,369	-5,910	-5,294	-2,648	-7,720	—	—	—
Maldives	-11	-18	-8	-37	-26	-57	-28	-31
Nepal	-225	-343	-390	-290	-245	-172	-415	-519
Pakistan	-1,965	-2,163	-4,348	-3,557	-1,701	-1,772	-1,531	-1,294
Sri Lanka	-860	-782	-677	-394	-224	-317	-1,280	-751
Pacific DMCs	517	687	441	-32	179	—	—	—
Cook Islands	—	0	5	1	2	—	—	—
Fiji Islands	-63	-19	61	6	27	10	—	—
Kiribati	1	-6	-7	—	—	—	—	—
Marshall Islands	5	2	4	16	21	—	—	—
Micronesia, Federated States of	13	46	62	64	67	—	—	—
Nauru	—	—	—	—	—	—	—	—
Papua New Guinea	573	673	312	-116	69	-23	-280	—
Samoa	5	8	11	17	10	—	—	—
Solomon Islands	-2	9	5	-24	—	—	—	—
Tonga	-8	-22	-11	-2	-19	-2	—	—
Tuvalu	1	1	—	—	—	—	—	—
Vanuatu	-8	-5	-1	6	—	—	—	—
Total	-5,658	-32,326	-38,980	14,323	106,135	91,819	48,432	14,145

Table A16 Balance of Payments on Current Account
(percentage of GDP)

Economy	1994	1995	1996	1997	1998	1999	2000	2001
Newly industrialized economies	2.0	1.4	0.3	1.6	9.3	6.4	3.7	2.4
Hong Kong, China	—	—	—	—	—	—	—	—
Korea, Rep. of	-1.0	-1.7	-4.4	-1.7	12.8	6.1	2.4	0.8
Singapore	16.4	17.3	15.9	15.8	20.9	18.5	17.8	16.0
Taipei,China	2.7	2.1	3.9	2.4	1.3	3.0	1.8	1.5
People's Rep. of China and Mongolia	1.4	0.2	0.9	3.3	3.0	1.2	-0.4	-0.9
China, People's Rep. of	1.4	0.2	0.9	3.3	3.1	1.2	-0.4	-0.9
Mongolia	-4.7	-4.6	-9.4	1.3	-11.9	-4.7	-9.5	-8.4
Central Asian republics	-5.4	-3.0	-5.9	-4.0	-4.5	-2.0	-2.4	-2.3
Kazakhstan	-8.6	-3.1	-3.6	-3.6	-5.5	-1.7	-1.5	-1.5
Kyrgyz Republic	-7.6	-15.7	-23.2	-7.9	-22.6	-12.0	-10.5	-8.8
Tajikistan	-20.5	-14.6	-7.4	-5.4	-8.8	-7.8	-3.0	-3.0
Uzbekistan	2.1	-0.2	-7.2	-4.0	-0.6	-1.3	-1.0	-2.0
Southeast Asia	-4.2	-6.3	-5.5	-3.4	7.0	7.6	3.3	0.8
Cambodia	-15.2	-14.5	-17.3	-8.8	-8.0	-8.4	-9.0	-10.0
Indonesia	-1.7	-3.3	-3.4	-2.3	4.1	3.5	2.2	0.5
Lao People's Democratic Rep.	-14.4	-13.0	-16.6	-16.8	-10.6	-10.3	-11.0	-12.0
Malaysia	-6.1	-9.8	-4.9	-5.0	12.9	14.0	11.3	8.1
Myanmar	-0.1	-0.2	-0.2	-0.2	-0.2	—	—	—
Philippines	-4.6	-4.5	-4.7	-5.3	1.7	9.1	6.3	5.6
Thailand	-5.4	-7.9	-7.9	-2.1	12.7	9.1	5.5	1.9
Viet Nam	-8.0	-11.0	-10.3	-6.5	-4.4	2.3	0.8	-1.4
South Asia	-1.5	-2.0	-2.4	1.4	-1.9	-2.2	-3.9	-3.0
Bangladesh	-0.3	-1.8	-3.3	-2.2	-1.2	-1.4	-1.0	-1.2
Bhutan	10.5	12.1	12.1	15.9	12.0	25.8		—
India	-1.1	-1.7	-1.5	-1.3	1.0	-1.5	-1.8	-1.8
Maldives	-4.7	-6.7	-2.5	-10.8	-6.8	-10.0	-6.0	-6.0
Nepal	-5.6	-8.1	-8.9	-6.0	-5.5	-3.5	-8.0	-9.5
Pakistan	-3.8	-3.5	-6.8	-5.6	-2.7	-2.7	-2.5	-2.0
Sri Lanka	-7.3	-6.0	-4.9	-2.6	-1.8	-2.6	-6.8	-3.8
Pacific DMCs	6.2	7.9	4.4	-0.9	1.8	—	—	—
Cook Islands	—	—	—	—	—	-7.0	—	—
Fiji Islands	-3.5	-0.9	2.9	0.3	1.7	0.6	—	—
Kiribati	2.9	-13.2	-13.6	-17.9	-3.3	—	—	—
Marshall Islands	5.1	1.5	3.6	16.9	22.2	—	—	—
Micronesia, Federated States of	6.5	22.3	28.6	30.0	31.4	—	—	—
Nauru	—	—	—	—	—	—	—	—
Papua New Guinea	10.6	13.6	5.9	-2.4	1.9	-0.7	—	—
Samoa	2.6	4.3	5.2	7.3	—	—	—	—
Solomon Islands	-0.8	3.0	1.4	—	—	—	—	—
Tonga	-5.1	-12.9	-5.9	-0.8	-10.4	-1.0	—	—
Tuvalu	10.0	4.7	2.7	—	—	—	—	—
Vanuatu	-3.5	-2.1	-0.6	2.2	—	-8.0	—	—
Average	-0.3	-1.2	-1.3	0.5	4.1	3.8	1.5	0.5

Table A17 Foreign Direct Investment
($ million)

Economy	1993	1994	1995	1996	1997	1998
Newly industrialized economies	9,848	14,865	13,820	17,594	20,802	14,183
Hong Kong, China	3,657	4,131	3,279	5,521	6,000	1,600
Korea, Rep. of	588	809	1,776	2,325	2,844	5,143
Singapore	4,686	8,550	7,206	7,884	9,710	7,218
Taipei,China	917	1,375	1,559	1,864	2,248	222
People's Rep. of China and Mongolia	27,523	33,794	35,859	40,196	44,261	45,479
China, People's Rep. of	27,515	33,787	35,849	40,180	44,236	45,460
Mongolia	8	7	10	16	25	19
Central Asian republics	1,326	758	1,195	1,255	1,694	1,375
Kazakhstan	1,271	660	964	1,137	1,321	1,158
Kyrgyz Republic	10	38	96	47	84	102
Tajikistan	—	10	15	16	4	30
Uzbekistan	45	50	120	55	285	85
Southeast Asia	11,294	11,125	14,424	18,085	18,098	14,178
Cambodia	54	69	151	294	204	140
Indonesia	2,004	2,109	4,346	6,194	4,673	-356
Lao People's Democratic Rep.	36	59	88	128	86	45
Malaysia	5,006	4,342	4,178	5,078	5,106	3,727
Myanmar	149	91	115	38	124	40
Philippines	1,238	1,591	1,478	1,517	1,222	1,713
Thailand	1,805	1,364	2,068	2,336	3,733	6,969
Viet Nam	1,002	1,500	2,000	2,500	2,950	1,900
South Asia	1,116	1,584	2,934	3,506	4,667	3,433
Bangladesh	14	11	2	14	141	317
Bhutan	—	—	—	—	—	—
India	550	973	2,144	2,426	3,351	2,258
Maldives	7	9	7	8	8	7
Nepal	4	6	5	19	23	9
Pakistan	347	419	720	919	714	497
Sri Lanka	194	166	56	120	430	345
Pacific DMCs	206	160	561	180	136	170
Cook Islands	—	—	—			
Fiji Islands	91	68	70	27	34	91
Kiribati	–	–	—	—	1	—
Marshall Islands	—	—	—	—	—	—
Micronesia, Federated States of	—	—	—	—	—	—
Nauru	—	—	—	—	—	—
Papua New Guinea	62	57	455	111	29	30
Samoa	2	3	3	1	20	10
Solomon Islands	23	2	2	6	21	10
Tonga	2	—	—	2	1	1
Tuvalu	—	—	—	—	—	—
Vanuatu	26	30	31	33	30	28
Average	51,313	62,286	68,793	80,816	89,658	78,818

Table A18 **External Debt Outstanding**
($ million)

Economy	1994	1995	1996	1997	1998	1999	2000	2001
Newly industrialized economies								
Hong Kong, China	—	—	—	—	—	—	—	—
Korea, Rep. of	—	—	—	—	—	—	—	—
Singapore	—	—	—	—	—	—	—	—
Taipei,China	—	—	—	—	—	—	—	—
People's Rep. of China and Mongolia								
China, People's Rep. of	100,457	118,090	128,015	130,787	138,000	157,749	175,425	195,777
Mongolia	474	504	542	605	742	848	946	1,024
Central Asian republics								
Kazakhstan	3,265	3,480	4,205	5,952	7,543	—	—	—
Kyrgyz Republic	414	585	733	957	1,177	1,333	1,496	1,654
Tajilkistan	760	817	867	1,104	1,178	1,062	—	—
Uzbekistan	1,107	1,782	2,331	2,550	3,222	3,800	—	—
Southeast Asia								
Cambodia	416	561	624	2,056	2,146	2,223	2,314	—
Indonesia	101,278	106,455	113,143	138,018	149,849	—	—	—
Lao People's Democratic Rep.	1,971	2,057	2,178	2,322	2,442	2,489		—
Malaysia	22,518	33,400	38,700	45,600	42,000	43,200	43,700	—
Myanmar	6,555	5,771	5,185	5,647	—	—	—	—
Philippines	38,700	39,400	41,900	45,400	47,800	48,100	—	—
Thailand	64,866	82,568	90,536	93,416	86,160	75,600	71,100	—
Viet Nam	5,434	6,452	8,283	10,465	10,358	13,107	13,844	14,650
South Asia								
Bangladesh	15,700	16,500	17,600	18,700	19,800	20,800	22,004	—
Bhutan	130	129	117	120	133	—	—	—
India	99,008	92,982	93,470	94,320	98,231	109,590	116,265	128,465
Maldives	126	152	164	156	172	172	—	—
Nepal	2,320	2,399	2,349	2,369	2,463	—	—	—
Pakistan	24,482	27,072	28,852	29,617	31,000	32,000	33,000	—
Sri Lanka	7,888	8,231	8,003	7,698	8,526	8,737	9,381	9,314
Pacific DMCs								
Cook Islands	—	—	—	—	—	—	—	—
Fiji Islands	284	250	218	219	193	—	—	—
Kiribati	—	—	—	—	—	—	—	—
Marshall Islands	158	149	133	125	117	—	—	—
Micronesia, Federated States of	129	119	110	111	113	—	—	—
Nauru	—	—	—	—	—	—	—	—
Papua New Guinea	2,792	2,513	2,507	2,589	2,692	—	—	—
Samoa	154	162	167	156	180	—	—	—
Solomon Islands	155	157	145	135	152	—	—	—
Tonga	64	70	70	61	65	—	—	—
Tuvalu	—	—	—	—	—	—	—	—
Vanuatu	47	48	47	48	63	—	—	—

Table A19 Debt-Service Ratio
(percentage of exports of goods and services)

Economy	1994	1995	1996	1997	1998	1999	2000	2001
Newly industrialized economies								
Hong Kong, China	—	—	—	—	—	—	—	—
Korea, Rep. of	—	—	—	—	—	—	—	—
Singapore	—	—	—	—	—	—	—	—
Taipei,China	—	—	—	—	—	—	—	—
People's Rep. of China and Mongolia								
China, People's Rep. of	12.6	12.6	12.6	12.6	12.6	9.6	—	—
Mongolia	16.3	12.1	11.8	6.3	6.9	5.0	4.8	5.0
Central Asian Republics								
Kazakhstan	4.7	9.1	17.6	27.5	26.3	25.0	—	—
Kyrgyz Republic	4.1	20.5	12.3	6.3	7.8	7.9	11.4	17.9
Tajikistan	9.6	30.4	34.4	12.4	11.4	7.6	9.3	10.5
Uzbekistan	10.5	7.0	8.3	9.0	9.0	11.0	26.2	27.3
Southeast Asia								
Cambodia	3.2	3.6	5.8	2.5	2.9	2.5	3.0	3.0
Indonesia	32.6	32.6	34.2	37.8	39.1	34.8	—	—
Lao People's Democratic Rep.	3.3	5.7	5.3	9.0	11.1	12.0	12.5	12.0
Malaysia	4.9	7.3	8.5	6.5	6.6	6.2	5.3	5.0
Myanmar	14.5	16.7	—	—	—	—	—	—
Philippines	17.4	15.8	12.7	11.6	12.7	13.1	14.3	14.5
Thailand	11.7	11.4	12.2	15.6	20.8	20.4	16.0	—
Viet Nam	13.4	12.2	11.0	11.4	13.2	11.1	12.0	10.9
South Asia								
Bangladesh	11.6	10.3	12.1	11.4	11.7	12.0	12.1	12.1
Bhutan	26.8	18.3	25.9	10.4	9.0	14.7	—	—
India	27.5	27.9	23.6	19.8	19.4	—	—	—
Maldives	4.0	3.9	3.3	7.2	3.9	3.9	—	—
Nepal	8.0	8.1	5.4	4.5	6.1	6.5	6.5	6.5
Pakistan	33.4	34.9	33.9	38.0	40.0	20.0	22.0	—
Sri Lanka	13.7	16.5	15.3	13.3	11.0	12.7	12.0	12.0
Pacific DMCs								
Cook Islands	—	—	—	—	—	—	—	—
Fiji Islands	8.6	6.0	3.6	2.8	3.6	—	—	—
Kiribati	—	—	—	—	—	—	—	—
Marshall Islands	38.6	37.9	40.1	36.9	41.1	—	—	—
Micronesia, Federated States of	18.8	21.4	25.3	25.8	26.8	25.0	—	—
Nauru	—	—	—	—	—	—	—	—
Papua New Guinea	30.8	20.8	16.4	20.5	8.6	—	—	—
Samoa	—	—	3.0	2.9	3.0	—	—	—
Solomon Islands	6.2	2.8	3.9	2.5	3.3	—	—	—
Tonga	4.7	5.2	5.0	7.0	—	—	2.7	—
Tuvalu	—	—	—	—	—	—	—	—
Vanuatu	1.6	1.5	1.4	1.0	0.9	—	—	—

Table A20   Exchange Rates to the Dollar
(local currency/US$, average of period)

Economy	Currency	1994	1995	1996	1997	1998	1999
Newly industrialized economies							
Hong Kong, China	HK$	7.7	7.7	7.7	7.7	7.7	7.8
Korea, Rep. of	Won	803.5	771.3	804.5	951.3	1,401.4	1,189.5
Singapore	S$	1.5	1.4	1.4	1.5	1.7	1.7
Taipei,China	NT$	26.5	26.5	27.5	28.7	33.5	32.3
People's Rep. of China and Mongolia							
China, People's Rep. of	Yuan	8.6	8.4	8.3	8.3	8.3	8.3
Mongolia	Tugrik	413.0	473.5	547.2	791.0	877.2	1,042.9
Central Asian republics							
Kazakhstan	Tenge	35.6	61.0	67.3	75.4	78.3	119.9
Kyrgyz Republic	Som	10.9	10.8	12.8	17.4	20.8	39.0
Tajikistan	Tajik rubles	—	135.0	298.0	564.0	773.3	1,230.2
Uzbekistan	Sum	9.8	29.8	40.2	67.7	94.7	124.9
Southeast Asia							
Cambodia	Riel	2,567.0	2,464.0	2,635.0	2,952.0	3,756.0	3,809.0
Indonesia	Rupiah	2,160.8	2,248.6	2,342.3	2,909.4	10,013.7	7,852.9
Lao People's Democratic Rep.	Kip	717.5	818.6	926.2	1,259.6	3,296.2	7,108.2
Malaysia	Ringgit	2.6	2.5	2.5	2.8	3.9	3.8
Myanmar	Kyat	5.9	5.6	5.9	6.2	6.2	6.3
Philippines	Peso	26.4	25.7	26.2	29.5	40.9	38.9
Thailand	Baht	25.1	24.9	25.3	31.3	41.3	37.8
Viet Nam	Dong	10,978.0	11,037.0	11,032.0	11,683.0	13,297.0	14,028.0
South Asia							
Bangladesh	Taka	40.0	40.2	41.8	43.9	46.3	48.5
Bhutan	Ngultrum	31.4	32.4	35.4	36.3	41.3	42.9
India	Rupee	31.4	32.4	35.4	36.3	41.3	43.1
Maldives	Rufiyaa	11.6	11.8	11.8	11.8	11.8	11.8
Nepal	Rupee	49.4	51.9	56.7	58.0	66.0	68.0
Pakistan	Rupee	30.2	30.9	33.6	39.0	43.2	50.1
Sri Lanka	Rupee	49.4	51.3	55.3	59.0	64.6	66.4
Pacific DMCs							
Cook Islands	NZ$	1.7	1.5	1.5	1.5	1.9	1.9
Fiji Islands	F$	1.5	1.4	1.4	1.4	2.0	2.0
Kiribati	A$	1.4	1.3	1.3	1.3	1.6	1.5
Marshall Islands	US$	1.0	1.0	1.0	1.0	1.0	1.0
Micronesia, Federated States of	US$	1.0	1.0	1.0	1.0	1.0	1.0
Nauru	A$	1.4	1.3	1.3	1.3	1.6	1.5
Papua New Guinea	Kina	1.0	1.3	1.3	1.4	2.1	2.6
Samoa	Tala	2.5	2.5	2.5	2.6	—	—
Solomon Islands	SI$	3.3	3.4	3.6	3.7	—	—
Tonga	T$	1.4	1.3	1.3	1.2	1.3	1.6
Tuvalu	A$	1.4	1.3	1.3	1.3	1.6	1.5
Vanuatu	Vatu	116.4	112.1	111.7	115.9	—	—

Table A21   **Central Government Expenditure**
(percentage of GDP)

Economy	1994	1995	1996	1997	1998	1999
Newly industrialized economies						
Hong Kong China	16.2	17.0	15.3	14.7	18.9	19.4
Korea, Rep. of	18.7	19.0	20.2	22.1	26.0	23.0
Singapore	16.9	19.7	21.3	17.4	20.0	—
Taipei,China	30.2	27.9	25.4	25.9	26.0	25.5
China, People's Rep. of and Mongolia						
People's Rep. of China	14.7	13.2	12.9	13.8	15.8	16.9
Mongolia	35.8	34.4	26.4	35.2	38.9	36.0
Central Asian republics						
Kazakhstan	18.4	20.8	18.6	27.7	25.8	24.7
Kyrgyz Republic	32.4	33.2	25.3	25.2	29.2	28.3
Tajikistan	—	—	17.9	17.0	15.8	16.2
Uzbekistan	36.7	38.1	39.9	32.0	34.8	32.6
Southeast Asia						
Cambodia	16.1	16.5	17.0	14.0	15.2	15.1
Indonesia	16.2	14.9	15.6	15.7	18.8	17.4
Lao People's Democratic Rep.	23.8	21.9	22.1	19.8	23.7	20.6
Malaysia	23.0	22.1	22.3	21.0	21.9	22.2
Myanmar	10.1	10.7	10.1	—	—	—
Philippines	17.8	17.3	18.4	19.2	19.3	17.9
Thailand	17.3	16.2	17.1	19.5	19.7	18.1
Viet Nam	26.1	24.6	24.2	22.4	20.6	19.2
South Asia						
Bangladesh	13.9	14.7	7.3	7.1	7.5	17.0
Bhutan	34.0	36.7	35.4	32.0	27.9	42.6
India	15.5	15.2	15.4	16.1	16.6	15.5
Maldives	48.7	53.8	47.7	48.5	47.6	49.5
Nepal	16.9	17.8	18.7	18.1	18.9	18.8
Pakistan	23.2	22.8	24.2	22.0	21.3	22.9
Sri Lanka	29.7	30.0	27.8	23.8	26.4	25.6
Pacific DMCs						
Cook Islands	46.9	40.6	34.5	30.3	—	—
Fiji Islands	27.4	26.1	30.0	33.0	34.6	—
Kiribati	108.7	141.4	103.4	105.3	—	—
Marshall Islands	88.1	90.1	62.0	62.9	62.3	—
Micronesia, Federated States of	85.8	82.2	75.9	72.4	70.0	—
Nauru	—	—	—	—	—	—
Papua New Guinea	29.7	27.9	27.0	32.2	30.9	—
Samoa	46.1	53.1	47.0	39.4	36.5	—
Solomon Islands	57.0	48.1	46.4	41.0	44.0	—
Tonga	25.6	47.4	35.3	41.6	42.7	—
Tuvalu	52.3	50.0	56.1	—	—	—
Vanuatu	26.5	29.4	25.3	23.7	25.5	—

Table A22 **Central Government Revenue**
(percentage of GDP)

Economy	1994	1995	1996	1997	1998	1999
Newly industrialized economies						
Hong Kong, China	17.3	16.7	17.5	21.2	17.1	16.5
Korea, Rep. of	19.1	19.3	20.4	20.6	21.8	21.2
Singapore	22.3	21.3	37.0	37.0	29.3	—
Taipei,China	24.5	22.5	21.2	22.1	22.8	21.3
People's Rep. of China and Mongolia						
China, People's Rep. of	11.9	11.1	11.3	12.0	12.8	13.4
Mongolia	30.4	31.8	23.5	26.2	27.3	26.0
Central Asian republics						
Kazakhstan	18.4	16.9	13.6	20.4	17.7	21.2
Kyrgyz Republic	20.8	16.7	15.9	16.2	18.0	18.1
Tajikistan	—	—	12.1	13.7	12.1	13.1
Uzbekistan	29.2	34.6	34.3	29.7	32.4	31.5
Southeast Asia						
Cambodia	9.5	8.5	9.0	9.8	9.2	11.6
Indonesia	16.6	15.5	15.8	15.7	15.1	15.1
Lao People's Democratic Rep.	12.3	12.2	13.0	10.9	9.8	11.3
Malaysia	25.3	22.9	23.0	23.3	20.4	18.4
Myanmar	7.7	7.6	9.1	—	—	—
Philippines	19.9	18.9	18.9	19.4	17.5	19.8
Thailand	19.2	19.3	19.5	18.6	16.3	15.1
Viet Nam	23.6	23.3	22.9	21.1	19.0	17.2
South Asia						
Bangladesh	9.3	9.4	9.4	9.8	9.7	9.0
Bhutan	19.6	18.8	18.2	16.7	19.1	20.7
India	15.4	14.3	14.3	10.6	15.5	15.5
Maldives	35.1	37.8	37.2	41.4	39.7	40.5
Nepal	9.8	11.2	11.2	10.8	11.1	11.0
Pakistan	17.2	16.9	17.2	15.6	16.0	18.9
Sri Lanka	19.0	20.4	19.0	18.5	17.3	17.6
Pacific DMCs						
Cook Islands	40.9	39.0	33.0	31.3	—	—
Fiji Islands	26.1	25.7	25.1	26.5	31.2	—
Kiribati	125.7	145.5	97.6	114.8	—	—
Marshall Islands	75.0	76.0	82.4	66.8	66.5	—
Micronesia, Federated States of	85.3	83.8	82.7	73.8	75.7	—
Nauru	—	—	—	—	—	—
Papua New Guinea	26.8	27.3	27.4	32.3	31.3	25.4
Western Samoa	38.0	45.8	48.5	39.7	38.2	42.0
Solomon Islands	31.0	30.4	26.0	24.5	29.4	—
Tonga	30.4	43.8	36.1	40.4	38.4	24.9
Tuvalu	56.2	54.6	55.0	—	—	—
Vanuatu	23.8	23.7	21.8	21.0	16.7	—

Table A23 **Overall Budget Surplus/Deficit of Central Government**
(percentage of GDP)

Economy	1994	1995	1996	1997	1998	1999
Newly industrialized economies						
Hong Kong, China	1.1	-0.3	2.2	6.6	-1.8	-0.1
Korea, Rep. of	0.4	0.3	0.3	-1.5	-4.2	-2.9
Singapore	9.1	6.6	8.6	9.6	1.6	2.5
Taipei,China	-5.7	-5.4	-4.2	-3.8	-3.3	-4.2
People's Rep. of China and Mongolia						
China, People's Rep. of	-2.7	-2.1	-1.6	-1.8	-3.0	-4.0
Mongolia	-5.4	-2.7	-2.9	-8.6	-11.5	-10.0
Central Asian republics						
Kazakhstan	-7.3	-2.7	-4.7	-3.8	-4.2	-3.5
Kyrgyz Republic	-11.6	-17.3	-9.5	-9.0	-9.9	-11.2
Tajikistan	—	—	-5.8	-3.3	-3.8	-3.1
Uzbekistan	-7.7	-4.1	-7.4	-2.2	-3.4	-2.2
Southeast Asia						
Cambodia	-6.8	-7.5	-8.3	-4.2	-6.1	-3.7
Indonesia	0.4	0.6	0.2	0.0	-3.7	-2.2
Lao People's Democratic Rep.	-11.5	-9.7	-9.1	-8.8	-13.9	-9.3
Malaysia	2.3	0.8	0.7	2.6	-1.5	-3.8
Myanmar	-2.4	-3.1	-1.0	—	—	—
Philippines	1.0	0.6	0.3	0.1	-1.8	-3.6
Thailand	1.9	3.0	2.4	-0.9	-3.4	-3.0
Viet Nam	-2.3	-1.5	-1.3	-1.7	-1.6	-2.0
South Asia						
Bangladesh	-4.5	-5.4	0.9	-4.5	-4.2	-5.3
Bhutan	-0.5	0.1	2.0	-2.4	1.0	-2.5
India	-0.1	-1.0	-1.2	-4.8	-5.0	-5.5
Maldives	-7.4	-9.4	-3.8	-2.0	-5.3	-6.0
Nepal	-5.8	-4.8	-5.6	-5.1	-6.0	-6.1
Pakistan	-5.9	-5.6	-7.0	-6.3	-5.6	-3.7
Sri Lanka	-10.5	-10.1	-9.4	-7.9	-9.2	-8.0
Pacific DMCs						
Cook Islands	-6.0	-1.6	-1.5	1.1	—	—
Fiji Islands	-1.3	-0.5	-4.9	-6.5	-3.4	-1.2
Kiribati	17.0	4.1	-5.9	6.3	24.0	-3.2
Marshall Islands	-13.1	-14.1	20.4	3.9	4.2	-9.0
Micronesia, Federated States of	-0.6	1.7	6.9	1.5	0.3	—
Nauru	—	—	—	—	—	—
Papua New Guinea	-5.9	-4.3	-1.9	-4.4	-5.6	-6.5
Samoa	-8.1	-7.3	1.5	0.3	1.7	0.5
Solomon Islands	-6.0	-5.7	-4.7	-5.1	-0.1	-6.1
Tonga	4.8	-3.6	0.8	-1.2	-4.3	1.1
Tuvalu	3.9	4.7	-1.1	—	—	9.0
Vanuatu	-2.7	-5.6	-3.5	-2.7	-10.3	-1.2